SOCIOLOGY IN GOVERNMENT

RURAL STUDIES SERIES

Leif Jensen, General Editor
Diane K. McLaughlin and Carolyn E. Sachs, Deputy Editors

The Estuary's Gift
An Atlantic Coast Cultural Biography
David Griffith

Sociology in Government
The Galpin-Taylor Years in the U.S. Department of Agriculture,
1919–1953
Olaf F. Larson and Julie N. Zimmerman
Assisted by Edward O. Moe

OLAF F. LARSON AND JULIE N. ZIMMERMAN

ASSISTED BY EDWARD O. MOE

SOCIOLOGY IN GOVERNMENT

THE GALPIN-TAYLOR YEARS
IN THE
U.S. DEPARTMENT OF AGRICULTURE
1919–1953

PUBLISHED IN COOPERATION WITH THE
RURAL SOCIOLOGICAL SOCIETY
AND THE
AMERICAN SOCIOLOGICAL ASSOCIATION

THE PENNSYLVANIA STATE UNIVERSITY PRESS
UNIVERSITY PARK, PENNSYLVANIA

LIBRARY OF CONGRESS CATALOGING-IN-PUBLICATION DATA

Larson, Olaf F.
Sociology in government : the Galpin-Taylor years in the
U.S. Department of Agriculture, 1919–1953 /
Olaf F. Larson and Julie N. Zimmerman ;
assisted by Edward O. Moe.
p.   cm. — (Rural studies series)
Includes bibliographical references and index.
ISBN 0-271-02298-1 (cloth : alk. paper)
1. Galpin, Charles Josiah, b. 1864.
2. Taylor, Carl C. (Carl Cleveland), b. 1884.
3. United States. Bureau of Agricultural Economics.
Division of Farm Population and Rural Life—History.
4. Sociology, Rural—United States—History—20th century.
5. United States—Rural conditions.
I. Zimmerman, Julie N.   II. Moe, Edward O.
III. Title.   IV. Rural studies series (University Park, Pa.)

HT415 .L37 2003
307.72'0973'0904—dc21
2003002369

It is the policy of
The Pennsylvania State University Press to use
acid-free paper. Publications on uncoated stock satisfy the
minimum requirements of American National Standard for
Information Sciences—Permanence of Paper for Printed
Library Material, ANSI Z39.48—1992.

Contents

Dedicated to *Charles Josiah Galpin (1864–1947)*,
a pioneer in rural sociology, Head of the Division of Farm Population
and Rural Life, Bureau of Agricultural Economics, U.S. Department of
Agriculture from its establishment in 1919 until his retirement June 30, 1934,
and vice-president of the American Sociological Association in 1932; and to
Carl Cleveland Taylor (1884–1975), Head of the Division 1935–52, President
of the Rural Sociological Society in 1939, and President of the
American Sociological Association in 1946.

Foreword

We all know the actions of our intellectual and generational predecessors affect us, but only through a thoughtful historical description and analysis can we really understand and appreciate those actions and their impacts.

When the Rural Sociological Society and the American Sociological Association committed to support and endorse the preparation of *Sociology in Government: The Galpin-Taylor Years in the U.S. Department of Agriculture, 1919–1953*, a history of these pioneers in the disciplines seemed to be a valuable idea. Its completion represents a major accomplishment.

Olaf F. Larson and Julie N. Zimmerman, with the assistance of Edward O. Moe, have written not just a history of sociology in government, but a history of the creation and application of the disciplines of sociology and rural sociology in the USDA and across the nation.

The goal of sociologists in the USDA during this period was to develop a cumulative body of knowledge but, even more so, a body of knowledge whose application would be "useful to progress and social action." The fields of research included demographic analysis of rural and farm populations, farm family levels of living and standards of living, and rural social organization and social structures and changes in these systems.

Professionals in universities often conducted these studies. Extension personnel in every county communicated and applied their findings and, in response to societal crises, America's leaders used them to create public policy for rural areas from the 1920s through a depression, World War II, and a postwar recovery to 1953.

These studies were not merely academic. They addressed issues of race, inequities in power and well-being, and the policies that could change these social structures and systems. Significant issues such as farm-labor shortages, tenancy, differential standards of living by race, and by size and type of farm and community prompted some administrators to distance themselves from the studies, and caused Congress to question their value.

In 1919, empirical sociological research in the U.S. was rapidly maturing. The USDA program addressed important disciplinary issues then and today—network analysis, demographic changes and social impact analysis, racial inequalities, community power structures and organizational change, and land use planning. Unfortunately, the cumulative effect of a series of controversial community studies brought about the political purge of rural sociology from the government in 1953.

Every student of community sociology and sociology of agriculture is familiar with the 1944 study of Arvin and Dinuba, two California communities which differed by size-of-farms. The comparative differences in socioeconomic attributes—proportion of farm operators, diversity of the business community, and family level of living—have become core arguments in support of family-scale farms. But controversy surrounded the study because of its implications for access to water from federal irrigation projects. It was finally published independently of the USDA in 1947.

Why is this important to sociologists? Because in 1946 Congressional debates about the establishment of the National Science Foundation (NSF) focused on the applied nature of social science research and its links to social policy, especially on contentious issues such as racial and social inequalities. When the National Science Foundation was established in 1950, social science research was permitted but not mandated. As former NSF program officers in Sociology (Zuiches) and Law and Social Science (Levine), we experienced in the early 1980s a second, albeit unsuccessful, effort to purge the social sciences from the government research agenda.

As sociologists involved in research administration at the NSF, and in colleges and our professional societies, we are proud to recognize many major institutional innovations in research administration and methodologies that occurred in the USDA from 1919 to 1953.

First, cooperative agreements for research were used extensively; for example, cooperative agreements funded twenty-one of twenty-five projects in 1932. During the 1919–34 period, such projects partnered public land-grant universities, state agricultural experiment stations, private colleges, and historically black colleges with the USDA in thirty-seven states.

Second, the research leaders in the USDA created collaborative funding models with many agencies to underwrite major research projects. These included: the Bureaus of Reclamation and Census, the Department of Treasury, Social Security Administration, Forest Service, Bureau of Employment Security, and the Works Progress Administration.

Third, through research and evaluation studies these scientists were actively involved in significant interdisciplinary social experiments, e.g., rural rehabilitation loan program, health and dental care delivery program, and the design and creation of a social and community infrastructure in the Columbia Basin.

Fourth, research methodologies were evolving: residence histories, sample survey methods, census projections, sociograms and sociometrics, classification schemes, and participant-observation strategies. Studies needed to be completed rapidly in six to eight months. Seventy-one counties became laboratory settings in seven rural cultural (type of farming) regions—a precursor to communities targeted for contemporary market analysis surveys.

Fifth, sociological innovations included the standard of living index, mechanisms to provide group services and neighborhood action groups for rural rehabilitation, and financial credit and technical assistance in developing farm financial plans or home plans. Such systems are still in place to assist and educate farmers and families through Cooperative Extension and the USDA Natural Resource Conservation Service.

A powerful example of the use of sociological knowledge occurred in postwar Japan when the Allied Forces required five agrarian reform programs, under the hypothesis that land reform would lead to democratization at the village level.

Finally, to read the names of authors and publications found in the references is like reading a *Who's Who of Sociology, Rural Sociology, Economics, and Demography:* Vera Banks, John D. Black, Gladys Bowles, Edmund deS. Brunner, Louis Ducoff, Douglas Ensminger, Varden Fuller, Charles Galpin, Walter Goldschmidt, Margaret Hagood, Paul Jehlik, J. H. Kolb, Olaf Larson, Charles Loomis, Lowry Nelson, William Sewell, Conrad Taeuber, and Carl C. Taylor.

Our intellectual predecessors were creative, topical, and politically influential, and they left a legacy of which we all can be proud. This volume reminds us of the debt we owe to these pioneers of the disciplines.

Felice J. Levine, Executive Officer
American Sociological Association

James J. Zuiches, Past President
Rural Sociological Society and
Dean, College of Agriculture and
Home Economics, Washington
State University

To a large degree, the rural social sciences were born, nurtured, and matured in the inventive first half of the twentieth century. Sociology, economics, history, and demography were established disciplines well before the end of the nineteenth century. But two world wars and powerful economic cycles—from the "golden years" of agriculture to the Great Depression—generated both pragmatic applications of social sciences to real problems and a period of unmatched institutional creativity. The epicenter of much of the institutional innovation and social science adaptation was the U.S. Department of Agriculture. Energy, ideas, and social science pioneers flowed freely between that epicenter and a small cluster of leading land-grant universities.

In 1909, Henry C. Taylor became the first professor of agricultural economics in the U.S. and in 1919 was called to Washington and eventually became the first Chief of the Bureau of Agricultural Economics (BAE). The American Farm Economics Association (later the American Agricultural Economics Association) was organized in 1919. The American Sociological Association (ASA) was established in 1905. The Rural Section within the ASA was formalized in 1922 and the Rural Sociological Society was established in 1937. In 1919, the Agricultural History Society was organized. Many of the same people were prominent in the early history of each of these organizations and in the USDA-Land Grant cluster.

From colonial days until the early twentieth century, the United States was primarily a rural nation and the dominant rural occupation was farming. The census of 1920 was defining in that it marked the first time that rural population dropped to less than half the total population. When rural and agricultural lifestyles were dominant characteristics of the general economy and population, there was little incentive to treat them as specialized areas of study. Both the growth of urban population and the industrial economy relative to rural population and the farm economy, the growing disparity in economic well-being between urban and rural people, and concern about quality of rural life and decline in rural communities generated interest—and increasing specialization—in the rural dimensions of the social sciences. The same phenomena also motivated policymakers to call on the emerging rural social scientists to apply their interests to policy issues of the day. Thus, there evolved in the rural social sciences a tradition of empirical research, data collection, and applied analysis, built on a base of sound theory.

It was in this stimulating and creative environment that rural sociology evolved in the U.S. Department of Agriculture. The story of that evolution, its supporters and detractors, and the giants upon whose shoulders later generations of rural sociologists and rural demographers still stand, is told in meticulous yet fascinating detail by Olaf Larson and Julie Zimmerman. Indeed, Olaf Larson is one of those giants. His life spans the period from the early beginnings of rural sociology to the present. With this book, he continues his legacy of rich insights into rural life, insights characterized by their usefulness and the lessons they teach. Julie Zimmerman is of a more recent generation. She has proven, via her several collaborations with Professor Larson, her respect for the roots of the science she practices so well today.

The story of the Galpin-Taylor years in the old Bureau of Agricultural Economics is more than a fascinating historical review. It reminds us that relevant science often requires courageous scientists. Further, we are reminded that the fortunes of any science, and the opportunities for scientists to make useful contributions to the public good, are heavily conditioned by the attitudes, biases, and courage of administrators who control resources and who must deal with favorable and unfavorable political winds.

The ups and downs of the fortunes of the Division of Farm Population and Rural Life and the diligent efforts of its staff to usefully address the pressing needs of rural people and communities are faithfully documented in this important book.

John E. Lee Jr.
Administrator (Retired), Economic Research Service,
U.S. Department of Agriculture, and
Professor and Head, Department of
Agricultural Economics,
Mississippi State University

Acknowledgments

This volume is the second major output of the project "Sociology in the U.S. Department of Agriculture: The Galpin-Taylor Years, 1919–1953." The first was *Sociology in Government: A Bibliography of the Work of the Division of Farm Population and Rural Life, U.S. Department of Agriculture, 1919–1953* (Larson, Moe, and Zimmerman, eds. Boulder, Colo.: Westview Press, 1992). This project was conducted under a cooperative agreement between the Agriculture and Rural Economy Division, Economic Research Service, U.S. Department of Agriculture, and the Department of Rural Sociology, New York State College of Agriculture and Life Sciences at Cornell University. We are grateful to both organizations for providing funds. Financial support has also been provided by the Cornell University Agricultural Experiment Station and by a grant from the Rural Sociological Society's 50th Anniversary Committee. The American Sociological Association, the editorial board for the Rural Studies Series of the Rural Sociological Society (RSS), and the Cornell University Department of Rural Sociology provided assistance for publication costs. We would also like to acknowledge the University of Kentucky for supporting the continued work of Julie N. Zimmerman in this project.

David L. Brown's interest and support, when he was Associate Director, Agriculture and Rural Economy Division, Economic Research Service, USDA was crucial in the initiation of this project. His active support continued when he became Associate Director of the Cornell University Agricultural Experiment Station and, subsequently, Chair of the Department of Rural Sociology at Cornell. John E. Lee Jr., as Administrator of the Economic Research Service (ERS), was instrumental in assuring that ERS funds were made available for the project. Eugene C. Erickson, while Chair of the Department of Rural Sociology at Cornell University, also had a role in the project's initiation. We gratefully acknowledge the encouragement given to this endeavor at an early stage by William V. D'Antonio, as Executive Officer of the American Sociological Association. We appreciate the continued interest and support by his successor as ASA Executive Officer, Felice J. Levine.

We benefited greatly from the helpfulness, knowledge, and wisdom of the comments on the manuscript chapter by chapter by an Advisory Panel comprised of persons who had been members at some time of the USDA's Division of Farm Population and Rural Life. They were Calvin L. Beale, Gladys K. Bowles, Louis J. Ducoff, Douglas Ensminger, Paul J. Jehlik, and Conrad Taeuber. We gratefully acknowledge the careful review of the completed manuscript by David L. Brown, Cornell University; Jess C. Gilbert, University of Wisconsin-Madison; and James J. Zuiches, Washington State University. We also thank David Brown, Cornell University, and Ann R. Tickamyer, Ohio University, for assessing the manuscript for the ASA.

A meeting of the Panel was supported by the Farm Foundation. Ready access to a collection of Division publications, fortunately retained by the Economic Research Service in Washington, was facilitated by Calvin Beale.

Numerous other former Division staff members assisted us. Charles P. Loomis granted an interview to Olaf F. Larson on April 20, 1990, in Las Cruces, New Mexico. E. B. Williams consented to a tape-recorded interview by Yvonne Oliver on August 3, 1990, in Atlanta, Georgia. Walter R. Goldschmidt and Irwin T. Sanders kindly checked a draft of sections of the manuscript that pertained to their research in the Division. Others who supplied copies of publications or other help included Mary Montgomery Clawson, A. Lee Coleman, Donald G. Hay, Helen Wheeler Johnson, Walter C. McKain Jr., William H. Metzler, James E. Montgomery, Henry W. Riecken Jr., Edgar A. Schuler, T. G. Standing, and Glenn L. Taggart.

We were also helped in locating publications or in verifying information by the following people: widows of former staff members, namely, Mrs. May Alexander, Mrs. Jane W. Hay, and Mrs. Virginia Longmore; Mrs. Lois R. Walz, secretary to Carl C. Taylor prior to his retirement as Division head; Allen D. Edwards, at one time on the staff of the Social Research Section, Farm Security Administration; and Wayne D. Rasmussen and Vivian Wiser, both agricultural historians in the Agricultural and Rural History Section of the Economic Research Service. Others who made a special effort to provide or search out pertinent information include Arnold W. Foster, State University of New York at Albany; Anthony A. Hickey, Western Carolina University; Daryl J. Hobbs, University of Missouri; John S. Holik, University of Missouri and Rural Sociological Society archivist; Margaret E. Martin, retired from the Bureau of the Budget; and Ronald C. Wimberley, North Carolina State University.

Our analysis has been sharpened by comments made and questions raised following papers presented individually, jointly, or collectively at the ASA's 1990 annual meeting in Washington, D.C.; at annual meetings of the RSS in 1989 in Seattle, Washington, in 1990 in Norfolk, Virginia, in 1992 at The Pennsylvania State University, in 1994 in Portland, Oregon, in 1996 in Des Moines, Iowa, in 2000 in Washington, D.C.; at the Eighth World Congress for Rural Sociology at The Pennsylvania State University in 1992; and at the Agricultural History Society's 80th Anniversary Symposium in 1999.

The editors of the Rural Sociological Society's Rural Studies Series have offered encouragement for this book. These editors have been, successively, Forrest A. Deseran, Lionel J. Beaulieu, Michael D. Schulman, and Leif Jensen. The great resources of the Cornell University Libraries system and the help of the Albert R. Mann Library staff have been much appreciated.

The authors would also like to acknowledge co-author Edward O. Moe, who is now deceased. He was a retired principal sociologist in the Cooperative State Research Service, U.S. Department of Agriculture. He encouraged the initiation of this project and was an enthusiastic participant in the early stages of the book. We are also grateful to Yvonne Oliver of Fort Valley State University for writing the chapter "The Division and Black Populations."

We are especially indebted to Mrs. Beverley A. Wells for her dedicated efforts in preparing the copy for this book and for her assistance on this project in many other ways.

Olaf F. Larson and *Julie N. Zimmerman*

List of Acronyms

AAA   Agricultural Adjustment Administration
ACLA   American Country Life Association
AES   Agricultural Experiment Station
AMS   Agricultural Marketing Service
ASA   American Sociological Association (formerly American Sociological Society)
BAE   Bureau of Agricultural Economics
Division Division of Farm Population and Rural Life (Welfare)
DFPRL   Division of Farm Population and Rural Life
DFPRW   Division of Farm Population and Rural Welfare
ERS   Economic Research Service
FERA   Federal Emergency Relief Administration
FmHA   Farmers' Home Administration
FSA   Farm Security Administration
FY   Fiscal year
GPO   United States Government Printing Office
HBCUS   Historically black colleges and universities
Mimeo   Mimeographed
RA   Resettlement Administration
RR   Rural Rehabilitation
RSS   Rural Sociological Society
SCS   Soil Conservation Service
SSRC   Social Science Research Council
USDA   United States Department of Agriculture
WPA   Works Progress Administration
[ ]   Information inside brackets not available in publication cited but provided by authors of this monograph

1

Introduction

Sociology started holding a small niche in the federal government system on a continuing basis about eighty years ago. Growing out of antecedents based in the U.S. Department of Agriculture, the first, and for a time, the only unit specifically established for sociological research was initiated in 1919. This unit was known for most of its thirty-four-year life history as the Division of Farm Population and Rural Life (referred to hereafter as the "Division"). It was located within the Bureau of Agricultural Economics (BAE) in the U.S. Department of Agriculture (USDA).

The Division has a unique place in the history of sociology. Despite its always small staff and budget and its placement at a subordinate level in the administrative organization of the USDA, it had a leading role in the development and promotion of the specialized area designated as rural sociology. It was a pioneer in the practice of sociology, that is, in the application of sociology to the public agenda in a federal government setting. In 1953, shortly after President Dwight Eisenhower's administration came into office, the BAE was abolished by order of then Secretary of Agriculture Ezra T. Benson in a reorganization of the USDA and, concurrently, the Division was dissolved. Some of the Division's work was continued within a new research agency of the reorganized USDA.

Until now, the Division's work was undocumented and had never been systematically assessed. The record of this important chapter in the history of sociology was at risk of being lost as the roster of living persons with direct Division experience has been greatly depleted. To prevent this loss, we first undertook to identify as completely as we could and catalog the work of the Division and its cooperators; the result was *Sociology in Government: A Bibliography of the Work of the Division of Farm Population and Rural Life, U.S. Department of Agriculture, 1919–1953* (Larson, Moe, and Zimmerman 1992a). The present volume is the first attempt to systematically examine the work of the Division. In this, we indicate the need for the research done, the problems or issues addressed. We undertake an analysis of the research and assess its contributions to substantive knowledge about rural society, to research methods, to sociological concepts and theory, to public policy development, to federal action and educational programs, and to the social science research system.

This historical analysis depends primarily on the literature identified in the some 1,500 citations to the Division's work listed in Larson, Moe, and Zimmerman (1992a). Living history also played an indispensable role in this research on the Division. Indeed, two of the authors of this project were former Division staff members. Olaf F. Larson served during 1938–46 as, successively, leader in a newly established regional office in Amarillo, Texas; in Washington, D.C., with major work in rural rehabilitation research; and as leader in a new regional office in Portland, Oregon. Edward O. Moe served on the Washington staff during 1940–42, working first on one of the "culture of a contemporary rural community" studies and later on investigations for use in planning the Columbia Basin irrigation project in Washington state.

In addition to possessing first-hand knowledge of the Division, these two authors provided contact with other former Division staff. Six of these were gathered together to form an advisory panel for the project. They were: Calvin L. Beale, Gladys K. Bowles, Louis J. Ducoff, Douglas Ensminger, Paul J. Jehlik, and Conrad Taeuber. Their service on the professional staff of the Division covered the period, collectively, from 1936—when its New Deal expansion years were just starting—through the Division's 1953 demise. The advisory panel served as both resource and reviewers. They recounted experiences and interpretations of events, personalities and programs, providing important insights into the Division.

UNDERSTANDING THE DIVISION

At the time the Division was established, sociology was a relatively new and not widely understood discipline. The emergence of sociology as a recognized specialty among the social sciences was symbolized by the formation of what is now the American Sociological Association (ASA) in 1905. The Rural Section within the ASA would be formalized in 1922 (Nelson 1969:126–27). The limited knowledge available about rural social organization and rural people was largely descriptive. Sociological research methods for data collection and analysis were primitive in comparison with even ten or fifteen years later.

The placement of the Division within the Bureau of Agricultural Economics meant that the Division's fate from beginning to end was linked with that of the BAE. This structural position meant that changes in function assigned to the Bureau and shifts in the Bureau's budget and political acceptability had direct and major consequences for the Division. All funding for the Division was channeled through the BAE. Congressional appropriations were made to the BAE for lines of investigation that might involve the work of more than one of the BAE's divisions; the Bureau's chief then determined each Division's budget. Likewise, the subordinate position of the Division meant that, in general, its lines of access to users or potential users of its work within government was channeled through or approved by the upper administrative level of the BAE. Fortunately, each BAE chief typically was a strong and crucial supporter of the Division and, at times, played a protective role. Each was, without exception, a highly regarded professional agricultural economist.

As a research unit in a federal agency, the Division was subject to the constraints imposed by the political process at the national level. This was expressed by actions of Congress and by decisions of political appointees who held administrative posts above the Bureau level in the governmental hierarchy. Based on his years of experience as Division head, Carl C. Taylor (1946b:390) tried to explain that in a federal agency the use of research funds is "restricted to types of activities specified by the Congress." The Congress could, and, in some instances did, impose prohibitions on what the Division and the BAE were doing. Through committee hearings and other means the Congress could exercise a chilling effect on social science research.

Between the Division, the BAE, and the Congress were intermediary decision-makers about budget and research program activities. As political leaders and appointees these intermediaries were identified with specific political ideologies. However, they also were tuned into the policy and program implications of shifts in the nation's economic and social environment. Especially important here were the Secretary of Agriculture, always an appointee of the President, and the President's budget people as represented during much of the time by the Bureau of the Budget. Some Secretaries and their close associates in the USDA were extremely supportive of the Division and its work; the most notable were David F. Houston and Henry A. Wallace.

FOUR PERIODS IN THE DIVISION'S HISTORY

The Division's fate during its entire life history was largely determined by factors and forces external to it—the changing economic and social context in the United States, including societal crises; the political responses to the changing context and the crises; the structural position within the

USDA; and the decision-making and influence of non-sociologists, especially of political appointees, at higher levels of the USDA's bureaucratic hierarchy. As a consequence, the thirty-four-year life span of the Division was clearly characterized by marked fluctuations in staff, funding, and in type and range of program activity. In reviewing this hectic and rocky history with colleagues at the 1948 annual Rural Sociological Society meeting, Carl Taylor (1948b:7) commented "no well planned research program with so short a history should have experienced . . . such marked epochs."

Reflecting these changes, we found it useful to divide the Division's life history into four periods. The first, when Charles J. Galpin was head, is what we have come to refer to as the Galpin years, 1919–34. Second is the depression-born New Deal years, 1935–41. Third is the World War II period, 1942–45, and fourth is the postwar period, 1946–53.

The Galpin Years

During 1919–34, the Division was always very small scale. It was a constant struggle to keep funds for the work in the annual appropriations by Congress (C. Taylor 1939). The professional staff never exceeded five persons. Funds from regular appropriations were less than $34,000 in the best of years. When the Division started, there were no farm population census figures, the farmer's level of living was not even a matter of statistical discussion, and there was only limited information on the dynamics of the small community's social structure. A distinctive contribution of the Galpin years was the start on building a knowledge base about rural life in the United States. Three fields of research were especially important: farm population (migration, gain or loss on farms, composition), rural organization (the community, neighborhood, and special interest group structure in rural areas), and farm family levels and standards of living. Another feature of the Galpin years was his success in getting sociological research under way at numerous land-grant and other universities and increased in the few places where it existed. The Division also had a role in developing professional resources in sociology through planning and supporting training to increase the methodological competence of sociologists.

The New Deal Years

During the depression-born New Deal period, 1935–41, the fortunes of the Division improved dramatically. Opportunities opened to provide sociological knowledge for policy development and programs aimed at improving the well-being of agriculture and rural people. The result was that the staff, in Taylor's words was "swamped almost to the point of confusion in attempting to render requested service far beyond its personnel and financial resources" (1939:225). The demand came from the new agricultural action agencies such as the Farm Security Administration (FSA), the Agricultural Adjustment Administration (AAA), and the Soil Conservation Service (SCS); from the new nationwide grassroots level agricultural planning system (called land-use planning) initiated by the BAE in cooperation with the land-grant colleges; and from nonagricultural agencies in the federal government, most conspicuously the Department of Interior's Bureau of Reclamation. Access was also opened to provide research findings to policymakers in Congress; over two-thirds of the items in the bibliography in the "Congressional testimony and reports" category fall within the 1935–41 period (Larson, Moe, and Zimmerman 1992a).

Some feeling for the ethos that prevailed in the Division is conveyed by excerpts from Taylor's talks to professional colleagues (1940:17–31; 1941a:154–59). For example, agricultural action agencies were "opening the gates of opportunity to the sociologist by furnishing real laboratories and elaborate funds for study and by asking questions to which their administrators need practical answers. . . . The sociologist has a rare opportunity to put himself on the spot and use his knowledge to be of service to both the public and to his science." Taylor also argued that there is a "valuable reciprocal functioning of research and action in the field of sociology. . . . Sociology as a science will probably grow only to the extent that it makes itself useful to programs of social action."

Several characteristics distinguished the New Deal years:

1. This period marked the high point in the unit's staff and budget. Professional staff reached a peak number of fifty-seven, about half in Washington and half in the regional offices which eventually were set up in nine locations. Funds allocated from all sources exceeded $400,000 in the later years of the period.
2. The staff was made up predominantly of sociologists but, by design, it was given a multidisciplinary mix by the addition of cultural anthropologists, social psychologists, human geographers, cultural historians, and economists. The research of the economists was largely in the area of agricultural labor, an area which in this period became a major one for the Division for the first time. The other new members of the unit were identified especially with community studies.

3. Because of the structural context, being in the BAE, and also by necessity and conviction, much of the Division's research and evaluation
work was conducted on an interdivision basis within the BAE, an inter-
agency basis within and outside the USDA, and with multidisciplinary
and interdisciplinary sets of researchers.

World War II

By 1940, requests for information began to come to the Division from the
federal agencies planning in case the U.S. became involved in World War
II. These national defense concerns began to reshape the Division's work.
The events of December 7, 1941, immediately led to a drastic redefinition
of priorities and programs for most federal agencies, including the USDA
and, therefore, the BAE and the Division.

On January 1, 1942, the BAE announced the immediate wartime work
program for the Bureau as a whole and for each of its 11 divisions. The
Bureau's program called for giving first priority to "all lines of work that
make significant contributions to winning the war" (USDA, BAE 1942:1).
The BAE's efforts to aid in meeting the farmers' labor needs were to center in the Division. Second to farm labor studies was the application of
the Division's expertise in rural social organization to assist in organizing
rural communities for wartime activities. This work was carried out in
cooperation with the Extension Service, the Office of Civilian Defense,
USDA War Boards and others. Studies of civilian participation in the war
effort and of the impact of the war on rural life and communities were
also significant elements of the Division's wartime activities. The January
1, 1942, BAE announcement gave second priority to those lines of work
which had the promise of making a practical contribution to the solution
of major problems of the immediate postwar period.

The shift in priorities forced by the wartime information needs of the
government resulted in a sharp curtailment of the Division's research then
underway. Some studies were dropped. For others, analysis and publication was not carried to the point envisaged in the original design. A high
proportion of the Division's wartime work was made available only to a
restricted group of users, e.g., policymakers and administrators within the
federal government. For example, 40 percent of the 482 citations for
1942–45 (excluding periodical publications of the Division and unpublished addresses) in Larson, Moe, and Zimmerman (1992a), were placed
in the "Restricted use" category. These restricted items, in mimeo, dittoed,
or typed form, were not intended for distribution outside of government

circles. Valuable research published in this form destined the reports to become "fugitive" literature. For example, during 1943–44 intensive studies of the impact of the war were made in 12 widely dispersed rural communities. Eight of the studies were issued in mimeo form by regional offices of the Division, one never got beyond a Ph.D. dissertation; the fate of the other three has escaped us.

The inter-division, inter-agency characteristic of the Division's activities not only continued but increased during the war period. The multi-disciplinary nature of the professional staff gradually diminished, however, as personnel was lost to the military service and to other wartime agencies and programs without replacement. By war's end, professional staff had dropped to 44 from the New Deal period peak of 57 and the annual budget had shrunk by one-third from its earlier peak. But harder times were ahead.

Postwar Period

As the Division entered the postwar period, 1946–53, its fortunes quickly took a turn for the worse. External political forces, congressional action, executive decisions at the top level of the USDA, and the structure that linked the Division's fate to that of the BAE all combined to bring about the retrenchment and, eventually, the demise of the Division.

The assignment of planning responsibilities within the USDA to the BAE and its land-use planning organization had come under fire from the Soil Conservation Service and the Agricultural Adjustment Administration within the Department of Agriculture and from the American Farm Bureau Federation outside (Hardin 1946; 1955:160–62). Weakening of the BAE began with congressional prohibition, in the appropriation act for fiscal year 1943, of use of any BAE funds for state and local land-use planning. Then, on January 1, 1946, all of the BAE's planning functions for the USDA were removed and restored to the Office of the Secretary, by then Secretary of Agriculture Clinton P. Anderson. Concurrently, Congress, in the appropriations act for fiscal year 1947, cut the Bureau's funds for economic investigations by $500,000, ordered the closing of the regional offices, and barred the use of any funds for "cultural surveys," (the referent for the Division's research in seventy-one "laboratory" counties). About this time, Howard R. Tolley, a strong supporter of the Division's work, was forced out as BAE chief. His successor, O. V. Wells from within the agency, was more in tune with the redefined much narrower BAE role, one limited to providing factual and scientific information for use by others (Hardin 1946; 1955:175–76). Another development counter to the Division's interests was the abolishment in 1946 of the Farm Security Administration—long in political hot water—and its reorganization into the Farmers' Home Administration. The FSA had been a significant user of the Division's work and had provided some of its funds at times; the new agency, reflecting the changing political climate, was permitted to operate only a much more restricted program than did the FSA.

With these reorganizations, Congressional-ordered cutbacks in funding and restraints on program activity, and the shift in political climate, user-demand by action agency clientele for the Division's work was diminished. The research program was narrowed in scope. Among the four approved broad fields of research, farm labor was best-funded. By about 1950, the work in rural organization was being phased out. Population studies continued, as throughout the Division's history, to be an important area. Work on farm family levels of living continued and, with the help of funds from the Research and Marketing Act of 1946, was broadened to include studies of health services available to and used by rural people.

Staff reductions occurred at a rapid rate. By 1948, the professional staff was down to twenty-three, about half that at war's end. Frustrated with the deteriorating environment in the BAE for the Division's work, Carl Taylor, head of the Division, retired in June 1952 to accept consultant assignments on rural development with the State Department and the Ford Foundation. His successor, Margaret J. Hagood, came from within the Division. By the decision of the new Secretary of Agriculture, Ezra Benson, little more than a year later on November 2, 1953, the BAE and, with it, the Division of Farm Population and Rural Life came to an end.

Characteristics Common to All Periods

While each of the four periods had activities and features unique to it, there were some characteristics common to all. These included:

1. A governing principle for the Division, as for the BAE, was the ideology, the faith, the belief that knowledge could be applied to the solution or alleviation of societal problems (Hall 1983); in fact, the rationale for establishing the Division was to conduct studies "with a view to facilitating advancement in the life of American farmers and their families" (USDA, Office of the Secretary 1919b:6).
2. Another governing principle was that the Division, like the Bureau within which it was placed, had a high order of professionalism (Hall

1983; McDean 1983). The Division's leadership and much of its staff previously held university positions as sociologists. The Division sought and maintained working relationships with land-grant and other universities nationwide. Its leaders were active in professional sociological organizations. And, it consistently sought to develop and improve research methods and add to the fund of validated knowledge about rural life.

3. The Division's program always had a mix, in varying proportions, representing both its applied orientation and its interest in discipline-building.

4. The Division had the benefit of continuity in leadership (Galpin for fifteen years, Taylor for seventeen years), leadership which had the respect of peers. For example, Taylor was elected to the presidency of both the Rural Sociological Society and the American Sociological Association.

ORGANIZATION OF BOOK

The remainder of this book is organized in the following manner. Chapter 2 relates the antecedents and events which preceded the establishment of the Division and reviews the conditions which led to the decision to have a unit within the federal government to undertake studies of farm life. Chapter 3 presents the Division as a research unit, its leadership and staffing, its budget, its organization, and its cooperative relationships within the government, with the states, and with the private sector. The determinants of the Division's research priorities and programs, the factors shaping research continuity and discontinuity, are examined in Chapter 4. In the latter chapter, we also touch upon some of the impediments and obstacles encountered by the Division in conducting research and publishing the results.

In the five chapters that then follow, the focus is upon substantive areas that were central to the Division's research program during all or part of its existence. In each chapter we highlight contributions to knowledge and its use—including the identification of public issues—together with contributions to research methods and to sociological concepts and theory. Chapter 5 covers farm and rural population, an area of emphasis throughout the Division's history. Chapter 6 pertains to farm and rural levels of living, another area of continuing program emphasis although the methodological approach shifted sharply over time. Several aspects of the social organization (or social structure) of rural society, also an area of continuing emphasis throughout the Division's existence, are considered in

Chapters 7 and 8. By the start of World War II, the Division was recognized as a major source within the government of farm labor information; this research area is the subject of Chapter 9. In Chapter 10 we cover the range of topics that fall under what has come to be designated as the sociology of agriculture, e.g., farm tenancy, types of farming systems, and agriculture and community.

The Division's studies of black populations and its relationships with historically black colleges and universities are examined in Chapter 11. During the time Carl Taylor was Head, the Division's research findings were frequently fed into the policy-making process at the federal level or used for program purposes by a diverse set of public agencies. In Chapters 12 and 13 we illustrate the Division's work done for or used by major agricultural and other action agencies and programs. The full scope of the Division's research extended well beyond the major substantive areas included in Chapters 5 through 13 as one may infer from the fact that a parsimonious assignment of keywords to the research citations in Larson, Moe, and Zimmerman (1992a) gave us 168 substantive area topics. In Chapter 14 we examine the research on some of the additional topics on a highly selective basis, e.g., studies of farm women, youth, and farmer attitudes and opinions.

Chapter 15 assesses the contributions of the Division to the development, strengthening, and maintenance of the social science disciplines and research system. In Chapter 16 we offer some reflections on the Division and sociology in a government setting. Finally, in the Epilogue we make a linkage between the Division and sociological work within the USDA agencies that succeeded the Bureau of Agricultural Economics.

This endeavor provides a record of an important piece in the development and history of rural sociology in the United States. Without efforts such as this one to rescue rural sociology's records, future attempts to document and provide interpretations will be stymied. It is important to recover the history of our own discipline, not only to preserve the past and the steps of those who came before us, but also as an expression of the value we place on this discipline.

2

Establishing the Division: The Background

On May 12, 1919, Charles J. Galpin was appointed by David F. Houston, Secretary of Agriculture for President Woodrow Wilson, as "economist in charge of Farm Life Studies."[1] This marked the beginning of sociological research in the USDA and in the federal government on a continuing basis. Prior to the Division's establishment there were important antecedents both within and beyond the USDA.[2] However, the 1919 establishment of the Division was the first time that sociological research was the sole focus for an arm of the federal government.

In starting Farm Life Studies within the USDA, Secretary Houston was acting on the report of an advisory committee he had appointed. This committee outlined research work it recommended the USDA undertake on the subject of farm life studies. The hoped-for outcome of such studies was to facilitate advancement in the life of American farmers and their families. Upon receipt of the advisory committee's report, Houston's action followed within little more than a week. The Secretary's speedy action was not, in a sense, precipitous. Rather it represented continuity with past efforts to improve rural life which had been interrupted by World War I.

THE COUNTRY LIFE COMMISSION REPORT

In 1908, President Theodore Roosevelt appointed his Commission on Country Life. Five months later, the Commission submitted its report, which contributed greatly to stimulating developments that culminated in starting the Division.[3] The Commission's *Report* (1944:24, 28) saw the problem of country life as one of reconstruction. It identified a number of remedies by the Congress, the states, and by voluntary organizations and institutions.

One of three great movements the Commission recommended be set underway was investigating in detail all agricultural and country life conditions through exhaustive study. From the time Houston became Secretary of Agriculture on March 6, 1913, he sought to have the USDA devote "much more attention than before to broad social and economic issues affecting farmers" (Harding 1951:63). His setting up the Rural Organization Service, a forerunner of the Division, in 1913 can be interpreted as one response to the Commission's recommendation to take stock of rural life.

A second great movement recommended by the Commission was "a campaign for rural progress" to be conducted through holding local, state, and even national conferences on rural progress, and the formation of organizations to unite diverse interests for the rebuilding of rural life was proposed. Soon local and state conferences under varying types of sponsorship began to be held in all sections of the nation (Carney 1912: 307–12, 384–87; Sanderson 1942:710–24), thereby building interest in rural life problems. The first state country life conference was held in February 1911, under College of Agriculture auspices at the University of Wisconsin. Henry C. Taylor, agricultural economist who later would be called by Houston to head the BAE, was Conference chair. Galpin reported on his initial work on the rural community (1911:12–18). The rural school movement and the rural church movement, both major components of the "campaign for rural progress," were given a boost by the Commission's *Report*.

The third great movement recommended by the Commission was the establishment of a nationalized extension program with work in each state's College of Agriculture.[4] This recommendation gave further impetus to the idea that the Association of American Agricultural Colleges and Experiment Stations had been advocating. That idea became a reality when Congress passed the Smith-Lever Act in 1914. The Act provided federal funding for an unprecedented cooperative arrangement between the land-grant colleges and the USDA to offer instruction and practical demonstrations in agriculture and home economics for persons not in college. One consequence of the resulting greater contact by agricultural college faculty with farmers was "a rapid increase in interest in rural sociology and agricultural economics" (Sanderson 1917:433).

THE RURAL SOCIAL SCIENCES EMERGE

At the time of the Country Life Commission's *Report,* there were signs that rural sociology might emerge as a specialized area within the still-young discipline of sociology. When Secretary Houston made his decision to reorganize the economics work within the USDA and to start what was to be the Division, there was a small core of persons dedicated to rural sociological research and teaching. These were strategically located in a number of land-grant colleges. A few were in other academic institutions. The growth of the rural social sciences between 1909 and 1919 had been aided by the *Report's* emphasis on fact-finding surveys, studies economic and sociological in content.

After the *Report,* both rural sociology and agricultural economics increasingly began to find a place in the teaching and research programs of agricultural colleges. Normal schools, which trained rural teachers, began to offer rural sociology courses. Some major Protestant denominational bodies, interested in strengthening the rural church, employed staff members with sociological training. Warren H. Wilson and Paul L. Vogt, for example, directed numerous church related rural life surveys (Buttel et al. 1990:11–15; Nelson 1969:45–46).

To train and broaden agricultural college faculties, the Association of American Agricultural Colleges and Experiment Stations had a practice of organizing month-long summer "graduate schools." At the school held in 1910, a course in rural economics and sociology was given for the first time. Henry Taylor discussed the scope and methods of agricultural economics. Kenyon Butterfield, who had first given a course in rural sociology in 1902 at the University of Michigan, outlined the field of rural sociology. The course was judged by the USDA's Office of Experiment Stations as "one of the most important enterprises" of the Fourth Graduate School of Agriculture (Allen 1910:406).

At the annual meeting of the American Sociological Association, held in 1916, Dwight Sanderson (1917:433–60) reported on his survey of the teaching of rural sociology. He found 31 land-grant colleges, 9 separate state universities, 30 normal schools, and 29 other colleges and universities were teaching rural sociology. The first separate department for rural sociology was the one authorized in 1915 at Cornell University. This department, named "Rural Social Organization," became active in 1918 with Dwight Sanderson in charge.

The persons engaged in rural sociology research and teaching first met together in 1912, during a conference on "Social Service and Country Life" sponsored by the Federal Council of Churches. A dozen people, among them Galpin, gathered informally several times in the room of Kenyon L. Butterfield (Brunner 1968:43–44). They decided to try to have rural life chosen as the theme for an annual meeting of the American Sociological Association. In 1916, this effort was successful. They also decided to try to organize a rural section of the Association. And in 1921, recognition as a section was gained.[5]

THE RURAL ORGANIZATION SERVICE

Within the USDA, the Division had antecedents that trace to the Rural Organization Service, set up in 1913 as noted earlier. The General Education Board had been financing some farm demonstration work in Southern states. When Houston became Secretary of Agriculture, the Board offered to finance some other work (Baker et al. 1963:73–74; Sanderson 1939:219–21). It was suggested that marketing was of great importance and that marketing required organization. The Board agreed to finance a preliminary study of the general problem of rural organization for one year, thereby providing the funds for a new nongovernmental Rural Organization Service closely integrated with the USDA's Office of Markets. In fact, the relationship was so close that the USDA directory of June 1914 showed the new unit as a part of the Secretary's office (USDA 1914:3–4).

Houston induced his friend, Thomas N. Carver, to take leave from Harvard to head the Rural Organization Service. Like many of his contemporaries, Carver had an identification with both economics and sociology.[6] When funding was not continued by the Board for a second year, the work was shifted to what first became the Office of Markets and Rural Organization, and later, in 1917, the Bureau of Markets. Carver stayed on for a year in the USDA as "Adviser in Agricultural Economics" before returning to Harvard. During this time, Carver published "The Organization of a Rural Community" in the 1914 USDA *Yearbook* (1915: 89–138). This was a detailed plan of organization to meet the business and social needs of rural communities.

Carver's work was continued by Carl W. Thompson,[7] who held the title "Specialist in Rural Organization Work." Thompson was first made responsible for two lines of investigation. One was "rural credit, insurance, and communication." The other was "rural, social, and educational activities." The object of the latter work was described in 1915 as the

> improvement of social and educational conditions in rural communities by the accumulation and dissemination of useful information growing out of a study of the social and educational needs of typical communities; the work of their existing forms of organization, and the possibilities for improvement through organized activity; the investigation of methods of encouraging social organization activities; and the study of means of improving social, economic, and educational conditions of women and children through the work of women's rural organizations. (USDA 1915:35)

At the time, Thompson had a "scientific staff" of three people: Anne M. Evans, J. Sterling Moran, and Leon E. Truesdell. Truesdell left to join the Bureau of the Census where he became a specialist in farm population. Evans, investigator in women's rural organizations for about three years, published *Women's Rural Organizations and Their Activities* (1918). Moran, field assistant for two years, prepared *The Community Fair* (1917). He also had collaborative arrangements with a small number of university-based social scientists.

By 1917, Wayne C. Nason joined the staff as an assistant. He, with Thompson, published *Rural Community Buildings in the United States* (1920). On July 1, 1919, Nason was transferred to Galpin's staff in the new Farm Life Studies unit. His work was likewise transferred to Galpin's unit.

COUNTRY LIFE IN 1919

Only a few months after World War I had ended, Secretary Houston started the actions that resulted in a sociological research unit within the USDA. Although the participation of the United States in the war had been short, the war brought major changes for American agriculture and rural life. A decade earlier the Country Life Commission had called for the reconstruction of country life. After the war, "talk of reconstruction policies was rife and agriculture shared in this" (Sanderson 1942:726).

During 1917–19 farmers benefited from unusually prosperous conditions as the prices for their products and their incomes rose (Elliott 1940:105–6; Genung 1940:292–94). The number of farms in 1919, about 6.5 million, had changed little in ten years. Farm tenancy, however, had been climbing since 1880 until close to two out of every five farm operators did not own the land they tilled. Farmers were in the early stages of substituting mechanical power for animal power. Nearly all depended entirely on horses or mules for plowing, cultivating, and other field tasks. In 1919, only 158,000 tractors (exclusive of steam and garden) could be found on farms (USDA 1964:29).

The rural population, numbering around 51 million, had continued its longtime growth. A landmark turning point, nevertheless, was at hand. The 1920 census would show the nation's rural population was outnumbered for the first time by the urban. The war had had an unsettling effect on the farm population. Farms are said to have supplied about one-fourth, or 1.1 million, of all men who entered the military during the war (Genung 1940:293). Some farm operators near cities and hired farm workers were drawn into higher paying factory jobs. There was an extensive movement of African Americans from southern farms to northern cities. With demobilization, the off-farm movement was reversed. Hundreds of thousands of war veterans suddenly reentered farm life, many wanting to find a farm of their own.

Some gains were being made in reducing the physical isolation of rural areas. Probably close to 30 percent of the farm families had an automobile (Schuler and Swiger 1947), and rural roads were being improved. Despite this, in 1925, the year for which road information was first reported by the Census of Agriculture, three-fourths of the farms were located on roads that commonly were impassable by auto in early spring because of mud. Winter snows also made auto use impossible for many for extended periods. By 1920, nearly 39 percent of the farms had a telephone but many were served by inadequate small cooperative or privately owned local companies. In 1919, radios were a curiosity.

The United States also lagged far behind in making electricity available to rural communities (Beall 1940:790–92). Farm dwellings with electricity approached 7 percent in 1919 (Schuler and Swiger 1947:28), but over half of these generated the electricity on the farm by engine, water, or wind. Electricity was the key to having the appliances that made some of the farm woman's homemaking tasks easier and the farm home more comfortable. In 1919, no more than one farm home in ten had running water.

Services used and social ties for the majority of country families continued to be predominantly local, the geographic limits set by horse and buggy, the team-haul, or walking. For example, although there had been substantial gains by 1919 in consolidation for elementary education, over 195,000 one-teacher schools remained in the countryside (Kolb and Brunner 1935:406). These small schools, within walking distance of children's homes, were "distinctly the institution of the rural neighborhood group" (Kolb 1921:27).

As a consequence of the war, rural America in 1919 saw some new and expanded social organizations. The wartime National Defense Council, through its state and county councils of defense, had pushed the formation of local community councils that conformed to the natural community rather political subdivisions (Sanderson 1942:707). While after the war, the Defense Council saw a need to preserve some voluntary type of such community organization (Smith 1919:36–46, 223–38), the effort collapsed in the absence of a wartime rationale. Social welfare work for rural areas was started when the American Red Cross organized Home Service Sections of local Red Cross chapters to assist families of men in military service. By 1919 there were 4,000 such sections with 10,000 branches in smaller communities. At the close of the war, the service was expanded to civilian families, especially in rural counties (Sanderson 1942:487; Steiner 1919:30–35).

The outbreak of war found the new system of cooperative extension workers at county, district, and state levels "constituted the only Federal machinery in intimate touch with the millions of people in the farming districts" (Houston 1926:336). There was a rapid expansion of extension workers on an emergency basis. On June 30, 1919, over 75 percent of the counties had an agricultural agent, 35 percent had a home demonstration agent (True 1928:151). The Extension Service's wartime work helped establish the system on a permanent basis. To support this extension work, organizations of farmers began to be formed in many counties under different names. The supporting county groups started to federate within states. Representatives meeting in 1919 laid the groundwork for a new general farmers' organization know as the American Farm Bureau Federation. Thus, an unanticipated consequence of the extension system was the rise of a third large farmers organization alongside the two existing such groups, the Grange (Patrons of Husbandry), which dated from 1867, and the Farmers' Educational and Cooperative Union, started in 1902.

The year 1919 also saw other actions concerned with rural life which contributed to the context for Secretary Houston's decision to create a farm life studies unit in the USDA. In January of that year, the first National Country Life Conference was held with "Country Life Reconstruction" as the conference theme.[8] Here a decision was made to form what was soon named the American Country Life Association (ACLA). The "campaign for rural progress," interrupted by the war, was getting under way again.

At the conference, several committees submitted reports (ACLA 1919: 51–160). One, chaired by Charles J. Galpin,[9] recommended a national program of cooperative research with projects funded by colleges, universities, theological seminaries and, philanthropic foundations. The Committee on Standardization would become a clearinghouse for national rural research plans and results. A committee on legislation, also chaired by Galpin, urged that the U.S. Census for 1920 include a "farm population" classification. In advocating this new classification, the committee noted "that a new science is arising, Rural Sociology, which is concerned fundamentally with farm population" (ACLA 1919:74).

About this same time, Galpin[10] also chaired a committee "Education and Improvement of Rural Life" set up by a new voluntary research organization called the American Association for Agricultural Legislation. Galpin solicited, by letter, the views of about 150 rural life leaders as to the chief social and economic rural problems in their respective states. The report on the findings stated:

> The country life movement . . . has reached the point when it seems desirable, for research purposes, to select from the mass of rural issues . . . a few problems that are fundamental to the main line of rural progress. These few issues . . . might well be standardized in detail by some central cooperative research bureau. Following this, certain uniform methods of study might be formulated. A wide employment of such standard problems and methods would eventually lead to a public policy of large rural improvement. (Galpin and Cox 1919:80)

Finally, we should note that in the United States in 1919 the ferment about rural life issues had an international linkage. At its first conference, the ACLA heard a report from its committee on the "International Country Life Movement" with Kenyon Butterfield as chair. Later that year the World Agriculture Society was founded with Butterfield as president (Zimmerman and Larson 1989). Also in 1919, the Interchurch World Movement was formed by Protestant groups (Buttel et al. 1990:14–15).

FARM LIFE STUDIES RECOMMENDED

When, in November 1918, Secretary Houston was looking for a new Chief of the Office of Farm Management, he accepted a suggestion that he appoint a committee to outline a plan for the future work of the Office (H. Taylor and A. Taylor 1952:422). The seven-member committee of leading men in agricultural economics and farm management included Henry C. Taylor, who was head of the Department of Agricultural Economics at the University of Wisconsin. On February 26, 1919, the committee presented its report. Seven lines of research work were recommended for the proposed Bureau of Farm Management and Farm Economics (USDA, Office of the Secretary 1919a). Farm life studies was one of the seven.[11]

Houston followed quickly by appointing Henry Taylor on March 8 to head what would be an expanded and reorganized program. Taylor then asked the Secretary to appoint a special committee to outline the work to be undertaken in farm life studies. On March 1–3, 1919, the committee met in Washington. Professor Thomas N. Carver, Houston's friend from

Harvard, chaired the committee. The twenty-eight members included seven women, indicative of the concern for the farm family and for women on the farm that Secretary Houston had expressed in his first annual report (Houston 1914). The group was composed predominantly of persons professionally engaged in working with rural people or who were students of rural life and its problems.

Eleven of the members were from within the USDA. They were: G. I. Christie, then assistant secretary but on leave from his administrative post in agricultural extension at Purdue; Henry Taylor, the newly appointed Chief of the Office of Farm Management; L. C. Gray, who had just come from George Peabody College for Teachers to be in charge of the new land economics program in Taylor's agency; C. W. Thompson, rural organization specialist in the Bureau of Markets; O. E. Baker, Office of Farm Management; James L. Dumas, a Bureau of Markets staff member stationed in the state of Washington; A. C. True, Director of the States Relations Service which then included both the Office of Experiment Stations and the Office of Extension Work; and four staff members from the Office of Extension Work, namely, C. B. Smith, chief for work in the North and West; Bradford Knapp, chief for work in the South; Florence E. Ward, in charge of work for women in the North and West; and Ola Powell, assistant in home demonstration and girl's club work in the South.

Nine members were drawn from land-grant colleges. Of these, five were identified with sociology; they were: E. K. Eyerly, Massachusetts Agricultural College; C. J. Galpin, University of Wisconsin; O. F. Hall, Purdue; Dwight Sanderson, Cornell; and George H. Von Tungeln, Iowa State College of Agriculture and Mechanic Arts. The others from the land-grant system were Alice M. Loomis, head of the Home Economics Department, University of Nebraska; Charles A. Lory, president of the State Agricultural College of Colorado, and, at the time, president of the Association of American Agricultural Colleges and Experiment Stations; Herbert F. Van Norman, dean of the University Farm School, University of California at Davis; and Edna N. White, head, Department of Home Economics and supervisor of home economics extension work, Ohio State University. White was also on the Committee on Instruction in Home Economics of the Association of American Agricultural Colleges. She was president of the American Home Economics Association, 1918–20.

The other seven members of the committee were E. C. Branson, University of North Carolina, prominent for his rural economic and social studies; Mabel Carney, Department of Rural Education, Teachers College, Columbia University, a longtime leader in the rural school movement;

Elizabeth Herring who was identified with the rural interests of the Young Women's Christian Association; H. N. Morse who made sociological studies of rural churches; Bruce R. Payne, president of George Peabody College for Teachers; Mrs. Oliver Wilson of Illinois, whose husband headed the National Grange, 1911–19; and F. O. Clark.[12]

THE SPECIAL COMMITTEE'S REPORT

On May 3, 1919, the special committee submitted its report to Secretary Houston (USDA, Office of the Secretary 1919b). The introduction advocated that people on farms should have the same opportunities for education, worship, recreation, and social contact as the people in cities and towns. Satisfactory hospitals and medical services should be within easy reach. Increased farm production and income made it now possible, in the committee's view, "to bring into many farm homes and rural communities the conveniences and institutions which make for comfort and an efficient, wholesome life" (USDA, Office of the Secretary 1919b:5). The subjects recommended for research were selected with a view that their study would facilitate advancement in the life of American farmers and their families.

Ten suggested fields of study were outlined sketchily and brief comments were made about each. The ten were: (1) rural home life, including the farmer's wife, the children, and the farmhouse; (2) opportunities for social contact in typical rural communities; (3) the relation of educational and religious institutions to farm life problems; (4) problems relating to geographical population groups; (5) rural organization without definite geographical boundaries; (6) social aspects of tenancy and landlordism; (7) social aspects of various types of farm labor; (8) the relation of various forms of disability to farm life problems (the aged was one of the forms of disability); (9) the social consequences of local disasters due to natural causes; and (10) the social consequence of thrift and agencies for promoting thrift. The fields were made more specific by topics listed under each. For example, under geographical population groups appeared: (a) definition, e.g., the neighborhood, the rural community; (b) planning and organization; (c) community centers and buildings; (d) the relation of urban and rural populations; and (e) the shifting of rural populations.

The committee recommended that the closest cooperation be sought with the Bureau of the Census to collect more information relating to farm population. The report indicated that the committee had discussed cooperation with the state colleges and experiment stations in carrying on farm life studies as well as lines of cooperation with other federal and social agencies, but no specifics were put into the report.

We have no account of the deliberations that went on during the committee's three-day meeting. But, aside from three of the fields of study, the listing was highly compatible with the objectives for country life that were summarized in the conclusions of the committees of the first National Country Life Conference a few months earlier (*Proceedings* 1919:15–24). It also had considerable resemblance to the list of rural social problems which came out of Galpin's survey of some 150 rural leaders (Galpin and Cox 1919:94). The highly ranked field of educational and religious institutions also reflected the interests of the rural school and the rural church movements. The work of the Galpin-chaired committees for the American Sociological Society and the first Country Life Conference clearly influenced the recommendations to study geographical population groups and to seek Census Bureau cooperation on farm population information. Likewise, the thinking Galpin did about the social role of the rural housewife and the rural child (Galpin 1918) was reflected in the special committee's top-ranked field—rural home life.

The report received Houston's hearty approval. On May 12, he had Galpin on the job to get the farm life studies research work under way. Not only was Galpin unusually well prepared for the task by virtue of the groundbreaking work he had done at the University of Wisconsin but he was the person Henry Taylor wanted for the position. After all, Taylor had selected Galpin for his staff eight years earlier to begin the study of country life problems in Wisconsin. In Galpin's view, the Division was a fulfillment, belated in time, of Theodore Roosevelt's desire for a government unit to study the needs of country life (Galpin 1924b:1).

Galpin began in the USDA's Office of Farm Management. Within a few weeks a reorganization effective July 1, 1919, made his "Farm Life Studies" unit one of the research sections in what was renamed the Office of Farm Management and Farm Economics. Secretary Henry C. Wallace created the BAE on July 1, 1922, when he consolidated all of the USDA's work in economics (Tenny 1947). At the same time, Galpin's unit was given divisional status and the name "Farm Population and Rural Life."[13] This title continued to hold except for July 1939 to November 1947, when "Welfare" was substituted for "Life."

SUMMARY

The organization in 1919 in the USDA of a "Farm Life Studies" unit headed by Charles J. Galpin was the beginning of sociological research in the federal government on a continuing basis. Clearly, the administrative action by Secretary of Agriculture Houston to start this work was well-grounded. The action was the end result of a set of social and political forces concerned with improving rural life going back at least to the *Report* in 1909 of President Theodore Roosevelt's Country Life Commission. That *Report* had called for the reconstruction of rural life. However, entry of the United States into World War I interrupted the country life movement.

The end of the war saw a conjuncture of: (1) a resurgence of organized activity on the part of rural interests, e.g., the organization of the American Country Life Association in 1919; (2) a renewed call from rural life interests for rural reconstruction; (3) the emergence during the preceding decade of rural sociology as a science which held the promise of providing a beneficial knowledge base; and (4) persons in decision-making positions in the USDA with deep and long-standing concerns for the human side of agriculture, namely, David F. Houston and Henry Taylor.

Notes

1. The title "economist" or "agricultural economist" continued to be used for appointments in the Division until the early 1940s, when "social science analyst" came into use. The U.S. Civil Service announced examinations for "rural sociologist," specifically for the Division, for the first time in 1940.

2. For example, there were instances of federally supported sociological research as far back as the field investigations by the black sociologist W. E. B. Du Bois undertaken in 1897. In 1897, Du Bois received support from U.S. Commissioner of Labor Carroll D. Wright to study the conditions of small, well-defined groups of the black population. The first study was in Farmville, Virginia (Buttel et al. 1990:2–3; see also Du Bois 1968: 202–4, 226–27). Du Bois, again under Department of Labor auspices, also made a study of black landholders in Georgia in 1901 and made, for the Census Bureau, a comprehensive analysis of the status of black farmers based on the 1900 U.S. Census. The Children's Bureau, U.S. Department of Labor, initiated a set of field studies in 1916 dealing with conditions surrounding childbirth and infancy in rural communities. The resulting reports included information on the work of rural mothers, family living conditions, and health practices. The reports, all in the Children's Bureau Rural Child-Welfare Series were: Elizabeth Moore (1917); Frances Sage Bradley and Margaretta A. Williamson (1918); Viola I. Paradise (1919); and Florence Brown Sherbon and Elizabeth Moore (1919). There was also a Children's Bureau Series called Dependent, Defective and Delinquent Classes which included two rural studies: Kate Holladay Claghorn (1918), and Walter L. Treadway and Emma O. Lundberg (1919).

3. The Country Life Commission report has had an enduring place in the rural social history literature. First published in 1909, it was soon reprinted by the Spokane Chamber of Commerce for use in the Northwest, then again by Sturgis & Walton (1911) with reis-

sues in 1911 and 1917. In 1944 the University of North Carolina Press reprinted. In 1958 the House Committee on Agriculture included the report with the record of the "Hearings Before the Subcommittee on Family Farms of the Committee on Agriculture, July 8 and 9, 1958." The complete report was reprinted again in Wayne D. Rasmussen (1975:1860–1906).

4. Liberty Hyde Bailey, Chair of the Commission, was dean of the College of Agriculture at Cornell University. Kenyon L. Butterfield, president of the Massachusetts Agricultural College and closer to being a rural sociologist than any other member of the Commission, was probably second only to Bailey in influencing the Commission's *Report*. Both were prominent in the leadership of the land-grant college association. Other members of the Commission were C. S. Barrett, from Union City, Georgia, president of the Farmers' Cooperative and Educational Union of America; William H. Beard, editor of the *Great Western Magazine*, Sacramento, California; Walter Hines Page, editor of *World's Work*, New York; Gifford Pinchot, U.S. Forest Service; and Henry Wallace, editor of the midwestern journal *Wallace's Farmer*.

5. For the sequence of events between the 1912 informal meeting and the formal organization of the Rural Sociology Section in December 1921, see Holik and Hassinger (1986).

6. Carver was one of the small group who in 1905 decided to form the American Sociological Association (Rhoades 1980:1, 7). He compiled *Sociology and Social Progress: A Handbook for Students of Sociology* (1905). His *Principles of Rural Economics* (1911) concluded with a chapter on "Problems of Rural Social Life." He also co-authored with Henry B. Hall *Human Relations: An Introduction to Sociology* (1923), and co-authored with Gustav A. Lundquist *Principles of Rural Sociology* (1927).

7. While at Minnesota, C. W. Thompson had co-authored with Gustav P. Warber (1913) the first of three pioneering social and economic surveys of rural areas sponsored by the Bureau of Research in Agricultural Economics in the University of Minnesota's Department of Agriculture.

8. The conference was called by a self-constituted committee of nine country life leaders chaired by K. L. Butterfield. The other members of the organizing committee were rural social scientist E. C. Branson, University of North Carolina; Mabel Carney, prominent in rural education, Teacher's College, Columbia University; P. P. Claxton, U.S. Commissioner of Education; A. R. Mann, Dean, College of Agriculture, Cornell University; C. W. Thompson, USDA; George E. Vincent, president, University of Minnesota and president of the American Sociological Association in 1916; Georgia L. White, Cooperative Extension, Cornell University; and Warren H. Wilson, rural sociologist with the Presbyterian Board of Home Missions. Dwight Sanderson, rural sociologist at Cornell University, was acting secretary.

9. The other members were Walter J. Campbell, YMCA College, Springfield, Massachusetts and rural sociologist Paul L. Vogt, Board of Home Missions and Church Extension, Methodist Episcopal Church.

10. In addition to Galpin, the other members were E. C. Branson, K. L. Butterfield, A. R. Mann, and H. W. Fogt; the latter was Rural Division Chief, U.S. Bureau of Education.

11. The other lines of research were cost of production, farm organization, farm finance, farm labor, agricultural history and geography, and land utilization.

12. We were not successful in locating information about F. O. Clark.

13. Henry Taylor, the first BAE chief, objected to the word "sociology"; he preferred the phrase "rural life," hence the name given Galpin's unit (H. Taylor 1948:123).

3

The Division as an Organization

To help understand the Division's research and related activities, it is important to understand the essential features of the Division as a research unit within the federal government and the context within which it operated.

The Division had the benefit of continuity in leadership by sociologists whose peers bestowed on them the highest recognition offered. The Division had wide and, sometimes, abrupt swings in money and staff. The professional staff fell to as low as two and rose to as many as fifty-seven. More than 140 persons held a professional appointment over the Division's life. Most were sociologists but during the reconstituted BAE the staff included some cultural anthropologists, social psychologists, and others. Women were among the first persons appointed as professionals. Finally, a system of cooperative research arrangements with universities was a special feature of the Division's organization.

THE DIVISION'S LEADERSHIP

The Division had remarkable stability in its leadership. Charles J. Galpin and Carl Taylor, between them, headed the Division for thirty-two of its thirty-four years. Margaret J. Hagood succeeded Taylor. She had served little more than a year when the BAE was abolished on November 2, 1953.[1]

Charles J. Galpin

In 1911, Galpin was chosen at age forty-seven by Henry Taylor to teach about rural social problems and the human factors in agriculture at the University of Wisconsin. Without formal training in sociology, Galpin began his "drift" into the work that made him one of the pioneers in the sociology of rural life.[2] Raised in a rural milieu, mainly central New York, his previous work experience included thirteen years as teacher and principal at the Belleville Academy in New York. He established an agricultural department there in 1901, certainly one of the first in any high school in the nation. Later he operated a forty-acre farm in the cutover sand wastes of Michigan for three years, a period during which he conquered insomnia.

In preparing to teach his first course, Galpin found no rural sociology text and little suitable material in the library (1938a:20). He began studies to get firsthand knowledge of the uncharted area. This led directly to his now-classic *The Social Anatomy of an Agricultural Community,* a landmark for studying the rural community (1915). His first book, *Rural Life,* was based on the discovery of a repeating socioeconomic unit of local territory and population (1918).

When Henry Taylor went to Washington in March 1919 to lead what became the BAE, he told Galpin that if all went well he would be back after him in about a year to head up the farm life work (H. Taylor 1992: 144). He had Galpin in Washington in only about two months! In his new position, Galpin became a central figure in developing the new field of rural sociology. He was successful in having the U.S. Census make farm population data available. Understanding of the social groupings in rural society was gained through studies of neighborhoods and communities. Galpin brought in staff members to conduct widespread studies of farm family living and to start research on the social psychology of farmers' economic organizations. One early study pertained to farm women.

In Washington as in Wisconsin, Galpin was a crusader for rural life. To this end, he had studies made to bring to light "the prideful features of rural life" (1938a:49). He made numerous speeches about rural life and the Division's research to a great variety of audiences, even using the new media of radio with its national and regional hookups.

Galpin was also active in the lesser remembered international agriculture scene. In 1926 he spent six months on official assignment visiting thirteen European countries. That year he was also a U.S. delegate to the General Assembly of the International Institute of Agriculture in Rome and to the International Rural Life Conference in Brussels.

While Division head, Galpin wrote two books (1924a; 1925) and, with P. A. Sorokin and C. C. Zimmerman, he co-edited the three-volume *A Systematic Source Book in Rural Sociology* (1930–32). It had been Galpin who secured the $6,000 from the BAE to finance the project at the University of Minnesota (Galpin 1938a:60–61). The first secretary of the American Country Life Association, he was also vice-president in 1923 and 1924. Always active in the Rural Section of the American Sociological Association (ASA), he was ASA vice-president for 1932. Upon Galpin's retirement in 1934, T. B. Manny, who had joined the Division staff in 1927, was made acting head.

Carl C. Taylor

Carl Taylor was a generation—twenty years—younger than Galpin. Unlike Galpin, he had a Ph.D. in sociology,[3] and virtually his entire career was as a sociologist. Farm-reared in the Corn Belt's Shelby County, Iowa, Taylor also had extensive experience in the South before joining the federal service. And he had worked in three of the New Deal action agencies before Secretary Henry A. Wallace chose him to be Galpin's replacement.

Taylor received his Ph.D. at the University of Missouri in 1918 where he had joined the sociology faculty a year earlier. Taylor's first book (1919) was on social survey methods. In 1920 he accepted an offer from the North Carolina State College of Agriculture and Engineering to initiate a program in rural sociology and agricultural economics.[4] Shortly thereafter a graduate school was established and he was made its first dean. One of Taylor's early research activities in the state was to help organize a study of North Carolina farmers. The study compared different tenure groups and included black farmers. While there he also wrote *Rural Sociology* (1926), one of the early texts in the field.

At North Carolina State, Taylor encountered trouble. Despite segregationist practices at the time, he openly invited an African American to a university function. He did not hesitate to take a position about controversial issues, using hard-hitting and forthright language (Mayo 1983:54). He had great energy and was a skilled public speaker. He gained much influence in the college and in the state. But as of June 30, 1931, his position was abolished by the Board of Trustees on recommendation of the college president. Taylor's dismissal was the subject of an investigation by the *Baltimore Evening Sun* and the National Association of University Professors (Larson et al. 1999).

After two rather difficult years financially, Taylor started his career in the federal government. When the Subsistence Homesteads Division in the Department of Interior was started in 1933, M. L. Wilson was made director. Wilson asked Taylor to join his staff (Conkin 1959:98). When Secretary of the Interior Harold Ickes ordered a policy change, moving from decentralized to centralized administration, Wilson left in protest. Taylor left with him (Conkin 1959:110–22), and in 1934, became regional director of the AAA's Land Policy Section in Raleigh, North Carolina. When the Resettlement Administration (RA) was established in 1935 with Rexford G. Tugwell as administrator, Taylor was made assistant administrator to direct the Resettlement Division. Taylor and Tugwell, however, had their differences. Tugwell was succeeded by Will W. Alexander and the agency was put in the USDA. In the meantime a social research unit was set up in the RA and continued in the successor agency, the FSA, with Taylor in charge. Even after Taylor became head of the Division, he continued to direct the FSA research unit as long as it existed.

Taylor came to the Division at an opportune time. The preceding New Deal years in the USDA had been gradually setting the stage for a vast expansion in the use of sociology for program and policy purposes. Taylor had the right characteristics, as a sociologist and personally, to have the Division take advantage of these circumstances. He became a "tower of strength in sociological matters within governmental circles" (Smith 1975).

Taylor's acquaintance with Secretary Wallace and M. L. Wilson went back to the 1920s. They, with BAE Chief Howard Tolley, saw the need for sociological research on the pressing problems facing agriculture and rural life. By the end of the 1930s, the Division had a budget and professional staff twelve times the maximum reached under Galpin. But World War II brought waning support and cutbacks as top-level USDA administrators changed and the BAE and the Division came under political fire.

Like Galpin, Taylor occupied a position of national leadership among rural sociologists. Taylor was president of the American Country Life Association in 1935, and in 1939 was the second president of the Rural Sociological Society. In 1946 he was president of the ASA. While Division head, he wrote *Rural Life in Argentina* (1948a)[5] and, with Division colleagues, was senior author *of Rural Life in the United States* (Taylor et al. 1949). His *The Farmer's Movement, 1620–1920* (1953) was the result of work over many years. In 1952, Taylor left the Division to do work in the area of rural international development.

Margaret Jarman Hagood

Margaret Jarman Hagood served briefly as head of the Division until Secretary Benson terminated the BAE. Hagood, a native of Georgia, came to the Division in 1942 from the University of North Carolina.[6] She earned an A.B. degree at Queens College, North Carolina, an M.A. degree with a major in mathematics at Emory University, and received a Ph.D. in sociology in 1937 at the University of North Carolina. Before coming to the Division, she had already written *Mothers of the South* (1939) and *Statistics for Sociologists* (1941).

From the time Hagood joined the staff in 1942, the Division relied heavily on her special technical expertise in statistics. She developed and applied sophisticated statistical methods in her work in population analysis (see Chapter 5), level of living indexes (see Chapter 6), and farm labor and wage and wage rate studies (see Chapter 9). When Hagood came into the Division, the USDA had already initiated a major statistical research program, working with the statistical laboratory at Iowa State College, to improve the accuracy of data needed by the USDA (USDA, Statistical Reporting Service 1969:84–88). By the mid-1940s, this had led to the development of the Master Sample for use in farm and open country areas plus unincorporated and incorporated places (King and Jessen 1945). The Master Sample had numerous applications for the Division's work in farm labor and population. Hagood, representing the Division, was in the mainstream of these important developments for social statistics, working with statisticians in the BAE and at the statistical laboratory in Iowa.

After the Division was abolished, Hagood continued her work in the new Agricultural Marketing Service. The quality of Hagood's work was recognized by her election to the Sociological Research Association in 1943, honorary membership in the International Population Union in 1947, and in 1949 being made a Fellow of the American Statistical Association. In 1950 she was elected vice president of the ASA. She was president of the Rural Sociological Society for 1955–56, the first woman elected to this post.

THE ADMINISTRATIVE CONTEXT

During its thirty-four-year life, the Division was affected directly or indirectly by the actions and policies of seven presidents, eleven USDA secretaries, and seven BAE chiefs. On organizational charts of the executive branch, the Division was a subordinate unit, the lowest officially recognized level of organization. Requests for funds appropriated by the Congress were filtered through successively higher levels of the executive branch starting with the BAE chief. The case for funds then had to be made with such key congressional committees as the Senate Committee on Agriculture and Forestry, the House Committee on Agriculture, and the subcommittees on agriculture for the appropriations committee in both the House and the Senate (Rasmussen and Baker 1972:202–10). At the end of this process, appropriated funds came to the BAE not to support specific divisions but for lines of work.

A new element in the administrative context was introduced by the Federal Reports Act of 1942. Now, any request for identical information made to ten or more respondents had to be reviewed and approved in the Bureau of the Budget. This was done by the Office of Statistical Policy.

For such reviews, the BAE was the liaison unit between all USDA agencies and the Bureau of the Budget. Even questionnaires for the Division's cooperative projects with the state agricultural experiment stations were subject to this review and approval process.

Access to the Division's work often had to be channeled through the USDA hierarchy. Funds for the Division from other agencies came through the BAE. Likewise, the hierarchy was the channel for information originating in the Division and provided to the Congress and other federal agencies. The hierarchy could provide a buffer, a filter, for external influences on the Division or could accentuate the impact of such influences. Much depended on the political climate and on the beliefs and orientation of the BAE chief and the USDA secretary at the time.

The Bureau of Agricultural Economics

The BAE provided the immediate administrative context for the Division. The number of divisions within the BAE changed from time to time as its activities were expanded or reduced. For example, the BAE had eighteen divisions in 1922 and twelve in 1939 (Baker and Rasmussen 1975:54, 59). Despite the ups and downs, the Division endured until 1953 when its parent agency in the USDA was abolished.

In contrast to USDA "action," educational, or regulatory agencies, the BAE was primarily a research agency. Henry Taylor, the first chief, established its guiding policies. "Its major functions are those of fact finding, information giving, and service rendering" (H. Taylor 1992:138, 148). As an agency of all the people, he further held that the BAE was obligated to take the national or social welfare point of view, not a purely agrarian standpoint. Taylor's position would put the BAE in a difficult spot when a succession of secretaries, starting with H. C. Wallace, turned to it specifically for economic analyses.

Galpin was not uncomfortable having his Division in an agency made up mostly of economists. In fact, he thought it was rather fortunate (Galpin 1938a:36). In the 1920s agricultural economics in the BAE was not a narrow economic specialty (Hall 1983:86). For BAE economists of that time, "economic adjustment was a means toward the larger goal of revitalizing the rural community" (Hall 1983:85).

Over the years, there were exceptions to the BAE's research mission.[7] For example, until 1938 the BAE also had market-related regulatory and service functions. At that time, Secretary Henry A. Wallace designated the BAE as the general planning agency for the entire USDA, a major addition to its research function. This continued until 1945 when Secretary Clinton P. Anderson removed the planning function from the BAE and returned it to the Secretary's office.

In the view of USDA historians Wayne Rasmussen and Gladys Baker, "of all the Department's research bureaus, the Economic Research Service and its predecessor, the Bureau of Agricultural Economics, have engendered the most controversy" (1972:77). On occasion, BAE work was opposed by powerful organized interest groups or aroused the ire of Congress. For example, during the BAE's first years, the Congressional Joint Committee on Printing blocked publication of sections of the historical *Atlas of American Agriculture*. The Cotton Bloc in Congress got a prohibition of any reports on the "intentions to plant cotton" into the appropriations act for the BAE (Tenny 1947:1025). Studies of settlement on submarginal land and on land values brought pressure from real estate interests and their spokesmen in Congress (H. Taylor 1992:59–65, 74, 79). Started in 1938, the state and county land-use planning program soon aroused the wrath of the American Farm Bureau Federation. This led, in 1942, to Congressional prohibition of any BAE funds for such planning work and a budget cut (Hardin 1955:155–63; Kirkendall 1966:195–217). Cotton interests appeared again when the report "A Conversion Program for the Cotton South," issued in 1945, proposed letting cotton prices drop to be competitive in the world market and with synthetics. Criticism of the report by many important southern groups was reflected by attacks in Congress on the BAE and Howard Tolley, its Chief. Tolley resigned in frustration (Baker and Rasmussen 1975:61–63; Kirkendall 1966:227–30, 240–43). A demotion of the BAE began in the USDA.

BAE Chiefs and the Division

The Division's fate—its resources, its program, its existence—was inextricably linked to the changing role and status of the BAE. The administrative decision-maker closest to the Division was the BAE chief, always an agricultural economist. This person was not a political appointee but was selected by the USDA secretary. The chief had to approve the Division's program and make the case to the USDA secretary and to Congressional committees for its funds.

Galpin worked with four BAE chiefs: Henry Taylor who served until forced out by President Calvin Coolidge in 1925; T. P. Cooper (1925–26); Lloyd S. Tenny (1926–28); and Nils A. Olsen (1928–35). Taylor's role was especially crucial for the Division.[8] It was he who wanted rural life studies in his agency. It was he who wanted Galpin to head up such studies. And it was he who fought to save the Division's small budget from cuts or elimination by the several Congressional committees. In 1922, when the Division's scientific studies of country life problems were being explained to an appropriations committee hearing, it was Taylor who took Galpin along, introduced him to the committee, and let him speak about the work (Galpin 1938a:44–45).

Galpin (1934a) had kind words at his retirement for the BAE leadership. This, despite the fact that the Division saw no gains in resources after BAE Chief Henry Taylor left. And, during Olsen's last years, a time of severe depression, the Division took more severe cuts than the BAE as a whole (Taylor 1941b [refers to Carl C. Taylor]; H. A. Wallace 1933:101; 1934:111).

Division head Carl Taylor had three BAE chiefs: A. G. Black (1935–38), Howard R. Tolley (1938–46), and O. V. Wells. Black was a strong supporter of New Deal programs and was picked by Henry Wallace for the post. Under Black, the Division's budget more than tripled from about $13,000 to $43,590 in three years. During the eight years under Tolley, also chosen by Wallace, the Division had its high point in resources, in the scope of its research, and in providing social science knowledge for the public agenda. Even prior to becoming BAE chief, Tolley had a record of support for sociological research. By the time he started in the post, the climate had become good for sociological research. Secretary Wallace and M. L. Wilson, his close associate, had made it that way. In a short time, the Division's budget was more than thirty-fold that in Galpin's last year. Tolley backed M. L. Wilson's idea that the Division add cultural anthropologists, social psychologists and others to complement the sociologists. Division staff members were included among BAE representatives presenting research findings to Congressional committees. But starting about 1941, the BAE came under frequent attack by its critics. Tolley's efforts to defend his agency could not prevent budget cuts and Congressional mandates restricting planning and research activities.

When Tolley elected to leave, Secretary Anderson replaced him with O. V. Wells, a career economist in the USDA. Wells was flexible (Kirkendall 1966: 257–58). He did not object to the limitations placed on the BAE (Baker and Rasmussen 1975:63). Under Wells, statistical work received more emphasis, research less. His inclination was to limit research involving social and psychological problems (Baker and Rasmussen 1975:65). He prohibited a new BAE journal from publishing articles dealing with agricultural policy (Wells 1949:9). Not only was the Division's research domain restricted, but there was an attrition of its resources. Carl Taylor began to feel harassed by the BAE leadership.

The Presidents and USDA Secretaries

Lines of authority among the BAE Chief, the USDA Secretary, and the President were clear enough. But relationships among the several sets of occupants varied greatly in harmony and compatibility. The consequences had an effect at the Division level.

Calvin Coolidge (1923–29) and Herbert Hoover (1929–33) appear to be the only ones of the seven presidents to have intervened directly in BAE affairs. Shortly after Coolidge took office, Secretary H. C. Wallace—a BAE supporter and father of Henry A. Wallace—died. Coolidge accused BAE Chief Henry Taylor of disloyalty on farm relief policy issues. When Taylor refused to resign, Coolidge ordered the incoming USDA Secretary to fire him (H. Taylor 1992:209–19). William Jardine (1925–29) did. Thus the Division lost its strongest backer in the administration. Hoover's controversies with the USDA, and especially the BAE, began when he administered the War Food Administration during the First World War. They continued when he was Secretary of Commerce in the Harding and Coolidge administrations. As President, in 1931, and after an earlier warning, he ordered the BAE to end all farm product price forecasts (D. Hamilton 1991:170–73). He "distrusted the farm economists, who . . . had too many socialistic ideas" (Conkin 1959:78). He also had the BAE's Division of Cooperative Marketing, with which the Division was cooperating in research, moved to his new Federal Farm Board.

Franklin Roosevelt (1933–45) had a major although indirect impact on the BAE and the Division. His election as president was followed by the initiation of unprecedented governmental measures for relief, recovery, and reform to cope with the Great Depression. In this context of ferment and change, the USDA under Henry A. Wallace (1933–40) embarked on bold new action programs to help farmers, the rural poor, and rural communities. These programs were started by either presidential order or congressional legislation. In this setting a reconstituted BAE and an expanded Division resulted.

Secretary Houston (1913–20) placed Henry Taylor and Galpin in their posts and in 1922, Secretary H. C. Wallace (1921–24) created the BAE and at that time Galpin's unit gained division status. But of all the USDA Secretaries, Henry A. Wallace had the greatest positive effects. Wallace's key appointments, the intellectual climate he fostered, and his reorganization of the USDA, turned out to be favorable for the social sciences in the USDA and for the Division. He had a broad concept of scientific research that "included the lifting of the social sciences to the same level as the natural sciences" (Culver 1996:25). Wallace selected M. L. Wilson, first as assistant secretary, then as undersecretary, and later as director of the Extension Service. Wilson supported a USDA program of discussion groups and "Schools of Philosophy" for farmers to provide a basis for informed democratic planning for agriculture.[9] He argued that rural sociology, social psychology, cultural anthropology, and political science should be developed commensurate to agricultural economics (Wilson 1938:1–7). He called conferences in 1939 on the question "What can the social sciences contribute to the work of the Department of Agriculture?" (Baker et al. 1963:239). One of these was specific to rural sociology (USDA, BAE, DFPRL 1939:3–20).

The positive effect of Henry A. Wallace would not be apparent at first. For instance, he kept on as BAE Chief Nils Olsen, who had been picked by William Jardine (1925–29). But Olsen was not sympathetic to the New Deal's agricultural policies. He soon found that Secretary Wallace bypassed the BAE for advice (Lowitt 1980:9–10). After two years, Olsen resigned.

After Olsen left the BAE, Wallace replaced him first with Black and then with Tolley, both supporters of the Division's work. In his annual reports to the President, Secretary Wallace's commitment to the social sciences emerged time and again (e.g., Wallace 1934:6; 1938:54–68, 87, 110–14). He also chose Carl Taylor as head of the Division to succeed Galpin.

After more than five years of administering an expanded department with action programs having divergent, even conflicting, themes (Gilbert and Howe 1991:210–18), Wallace made two major organizational moves. The first, the Mount Weather agreement of 1938 with the land-grant colleges, was intended to establish a system of democratic planning for action programs, adapt national policies and programs to local conditions, and provide better coordination on agricultural problems (Wallace 1939:73–76). A system of state and local "land-use" (in reality, agricultural) planning committees were to be set up.[10] The BAE was given a leading role in this new effort. The Division gained staff which was located in regional BAE offices in support of the planning committees through data, research, and training.

In the same year, Secretary Wallace reorganized the USDA. His aim was to ensure that the USDA's action programs were coordinated when they reached the farm. In addition to its research functions, the BAE was reconstituted as the central planning agency for the USDA (Baker et al.

1963:260–65). At the time, Undersecretary M. L. Wilson characterized the BAE as "the heart of the new Department structure" (Baker et al. 1963:261.) The Division was strategically placed in the USDA structure to have its social science expertise drawn upon by USDA agencies and by policy-makers. During this time with Tolley as BAE Chief, Carl Taylor succeeded in bringing the Division to its life-history high point in resources and in scope of activity.

Wallace's two big moves brought controversy for the BAE. The heady days for the social sciences did not last long. Wallace resigned in 1940, drafted by President Roosevelt to be his running mate. Fortunately for the Division, before Wallace left the USDA, he shifted M. L. Wilson from undersecretary to director of the Extension Service.

While his successor, Claude R. Wickard, lacked appreciation for the social sciences, he did not, however, cut the Division's budget (Kirkendall 1966:222). Harvard economist John D. Black (1947:1033) asserted that Wickard was "largely unable to use any kind of policy-making machinery." In regrouping the USDA for World War II tasks, he passed over the land-use planning committee system and set up a structure of defense (later, war) boards chaired by AAA staff (Baker et al. 1963:285–88). Wickard pushed the BAE and Tolley aside (Kirkendall 1966:207).

During Wickard's time in office, the BAE land-use planning and general planning functions increasingly came under attack. When Clinton P. Anderson, member of Congress from New Mexico, became Secretary in 1945, he soon transferred responsibility for general agricultural program planning from the BAE back to the Secretary's office. The reversal of Wallace's reconstituted BAE was complete. When Tolley resigned the following year, the Division again lost a strong supporter in the administrative hierarchy. In 1953, when Republican Ezra Benson became Secretary the BAE had been losing ground for more than twelve years. Benson went one step further. Within less than a year, he abolished the BAE and, with it, the Division.

RESOURCES AND STRUCTURE

Professional Staff

During the Division's history more than 140 persons served on its professional staff (see Appendix). Of these, over twenty-five were women. The great majority were sociologists. Some served only a few months or a year, usually by design.[11] A few, like Galpin and Taylor, had a large block of their career with the Division. The number of professionals varied from as few as two in 1933–35 to a maximum of fifty-seven in 1939–40. Staff turnover was high during the 1940s. Younger men were drawn into military service. Senior staff members were lost to wartime agencies. The postwar rehabilitation and rural development agencies also recruited from the Division. Lastly, postwar budget cuts came at a time when there was a stepped-up demand by universities for faculty.

The staff may be characterized overall as being well-trained social scientists, having a high order of professionalism, and as having close ties with research-oriented universities. After all, the majority had their training at these institutions, were recruited from their graduate students or faculty, and many returned to them immediately, or eventually after their work with the Division. Many of the staff had distinguished careers. In addition to Carl Taylor, ASA presidents included one-time staff members Kimball Young (1945) and Charles P. Loomis (1967). Conrad Taeuber, the first recipient of the ASA's Distinguished Career Award for the Practice of Sociology, had a major role on the Division staff for nearly eight years. The list of past presidents of the Rural Sociological Society includes thirteen with Division staff experience.[12]

When the Division was started, the professional staff came from a variety of sources. Wayne Nason, for example, was transferred from within the USDA. Galpin brought in three of his former graduate students from Wisconsin: Walter Baumgartel; Emily Hoag (Sawtelle); and Veda Larson (Turner). When E. L. Kirpatrick completed his Ph.D. at Cornell under Dwight Sanderson, he was added to study farm family living. In 1927, T. B. Manny, also Wisconsin-trained, was brought in to work on the social psychology of farmers' organizations and in the area of local government.

The new staff under Taylor came at first, in part, by transfer from within the BAE or other agencies. In early 1936, BAE Chief Black shifted the research in farm labor and that part of farm population which had been in the Division of Land Economics to the Division. This change brought O. E. Baker and J. C. Folsom to the Division. In mid-1939, W. T. Ham and his staff who had been doing farm labor and tenancy studies in the AAA were also placed in the Division. While Taylor was concurrently head of the social research unit in FSA and of the Division, he brought several of the FSA sociologists into the Division.

Just before Henry A. Wallace reconstituted the BAE, the Division was able to place a staff member in each of five BAE regional offices for its land utilization program. By the end of 1939, the Division had staff in seven BAE regional offices in connection with the state and county land-use planning program. In time, there were nine regional offices, each with a leader and one to three other professional staff. In 1939, with the encouragement of BAE Chief Tolley and Undersecretary Wilson, the Division began to add a few cultural anthropologists, social psychologists, and historians to the Washington staff.

A number of special staffing arrangements were made with other USDA agencies. When the Extension Service made the first step to develop a rural sociology extension program in 1935, Ella Gardner was housed with the Division under a cooperative agreement. A year later, O. E. Baker started to give one-fourth of his time to the Extension Service. After M. L. Wilson became Director of Extension, an arrangement was made, lasting until 1951, for Douglas Ensminger to divide his time between the Division and the Extension Service. Ensminger's special area was community organization. He became closely associated with Wilson who was, in his view, trying to change the Extension Service from a technical service agency to an educational institution.

There were other types of special arrangements. Loans of staff were made to the Division. For example, Blanche Halbert from the RA helped revise a USDA bulletin on rural hospitals. Later, Margaret Lantis from the FSA was detailed to assist in a Division study of the USDA's experimental rural health programs. A variant was the employment by the Division of social scientist John P. Shea and detailing him to the SCS, under Division supervision, to research community organization aspects of SCS work. But changes in professional staff numbers also corresponded with variations in available funds. During the Division's life, the budget ranged from less than $13,000 in the leanest of years, FY 1934–35 (Taylor 1941b), to more than $400,000 in the best of times, FY 1939–41 (Nichols 1955).

Funds

Annual appropriations by Congress to the BAE were the basic source of funding for the Division. Through the annual appropriations procedure, the Congress controlled the scope in content and size of the BAE's work, could emphasize or prohibit any program it chose, and could terminate an activity entirely (Gaus and Wolcott 1940:408). The BAE and the Division within it experienced all these possibilities. The Division also was able to receive funds, through the BAE, from other agencies for specific tasks.

The Division began with a budget of $20,390 for FY 1919–20. However, the very next year, the USDA was caught in a post–World War I congressional economy drive (Baker et al. 1963:100) and the Division's existence was at risk. Although not the $100,000 budget Galpin had optimistically been hoping for, Henry Taylor was able to secure $25,000 the second fiscal year. This covered Galpin's salary, now up to $4,500, and the salaries of the other four professionals and of the support staff. It even left some money for cooperative projects with universities. Thereafter, budget time was a "nightmare" for Galpin (1938a:44).

Before appropriation hearings began in 1923, the Division's funds were again in danger of being cut (H. Taylor 1992:146). Henry Taylor was assured by Secretary H. C. Wallace that he would back the work. Taylor took Galpin with him when he made the case for the Division before the House committee handling USDA appropriations. At the close of Henry Taylor's statement, the committee chair observed that he thought the statement had cost the committee $30,000. In fact, the Division received $31,200 or so for the next ten years.

In the first years of the New Deal, and Galpin's last as head, funding was cut to its lowest point. However, in 1936, a turn-around began. Due to personnel transfers and increased appropriations, $59,665 available in FY 1935–36 grew to $246,590 in FY 1936–37 (Taylor 1939:224). The next year, funds dropped back to $82,323 because of reduced transfers from the FSA. In the setting of the reconstituted BAE, the total funds available jumped dramatically to $428,000 in FY 1939–40 and $417,000 in FY 1940–41 (Nichols 1955).[13] The budget was then reduced but remained fairly stable until 1946. The range was between $336,000 in 1941–42 and $289,000 in 1943–44. As the BAE and the Division came under intense attack by interest groups and Congress, drastic cuts began. The first cut was from $250,000 in 1946–47 to $171,500 the next year. In 1950–51, the Division was down to a little over $50,000 for its entire program.

Transfers from other agencies varied widely from year to year. In some years they exceeded appropriated funds. In other years there were no transfers. Overall, the fact that the Division could receive such transferred funds increased its research capacity. As examples, the RA-FSA allocated $40,000 in FY 1935–36, $143,000 in 1936–37, $28,733 in 1937–38, and $2,970 in FY 1938–39 (Taylor 1939:224) for such transfers. Title III of the Bankhead-Jones Farm Tenant Act was the source, through the BAE, of $10,000 in FY 1937–38 and $38,500 in 1938–39. The Works Progress Administration (WPA) gave $10,000 for farm labor studies in FY 1936–37. Starting in 1939, the WPA supplied well in excess of $100,000 for a study of FSA borrowers. The Research and Marketing Act of 1946 was the source of support for research in rural health and medical facilities and for a study of the effects of mechanization in plantation areas. The Bureau of Reclamation in the Department of Interior underwrote studies in the 1940s for the Columbia Basin irrigation project.

Structure

When the staff expanded in the late 1930s, the Division began to have a differentiated structure. The Washington staff, for instance, was grouped informally into "sections." Each section was comprised of the staff working in a designated research area. The number and descriptive titles of the sections changed from time to time, reflecting such factors as shifts in areas of research emphasis and staff changes. Thus, in fiscal year 1940, there were sections for anthropology, community organization, farm labor, history, population, and social psychology (Nichols 1955:6). In 1948 when the postwar downsizing was underway, there were sections on farm labor, levels of living, population, and rural organization (Taylor 1948b:8–11).

In 1938, the Division began to place staff in regional offices. This started with a professional in five of the BAE's Land Utilization Program offices. Shortly, the function of these and additional regional offices was to support the BAE's new state and county land-use planning program. In time, there were nine regional offices working with the forty-eight states. These were located in Amarillo, Texas; Atlanta, Georgia; Berkeley, California; Lincoln, Nebraska; Little Rock, Arkansas; Milwaukee, Wisconsin; Portland, Oregon; and Upper Darby, Pennsylvania. There was also an office for the Appalachian region located in Washington. The Divisions of Farm Management and Costs and of Land Economics also had regional representation. In this arrangement, the field staff performed as "generalists," while the Washington staff took a "specialist" role. There was, however, interchange of staff between Washington and the field. When the land-use planning program was stopped by Congress, the regional offices continued until they, too, were abolished by Congress effective July 1, 1946. After the closing of the regional offices, some of the retained professionals were continued in the field by locating them at land-grant institutions where they had cooperative research.

COOPERATIVE RELATIONSHIPS

During its lifetime, the Division sought and secured cooperative arrangements. Formal cooperation was primarily with governmental agencies or colleges and universities. There were exceptions. The Division cooperated with the Institute of Social and Religious Research in the 1920s. Also, the magazine *The Farmer's Wife* was one of the cooperators in studies of farm family living.

Cooperation with Universities

Cooperative research arrangements with universities was a distinctive feature of the Division. Galpin quickly adopted a policy of seeking cooperation with responsible research agencies as a means of accumulating a body of scientific knowledge on the problems of farm population and rural life. This also had the effect of stretching available research dollars, and Henry Taylor (1992:22) endorsed this policy for the BAE. Galpin's belief was that a greater gain was to be made developing a broad rural sociology in the United States "by giving each cooperator his head, wide scope, freedom to discover and invent" rather than by "compelling adherence to a rigid form under central supervision" (1938a:51). In 1920 Galpin worked out cooperative agreements for research with six land-grant universities (Taylor 1941b): Cornell University, Iowa State College, University of Montana (now Montana State University), University of Nebraska, University of Wisconsin, and West Virginia University. A few more states were added year by year.

With this experience, Galpin laid out the Division's policy on cooperative research agreements (Galpin 1924b). A written agreement was required. In any state, the College of Agriculture would have the first chance to be a cooperator. The research problem selected should have value to the state and, at the same time, fit into a scheme of national problems having the possibility of regional comparisons. The Division would expect to pay half the cost of a study.[14] In this, a study longer than one year would be an exception. The unstated assumption was that the research would require field investigation. Direct supervision of the field work was a function of the project leader in the cooperating university. Publication could be joint with the Division or by the cooperator alone.

In 1932, twenty-one of the Division's twenty-five projects were in cooperation with universities. During the Galpin years, there were one or more agreements with forty-seven institutions in thirty-seven states (Galpin 1934a). The ten non-land-grant institutions were Alabama College, Brigham Young University, Boston University, Hampton Institute, Hendrix College, North Carolina College for Women, Northern Illinois State Teachers College, Ohio Wesleyan University, Tulane University, and Western

State Normal in Michigan. After 1933, however, budget cuts forced an end to this cooperation until Taylor became head.

Taylor revived the policy of cooperative agreements as soon as funds permitted. As of mid-1938 the Division had twenty-one cooperative agreements with universities. Most were with reference to estimates of farm population but two dealt with farm labor, two with selective rural-urban migration, one with rural youth, one with the analysis of a state's population, one with attitudes of farm people, and one with social aspects of farm tenancy. After the closing of the regional offices, the plans for 1948–49 called for projects with seventeen states involving nine Division staff located in the field at various universities.

Within the Federal Government

The Division also had cooperative arrangements within the federal government. During Galpin's fifteen years, the Division cooperated within the BAE on studies with the Divisions of Agricultural Finance, Cooperative Marketing, Crop and Livestock Estimates, Farm Management and Costs, and Land Economics. In other parts of the USDA it had studies with the Bureaus of Plant Industry, Home Economics, Chemistry and Soils, Public Roads, the Forest Service, Extension Service, and the Office of Experiment Stations. Outside the USDA there were studies with the Bureau of the Census, the Farm Board, the Office of Education in the Interior Department, and Public Health in the Treasury Department.

Carl Taylor's experience in the reconstituted BAE led him, in that context, to stress the impossibility of any division making its full research contribution, even in the field of its own competence, without appropriate inter-division and inter-agency cooperation (1946c:10–12). Within the BAE, the Division worked especially with Farm Management and Costs and other older divisions such as Agricultural Finance, Agricultural Statistics, Land Economics, and Statistical and Historical Research. It worked with newer units such as Program Surveys and State and Local Planning. Work with agencies in other parts of the USDA included that with the RA-FSA and the Extension Service but also the AAA, the Bureau of Home Economics, the Forest Service, and the SCS. Before the war, there was work with the Division of Social Research in the Works Progress Administration, the National Resources Planning Board, and a start on a major project for the Bureau of Reclamation, U.S. Department of Interior. Defense and wartime brought cooperative work with a host of new USDA agencies such as the Office of Agricultural War Relations. Outside the

USDA, there was extensive work with the Bureau of the Census. The wartime situation resulted in work with such non-USDA agencies as the Farm Placement Service of the Bureau of Employment Security, the Office of Civilian Defense, and the Office of Indian Affairs in the U.S. Department of the Interior. In the postwar period, the Social Security Administration was an addition to the roster of cooperators.

SUMMARY

Over its lifetime, the Division experienced dramatic ups and downs. The context within which the Division operated was important to the Division's changing fortunes. The immediate administrative context was provided by the BAE. Beyond the BAE, decisions made by the USDA Secretary and even, at times, the President affected the Division. Presidents Coolidge and Hoover both took actions with respect to the BAE which, indirectly, hurt the Division. Franklin Roosevelt's New Deal contributed to a setting favorable for the social sciences in the USDA. Agriculture Secretary David F. Houston created what became the BAE and the Division. Secretary H. C. Wallace strengthened the BAE and backed the Division when its budget was in question. Secretary Henry A. Wallace, with his assistant, M. L. Wilson, had a notable positive impact on the Division. His reconstitution of the BAE in 1938, adding a planning function for the USDA, was a watershed in the expansion of resources and opportunities for the Division. In contrast, in 1946 Clinton P. Anderson removed the planning function from the BAE. And in 1953, Secretary Ezra Benson abolished the BAE and the Division.

Notes

1. Secretary of Agriculture Ezra Benson's rationale for abolishing the BAE in 1953 and critiques of the breakup may be found in a set of seven papers published under a symposium titled "The Fragmentation of the BAE" (Wells et al. 1954:1–21).

2. For further information on Galpin see his *My Drift Into Rural Sociology* (1938a); Nelson (1969:34–44); and the June 1948 issue of *Rural Sociology* honoring Galpin.

3. For additional information about Carl Taylor and appraisals of his work see obituaries by T. Lynn Smith (1975) and by Conrad Taeuber (1975). Also see Nelson (1969:65–66, 183–84), Howard W. Odum (1951:224–26) and Larson et al. (1999).

4. Carl Taylor's work at North Carolina State is described in Selz C. Mayo's "A history of sociology at North Carolina State University, 1920–1981" (1983).

5. When Carl Taylor went on a special research assignment in Argentina for the State Department in 1942–43, Conrad Taeuber became acting head of the Division. Taeuber, a senior staff member, had come to the Division in 1935.

6. One of the most complete sources about Margaret J. Hagood is Carl Taylor's memorial statement (1964). See also Fern K. Willits et al. (1988) and Julie N. Zimmerman (1999).

7. A concise historical account of the BAE is given in Gladys L. Baker and Wayne D. Rasmussen (1975). Also see John D. Black (1947) and Lloyd S. Tenny (1947).

8. For Henry Taylor's own account of his work in the BAE, see his *A Farm Economist in Washington 1919–1925* (1992). A brief statement about him is given by Clyde C. Jones (1958). A professional chronology and citations to his papers is given in Anne Dewees Taylor (1958).

9. This program of adult education originated in 1935 through the efforts of Secretary H. A. Wallace and then-Assistant Secretary M. L. Wilson. The Division of Program Study and Discussion was headed by Carl F. Taeusch (1940), who had been a philosophy professor at the University of Chicago. For a historical account and evaluation see David Lachman and Jess Gilbert (1992).

10. An account of the new system after its first year is given from the perspective of two participants in the BAE's Division of State and Local Planning in Ellery A. Foster and Harold A. Vogel (1940). For an analysis of this four-year experiment in democratic planning, some fifty years after it was killed by Congress, see Jess Gilbert (1993).

11. University-based scholars who held short-term appointments, typically about one year, with the Division included social psychologists Edward Hulett Jr., University of Illinois; Raymond F. Sletto, Ohio State University; Kimball Young, University of Wisconsin; sociologists C. Horace Hamilton, North Carolina State University; Homer Hitt, Louisiana State University; Wayne Neeley, Hood College; Irwin T. Sanders, University of Kentucky; and Nathan L. Whetten, University of Connecticut.

12. Besides Carl Taylor, Rural Sociological Society presidents with Division staff experience were Lowry Nelson, Charles P. Loomis, C. Horace Hamilton, Nathan L. Whetten, Margaret J. Hagood, Irwin T. Sanders, Olaf F. Larson, Harold Hoffsommer, Paul J. Jehlik, A. Lee Coleman, Robert McNamara, and Edward O. Moe.

13. Budget figures in Nichols (1955) for 1939–40 and later are complete for the total allotment but do not fully differentiate appropriated and transfer funds.

14. During the Galpin years, the Division's share for a project was usually $400 to $600 per year (Taylor 1939:235). In practice, this ranged from $150 for a small to $750 for a large one-year study.

4

Research Priorities and Programs: Continuities and Discontinuities

The Division was established to do research on the social aspects of farm life and rural communities. The intent was that such research should contribute to improving the well-being of American farmers and their families. Being a unit in the federal government, the Division was called upon for a variety of services. However, research was central. Both the scope of this research and the specific lines of work were influenced by external and internal factors, some of which worked at cross-purposes. A few categories of research had remarkable continuity during the unit's thirty-four years; others experienced sharp discontinuities, especially as the political process was brought to bear, as was evidenced in the Arvin-Dinuba and Coahoma County controversies.

THE DETERMINANTS

Overall, ten major factors shaped the Division's research priorities and programs, not including the ever-present budgetary restraints.[1] Four factors internal to the Division affected its research priorities and programs. These guided especially the early years, but remained goals and concerns throughout the Division's life span. These internal factors were: (1) the goal of adding to the fund of validated knowledge about rural life in the United States; (2) the goal of contributing to the improvement of rural life through research, its interpretation, and application; (3) the areas of interest and of specialized competence of the professional staff which shaped the first two internal factors; (4) the goal of getting rural sociological research established in colleges and universities through the strategy of cooperative research agreements.

There were six factors external to the Division that affected its research priorities and programs. Of these, two were discipline-related: (1) the state of scientific knowledge about rural life and the state of research methods to acquire this knowledge; and (2) the recommendations of external advisory or peer groups of social scientists and others that suggested guidelines for the Division's work.

The remaining four external factors were especially powerful. At times, these factors dominated, and actually overrode other determinants. These four were: (1) the overall context represented by the economic, political, and other aspects of the societal environment, referring not only to the agricultural and rural life context but to that of the larger society as well; (2) the permitting, mandating, or even prohibiting given lines of research by the Congress; (3) actions taken by the executive hierarchy, especially within the USDA, which encouraged, requested or prohibited specific research; (4) the placement of the Division as a subordinate unit within the BAE, which meant that changes in functions assigned the BAE and shifts in its status had direct consequences for the Division's research.

THE DETERMINANTS ILLUSTRATED

The impact of each of the ten factors was not constant and worked in differing combinations to affect the Division's research priorities and programs. During the Galpin years, there were few competing demands on the Division, research continuity was more easily maintained. Therefore, the discipline-oriented external factors and the factors internal to the Division weighed heavily in the research choices made. As a result, Galpin was able to shape the Division's research, not only providing continuity, but aiding to establish its legitimacy.

The report of the special committee appointed by Secretary Houston and chaired by Professor Carver had special importance for what the Division did in its early years (USDA, Office of the Secretary 1919b). Galpin asserted, after his retirement, "this eight-page pamphlet has served as the official charter under which the Division of Farm Population and Rural Life has operated for nearly nineteen years" (Galpin 1938b:205). Of course, the committee's "suggested fields of research" had to be translated into specific research activity. But, as a member of the twenty-eight-person committee, Galpin was privy to the deliberations that had resulted in its recommendations and was, therefore, in an excellent position to interpret the committee's statement.

One of the special recommendations of the committee was that the closest cooperation be sought with the Bureau of the Census to collect more information relating to the farm (as distinguished from rural) population (USDA, Office of the Secretary 1919b). Work in farm population quickly became a distinguished and continuing area of research activity. Of the ten major areas outlined sketchily by the Carver committee, "problems relating to geographical population groups" became an area of continuing emphasis for the Division and its cooperators in the form of locality group studies—the social organization of communities, neighborhoods, villages, and trade areas. Both locality groups and farm population were of interest to Galpin and judged by him, preceding his coming to the Division, to be of great importance for building useful knowledge about rural life.

Comprehensive studies of farm family levels and standards of living were initiated by the mid-1920s. This reflected the committee's recommendation to study rural home life. Because of the special competence he had demonstrated in his ground-breaking dissertation research at Cornell, E. L. Kirkpatrick was recruited to take the lead in this work.

These areas of population, locality groups, and levels of living were reaffirmed by the Special Committee on Rural Social Organizations and Agencies, established to develop guidelines for the new money appropriated by the Purnell Act (Joint Committee 1925:23–25). The fourth recommended research area was rural youth. Further, the committee gave special recognition to the study of rural local municipalities already underway by the Division and cooperators. Galpin had been one of the six members of the special committee chaired by G. I. Christie.[2]

In some instances, leadership for suggested fields came from the cooperators in colleges and universities. For example, J. H. Kolb and A. F. Wileden at Wisconsin were investigators for a study of rural special interest groups, T. B. Manny at Hendrix College initiated studies of local government, and J. O. Rankin in Nebraska undertook research on the social aspects of land tenure. The goal of improving rural life and identifying some of the best things in country life were both represented in staff member Wayne Nason's popular USDA Farmers' Bulletins. Based on studies of successful cases, topics included rural community buildings, rural hospitals, rural libraries, and rural planning.

Not all of the ten areas suggested by the Carver committee were ever pursued. As Taylor observed early in his tenure as head, the Division "has never fully occupied the field outlined by the committee report" (1939:228). No work was done on three areas listed last among the committee's ten: the relation of various forms of disability to farm-life problems; the social consequences of local natural disasters; and the social consequences of thrift and agencies for promoting thrift.

In contrast to the continuity which marked the Galpin years, while Taylor was Division head four factors external to the Division had great influence. These created much of the discontinuity in the Division's research priorities and programs during this time. The Great Depression and World War II provide prime examples.

The initial impact of the 1930s depression was disastrous for the Division. The budgetary response to the economic crisis by Congress, the Roosevelt administration, and USDA-BAE administrators eroded the Division's funding. Its allocation fell from $32,825 in FY 1931–32 to $12,765 in 1934–35. At the low point, about all that remained of the research program was the annual estimates of farm population. Cooperative research with the states came to a halt.

However, only a year after this low point, a dramatic reversal in resources began. By 1939–41, the Division had reached its high point in staff and activity. This, because the New Deal agricultural agencies generated a large demand for information which could only be provided by sociological research and evaluation.

Rural sociology research was "profoundly" affected by entry of the United States into World War II (Leonard 1944:142). Following December 7, 1941, a drastic reordering of priorities began throughout the federal government. On January 1, 1942, BAE Chief Tolley announced the agency's priorities for the months immediately ahead (USDA, BAE 1942). Central to the BAE's efforts to meet the farmer's labor needs, the Division was to place major emphasis on the compilation, analysis, and interpretation of farm labor data. Work on community and neighborhood identification was to be reoriented to support efforts of the Extension Service and wartime agencies in mobilizing rural areas. Even postwar planning was given priority.

The war brought demands for facts, such as in the areas of farm population and agricultural employment (Taeuber 1945:170–73). The need for speed and precision in providing these facts led the Division and other units of the BAE to sharpen definitions, refine concepts, and improve technical sampling methods. The Division's 1941–42 annual report noted "many of the special studies in progress earlier in the year have either been greatly curtailed or abandoned entirely" (USDA, BAE, DFPRW 1942:15). Because of the war-induced shift in priorities, for example, the overall summary of the six studies of the "Culture of a Contemporary Rural Community" was never prepared.[3] Among others, the reports on field studies of some ten new settlement projects, made for the Columbia Basin Joint Investigations, were never completed (Taylor 1947a:v).

Congress held the ultimate authority and power to shape the Division's research if it so chose. For example, before the end of 1944, Congress made a supplemental appropriation to the BAE for detailed data on agricultural wages and wage rates. This funding made possible the series of reports on wages and wage rates of hired farm workers in which the Division had a major role.

The negative impact of congressional action was most vividly demonstrated in 1946. That year's appropriations for the BAE included a prohibition that no part of the funds could be used for conducting cultural surveys. This mandate was aimed specifically at one of the Division's most promising major and long-term projects. The same appropriations bill put an end to the BAE's regional offices. This experience had a chilling effect on the Division for the rest of its existence.

Being a subordinate unit within the BAE also had both positive and negative effects for the Division. For instance, the requests from the FSA for a critical appraisal of subsistence homestead projects (Lord and Johnstone 1942) and for a study of the standard rural rehabilitation loan program (Larson 1947a) were channeled through the BAE. The same held for the Bureau of Reclamation's requests for studies for irrigation projects planned for California's Central Valley and Washington's Columbia River Basin. The negative side was demonstrated by what happened to the BAE-led land-use planning program. The Division, especially its staff in regional offices, was one of four divisions most actively involved in this program. In 1942 this participation was halted when Congress stipulated "that no part of the funds herein appropriated or made available to the Bureau of Agricultural Economics shall be used for State and county land-use planning." The accompanying budget cut further hurt the Division.

RESEARCH AND PUBLICATION CONTROVERSIES

A number of research controversies and publication problems were caused by factors external to the Division. Directly or indirectly, all of the incidents involved the political process. They occurred under both Democratic and Republican administrations. Each incident centered around a specific research activity or research report. In the most controversial cases, if a dominant socioeconomic group perceived that its economic self-interest, privileged social status, or deeply held values and beliefs were, or even might be, threatened by the research results, it sought sanctions against the BAE and the Division. When such efforts were successful, USDA and BAE administrators became fearful of political reprisal. At the worst, these incidents of controversy abruptly halted research, providing an important source of discontinuity in the Division's research program.

Galpin's Blocked Manuscripts

The Division was barely under way when Galpin ran into problems with two manuscripts. The first was for a cooperative project with the University of Missouri to study farm tenancy among white families in a Southeast Missouri community. The resulting manuscript (Taylor, Yoder, and Zimmerman 1920), intended to become a USDA bulletin, created a veritable hornet's nest for the Division (Galpin 1938a:51–52). The contrasts reported in the living conditions of farm owner-operators, of farm tenants, of croppers, and of hired men were striking. But when the Dean of the cooperating college saw the photographs portraying the unsuspected sharp contrasts between the houses, churches, and school buildings of landowners and those of tenants and hired men, he "washed his hands of the whole affair" (Galpin 1938a:51). USDA decision-making about publication became timid. In the end, averse to putting the Division's young life at risk over the issue, the manuscript and photographs were filed away in the hope that someday such topics could be brought to public view without fear of reprisal.[4]

The second time Galpin ran into problems was when the manuscript on the use of time by farm men and women was killed on the floor of the House. The Carver committee had included the social life of farm families among its suggested topics, in part because of the social isolation of the farm home. Galpin thought that knowledge of the use of time, season by season, would help in planning recreational and cultural activities for farm families (Galpin 1920:159). Detailed records from USDA farm cost studies were the basis for a manuscript titled, we believe, "The labor and leisure year of the farmer and his wife."[5] Included were a dozen color charts indicating the use of time on these farms. When the manuscript reached the public printer, he hesitated at the color charts because the cost would be more than that for black and white. He sent the manuscript to the chair of the House Committee on Printing. The next day the chairman took the floor, flourished the manuscript in his hand, and "boomed, 'this is the stuff the Department of Agriculture wants to print. It tells the farmer that the sun rises in the morning and sets in the evening'" (Galpin 1938a:41–43). There were no defenders. The laughter of the House members sent the manuscript back to the files in disgrace.

The Arvin-Dinuba Study

In 1944, a study for the Bureau of Reclamation of the Arvin and Dinuba communities in California's Central Valley provoked a political storm which would be continuing at the time of the Coahoma County controversy. Walter R. Goldschmidt was the principal investigator on the Arvin-Dinuba study, one of what was to be a set of studies on the Central Valley.[6] Ironically, when Goldschmidt subsequently used the study in his *As You Sow* (1947; 1978a), the Arvin-Dinuba study proved to be a classic in the literature on the sociology of agriculture and on rural communities.

To foster family-scale farms, reclamation law since 1902 had limited the water a land owner could legally get from a federal irrigation project to only the amount needed to irrigate 160 acres. The law was not popular among many land owners in the Central Valley where much of the land was held in large tracts. The Arvin-Dinuba study was designed to determine the potential social consequences of the acreage limitation law. Large land owners feared that the study would provide evidence to support enforcement of the acreage limitation for subsidized water. A preliminary report which showed marked differences of social and economic conditions in the two communities, concluded, "the basic cause, the one all important cause is . . . size of farm operations" (Goldschmidt 1944:225).

In essence, following Goldschmidt's (1972; 1978a:458–87; 1978b) reconstruction of events, the Arvin-Dinuba study met with attempted sabotage from the start, attempts to suppress publication of the full report, and attempts to discredit the study after it was published. Plans to study additional Central Valley communities were dropped by the BAE. The decision about publishing Goldschmidt's report went up the USDA hierarchy to Secretary Anderson who decided against publication. As Chair of the Senate Special Committee on Small Business, Senator James E. Murray, a Democrat from Montana, got Anderson to release the report for printing by the committee. Secretary Anderson's condition was that no mention be made of the USDA's involvement with the study. In practice, Goldschmidt submitted his manuscript to the committee as a private citizen; he learned that he had been terminated while on leave for a temporary appointment at UCLA (Goldschmidt 1978a:477). After publication by the committee, charges were brought as to the accuracy of the facts and conclusions of the study. Some of these attacks were led by Senator Sheridan Downey, Democrat from California, in his fight against the acreage limitation law as it applied to California.

The Coahoma County, Mississippi, Report

In late 1945 a serious controversy erupted with costly consequences for the Division. The immediate cause was the objection of a few members of Congress from Mississippi to an unpublished manuscript, "Cultural

Reconnaissance Survey of Coahoma County Mississippi," prepared by the investigator, Frank D. Alexander, for review prior to publication (1944). The objections centered on statements about the "race question" and "segregation."

Coahoma was one of the seventy-one counties selected in 1944 as sites for a series of studies to be made over a three to five year period. Each county represented one statistically determined strata of each of the nation's seven type-of-farming areas. Coahoma was a Cotton Belt county whose population was predominantly black. The first phase of this new research was a "cultural reconnaissance" survey to provide an overview of each county with respect to such features as the physical environment, techniques and patterns of making a living, social organization, and value systems. The thirteen-page guide for preparing the reports made no reference to "black" or "negro." But to faithfully report his findings, Alexander compared blacks and whites and described black-white relations in his descriptions of man-land relations, levels of living, class and status groups, schools, value systems and some other areas. The concluding statement in his report read:

> There are two dominant features of the culture of the people of Coahoma County—one is Negro-white relations, the other is the plantation system of farming. Almost every phase of the people's thoughts and behavior is influenced by these two complexes. Schools, churches, families, law enforcement, public welfare, earning a living are all under the domination of the plantation economy. Similarly all of these institutions and activities are carried on within the definitions of white supremacy and racial segregation.

Procedures routinely called for draft reports to be circulated for review and criticism prior to submission for approval within the USDA for publication. Alexander dittoed thirty-five copies of his Coahoma County report, labeled "For Administrative Use." Four went to persons outside the USDA. One of these was passed to the extension service director of Mississippi, a person who had been critical of the BAE's planning and research activities (Kirkendall 1966:235). He, in turn, passed the copy on to congressmen from the state. They then extracted a few paragraphs about race relations and circulated them among other Southern congressmen. Trouble for the Division, the BAE, and the USDA was not far behind.

Secretary Anderson, new to his post and a former congressman, was contacted in 1945 by Congressman Dan R. McGehee from Mississippi, with the statement that "ninety percent of the stuff in this proposed bulletin is nothing but ball-faced damn lies" (Kirkendall 1966:236). Secretary Anderson assured there was no intention of publishing the report, ordered no further studies of this type be made by the BAE, and reprimanded Alexander. One month later, Division Head Carl Taylor along with Arthur Raper (Washington staff member with a major responsibility for the seventy-one-county project) met with Mississippi Congressman Abernathy and provided him with a detailed explanation of the work. Abernathy's views were unchanged.

When BAE Chief Tolley appeared to testify on the Bureau's budget request, he was quizzed on the Coahoma County report (U.S. Congress, House 1946:234–42). They refused to accept Tolley's statement that the report was not published. Statements were made that "the value of this report . . . is worse than nothing," the work was "a misuse of public funds," and "that statement is an indictment of the people of Coahoma County" (U.S. Congress, House 1946:234–42). Tolley agreed to meet the request for copies of the draft reports for the remaining seventy counties.[7] Soon, the American Farm Bureau Federation publicly joined the attack (U.S. Congress, House 1946:1644). It recommended that the BAE be prohibited from conducting "social surveys" and that the regional offices be eliminated.

Indeed, the ensuing appropriations bill for the BAE banned use of any of the funds for *cultural* surveys. It also abolished the BAE's regional offices and funding was reduced. The congressionally mandated ban meant that the USDA did not publish *any* of the seventy-one-county cultural reconnaissance reports.[8] The reports planned for each of the seven type-of-farming regions were not even prepared. As a salvage measure, the project was converted into a politically safer study of rural social organization in twenty-four of the counties, a few from each type-of-farming region. Of these, only sixteen reports saw publication. The reports which were not published by the USDA included three of the four Cotton Belt county studies; the fourth was printed by a nonland-grant college press (Lewis 1948). The two California county studies also did not result in publication. Finally, the Division's 1949–50 project statement indicated that the year would bring studies in the field of rural organization to a close.

More Manuscript Problems

The influence of external factors on blocking or delaying publication is further evidenced by the Division's experience during the 1940s with three additional manuscripts. For instance, in an exploratory study to apply the cultural approach to the study of farm life, Horace Miner examined the aspects of Corn Belt culture involved in the relations between farmers and USDA action agencies and programs in Hardin County, Iowa. Miner's report, submitted in 1940, provoked controversy within the USDA over the advisability of publication. While Division Head Carl Taylor opted for publication, wartime exigencies resulted in prolonged delay. After the war's end, because of the Coahoma County and Arvin-Dinuba controversies and attacks on the BAE for land-use planning and other activities, the new BAE Chief—O. V. Wells—and Secretary Anderson were super-cautious on sociological and economic studies. The Division decided to release the report to Miner to seek outside publication. Nine years after the original submission, Miner's report was published by a university press (1949).

Another case occurred when the Division engaged Irwin T. Sanders to prepare a handbook on rural community mobilization using recently completed studies in six communities. The Coahoma County furor had occurred by the time the manuscript was completed. The USDA publications office decided against putting out the handbook. "The spelling out of good community organization procedures sounded," at the time, "too much like the Department of Agriculture telling its agents how to 'manipulate' people" (Sanders 1990). The Division did gain approval for Sanders to publish under another aegis. The book was issued by the University of Kentucky Press (1950) where Sanders was on the faculty.

Our final manuscript case is about Olaf F. Larson's report (1947a) on a comprehensive study of the RR-FSA rural rehabilitation program. The approval process also reflected the caution of the post-Coahoma County report climate as well as the caution in the USDA created by the political controversies surrounding the FSA. Division head Carl Taylor was unable to gain approval for publication in the format originally planned; that is, printed for wide circulation. He had to settle for "a few copies" in mimeographed form which were to be "made available to interested research workers, administrators, and to libraries," (Foreword in Larson: 1947a). However, before the mimeo copies could be produced, BAE Chief O. V. Wells insisted on personally reading and editing the 400-plus page manuscript. He wanted insurance that it contained no terms such as "culture" or other language which could result in a political backlash costly to the BAE. Publication for general distribution was finally achieved when the report was reissued by the Indian Society of Agricultural Economics to be a resource for those responsible for India's rural reconstruction policy (Larson 1951).[9]

SUMMARY

Aside from funding considerations, the Division's research priorities and programs were shaped by a complex set of factors, external and internal. These factors could be positive for the Division as well as negative. Of the external factors, the contextual factor, congressional and USDA-BAE executive actions, and the Division's structural position were especially potent in causing program discontinuities.

Overall, the internal and discipline-related external factors tended to support continuity, while the external factors were a force for discontinuity. Despite difficulties, the Division managed to maintain a high degree of continuity in its research in population, in levels of living, and—until near the end—in rural social organization. The same holds for farm labor research after it was started. But for many other areas, research was episodic or short term (farm women, rural health services, local government, farmer cooperative and marketing organizations, rural industries, the rural disadvantaged, rural youth, and land tenure).

In particular, seven instances occurred which involved the political process and gave rise to controversy about the Division's research. Each controversy, each publication problem, had its own set of circumstances. Six of the seven cases resulted in a research report *not* being published by the USDA. The Coahoma County study actually contributed to the Division's curtailment and demise.

Notes

1. This section is a major revision of Larson (1989).

2. Other members were F. B. Bomberger, assistant director of extension, University of Maryland; A. E. Cance, head of the Department of Agricultural Economics and Rural Sociology, Massachusetts Agricultural College; rural sociologist Dwight Sanderson, Cornell; and Carl C. Taylor, North Carolina Agricultural College.

3. In 1943, Irwin T. Sanders, on leave from the University of Kentucky, was to analyze the six community studies in terms of what they contributed to social science theory (Sanders 1990). The assignment was shortly changed, however, to use information from the studies in the preparation of a "Handbook on Community Organization During War and Peace" to assist the war mobilization effort in rural areas.

4. Fred R. Yoder, an instructor in sociology, and Carle C. Zimmerman, a graduate student at the time, assisted Taylor in the study. Years later they recorded some recollections about the refusal of both the USDA and the university to publish the report (Nelson 1969:177–80). Taylor later used some of the data from the Southeast Missouri research in a chapter on "The problem of tenancy and ownership" in his *Rural Sociology* (1926:164, 169–73, and 176–88), Zimmerman (1938:117–36) used this study as the "Resettlement" case in his *The Changing Community*, but with an interpretation which differed from the original.

5. Several drafts of the manuscript are in the National Archives. Division staff member Walter Baumgartel devised a method of converting the data for a twelve-month period into a graphic presentation. However, on the basis of manuscripts in the National Archives and Galpin's introduction attached to one draft, we have credited Oscar Ajure and Ilene M. Bailey with authorship.

6. This case has also been reported in detail from the perspectives of the BAE economist who coordinated the set of Central Valley studies (Clawson 1946:330–32; 1987:150–60) and an historian (Kirkendall 1964:195–218). Goldschmidt (1978a:467–73) was critical of Kirkendall's treatment of the Arvin-Dinuba study controversy.

7. Reports were immediately submitted for the fifty-seven counties available in the Division's Washington office.

8. Despite this, use was made of the cultural reconnaissance and associated reports in the chapters on rural regions in Carl Taylor et al. (1949).

9. It is probable that the Indian Society of Agricultural Economics became aware of the report through Douglas Ensminger of the Ford Foundation staff in India. Ensminger had previously been a Division staff member.

5

Farm and Rural Population

Research in farm and rural population was a major, continuing, and distinguished area of work for the Division. More than three decades later, Garkovich (1989:167) asserted that "the roots of a rural sociological perspective on American population studies can be traced to" the Division's early work. Throughout its life, high priority was assigned to this area. Indeed, unique and major contributions to the field were made by Division-sponsored research. Population research had more continuity than any other area of research. And, in contrast to some other areas of work, the studies did not cause trouble for the Division from external sources.

The Division's emphasis on population studies was in tune with the attention demographic problems were being given by social scientists in the United States. Rural to urban migration during and after World War I, the movement of African-Americans from Southern farms to Northern cities, and the depression and drouths of the 1930s all raised demographic issues for the research community. For example, beginning in 1924 the Social Science Research Council (SSRC) set up a sequence of committees on population research. A major publication from this SSRC impetus was the policy-oriented *Migration and Economic Opportunity* (1936) by Carter Goodrich and associates.

THE 1920 CENSUS OF FARM POPULATION

When the Division started, there were no farm population figures available for the United States. Credit C. J. Galpin with convincing the Bureau of the Census to employ the farm population classification. He arrived in Washington on the eve of final decisions for the 1920 census enumeration. It was only through his "supreme effort" that the Bureau of the Census agreed to include the farm population classification (H. Taylor 1939:701). However, Census administrators decided that the data should be tabulated only by a few characteristics and only at the state level. Thereupon, Galpin initiated a cooperative arrangement, at the Division's expense, with the

Census Bureau to demonstrate the value of farm population data at the county level (Galpin 1938a:45–47).

Eight counties were selected for these special tabulations. The intent was that they represent, as far as so few could, factors such as different geographic locations, different types of agriculture, different farm tenure conditions, and the presence or absence of cities. Galpin planned and Veda Larson (Turner) directed the tabulations made from the census enumeration sheets.[1] For experimental purposes, farm population was defined more inclusively than the census had done in its tabulations. This definition included not only all persons living on farms without regard to occupation (as did the Census) but all persons engaged in agricultural occupations but not living on farms, together with their family households. Three residence classes were used, namely, living (1) on farms; (2) not on farms but outside incorporated places; and (3) not on farms but inside incorporated places.

This demonstration resulted in 30 detailed tables on the farm population of each of the eight counties. Leon Truesdell, Bureau of the Census, wrote most of the introductory text for the resulting compilation *Farm Population of Selected Counties* (Galpin and Larson (Turner) 1924) printed by the Census Bureau. The tables were reprinted in Truesdell's census monograph *Farm Population of the United States* (1926). They were also the basis for his chapter suggestive of the analysis made possible by farm population data for counties.

After his retirement, Galpin ranked establishing the value of farm population statistics as one of the Division's major accomplishments in the early years (1938a:47). Due to the special tabulations, the 1925 and 1935 Censuses of Agriculture included farm population in the county tables. In 1930, the Census of Population adopted county tables using the rural-farm classification. The acceptance of the rural-farm classification led to the rural-nonfarm classification being used for the remainder of the rural population. Furthermore, the special eight-county tabulations also revealed substantial numbers of farm family members employed in a great variety of nonagricultural occupations. This finding, along with other research, led to introducing a question regarding off-farm work into the 1930 Census of Agriculture.

FARM POPULATION ESTIMATES

The early 1920s saw a demand for more frequent information on the status of the farm population than could be provided by a decennial census.

In response to this need, the Division devised a procedure for making annual estimates of the nation's farm population and of the movement to and from farms. This work on farm population estimates was one of the Division's most distinctive contributions. The estimates, issued yearly starting in 1923, helped establish the Division's reputation as the nation's most authoritative source on the current farm population situation and trends. Furthermore, estimates of income parity for agriculture, required under the New Deal could not have been calculated without knowing the number of people living on farms each year (Hagood and Bowles 1957a:2).

The farm population estimates were based on innovative data collection and data processing methods explained in detail by Margaret J. Hagood and Gladys K. Bowles (1957a). To collect the basic data needed, Galpin arranged to "piggy-back" onto an ongoing BAE data collection system. The Division of Crop and Livestock Estimates had developed a system for agricultural forecasting in which rural mail carriers distributed and collected BAE-prepared questionnaires to a sample of farmers along their routes. The Division's questionnaire, distributed annually, asked the same farmer reporters to provide information for their own and each adjoining farm on the number of persons at the beginning and end of the specified year, the number of births, the number of deaths, and the number who had moved to and from other farms, cities, towns, or villages.

The farm population estimates were reported in *Farm Population Estimates*, issued annually 1923–40, 1943–45, and 1948–49 with data for the nation, census regions, and census divisions. For the state level, annual estimates, retroactive to 1920, were developed after the 1940 census. Revisions in the estimates were made following the 1930 and subsequent censuses. In time, procedures were developed for using birth and death data from the National Office of Vital Statistics.

Early on, deficiencies in the sampling technique became evident. The coverage varied widely year to year. Galpin and Manny (1932:3) stated "it is probable" that the farmer reporters "live on somewhat larger than average farms and that the number of persons living on their farms exhibits a little greater stability than obtains for the average."

Efforts were made to improve data collection. The periodical *Farm Population and Rural Life Activities* reported on several of these (1938[2]:19–20). Three questions were added to the 1934 mailed questionnaire that would permit direct comparisons with the 1935 farm census. In the late 1930s, the Division had cooperative projects to test data collection methods with as many as thirteen state agricultural experiment stations. Translating the schedule was tried to reach a non-English-speaking group. Having reports apply only to the square mile section in which the reporter lived, reporting for an entire school district, and obtaining information by personal interview were also tried. Carefully selected sample areas promised to become the most useful approach.

During the early part of World War II, migration from farms led, starting in 1944, to new methods of arriving at farm population estimates.[2] This work was done jointly by the Bureau of the Census and the BAE. The basis for the Joint Series was the enumerative surveys made by the Census Bureau for its Monthly Report on the Labor Force, later named the Current Population Survey. The joint series provided not only the estimates on farm population numbers and movement to and from farms but some data on age, sex, labor force status, as well as other topics. At the time, the Division also continued its mail questionnaire survey of farmer reporters.

Issued on a timely basis, the Division's estimates tracked year-by-year changes in farm population. These estimates were presented each year as a record of what was happening to the farm population during depression and prosperity, defense and war. Galpin (1927a:591) asserted "the movement of people from farms to cities and the reverse movement from cities to farms constitutes at any one time a fair index of the agricultural situation." Thus, the estimates reported net migration from farms throughout the agricultural depression years of the 1920s with the slowing up of that loss starting in 1927 (Banks and Beale 1973:32). They showed the net back-to-the-farm movement during the Great Depression years of 1931 and 1932. During 1933, 1934, and 1935 the number of people on farms was almost back up to the peak level reached just prior to the First World War. Except for a short-term reversal after World War II ended, the estimates recorded the resumption of farm population losses. The procedures used also identified the sharp increase in the farm births immediately after World War II was over (Hagood 1949:9). Comments volunteered by farm reporters likewise provided insights which helped interpret the ongoing demographic processes. For example, mechanization as a factor in farm population displacement, especially in the winter wheat area of the Great Plains but also in the spring wheat area, the Corn Belt, and in some parts of the Cotton Belt, was mentioned in the reports for 1937 more frequently than before (Taeuber 1938:11–12).

MIGRATION STUDIES

Of all the demographic processes, migration received the most attention, in part because it most greatly affected and reflected change in rural America. The Division's work in migration went far beyond counting the numbers who moved to and from farms. The first three migration studies undertaken were contrasts in scope and method.

For the first study, Galpin sent Emily Hoag to the farming community of Belleville, New York, for five months. Because he had taught there, Galpin knew that the academy (high school) had a record of its students covering nearly a century. Hoag used these records and local interviews to trace the final residence, occupation, and achievements of the students who had attended between 1824 and 1920. From this, Hoag was able to determine the final residence of 68 percent of the 3,064 former students. The result was her *The National Influence of a Single Farm Community: A Study of the Flow into National Life of Migration from Farms* (1921). This simple but pioneering study demonstrated the influence, through migration, of an obscure farming community on the life of the nation. Henry Taylor called the study a "classic" (1992:145). The same community was chosen about twenty years later for a Cornell University Agricultural Experiment Station study of selective migration in which the Division cooperated (Gessner 1940).

The early work on farm population estimates led to the Division's second early migration study; a national study in 1926 and 1927 to learn more about the people moving to and from farms and the reasons for the moves (Galpin 1927b).[3] A "random" list of 120,000 farmers was requested by mail to provide the names and addresses of neighbors who had recently given up farm operations and had relocated in cities, towns, or villages. This yielded 20,000 names of out-migrants. The "random" list of 120,000 farmers also generated the names of 10,000 who had moved to farms. Both out-migrants and in-migrants were mailed questionnaires. There were 2,745 responses from those who had left farms and 1,167 from those who had moved to farms. Galpin cautioned that no claims could be made that the respondents were a representative sample (1927b:1).

The first of the Division's census-based migration studies indicated the volume and direction of interstate migration of the native white population without regard to farm or rural residence (Galpin and Manny 1934).[4] The "excellent and widely used series of maps" (Isabell and Thomas 1938:193) showed for each state, for each census 1870 through 1930, the state destination of persons born in the state but living elsewhere as well as the state of origin of persons living in the state but born elsewhere. The study corroborated the generalization that migrants tend to travel short distances (Taeuber and Taeuber 1938:503).

The most comprehensive rural migration publication in the 1930s was *Rural Migration in the United States*, by Lively and Taeuber (1939). The study was initiated in the rural research unit of the Federal Emergency

Relief Administration (FERA). The purpose was to provide a better understanding of the extent and nature of rural population movements and of
the relation of these movements to social and economic factors. The study
had three parts.

In the first part, net migration for 1920–30 was computed, with the
help of census data and life tables, by age-groups for the rural-farm, the
rural-nonfarm, the rural white, the rural "colored," and rural male and
female populations of the United States. Net migration was also computed
for the rural-farm and rural-nonfarm population of each state and for the
rural population of counties. Counties were classified into one of three
groups, based on the net migration and natural increase of their rural population: (1) depopulation; (2) dispersion; and (3) absorption. Net rural
migration was analyzed in relation to such factors as rural fertility ratios,
quality of land, educational facilities, a rural "plane" of living index, and
distance to cities. This analysis showed how complex the relationships
were between rural migration and the selected socioeconomic factors.

A second part of the study used data from the 1935 Census of
Agriculture question "How many persons on this farm were not living on
a farm five years previously?" Taking into account the natural increase in
the farm population, the extent of net migration to and from farms during 1930–34 was estimated for every county. Wide variations in this net
migration were found among the census geographic divisions. Another
finding was "the movement was largely one of white persons to farms near
the larger industrial centers and was less important in those areas where
Negroes normally comprise a large proportion of the population" (Lively
and Taeuber 1939:45).

The third part of the study was based on field interviews with over
20,000 rural family heads in sample areas within seven states.[5] Residence
histories were obtained for 1928–34 in three states and for 1926–35 in
four. In interpreting the social significance of rural migration, Lively and
Taeuber asserted that the interchange of rural-urban population was a crude
index of comparative rural-urban prosperity (1939:119), much as Galpin
had concluded earlier (1927a:591). They related rural migration to contemporary public policy issues such as public works and relief programs,
overpopulation of much of the nation's poorer farmland, and populations
stranded by the exhaustion of natural resources. They warned against viewing migration as a panacea for the problems of rural areas, concluding that
"a combination of directed migration, reduced birth rates, and improvement of basic social and economic conditions within overpopulated areas
seems to offer the soundest approach to solving the longtime problems of
widespread rural destitution" (Lively and Taeuber 1939:133).

A groundbreaking study in selective migration was made by Margaret Hagood in cooperation with Donald Bogue of the Scripps Foundation of Miami University. The study, *Differential Migration in the Corn and Cotton Belts* (1953), was based upon special experimental tabulations from the 1940 Census of Population which asked for every household resident "In what place did this person live on April 1, 1935?" The tabulations were as elaborate as those then available for any other nation. The migration from rural-farm, rural-nonfarm, and urban places to Corn Belt and Cotton Belt urban areas was examined. Twelve basic differentials such as age and sex were analyzed individually and by cross-tabulations for selectivity. For comparative purposes, an index of differential migration was devised. Differentials were computed for areas of origin and for areas of destination. Nine generalizations from the analysis of short distance migration were stated in a way designed to contribute to the development of a general theory of migration selectivity.

Throughout the Division's history, times of crisis generated increased interest in rural migration. Severe droughts in the Great Plains between 1930 and 1936, with the associated human distress and federal assistance programs, led to a notable set of studies in the drought-stricken states and in the Western areas where many refugees from the drought resettled. In *The People of the Drought States,* a joint WPA, RA, and Division project, Taeuber and Carl Taylor (1937) placed each of 803 Great Plains counties in one of five net migration categories. This was done on the basis of the rate of natural increase for the farm population during 1930–35 and for the total population for each decade 1890–1930. The high degree of mobility revealed as a Great Plains characteristic was taken to indicate an unsatisfactory adjustment between man and the natural environment. The authors' concluding analysis was quoted in full by the president of the Ecological Society of America as similar to ecological thinking about man's adjustment problems in the Great Plains environment (Hanson 1939:116).

In the West, social problems popularly associated with the drought refugees and other disadvantaged rural people were widely discussed. To develop a factual basis for policy regarding these problems, the Division's regional office joined with the BAE's Divisions of Land Economics, Farm Management and Costs, and other cooperators.[6] As a result, several studies were made of migration and resettlement in Arizona, California, Idaho, Oregon, and Washington (McEntire and Whetten 1939).

Data for these studies were collected from a variety of sources. One information source was questionnaires completed in grade and high schools by children of migrants. Another was data obtained by enumerations at plant quarantine stations of persons entering Arizona and California. In

California detailed studies were made of 1,000 resettled migrant families who had some experience in agriculture (Fuller and Janow 1940). In the Yakima Valley of Washington, 250 recently settled families with agricultural experience were also studied (Reuss and Fisher 1941). All of the studies provided information on the nature, dimensions, and geographic distribution of migration-related problems in the five Far Western states. Some findings ran counter to widely held views, e.g., that the volume of in-migration during the 1930s was unprecedented and that the in-migrants were predominantly tied to agriculture.

In the 1930s, the unguided settlement of perhaps 20,000 families in the poorly drained cut-over areas of the Mississippi Delta drew the Division into a cooperative study with the Louisiana AES (Hitt 1943). With the marketable timber cut, the lumber companies and other large landowners tried to sell the undeveloped land. Settlement became more attractive because annual flood dangers had been reduced by new federally built dams, floodways, and levee work. The situation caught the interest of the BAE about the time it was given a major planning function (USDA 1941). The USDA and the Louisiana AES made several studies of "new ground" settlement questions. The one in which the Division participated concerned the process of migration into the area during 1929–39, comparing recently settled new ground families with their neighbors residing on plantations and on long-cultivated family-size farms. The study found a changing racial balance in the Delta as the majority of new ground farmers were white, holding implications for institutions such as local government.

Entry of the United States into World War II shifted the focus of much of the Division's migration work. The status of the Division's demographic work among social scientists at that time is suggested by the action of the SSRC. This organization promptly arranged for the rapid preparation of memoranda to assist in planning research on the social aspects of the war. The SSRC turned to the Division's Conrad Taeuber, in cooperation with Irene Taeuber of the Princeton University Office of Population Research, to prepare the "research memorandum on internal migration resulting from the war effort" (1942).

Several of the Division's wartime studies are worth noting. For example: the migration of males from 24 Spanish-speaking villages in New Mexico between 1939 and 1942 (Loomis 1942); migration of FSA borrowers from farms during 1942 (Jehlik and Larson 1943); and migration from the rural-farm population in Eastern Kentucky during 1940–42 (Larson 1943a). The New Mexico study was intended to provide public farm labor recruitment and placement agencies with information about the labor supply remaining in the villages. Base year information was available in schedules provided by New Mexico State University, the Forest Service, the FSA, and the SCS. The SSRC provided travel funds for a resurvey of these villages. This study showed that over half the males who had left were in the armed forces or in defense work. Few remained to be recruited for farmers and ranchers who customarily depended on Spanish-speaking workers.

The data for the FSA borrower study (Jehlik and Larson 1943) came from annual reports required for all FSA borrowers and submitted by the county FSA supervisors for more than three thousand counties. The analysis was made to get a clue as to the response of low-income farmers to the war-related employment opportunities which were opening up. During 1942 about 4 percent of all active standard RR borrowers had left their farms and counties.

In 1942, the BAE had used 1940 census data to estimate the number of low-income farm families potentially available for "more productive" work than on their present farms (Taeuber 1942). However, because of population shifts since 1940, there was a suspicion that the estimates might no longer hold. By these estimates, Eastern Kentucky was one of the important rural labor reservoir areas. To determine the current situation, the Division in cooperation with the Kentucky AES and the BAE's Division of Farm Management and Costs made a quick study of a thirty-three-county area (Larson 1943a). By interviewing local informants such as country storekeepers, a population census was taken for the 2,007 households in five magisterial districts (minor civil divisions). Each informant reported on all families in a recognized neighborhood. Concurrent interviews by the farm management professionals with a sample of the families permitted the informant data to be adjusted for under- or over-enumeration. Ratios for the five districts were extended to arrive at estimates for the total area. Furthermore, reconnaissance surveys were made in twenty of the other counties as a check on the five-district data. Even the low estimate of the number of unemployed or "unproductively" employed workers remaining on Eastern Kentucky farms in December 1942 was larger than the BAE estimates based on the 1940 census. Reported barriers to the out-migration and employment of the workers included size of family and family ties, property ties, limited education, and lack of skills with more complicated farming equipment.

Midway through World War II, it was thought that knowledge of county variations in migration during the prewar years could find application in planning for the postwar period. This led Eleanor Bernert to prepare estimates, using census data and life tables, of the amount and rate of net migration during 1930–40 from the rural-farm population. This was done for age, sex, and race at the level of the nation, geographic divisions, and states (1944a). Estimates were also calculated for the rural-farm population of each county (1944b). A reviewer, Horace Hamilton, evaluated the work as exemplifying "the progress being made in the application of advanced statistical methods to sociological research in the rural field" (1944:187). For Hamilton, the pattern of excessive rates of migration from farms raised questions such as "What sort of social system do we have that makes such radical continuous population migration necessary?" (1944:187).

Finally, the national sample of seventy-one "laboratory" counties mentioned in Chapter 4 were the site for special studies pertinent to the Division's wartime and postwar planning work. The first, on current and anticipated migration problems, was based on interviews with key informants and on sources such as war ration book data and Selective Service records. Instructions for a second report (USDA, BAE, DFPRW 1945) included questions such as "What is the outlook for postwar migration and re-employment opportunities (in this county) during the next two years?" None of these county reports were published. They were prepared solely for administrative use within the federal government. They did, however, provide the basis for a brief national report following the end of the war (Hagood 1946). They were also drawn upon for reports on regional postwar trends prepared in the Division's regional offices.

Over the years some of the cooperative migration studies with state AESs clearly reflected a special interest of the state investigator, especially during the Galpin years. An instance is *Migration of Farm Population and Flow of Farm Wealth*, authored by Fred Yoder and A. A. Smick, both at the State College of Washington (1935). The study was an exploratory test of the hypothesis that transfers of wealth follow movements of people. In another cooperative project, *Rural-Urban Migration in Wisconsin, 1940–1950* (Hagood and Sharp 1951), late in the Division's life history, the research leadership clearly rested with Margaret Hagood. The work was done while she was a visiting staff member for a semester in the University of Wisconsin's Department of Rural Sociology. Net migration for the decade was determined by taking the 1940 enumerated population, adding the births, subtracting the deaths, and comparing the resulting population with that enumerated in 1950. This was done for the rural and urban population of each county in the state. County data were also aggregated for the economic areas of Wisconsin, newly delineated by

Donald Bogue for the Bureau of the Census. This approach and the analysis accompanying it served as a prototype for similar reports from other land-grant universities.

ADDITIONAL AREAS OF WORK

While studies in migration dominated the Division's demographic research, the work in population also included other areas such as fertility, replacement rates, and projections. Conventional data on population composition and trends were woven into numerous reports and addresses. A population component can also be found in research in other substantive areas such as locality groups, rural youth, and the labor force.

The first general study of the composition, characteristics, and occupations of the village population of the United States was *A Census Analysis of American Villages* (Fry 1925). The Institute of Social and Religious Research made a field study of 177 incorporated "agricultural" villages located throughout most of the nation. Edmund deS. Brunner, the director, wanted to supplement the field study with census data. The Division arranged the special tabulations from the 1920 census. An unexpected finding was the extent of differences between the village and the total rural population within regions (Fry 1925:160).

Rural reproduction was included in the Lively and Taeuber (1939) analysis of migration previously noted. Fertility ratios were computed from the 1930 census for all counties for the rural-farm and rural-nonfarm population, by race. The methodological notes included an illustration of a "net replacement quota" to indicate future population change in the absence of migration. By this measure, during the thirty-year period 1930–60, the native white rural-farm population had the potential to increase by 77 percent.

Wartime labor force and postwar planning information needs were served by the calculation of replacement rates during 1940–50 for rural-farm males for all counties (Taeuber 1944). The rates were also computed for whites and nonwhites on a state basis. Results indicated that the number of farm males reaching the age of twenty-five was far beyond the number needed to replace farm men who died or who, at age seventy, were expected to retire from farming.

The Division even became involved in population projections and their use, in part because of their relevance for the BAE's economists who were studying long-range trends affecting American agriculture. Margaret

Hagood, with Jacob Siegel at the Census Bureau (1951), adapted the "ratio-to-United States" method to develop projections for 1955, 1960, and 1975 of the total population for each of the nine census divisions. These were believed to be the first such official projections for the nation's geographic subdivisions. A procedure was also developed to project the age and sex composition of the total population for each of the four geographic regions of the U.S. The quality of this work and the range of its application is suggested by Hagood and Siegel's (1952) presentation in 1951 to the annual meeting of the Business and Economic Statistics Section of the American Statistical Association. They reviewed the types of population projections available in the United States and indicated types of problems in the use of such projections by sales forecasters for commodities.

In response to requests for correlation of data for farm households from the 1950 Censuses of Population, Agriculture, and Housing, the Division worked with other units of the BAE, the Bureau of Human Nutrition and Home Economics, and the Census Bureau. Individual reports were matched for a sample of some eleven thousand farm operator households. Division staff member Helen White prepared the population report on farm operator households (1953).[7]

Finally, two unique pieces of research are worth noting. Farm population density in the Northern Great Plains and the implications of it for community life and adequate services was examined by the Division's staff in the region (Anderson 1946; Anderson 1950). A statistical picture of the foreign-born population of Connecticut was the distinctive feature of Whetten and Riecken's cooperative project (1943). The study used special tabulations from the 1940 Census of Population to delineate the importance of major European nationalities in each Connecticut town.

PUBLIC SERVICE

The farm population estimates got the Division off to a good start with a wide range of users. In 1926 Henry Taylor observed that "The press is very much taken with the studies of migration from farm to city" (1992:145). Theodore Manny said the reports had been one of the Division's most popular releases, widely sought after by leaders of farmers' organizations, commercial interests, city planning bodies, and professional people (1936:12). Over the years, substantial resources were devoted to compiling, analyzing, and interpreting census data to meet specific requests.

Requests for assistance came to the Division from a variety of sources. For example, in the early 1930s the USDA responded to a request by religious and private social service agencies for a comprehensive survey of economic and social conditions in the Southern Appalachians. The Division prepared the section on population distribution and changes (Manny 1935). The county planning program under BAE leadership generated numerous requests for population data from state and county planning committees. At the request of the Kansas agricultural planning committee, an analysis was undertaken in 1940–41 of data collected by the Kansas state census.

The defense and war years in particular brought urgent requests for service. Special surveys and spot field checks pertaining to rural migration and defense and allied employment were made in the Far Western states. These were in response to the House Select Committee Investigating National Defense Migration, the FSA, and others. To assist local committees on problems of families displaced by land acquisition for a military camp, an ordinance plant, and other military and industrial uses, schedules were prepared and information collected for at least eight areas in Arkansas, Iowa, Kansas, and Missouri.

The Division's population work was also the basis of testimony by staff members before House and Senate committees. Topics included drought migration (Hay 1940), defense migration (Hay 1941; Taeuber 1942), and farm population trends (Taeuber 1940; Taeuber 1942). Congressional bodies included the House Select Committee to Investigate the Interstate Migration of Destitute Citizens and the Senate Committee on Education and Labor.

SUMMARY

During the Division's lifetime, dramatic changes took place in the nation's farm and rural populations, and in the rural-urban balance. Around 1920, the nation's population started its shift from a rural to an urban majority, just at the time the Division came into being. From 1919 to 1953, farm population decreased by 36 percent (Banks and Beale 1973:14–15). However, the total rural population during these years held up because of the rural-nonfarm growth. The rural population, 51.4 million in 1920, was counted in 1950 as 54.2 million by the "new" census definition (U.S. Bureau of the Census 1933; 1953).

Research in farm and rural population was a major, continuing, and distinguished area of work for the Division. This emphasis on population research was in tune with the attention given by social scientists in the United States. Between censuses, the Division was the only source of current information on farm population changes. While the Division's program began with a special focus on farm population, the work was quickly broadened. Indeed, work by the Division helped bring to light the growing importance of changes in the rural-nonfarm population.

While migration dominated the Division's population research, the program was not limited to that area. Other research included fertility, replacement rates, and projections. Population components were also woven into other reports and addresses. This was especially true for research on population composition and trends. Over the years, the Division was a much-used and highly regarded resource for its population research, leaving an indelible mark on this field.

Notes

1. Veda B. Larson (Turner), Division staff member from 1920 until her resignation December 31, 1925, had a major role in developing the farm population estimating procedures used initially.

2. In response to World War II, migration categories were expanded to include movement between farms and the armed forces.

3. A decade earlier a BAE predecessor agency had sent a mail questionnaire to about forty-five thousand crop correspondents requesting them to report on migration from cities and towns to the country (Holmes 1915).

4. This project started after the 1920 census with the preparation of maps for state-of-birth data for a few states. The interest these received led to continuing the work as resources permitted. It was not until the New Deal's Civil Works Administration that there were funds to hire unemployed draftsmen and complete the work.

5. Reports for the mobility field surveys in three of the states listed the Division as a cooperator, namely, Kentucky and North Carolina (Dodson 1937) and South Dakota (Kumlien, McNamara, and Bankert 1938).

6. Cooperators in different phases of the study included the departments of education in the five states; the agricultural experiment stations in four states; the U.S. Bureau of Reclamation; the Department of Economics at the University of California; and the California Division of Immigration and Housing. The Division's regional office in Berkeley had the lead role in these studies.

7. When the Bureau of the Census and the BAE began to issue farm population estimates and related statistics cooperatively in 1945 as Series Census-BAE, Nos. 1, 3, and 6 reported age, sex, occupational, and off-farm work data.

6

Levels and Standards of Living

No comprehensive studies of the living conditions of farm families in the United States had been made before the Division was established (Kirkpatrick 1923:31–32). During the 1920s, Galpin moved quickly to make levels and standards of living a major area of work. Research in this area, by Division staff or through cooperative projects, would continue throughout the Division's history.

Galpin realized that some areas of farm family living research bordered between home economics and rural sociology (1938a:53–54). An accommodation had to be worked out between the relevant units within the USDA. One result was that home economists, both in the USDA and in the states, were cooperators in numerous Division projects, especially during the 1920s. Acknowledging the close relationship of the farm family and the farm business, agricultural economists specializing in farm management research were also frequent cooperators.

Over time, the Division's research in levels and standards of living would undergo major changes. Concepts would become more clearly defined. The unit of analysis shifted from the family unit to aggregates of families. Data sources changed. In the end, work in the 1940s by Margaret J. Hagood would be markedly different from the early studies conducted by E. L. Kirkpatrick and his associates.

FARM FAMILY LIVING STUDIES

Early Studies

As mentioned in Chapter 2, Secretary Houston's advisory committee had assigned rural home life first place in its suggested fields of rural life study. Consistent with this recommendation, Galpin made farm family living research one of the major areas for the Division. Prior to this, information about family living status in the United States had come largely from studies of the cost of living of industrial workers and city dwellers. But this information clearly was not applicable to farm families. The Division's work in the 1920s made a start on providing the needed data on farm family living. Furthermore, the collapse of agricultural prices in 1920 underscored the importance of learning about the living conditions of farm families. Such information was also needed for developing extension programs for farm homemakers. There was also an interest in the relationship between living conditions on the farm and farm-to-city migration.

The nation's first published comprehensive study of farm family living was E. L. Kirkpatrick's *The Standard of Life in a Typical Section of Diversified Farming* (1923).[1] This research would influence the content and methods of subsequent studies of farm family living by the Division, the state AESs and others. A cooperative project with Cornell University, Kirkpatrick's research was based on interviews with farm families in Livingston County, New York. Following traditional gender roles, information on the "business" of the household was obtained from women and that regarding the farm business was obtained from men, with few exceptions. The USDA's Office of Home Economics gave financial support to the project and provided two home economists to assist in the interviews. At the time of the research, Kirkpatrick was a graduate student at Cornell. The resulting publication was based on his Ph.D. thesis, which was directed by Professor Dwight Sanderson in the Department of Rural Social Organization.

In 1922, Galpin added Kirkpatrick to the Division staff where he took the lead in early work on the living conditions of farm families. For the next six years, Kirkpatrick's research was devoted almost exclusively to farm family living studies designed on the basis of what had been learned in the Livingston County work. Cooperative projects were conducted during 1922–24 in 11 states. The interview schedules were prepared jointly by the Division and the new Bureau of Home Economics in the USDA. Soon after a study was completed in a state, a preliminary report in mimeo form would be issued.[2] This was consistent with Galpin's practice of trying to get research findings out promptly so they could be put to use. The combined results of these studies were published by Kirkpatrick in the USDA bulletin, *The Farmer's Standard of Living: A Socioeconomic Study of 2,886 White Farm Families of Selected Localities in 11 States* (1926). A magazine for farm women, *The Farmer's Wife,* supported the preparation of special reports for the four North Central states in this study. Each of these four reports dealt with one category of expenditures or consumption such as clothing or household furnishings and equipment.

The data for two other reports came from a USDA land tenure study in three Southern states made before Kirkpatrick's arrival in Washington. The first of these was on the cost of living among 154 "colored" farm families (Kirkpatrick and Sanders 1925; see Chapter 11). The second looked into the relation of ability to pay and family living for 861 white farm families (Kirkpatrick and Sanders 1926). Unlike the field studies directed by Kirkpartrick, living information in the land tenure study was usually obtained from the farm operator—a male.

Before Kirkpatrick left the Division to join the University of Wisconsin staff in rural sociology, he was afforded the opportunity to put in book form the results of investigations of farm family living by the Division and others (*The Farmer's Standard of Living* 1929). The research Kirkpatrick drew upon for the book generally examined factors that were related to, or conditioned, the total cost of all goods consumed by the family, and the percentage allocated to groups of goods such as food or "advancement." He classified these factors into three sets: (1) those indicative of the family's ability to provide economic goods, e.g., net worth; (2) those regarded as influencing the demands or desires for goods, services, and facilities, e.g., age and number of family members and formal schooling; and (3) those involving use of time for work, rest, and relaxation. Kirkpatrick concluded that the measures of economic ability to provide seemed to bear about the same relation to the family "standard of living" as did the measures of demands or desires. Interestingly, the data suggested that there was not a significant relationship between the measures of time use and the farm family "standard of living." The analysis also identified an important relationship of the life cycle of the family with economic means. Kirkpatrick also called attention to the accessibility of goods, services, and facilities as a factor in farm family living.

During the Galpin years, cooperative projects on family living were also supported in at least nine states. Leadership for these lay with sociologists in land-grant or other universities. These studies included, for instance, the comparison of living conditions by farm tenure status in Southeast Missouri (Taylor et al. 1920), and a comparison in North Carolina of farm homes and home-produced food supplies by tenure status and race (Taylor and Zimmerman 1922).

Taken as a whole the most sociological and most provocative for theory was the cooperative research initiated in Wisconsin by Kirkpatrick after he left the Division. Building upon the knowledge gained in his previous work, he made the most exacting test to date of relationships associated with different levels of living. For this, a 900-family sample was interviewed, taking into account the state's six major type-of-farming areas. The sampling also took trade and service areas into consideration. The first part of the study was unique in its examination of the inter-relations of family standards of living, as measured by cost, with income and participation of family members in home and community activities (Kirkpatrick et al. 1933). The second part constructed stages of development —the life cycle—of the farm family as a framework for analysis of the goods and services consumed (Kirkpatrick et al. 1934).

Research Decisions

Kirkpatrick's Livingston County study (1923) was not only the first comprehensive study of farm family living, but as such, laid the ground work for research to come. Kirkpatrick was aware of the cost of living studies that had been done in America's urban areas. He was also informed about the extensive work in Europe, notably F. LePlay's case studies of families and the statistical analyses by Ernst Engel and others (Kirkpatrick 1923:28–31). But these offered only limited guidelines for pioneering sociological research on farm families in the United States. From defining concepts to methods of analysis, research decisions needed to be made.

Rather than the commonly used "standard of living" or other concepts such as "level" or "scale" of living, for his first study, Kirkpatrick preferred the concept "standard of life." For Kirkpatrick, "standard of life" was unique in that it was an inclusive measure of life in terms of the sum total of values enjoyed by the family. He measured this through the acquisition and expenditure of income, and through the use of time in the satisfaction of wants for things, both material (as food, clothing, and shelter) and spiritual (as education, music, and art).

Use of the concept "standard of life" was short-lived as the term "standard of living" was adopted in the Division's publications. This was defined as the cost or value of goods and services used. Later, in the 1930s, the Division moved to use "level of living" to refer to the actual content of family living and to reserve "standard of living" for what the family aspired to for its living.

The basic thesis of Kirkpatrick's Livingston County study was that the standard of life was dependent on various aspects of socialization, including education, rather than solely on the family's economic assets. The nine-page "blank" used in the interviews with families included a sweeping array of items. Provisions were made for recording the quantity and cost or value of all family living items, purchased and farm-furnished, for the year preceding the interview. Information was also sought on the use of time by the homemaker and other family members and on their participation in community organizations. Among other items, the schedule asked for data on the home, its conveniences and furnishings, the grounds, and even for a list of the children's pets.

Few farm homemakers kept accounts of family expenditures so interviewers were trained in techniques to obtain the best possible estimates of goods used and their annual cost. Methods were also developed for placing a money value on the food, fuel, and housing furnished by the farm. In the end, Kirkpatrick believed the figures were "sufficiently accurate for all practical purposes" (1923:9).

To facilitate analysis and comparison, a classification system had to be devised to place in a few groups the many expenditure items. Nine groups, such as food, clothing, and "advancement," were used in the Livingston County study (1923:32–33). This classification would undergo some changes in subsequent research (Kirkpatrick 1926:11–12; 1929:29–30). While "advancement" was a key concept for Kirkpatrick's analysis, what to include proved to be especially difficult. There was also uncertainty as to what to include as "savings" for farm families (Kirkpatrick 1929:264–81).

The families in the New York study varied in the number, ages, and gender of members and in the presence of hired men and other non-family members. Presumably, these variations would have a bearing on the quantity and, therefore, cost of items consumed. To establish equivalent units for analysis purposes, much attention was given to constructing and testing cost-consumption scales (1923:40–48). Scales were devised for food, clothing, advancement, and the other six expenditure groups. However, most of the scales were found to be of questionable applicability. Thereafter, Kirkpatrick usually just accepted the family or household as an adequate unit for analysis.

Kirkpatrick also developed a scale to get a quantitative measure of a family's standard of life. The scale was developed with advice from a panel of some 100 persons knowledgeable about farming and rural life. The 118 items encompassed three main groupings: expenditures for necessities, comforts, and luxuries; education of children; and social values manifested through disposition to improve environment, use of time, and participation in community activities. Each item was assigned a weight so that a family's highest possible score was 1000. The researcher concluded, however, that this scale was far from satisfactory in many respects as a measure of standard of life and did not use it in subsequent studies.

An important contribution of Kirkpatrick's Livingston County study was that he broke new ground for data analysis. Largely, Kirkpatrick depended upon numbers and percentages presented in graphs and tables. But he also reported results from simple correlations. This was one of the first times, if not the first, that this statistical test was used in rural sociological research. A decade later, partial and multiple correlation would be used in the analysis for a cooperative project in Wisconsin (Kirkpatrick et al. 1933:9–10).

The experience gained and the testing done in the Livingston County study would be reflected in subsequent studies. For example, they were more streamlined in content. They emphasized the quantity and cost of goods and services used. Procedures for data collection by the survey method, for classification, and for analysis also reflected lessons learned from the Livingston County work.

Contributions of Work Done in 1920s

Before the end of the 1920s, the Division and its cooperators had made detailed studies of the annual family consumption and expenditures of about five thousand farm families in fifteen states (Galpin (1929:73). These studies provided a body of quantitative data about the value of the goods, (purchased and farm-supplied), used for family living. They showed wide variations among families in the total value and in the distribution among groups of goods. They also showed that it was not unusual to find that farm family living costs exceeded income available in a given year. In such cases, the family had to use savings, go into debt, or seek assistance from private or public sources. The studies also revealed the importance of non-farm income to cover the living costs of a substantial percentage of farm families. Furthermore, the studies explored the relation between living expenditures and family, farm, and community factors. They also drew attention to the importance of farm-furnished food and housing for farm family living although there were differences of opinion as to the soundness of Kirkpatrick's method for putting a money value on these items (Duncan 1941:305).

The data collected in Kirkpatrick's eleven-state study were used to determine items included in an early BAE index of the prices of commodities farmers buy for family use (F. M. Williams 1935:11). The localities for the study were intentionally chosen to represent "average" economic conditions for farming and farm families. The intent, in this early work, was to avoid painting a picture which was "too dark or too light" (Kirkpatrick 1926:6).

Writing in 1926, Henry Taylor stated that "No single type of rural study has awakened more thought than the study of the standard of living and cost of living of farm families. The results have been taken back to the communities and made the basis of a better living program" (1992: 145–46). Highlights from the research were used in brief articles in the USDA's annual *Yearbook*. One, for instance, reported on living conditions in a relatively poor farming section in southeastern Ohio (Kirkpatrick and Hawthorne 1928:293–95). The research was also the basis for a section on the farmers' standard of living prepared for the report of a committee on recent economic changes in the United States chaired by Herbert Hoover (Galpin 1929:70–76). "Standards of living" was the theme for the 1930 annual meeting of the American Country Life Association (ACLA) attended by an estimated two thousand people (ACLA 1931:vii). Materials prepared specifically for the ACLA conference by the BAE (Bercaw 1931) and by the University of Wisconsin (Kirkpatrick 1930) made extensive use of the Division's research.

Level of Living

A set of six studies of targeted groups and special problem areas published during 1937–40 marked the beginning of Carl Taylor's effort to have the Division's work make a sharp and consistent distinction between standard and level of living. Level of living was to pertain to what was purchased, consumed, or used, while standard of living was to refer to what families desired or preferred. Taylor also stressed that family living expenditures measured chiefly the material aspects of living.

The six studies were made by the Division and the FSA's Social Research unit, both headed by Carl Taylor.[3] All of these used the data collection and analysis methods developed earlier in the Division. One of these studies looked at families in seven of the New Deal's recently established rural resettlement communities (Loomis and Davidson 1938). While the original purpose was to construct a benchmark against which to measure changes in living conditions, the resettlement projects fell into political disfavor too quickly to allow time for a restudy. With the measurement of change in mind, the studies of two of the seven resettlement projects also included a sample of neighbors for comparative purposes.

A comparison of the levels of living in two very dissimilar communities was another of the six studies (Loomis and Leonard 1938). In one community, most were farm operator families relocated on a Bureau of Reclamation planned irrigation project in California and Oregon. The other was comprised of Indian-Mexican farm laborer families in a long-established village in New Mexico. The Indian-Mexican families had an average value of family living in 1935 of $347 as compared with $2,843 for the irrigation project families.

Rural problem areas were the focus of three of the studies. The Southern Appalachian work determined levels of living of rural families in high-relief counties which also had a large farm population increase from 1930 to 1935 (Loomis and Dodson 1938). In another study, a sample of both open-country and village families was used to examine levels of living in the once-timbered "cut-over" areas of Michigan, Minnesota, and Wisconsin (Loomis et al. 1938). In South Dakota, the main purpose of the research was to provide information requested by federal agencies about people in the states severely affected at that time by drought (Kumlien et al. 1938).

The last of the six studies pertained to farm and town white families in Virginia (Davidson and Hummel 1940). The objective was to increase knowledge of the levels of living of various segments of the state's population. The researchers suggested that such studies might be a basis for evaluating the effect of the New Deal's farm-focused action programs on the farmer's level of living.

Beyond these six studies, other research at the time also contained a family living component. For example, an attempt was made to determine both the level of living and the standard of living for more than 2,400 Corn Belt and Cotton Belt farmers (Schuler 1938b:52–61, 216–30). Rather than expenditure data, the measures relied on were the presence of, or the desire for, specified housing items and possessions. The data were analyzed by tenure status and, in the Cotton Belt, by race. In another study, participation in religious and other organizations was interpreted as a measure of the nonmaterial element in the level of living among black sharecroppers and wage laborers on plantations in selected localities (Leonard and Loomis 1939). A study of the influence of drought and depression in Haskell County, Kansas, had two special features (Edwards 1939:56–67). First, historical records were used to portray living conditions of settlers, 1875–1900, and changes, 1900–1936. Secondly, the farm families interviewed were asked how expenditures in 1936 compared with the "usual" year. They reported a 51 percent increase in health expenditures and nearly a 30 percent cut in "advancement" and clothing.

LEVEL-OF-LIVING INDEXES

The approach used by social scientists to measure the status of family living and changes in that status began to shift drastically in the 1930s. The policy and planning activities generated by the New Deal needed information that applied to farm families in every county in the nation. Such information could not be supplied cheaply or quickly by the methods used by Kirkpatrick and his colleagues. But data collected by the U.S. Census from every farm family was seen as opening the way to new measurement approaches. The result was the development by the Division and others of level-of-living indexes. In constructing these indexes, the county, not the individual family, was the basic unit of analysis.

The early indexes were simple. The first published for farm families for all counties in the United States was developed jointly by the FSA and the Division (C. Taylor et al. 1938:108–24).[4] The index value for any county was the average of the percentage of the farm homes having an automobile, electricity, radio, running water, and telephone. For this, data came from the 1930 Censuses of Agriculture and Population. On a map of the United States, graphic presentation of the county index values identified in a visually striking way the rural areas in which farm families with low index values were concentrated.

Rural sociologists at Ohio State University also developed an index based on census data. Lively and Taeuber (1939:73–77, 167–68), in another cooperative project, adapted this index as a measure of economic well-being at the county level. Index values were computed so that the percentages placed each county in relation to the national mean. The index, called "plane of living," was calculated for 1930 for the rural-farm, the rural non-farm, and the total rural population of each county.[5]

The most notable achievements in developing level-of-living indexes for rural America were those of Margaret Jarman Hagood after she joined the Division in the early 1940s. Her indexes permitted comparison of living conditions among counties or groups of counties. When used as time series, they also gave a measure of change between two points in time. The items used in the indexes all came from readily available census sources. Further, the index for a county was a relative measure as it was always expressed in relation to the corresponding attainment of a defined group, e.g., the average for all farm operators in the nation at a given time. In 1943, using the 1940 Censuses of Agriculture, Housing, and Population, the first of these indexes was published (Hagood 1943b). While separate indexes for the rural-farm, the rural non-farm, and all rural families of each county were used, subsequent published work was limited to farm operator families.

A farm-operator family level-of-living index was constructed for every county for the years 1930, 1940, 1945, and 1950 (Hagood 1952). Four items, all from the Census of Agriculture, were the basis for the index: the percentage of farms with electricity; with telephones; with automobiles; and the average value of products sold or traded in the year preceding the census (adjusted for changes in the farmers' purchasing power). These farm-operator family indexes were published not only for counties but for state economic areas, states, and census divisions and regions. Starting in 1951 and until the Division was ended, annual indexes were available within the USDA.

Margaret Hagood and Gladys Bowles (1957b) explain the assumptions underlying the indexes, their development and construction, and the Division's assessment of their limitations. In the early stages, the selection of items for the indexes involved extensive experimentation and testing. For example, using correlation analysis the fourteen items suggested for the 1940 rural-farm index were reduced to five (Hagood 1943a). As a basis for putting the separate items together in a composite index, factor or component analysis was used to derive the relative weight for each item. A coding procedure was then used which gave an index a value of 100 for the United States mean. Thus, the index value for any county could be compared directly in relation to the national average.

The limitations and problems of the indexes were recognized by Hagood and her associates. For example, quantitative data available for index items were far from encompassing the range of phenomena coming under the level of living concept. Although efforts were made to select index items that were most uniformly valid indicants of level of living in every region, this was not completely successful. Further, the value of items used in the indexes could change over time. For instance, the value of electricity as a differentiating factor was reduced as the percentage of farms with electricity increased. There were also special problems with the data for some censuses of agriculture. The 1950 census, for example, obtained data on electricity, telephones, and automobiles only for very large farms and a 20 percent sample of the rest. This data problem meant that special procedures were required for constructing the 1950 farm family index.

The indexes were not without their critics. Sociologist Horace Hamilton (1944:184–86) contended that Hagood's rural-farm index for 1940 was overloaded with cash-farming factors and, therefore, obscured important regional differences. For example, it gave lower index values to areas such as the Southern Appalachians where subsistence farming was important. Further, he would eliminate multiple correlation analysis and unequal weighting of index items, favoring an index of equally weighted items. The 1930–50 farm-operator level-of-living indexes were also criticized.

Agricultural economist Vernon Ruttan (1954:44–51) argued that, except for lower-income counties and states, the indexes were not closely related to another measure of rural welfare: average income per farm operator. Ruttan further noted that the Hagood index did not take into account the quantity or quality of the consumption items she used.

The critics, however, also acknowledged the wide usefulness of Hagood's indexes. For example, the indexes pointed to an upward trend in farm-operator level-of-living in all parts of the country during 1930–50 (Hagood 1952:3–4). Even during the depression decade it was only the drought-hit North Central census division that registered a decrease. The increase in the percentage of farms with electricity was an especially important factor in the index increase. The rise in level of living among farm-operator families during 1940–50 was generally most rapid where mechanization, as measured by increases in the number of tractors on farms, was most rapid. At the same time, the indexes indicated persistence in the areas having a concentration of counties with low or high index values. Findings from the research on level-of-living indexes were used in a report on long-range agricultural policy prepared by the BAE at the request of the House Committee on Agriculture (USDA 1948:66–67). The index formula for 1945 was also adapted for use at the minor civil division level for research projects in at least nine states (Hagood 1952:81–82).

OTHER NEW APPROACHES

Although the development by Margaret Hagood of the widely used level-of-living indexes was an outstanding contribution, Carl Taylor also fostered other distinctive research on levels and standards of living by Division staff. Some of this work was a direct consequence of a request to assist the Bureau of Reclamation in planning for the Columbia Basin irrigation project in the State of Washington.[6] The project area covered 2.5 million acres. Of this, over one million were suitable for irrigation farming. At the time, the area was sparsely settled, used mostly for large-scale dry land wheat farming. The goal of the project was to convert the land into not less than ten thousand new family-type irrigated farms with water from the Grand Coulee Dam.

To help develop plans for the development and settlement of the area, the Bureau of Reclamation sought the help of experts from numerous federal and state agencies. Twenty-eight specific problems were identified for studies and reports (Taylor 1946a). One of the problems addressed levels of living for the Columbia Basin settlers on the new farms. The Division refused to prescribe what level of living settlers should have but Carl Taylor agreed that it would conduct investigations aimed at answering the overriding question, "What level of living will settlers demand and without the attainment of which will be dissatisfied?" (Taylor 1947a:iv). The answer to this question was important to farm management specialists who had to deal with minimum income objectives in recommending the best type and size of farms for the project area. It was assumed that if the settlement was to be successful, the capacity of farms and communities in the settlement area had to be sufficient to support the settlers past habits of consumption and fulfill their expectations. Otherwise, turnover of settlers would probably be high and their morale would be low.

A multiple-part study was made of levels of living for the Columbia Basin project. The first part reanalyzed family expenditure data from the Consumer Purchases Study conducted in 1935–36 by the USDA's Bureau of Home Economics (Fisher 1947:1–27). The data were analyzed for a sample of families located in three main areas of prospective settlers. There were 948 native-born, non-relief families in Oregon and Washington on small full-time farms, 984 native-born, non-relief families in North Dakota and Kansas on relatively large full-time farms, and 383 native-born, non-relief, part-time farmers in Western Oregon. The most significant finding from the analysis was that there was a "critical point" at which, in a given cultural area, farm families resolved the conflict between unmet desires and lack of income for family living by going into debt. Below this point they refused to sacrifice an accustomed and desired level of living. Also, just above this critical point they began to accumulate savings. This finding was confirmed by the records of 122 farm families who had been living on two new irrigation projects in Eastern Oregon. The critical point, expressed by the income level, was higher for the Great Plains sample than for the Northwest. It was lowest of all for the families on the new Oregon irrigation projects. The "critical point" procedure was proposed as a preferred method of determining the minimum farm income that would meet the minimum requirements of family living (Fisher 1943; 1947:23–26).

The second part of the Columbia Basin levels of living study was designed to predict what types of goods and services the prospective settlers would demand, and the order in which they would desire to secure them (Swiger and Schuler 1947:29–48). The method used was adapted from previous work by Schuler (1944) in which he drew upon the 1935–36 Consumer Purchases Study. Data came from the same sample of full-time farmers used for the "critical point" determination described above.

Twenty-seven expenditure items were selected for grouping into one of four categories: cultural necessities, cultural luxuries, cultural rarities, and cultural substitutes.[7] Categorical placement of the items was done by comparing the proportion of low and high income families reporting the item. For example, cultural necessities were the items purchased by both high and low income families. Cultural luxuries were used mostly by families with above average incomes. These included running water, telephone, dentist, and life insurance. Cultural rarities were reported by only a few high income families. Examples included central heating and household help. Interestingly, three items which were necessities in the Northwest were rarities or luxuries in Kansas and North Dakota. These were electricity, kitchen sink with drain, and flush toilets. And no cultural substitutes were discovered among the families sampled.

To obtain further insights as to the likely goods and services desired and consumption habits of prospective settlers, field studies were made of families in ten newly settled reclamation projects. The results showed, for example, that families complained about being supplied goods and services different from those to which they were accustomed or that were not regarded as necessities in the new place of residence (Taylor 1946a: 324–25).[8] Also, a family's order of preferences for level of living items and farm operation expenditures often differed from that prescribed by project planners and administrators.

Most of the initial interviews for the study of reclamation project settlers were with men. They were made by pairs of researchers, one interviewing, the other recording the answers. There was some doubt as to whether the farm women settlers had the same opinions and attitudes as the men. Accordingly, a woman interviewer was sent back to interview only farm women. The results showed that the women settlers had about the same views as the men (Taylor 1946a:324–25).

Building on the Columbia Basin research, Longmore and Taylor (1951) expanded on the argument that because farming was a predominantly family enterprise, farm family and farm production expenditures automatically competed for budget shares. The theory was that the lower the family income, the keener the competition would be between farm and family expenditures. Further, savings and investments were considered residual after farm and family necessities were met. They hypothesized that of the three expenditure categories, expenditures for family living would tend to have top priority and would be the least flexible. Their test data came from the incomes and expenditures in 1946 for a sample of 4,057 families representing the farm population of the United States.

Using the coefficient of income elasticity, they found that farm production expenditures had a coefficient of unity; they generally increased as rapidly as gross cash income. Savings, too, were highly sensitive to changes in income. However, family living expenditures were found to be "rigid"; they had an income elasticity well below unity. Wide variations were found by regions in level of living expenditures, in farm production expenditures, and in savings practices at specified income levels. The "critical point," the average income below which indebtedness started and above which savings began, was seen by Longmore and Taylor as a turning point in the decision-making process of farm families. They interpreted the "critical point" as a culturally determined standard. The cultural referent was in keeping with the importance attached to the concept of culture which characterized much of the Division's work under Carl Taylor's leadership.

The level-of-living indexes developed by Hagood were excellent for comparative and sensitizing purposes, but were difficult for many users to visualize what they meant in real-life situations. Therefore, as a supplement to the indexes, the Division prepared readily understandable time series for specific items which provided measures of farm family living (Schuler and Swiger 1946; Flagg and Longmore 1952). Examples of items were the percentage of farms with electricity and with telephone. This material was intended for use by persons concerned with rural welfare such as extension workers and farm people in general.

In the 1940s, the Division undertook a parity approach to the study of farm family living. McKain and Flagg (1948) used a wide variety of data sources which had become available to compare farm families with rural-nonfarm and urban families. The range of measures used included per capita income, nutrition, health and medical services, and material possessions. The data, mostly for around 1940, found farm families disadvantaged on most of the level-of-living items as compared with urban families. The most significant output from this comparative analysis was *Trends in Rural and Urban Levels of Living* (Flagg and Longmore 1949). The basic question was to determine the influence of the relative dominance of farming on the level of living in a county. All of the nation's counties were sorted into class intervals based on the percentage of their population in 1940, which was rural-farm. The level of living indicators was tabulated in most cases for 1930, 1940, and 1945, for each class of county for each census division. Almost without exception, the analysis demonstrated a relation between farm levels of living and degree of rurality. Proximity of farm homes to urban centers was seen as primarily influencing the results found. For the researchers, the results pointed to the interlocking nature of the modern rural community with expanding urban centers.

SUMMARY

Research on the living conditions of farm families was one of the major and continuing areas of work for the Division. Aspects of this research were on the border between rural sociology and home economics. This led to numerous cooperative projects with home economists, especially during the 1920s when levels and standards of living work was new. The close relationship between the farm family and the farm enterprise was recognized. Thus, some Division studies also had a close linkage with agricultural economists who specialized in farm management.

Over the years, the Division's research on levels and standards of living underwent many changes. Concepts and their definition were one such area of change. The initial study used a quickly discontinued concept, "standard of life." This was a values-oriented concept, related to satisfactions derived from both the material and non-material components of family living. Soon, however, "standard of living" was commonly used. Later, Carl Taylor sought to make a sharp distinction between "standard of living" and "level of living." The first referred to what was actually used or consumed, the second to what was preferred by the family.

The unit of analysis, data collection, and statistical treatment of data also changed. Early research was based largely on collecting information by interview from relatively small numbers of farm women. Later, emphasis shifted to relying upon secondary data such as that provided by the Bureau of the Census. These secondary data were subjected to increasingly complex statistical analyses to develop level-of-living indexes. Such indexes provided indicants of the level-of-living for aggregates of families for county or larger geographic units.

The Division's work on farm family living was influential. Prior to E. L. Kirkpatrick's research, there had been no comprehensive sociological study of American farm family living. His studies provided a vast amount of data on the cost and other aspects of living for limited numbers of farm families in the 1920s. They led to examining the relationship between family living and such family characteristics as stage of the life cycle. Later, the indexes developed by Margaret Hagood made it possible to provide information, useful to policy-makers, about farm family living conditions and changes for every county in the nation. Measures were also devised to compare farm family living with that of rural-nonfarm and urban families.

Notes

1. Expenditure records for 106 farm homes in Livingston County, New York, had been collected by mail survey in 1909 by the Cornell Department of Farm Management. There were also reports of studies of consumption items furnished by the farm (Kirkpatrick 1923:31).

2. Abstracts of the preliminary reports for the studies in the 11 states may be found in Bercaw's *Rural Standards of Living: A Selected Bibliography* (1931).

3. The state AESs in Minnesota, South Dakota, Virginia, and Wisconsin cooperated in the research in their respective states. The WPA's Rural Research unit initiated one of the studies and WPA provided funding for two others.

4. Prior to the farm family living index used by Carl Taylor and his associates, a three-item "plane of living" index for the total population of all counties had been constructed for use in Carter Goodrich's Study of Population Redistribution (Goodrich, Allin, and Hayes 1935:13–25).

5. The spurt of development of indexes led Division staff member Walter McKain Jr. (1939) to critically examine the assumptions implicit in a "plane of living" concept and in the construction of an index. His test comparison of a weighted and an unweighted index for Vermont counties yielded widely divergent results.

6. The Division also met requests from the FSA for work on levels of living for that agency's policy and evaluation purposes (see Chapter 12).

7. Kirkpatrick (1923:26–28, 49–53) made limited use of "necessities," "comforts," and "luxuries" as family living categories in his first study.

8. The World War II situation prevented completion and publication of this study of reclamation project settlers but results were furnished to the Bureau of Reclamation officials in charge of settlement policy and administration (Taylor 1946a:325).

7

The Social Organization of Rural Society:
Locality and Other Groups

The Division's research ventured into virtually every aspect of the social organization of rural life in the United States. Rural social organization is used here in an inclusive sense. In this chapter we focus on geographically based groups, on their identification, characteristics, functions, relationships, and changes. Such groups range from country neighborhoods to rural cultural regions. In the next chapter we review the Division's research on other aspects of rural social organization such as institutions and functional groupings or special interest associations.

Locality groups, especially community, were central to the third core and continuing area of study for the Division. At the time the unit was started in the USDA, the social institutions of farm people were, generally, of a neighborhood type and scale (Galpin 1915:22). So were their social relationships. The automobile, improved roads, and the accompanying shifts in farm family spatial arrangements were, however, changing the neighborhood scale of things. But there was a great scarcity of research-based knowledge about the actual rural locality group situation. Accordingly, Secretary Houston's special committee on rural life studies gave a high priority to research on the neighborhood, community, village, and other geographic social units (USDA, Office of the Secretary 1919b:6–8).

Galpin was ideally suited to assume the leadership for the recommended studies. The one notable exception to the lack of empirically based research on the topic was his widely recognized and now classic *The Social Anatomy of an Agricultural Community* (1915). For this, he had used an ecological-type approach. Galpin's simple survey method in Walworth County, Wisconsin, of finding the boundaries within which farm families used specific economic and social services located in population centers and the dramatic maps which resulted caught the imagination of social scientists.[1] Interpreting what he found, Galpin asserted it was difficult to avoid the conclusion that the trade zone around a rather complete agricultural center formed the boundary of an actual, if not legal, community. Within this space, country and center residents had a fairly unitary system of interrelatedness (Galpin 1915:16–19; 1918:86–87). Soon he went on to hinge his theory of rural life on "the discovery of a repeating socioeconomic unit of local rural territory and population," the basic building block, beyond the family, of rural social structure (Galpin 1918:vii). Further, Galpin spelled out the implications of this community research for revamping the geographic base for institutions and agencies such as local government and high schools to benefit farm families.

AN OVERVIEW—THE GALPIN YEARS

During the Galpin years the special emphasis was on identifying and studying the structure and dynamics of what he referred to as "farm population natural groupings." All of the Division's locality group work during these years was conducted through cooperative projects. In these, the university researcher was always the principal investigator. Galpin's name did not appear as author or co-author of even one of the research reports resulting from these projects. Rather, his role was to counsel, to facilitate exchange of ideas among the researchers, to encourage, and to provide a few dollars of support.

The Search for Neighborhood

The presence and importance of neighborhood groups was mentioned in Galpin's *The Social Anatomy of an Agricultural Community* (1915), but they were not the object of his study. Neighborhoods were, however, the planned focus of the first important set of locality group studies the Division initiated on a cooperative basis. This work of sociological discovery was undertaken for six counties, one each in Missouri, Montana, New York, North Carolina, Washington, and Wisconsin. All had a common objective, to determine the primary population groups and their fundamental characteristics in the chosen counties (C. Taylor 1948c:150).

J. H. Kolb, who had succeeded Galpin at the University of Wisconsin, led off with a study in Dane County. His *Rural Primary Groups: A Study of Agricultural Neighborhoods* (1921) became a basis for comparison for the others in the set of six. Kolb attempted to distinguish between neighborhood and community. He defined neighborhood as "that first rural grouping beyond the family which has social significance and which is conscious of some local unity" (1921:5–6). These small locality groups were essentially a psychological thing, in Kolb's view, but for objective purposes had to be described and measured with geographic areas and terms. He adopted Charles H. Cooley's primary group concept as applicable to the Dane County country neighborhoods because of their intimate face-to-face relationships (1918:23–31).

There was no precedent for the sociological study of country neighborhoods. To start with, how were the rural primary groups of Dane County to be discovered? Kolb arranged to have farm families in the county sent a card via the teachers in the country schools. Families were asked the question, "By what name is the country neighborhood called in which you live?" There was an explanation of what was meant. The answers were plotted on base maps which showed the location of all farm units. This procedure resulted in 121 named neighborhoods. But a place name was not enough to identify a neighborhood as defined. Interviews with an informed person in each of the 121 localities revealed 26 were nonfunctional (later called "inactive"). Some 95 satisfied the definition; later they were termed "active." Kolb's research went far beyond identification. The origins, changes, group processes, functions, and binding factors were among other aspects studied.

Dwight Sanderson and Warren S. Thompson, at Cornell, studied Otsego County, New York (1923), to ascertain just what forms a rural neighborhood and how the neighborhood group functions in rural life. Methods for discovery and mapping were similar to those used by Kolb. One modification was that boundaries of the identified neighborhoods were only approximate because the maps available did not show individual farms and, unlike Wisconsin, farm boundaries did not run on section lines. Their procedure gave 222 country localities in the county. In addition, numerous farms were so near village centers that 43 of these were named by farm families as their neighborhood. To obtain evidence on the consciousness of local unity and the common activities of the named groups, country school teachers were sent a questionnaire. The researchers also made a personal study of 16 neighborhoods judged representative of different types of these groups, e.g., institutional, topographic, hamlet. Sanderson and Thompson concluded that in Otsego County, the rural neighborhood was ceasing to function as a social unit except where social life was centered on a local institution such as school, church, or grange.

A sharp contrast to the Wisconsin and New York studies, in social setting and conclusions, was offered by *Rural Organization: A Study of Primary Groups in Wake County, N.C.* (1922) by Carle Zimmerman and Carl Taylor (also see Chapter 11). Wake County was biracial, about 60 percent white and 40 percent nonwhite. It was a cotton- and tobacco-growing area with distinct economic and social strata. Much as Kolb had done, neighborhood names were obtained from farm families and the responses mapped. The groups thus located were locally referred to as communities. There were eighty-three such groupings for whites, fifty for "colored." After systematic study of these groupings, the conclusion was that in the Wake County situation the economic and social strata precluded the geographic community (neighborhood). Rural people there were organized on a different basis "than local and geographical" (Zimmerman and Taylor:32); rural organization was functional.

Boone County, Missouri, the setting for Morgan and Howells' (1925) analysis of rural primary groups, had eighty-nine black families remaining in the open country. "Family-sized," owner-operated farms were predominant. With the help of rural school teachers, county newspapers, and personal interviews, fifty-nine white and four black neighborhoods were found. The intensity of primary group consciousness of each neighborhood was indicated using five levels from low to high. The ratings were recognized as subjective.

Whitman County, Washington, is larger than the state of Connecticut. At the time of study (E. Taylor and Yoder 1926), it was essentially rural, sparsely settled, with relatively large-scale wheat farming. Interviews with about one thousand farmers included a question as to the neighborhood to which they belonged. The neighborhoods so found had from four to 40 families. The country school was the activity or service most frequently holding the neighborhood together. Each neighborhood was assigned one of three levels of intensity of group consciousness. A general conclusion was that the old type of neighborhood association was largely gone in this wheat farming area and that the town was the farmer's natural community center (E. Taylor and Yoder 1926:46–47). The study of rural community organization in Ravalli County, Montana, enumerated and described what the researcher termed "enclosing institutions" in contrast to "ramifying institutions" (Baumgartel 1923:4–5). The former covered a well-defined area and included the entire population; farm neighborhoods were an example. Lodges were an example of a ramifying institution, belonged to by choice. Some 53 areas with a local neighborhood name were identified in Ravalli County but the majority of these were designated as "topographic," lacking social bonds. Neighborhood groups were in transition as trade and personal service agencies were being concentrated in village and city centers.

Beyond Neighborhood

Each of the six researches reviewed above went beyond the neighborhood in exploring the rural locality group situation. Basically, all examined the relationships between farm families in the countryside and the population centers where many of the services were located which they used. They produced maps, as Galpin had done, showing the open-country territory within which the families used services offered by the centers. Except for the North Carolina study, all pointed in some way to the existence or development of a town-country community. In keeping with Galpin's practice of giving cooperators a free hand, data collection procedures varied. Governing concepts and ways of classifying centers also varied.

Before Galpin's retirement in 1934, more than a score of other publications on different aspects of locality groups resulted from cooperative projects in a dozen states. This volume of output reflected recognition that understanding locality group arrangements and how they were changing was knowledge important for planning improved social and economic services for farm people; the interest among researchers stimulated by the six exploratory neighborhood studies and by Galpin's own Walworth County work; and support for rural sociological investigations in state agricultural experiment stations aided by federal funding provided by passage of the Purnell Act of 1925.

Among these studies beyond the neighborhood, one line of work that received relatively high emphasis pertained to the services offered by centers and the relationships between farm families and the centers. A pacesetter in method of researching town-country relations and in a theoretical formulation of these relations was J. H. Kolb's *Service Relations of Town and Country* (1923). Kolb first analyzed the commercial and the non-commercial services available in the centers of Dane County and in two centers in other counties. He attempted to determine the share of commercial services business accounted for by farmers. Likewise, he sought to measure the percentage of participation and leadership accounted for by farm families in several types of agencies. Then, for six selected centers, farm families living at the margins of a center's influence were interviewed. They were asked where they went for various categories of service and the reasons for using a particular center for the service. On the basis of his findings, Kolb offered a "temporary" classification of centers. There were five types, each characterized as to services offered, population, and size of both general and specialized trade areas.[2] A representation of the theoretical distance relations among the five types of centers was presented in graph form. A second graph added primary and secondary service areas to the theoretical distance factor (Kolb 1923:7–8).

The most extensive and painstaking research on rural social and economic areas during the Galpin years was that in New York by Dwight Sanderson and his graduate students at Cornell University. Sanderson summarized this cooperative work in a 100-page experiment station bulletin *Rural Social and Economic Areas in Central New York* (1934). The primary purpose was to obtain accurate knowledge of the geographic basis of the social organization of rural society. Among the six specific objectives was (1) determining "the extent to which the economic and social life is carried on at one center in a given area, or to which, and for what purposes, it is divided among several centers," and (2) "the extent to which cities and large villages are drawing business and social activities from the smaller center" (Sanderson 1934:3–4). These objectives reflected sensitivity at the time of this work (1927 to 1931) to the impact on the behavior patterns of open-country residents and the rural community of ongoing technological and economic factors. These included the auto and the introduction into larger centers of chain grocery stores.

Some theory of rural community was accepted as basic from the first of the seven-county series. A distinction was made between the geographical or ecological concept of community and the psychological concept based upon collective behavior (Wakeley 1931:5–8). In the summary report, however, Sanderson stated that "From a sociological perspective the rural community consists of the interaction of the people in its area in their common activities" (1934:90). The collective behavior was the psychological aspect of community. Mapping geographic areas was a way of revealing the gross structure of rural community arrangements.

Sanderson's summary report was based, for the most part, on the five counties in which records were secured, by mail or interview, from some twelve thousand open-country families as to place of buying specified goods, obtaining certain services, or attending activities of organizations.[3] A refinement of the method devised earlier by Galpin (1915) was used to prepare maps for each service for each center. In this instance, the territory within which the majority of the respondents used a center established the boundaries for the service. Territory within which there was no clear majority for any one center was designated as an "interstitial" or "neutral" zone. Planimeter measurement of the maps gave the square miles in each service area.

In two of the five counties, families were also asked to identify the center visited most frequently. The maps, based upon the answers to this question, corresponded closely to "primary" areas, the area within which a majority of the families obtained a plurality of four common services at the local center.[4] Sanderson believed that these procedures identified the areas commonly called rural communities, areas of interrelated common interests (1934:90).

Tabulations were made of the survey data collected from the 12,000 families.[5] Seven classes of centers, by population size, were used for some of the comparisons. Economic and social services were differentiated. Simple and partial correlation techniques were applied. The tables showed, for example, the percentage of country families patronizing given types of centers for specified services, the average distance to the places patronized, and the relative use of local as compared with city centers.[6] The concepts of secondary areas and secondary centers, in addition to primary areas and centers, were introduced.[7] Sanderson saw the relevance of a systematic mapping of secondary areas for locating central rural school districts (1934:87). The New York study also dealt with change in the number of economic services in the centers in the study counties. The current situation was compared with 1900 and 1915 for classes of centers. The R. G. Dun Company *Mercantile Agency Reference Book* was the data source for the first two time periods. Current data came from the researchers enumeration in each center.

From the analysis of a vast amount of empirical data, it was evident to Sanderson that rural communities in Central New York were not all alike (1934:90). Types, based on essential structural and functional differences, had to be established to consider characteristic relationships among communities. Seven types were identified. Only villages of from 1,000 to 2,500 inhabitants could, at that time, be considered complete service centers. Only the areas of villages of less than 2,500 were considered to be rural communities. Larger places had rural social and economic service areas but were not, strictly speaking, generally rural communities unless they were chiefly agricultural centers. The relations of an average open-country family to different types of centers were portrayed in diagram form (1934:95). Country families, typically, used multiple centers but used their local center most for services. There was little evidence that the competition of the city was responsible for the decline in services and population of many rural communities. Distance was still a limiting factor in the social life of these people. They continued to prefer to congregate in the smaller villages for non-economic purposes. The projection, however, was that the larger villages were likely to continue to grow at the expense of the smaller and that the smaller rural communities would continue to be absorbed by larger centers (1934:97).

The emphasis in some other cooperative projects, for a time, was on trade centers and their services in an entire state. Examples are those in New York (Melvin 1929) and South Dakota (Landis 1932). The New York study made a statistical analysis of agencies, institutions, and organizations found in 1925 in the state's villages of 50 to 2,499 in population. Data on economic agencies came principally from the Dun Company *Mercantile Agency Reference Book* and from Bradstreet's *Commercial Ratings*. The source for non-economic agencies came from questionnaires sent to each village and from correspondence with the headquarters of several organizations. The study embraced sixty-five agencies as varied as grocery stores, libraries, churches, movies, and undertakers. The analysis showed, for instance, the number of each type of agency per ten villages, with the villages classified by population size. When villages were analyzed by type of county in which they were located—farming, urban, suburban, and mountain—the county type markedly influenced the agencies found in the villages. Agency numbers and village population size were subjected to simple correlation analysis. A close relation existed between population size and the number of economic agencies and the number of professional people in villages. But the correlation between village size and the number of religious, educational, or social agencies was low.

In contrast to the one point in time used by Melvin in his New York study, the South Dakota research took an historical, a social change approach. It covered a thirty-year period, 1901–31. The purpose was to study the effects of cultural or life habit changes and geographic changes, especially rainfall variability, on town-country relations. Trade was seen as the basic factor in the cultural ties between town and country. A trade center was defined as any sort of hamlet or larger place with one or more business units as listed by Bradstreet's *Ratings*. The study was limited to business enterprises which sold merchandise plus a few special services such as bank and post office. Tabulations were made for every type of merchandising enterprise for all trade centers in the state at five-year intervals 1901–31. The geographic factors, especially rainfall, affected the territorial distribution of trade centers through the effect on population density.[8] A trend toward specialization of merchandising was evident, e.g., the decline of the general store. A rapid increase in chain stores was found. The trends in merchandising, in shopping habits, and in related factors worked to the disadvantage of smaller trade centers.

Community Case Studies

Case studies of individual communities added to the diverse settings and differing research approaches in locality group research which received Galpin's support. The studies of three Mormon farm-villages—Escalante, Ephraim, and American Fork—in Utah by Lowry Nelson (1925, 1928, 1933) stood out among these.[9] The Escalante study was the first attempt made to describe a Mormon community in detail, especially with respect to land settlement patterns and settlement techniques. Topics included in the studies dealt with historical development, the physical layout of the community, agriculture, levels of living, and some aspects of social organization. The research was pertinent to such basic questions as to why the farmers lived in villages rather than on dispersed farmsteads and how to account for the relatively equal distribution of land and water rights. Nelson concluded that the Mormon farm-village arrangements were a social invention of the Mormons, the product of group ideologies (1952:38, 40). They resulted from the ideologies of millennialism, communism, and nationalism which came out of the social environment of the early nineteenth century and the Old and New Testaments.

A comparative analysis of a Quaker with a non-Quaker farming "community" in Illinois indicated need for further work on the issue of whether or not the development of strong community organization was a characteristic of Quaker communities (Whittaker 1929). The two localities were similar in agricultural factors when settled a hundred years earlier but, over time, the Quaker group had effective and persistent organization at the community level whereas the other had weak and intermittent organization. At the time of the survey, the Quaker group was superior to the other in such measures as agricultural efficiency, population stability, household conveniences, and college experience. Brunner interpreted the results of this work, little noted in the sociological literature, as raising a fundamental question as to the persistence of social values in a community (1957:28–29).

Other case studies were expressions of Galpin's desire to bring to light the prideful features in rural life, the success stories, and the reasons for the success (Galpin 1938a:48–49). One example is the study of three black farming communities in Tidewater Virginia (Doggett 1923; see Chapter 11). Another is a simple historical and descriptive account of the West Virginia farming community which scored highest in the state on a community self-rating measure (Dadisman 1921).

Locality Group Restudies

The appointment by President Herbert Hoover in 1929 of a Research Committee on Social Trends led to the Division's cooperation in intensive restudies of neighborhoods and town-country relations. The Committee, composed of social scientists, arranged for Edmund deS. Brunner, Columbia University, and J. H. Kolb, University of Wisconsin, to make a national study of recent changes in rural life. Galpin's assistance in this was acknowledged (Brunner and Kolb 1933:319). The Division had a part in the neighborhood restudies in Dane County, Wisconsin (Kolb 1933) and Otsego County, New York (Sanderson and Dorn 1934), ten years after the original field work.[10] It also cooperated in the restudy of Walworth County, Wisconsin, communities (Kolb and Polson 1933), sixteen years after Galpin's research there.

These restudies followed the plan of the original research as far as possible. The Dane County restudy used the same definitions and the same field and laboratory procedures. Kolb had retained all the original schedules, field notes, interview lists, work maps, and analysis sheets. The same schedule was used in 1931 as in 1921, and it was circulated through the country schools in the same manner. The results showed that country neighborhoods had persisted in Dane County during the 1920s despite the increase in farm family relationships with village, town, and city. About two-thirds of the rural primary groups active in 1921 were still active in 1931. The number becoming inactive during the ten years was equalled by the appearance of new neighborhoods or formerly inactive groups again becoming active. The findings led Kolb to search for the factors explaining persistence and change. One refinement in the classification of neighborhoods was the addition of a "distinctive" category based on performing more services than the average neighborhood (Kolb 1933:9–11). Kolb concluded that country neighborhoods and town-country communities could flourish side by side, complementing each other. He presented a theoretical graph showing the country family and its neighborhood, community, urban, and special interest group relationships.

The results of the New York restudy differed from those in Wisconsin about neighborhood changes over the same ten-year span. The tone of the researchers' interpretation also differed. In Otsego County, the neighborhood as a social unit was held to be of decreasing importance. Reasons given for the loss of all common activity or weakened activity among the more important neighborhoods as of 1920 included population decline, in-migration of people who maintained social contacts elsewhere, abandonment of neighborhood organizations and institutions such as churches and granges, and the organization of central rural schools and other forms of the movement toward organizing rural life on the basis of areas larger than the neighborhood.[11] The tendency toward neighborhood decline noted in the first study of this county continued during the decade of the 1920s. Units which remained were centered around some institution, organization, or hamlet. Surviving neighborhood organizations were typically linked to an outside organizational structure from which the locals received stimulation.

The restudy of communities, of trade areas, in Walworth County followed closely the data collection and mapping methods used earlier by Galpin (Kolb and Polson 1933:34–36). The implied hypothesis was that the changes over time in the service areas of centers would indicate trends in town-country service relations. The technique was to compare the service areas in 1929 for seven services for 12 centers with those for 1913. This was possible because Galpin's original maps and family information cards had been preserved. Planimeter readings of the maps gave, in square miles, information such as size of area in 1913, net change to 1929, and expansion or contraction in area, 1913–29. Expansion was found to be the general trend for all seven services for each of the 12 centers. Of the seven, library service areas expanded the most, banking areas the least. Interviews revealed that each farm family used an average of almost four service centers. Three major types of service centers were recognized: the rural or country center, the "rurban" or town-country center, and urban or city centers. Kolb and Polson's theoretical graph of service areas, unlike Galpin's, provided for country centers at the periphery of the "rurban" center service areas and also for areas of influence of metropolitan centers (1933:30–31). Running through the analysis was the thread of increasing specialization and interdependence of centers. The researchers generalized that the "rurban" type of center and service area was still the most important of all for country residents. They cautioned, however, that these were not complete or self-sufficient units now and had not been when Galpin first identified them.

The restudy of Dane County neighborhoods did not stop with these primary groups. It also examined the ten-year changes in some of the service relations of town and country. This was a way of placing neighborhoods in a larger set of group relationships as portrayed in his theoretical graph (Kolb 1933:34–51). This part of the restudy was limited to four of the service relationships: high school, trade, church, and the country weekly newspaper. For each of these, for each center, the 1931 service map was laid over the 1921 map for comparison. The trade area for Madison, a city center, expanded by over 40 percent whereas that for small village centers with incomplete service had a 15 percent loss. Among the four services, high school was found to be the most important factor in town-country relations. Use of village and small-town churches, rather than neighborhood churches, was becoming more frequent but, on the whole, such adjustments were being made slowly.

THE TAYLOR YEARS—A DIFFERENT FOCUS

Shortly after Carl Taylor became head, the Division became involved in a third study of the 140 agricultural communities last surveyed in 1930. Only this time, unlike the two previous studies, the Division was a formal cooperator. This time it joined with the Columbia University Council for Research in the Social Sciences. Leadership rested, however, with the university's E. deS. Brunner and Irving Lorge. The first purpose of this 1936 study was to discover what changes the depression had wrought on American rural communities. A second purpose was to relate the depression years changes, 1930–36, to the development and history of these village-centered communities as found in the two earlier surveys.

About a hundred interviews were conducted in each community to complete community, school, and church schedules. The field work in an average community required about one week. Division staff did the surveys for 11 of the 140 communities.[12] The fieldwork and secondary sources provided a vast amount of quantitative data used by Brunner and Lorge in their 397-page monograph *Rural Trends in Depression Years* (1937). The topics covered included agricultural adjustments, rural relief, population changes, village-country relations, and changes in the major institutions and agencies. In their concluding chapter, the investigators indicated what the study findings suggested as to policies or experimentation to achieve a larger measure of socioeconomic well-being in rural America.

Locality group research was quite different during the Taylor years, for the most part, than when Galpin was Division head. First, the work was typically done or led by Division staff whereas previously locality group studies were all conducted as cooperative projects with the university researcher taking the lead. This changed practice was possible because of the greatly enlarged staff and resources. Also, it was necessary if the demands by action agencies were to be satisfied on a timely basis. Second, the professional staff working on community studies was made multidisciplinary during the Division's heyday. Cultural anthropologists and social psychologists were added. M. L. Wilson, when Undersecretary of Agriculture, was instrumental in this move. He was on record as seeing cultural anthropology and social psychology as necessary social science tools for use in agricultural planning (Wilson 1938). Carl Taylor had a long-standing interest in social psychology, dating back to his graduate school courses. Among those added, to give the Division staff the desired disciplinary mix were anthropologists Earl Bell, Walter Goldschmidt, Oscar Lewis, Horace Miner, and John Provinse and social psychologist Kimball Young. Third, an important share of the Division's locality group work during the New Deal and the war years was devoted to service to increase the effectiveness of programs such as land-use planning, the SCS, and civilian defense (see Chapter 13). Much of this type of service work was based on community and neighborhood concepts and discovery methods developed previously by Galpin, the Division, and its cooperators. Efforts were also directed to evaluation studies of planned communities and to planning for the Columbia Basin irrigation project (see Chapter 13). And, fourth, the Division broke new ground in locality group research. Instances are the studies of community stability and instability and of rural cultural regions. Other examples include studies of the community and agriculture (see Chapter 10).

Innovations in Methods

Two innovations in rural locality group research methods deserve special note at this point. Both resulted from seeking a solution to a research issue encountered in the study of specific community situations. In the first instance, when Taylor was director of the social research unit in the FSA and also Division head, a study of seven recently established resettlement communities was initiated (Loomis 1940; also see Chapter 12). One of these, Dyess in Arkansas, was having a high turnover rate among the settlers. What was the reason? In seeking an explanation, Charles Loomis turned to J. L. Moreno's sociometric methods for discovering patterns of social relationships (Hare 1979). Loomis was aware of Moreno's theory and methods as a result of being the Division's major contact with him. Sociograms were constructed for the Dyess settlers, revealing the patterns of informal relationships among families for visiting, work exchange, and borrowing purposes. Previously, the Dyess turnover problem had been approached with theoretical conceptions about community bonds from P. Sorokin, F. Tonnies, and E. Durkheim (Loomis and Davidson 1939b).

The same sociometric procedure was followed in an analysis of the other six constructed communities. Subsequently, the Division used sociometric procedures extensively to understand the informal structure of neighborhoods and communities and in identifying informal leaders. Loomis recalled that the sociometric analysis was very saleable to resettlement project administrators (Larson 1990). It made sociology understandable to them.

The second instance was the invention of the neighborhood cluster method of delineating rural communities. Chilton County had been selected for a cooperative project with Alabama College to increase understanding of Alabama communities. When Irwin Sanders and Douglas Ensminger (1940) used the generally accepted service area method to determine community boundaries, the results did not seem to conform to the natural sociological communities. This was a county where rural neighborhood loyalties had been maintained. So, the researchers first mapped the neighborhoods and then determined the attachments of whole neighborhoods, rather than of individual families, to given centers. In this situation, the neighborhood cluster method was found to have a comparative advantage in community delineation. Subsequently, the method was frequently used in the Division's service and training work with action and educational agencies.

Community Stability and Instability

The Division's most extensive use of a multi-disciplinary approach in community research was initiated in 1939 in a project titled "Cultural, Structural, and Social-Psychological Study of Selected American Farm Communities" (Taylor et al. 1940). The project leaders were sociologists Carl Taylor and Charles Loomis, anthropologist John Provinse, and social psychologists, J. E. Hulett Jr., and Kimball Young. This project used six communities, selected on the basis of the presumed stability and instability of their community life and type of farming, for the purpose of investigating "the cultural, community, and social psychological factors in land use and rural life, with special reference to those factors which either facilitate or offer resistance to change, contribute to adjustments and maladjustments, and to stability and instability in the individual and community life" (Taylor et al. 1940:1). The mission-oriented aspect was not overlooked in the project plan. An attempt was to be "made to ascertain the implications of the findings with reference to extension services; agricultural monetary benefits; subsidies, grants, loans, etc.; rural rehabilitation; soil conservation; county land-use planning, and any other service or action programs of the United States Department of Agriculture" (C. Taylor et al. 1940:2). The six publications that resulted were issued by the BAE as a Rural Life Studies series under the common title "Culture of a Contemporary Rural Community." A seventh report was planned to present the methodology used and the generalizations from the six studies. This report was never published, a casualty of new priorities forced by war.

The community stability-instability studies were an outgrowth of the May 1939 conference of social scientists, chaired by Under Secretary M. L. Wilson, on the question, "What can the social sciences contribute to the work of the Department of Agriculture?" (FPRLA 1939[4]:3–20).[13] The hope in the USDA was to find out how the social sciences might contribute to the development of agricultural planning and policymaking and in the educational and service activities of the USDA in general and of the reconstituted BAE in particular. By August the Division had anthropologist Horace Miner in a Corn Belt County in essentially an exploratory study. The research evolved in the field with the guidance of Carl Taylor and other Division staff and the advice of eminent social anthropologists Robert Redfield and W. Lloyd Warner, both at the University of Chicago. A decision was made to point the study toward the aspects of Corn Belt culture involved in the relations between farmers and USDA action agencies. The hypothesis was that the nature of a culture sets limits on the type of change which can be introduced (Miner 1949:3). The field methods were largely anthropological—living in the area, informal contacts. Miner's report, when submitted, was not published by the USDA despite the support given by Carl Taylor (see Chapter 4).

The six Rural Life Studies communities were not a geographic sampling in any sense. They were purposively selected to represent a continuum of high to low community stability. The choices were a matter of judgment. The Old Order Amish in Lancaster County, Pennsylvania, was assumed to be the most stable (Kollmorgen 1942). Sublette, a Dust Bowl community is Haskell County, Kansas, was at the other extreme (Bell 1942). Irwin, in Shelby County, Iowa, was selected as midway on the continuum (Moe and Taylor 1942). The other three, El Cerrito, New Mexico (Leonard and Loomis 1941); Landaff, New Hampshire (MacLeish and Young 1942); and Harmony, Georgia (Wynne 1943), proved to have attributes or a history which made it difficult to place their stability so precisely. These sample social units did not closely resemble the village-centered rural communities such as discovered earlier in New York and Wisconsin, except for Irwin in Iowa with its village center of 345 people. The Pennsylvania Old Order Amish were, in fact, a socio-religious community of non-contiguous farming families, a cultural island. Sublette's center, population 582, was the county seat for a county of about two thousand. The community could not be studied independently of the county. Spanish-speaking El Cerrito was a village community located on an isolated land pocket in the Pecos River valley. All families lived within a stone's throw of each other. This, too, was virtually a cultural island. Landaff, a community of about 400 people, was a New England township without a well-developed trade center. Harmony was a racially divided locality, about fifty black and twenty white families.

The fieldwork was done and the report prepared by one or two persons for each locality. Of the nine researchers, five were sociologists, three were anthropologists, and one a social psychologist. The procedures to be used and the information to be obtained was specified in detail in a 105-page field manual (Taylor et al. 1940). Major reliance was placed upon the participant observation method. Repeated interviews were to be made with carefully selected informants, twenty to fifty in each community. At the start of the work, pertinent statistical data for the county and its subdivisions was to be collected and analyzed. Also, a rapid reconnaissance survey of the county's communities, neighborhoods, and culture patterns was to be made.[14] In practice, the field workers were given wide latitude in making observations and considerable leeway in the organization of their reports. The principal observer in each case spent from four to six months residing in the community. Brief return visits were made in at least three instances. Both El Cerrito observers were Spanish-speaking. The Old Order Amish observer spoke High German, the language of the Bible used by the sect.

The six reports shared in common major sections on the history and background of the group; people on the land and making a living; the community, its organization, and values; the farmer's expanding world; and integration and disintegration in community and individual life. The community section of the El Cerrito report, for example, covered spatial distribution, patterns of informal association with sociometric analysis, recreation, patterns of formal association, the school, the church, farm organizations and cooperatives, local politics, leadership and class structure, youth as the critical age-group, the value system, and integration and conflict (Leonard and Loomis 1941:37–65). Some of these subjects were given no coverage in other reports in the series or were given quite a different emphasis.

One of the tragedies of the Division's life history was that wartime priorities meant the failure to prepare the summary volume planned for these six studies. What generalizations, for example, might the multi-disciplinary researchers have arrived at with respect to factors in community-level stability and instability, integration and disintegration? Irwin, Iowa, for instance, was seen as having a high degree of stability in the midst of constant change. It was "integrated by the occupation and enterprise of, and thinking about, farming" (Moe and Taylor 1942:89). In contrast, in El Cerrito the factors most instrumental in holding the community together were the institution of the family, followed by the church (Catholic), and the sense cultivated from childhood of belonging to the community. Disintegrating influences in El Cerrito were the recent and rapid loss of land that formerly supported the community and the adverse consequences of the work relief programs initiated by the federal government (Leonard and Loomis 1941:70–72). The Haskell County, Kansas, situation offered a further contrast. This was a locality in which instability had been the dominant theme of its history: instability in population numbers, in institutions, and in agriculture. Such instability was rooted in wide variations in annual rainfall and erratic fluctuations of rainfall within a year together with the failure of farmers to adopt to such uncertainty (Bell 1942).

This set of studies made a significant contribution to the literature on community and rural life. The monographs found wide use for teaching purposes. The findings were put to both theoretical and applied use. For example, the El Cerrito and the Old Order Amish cases were used to illustrate Loomis' social system conceptual model (see Loomis and Beegle, *Rural Social Systems* 1950; Loomis, *Social Systems* 1960). In his *Community in America* (1963), Roland Warren chose El Cerrito as one of four cases in his description and analysis of the "great change" in American communities. In a down-to-earth handbook for community organization, *Making Good Communities Better*, Sanders (1950, 1953) drew on the reports to illustrate how communities show differences in such attributes as types of leadership confided in, importance of social ranking, methods used to make individuals conform, and systems of social values. The six studies have served as benchmarks for subsequent research, some initiated about 50 years after the original research.[15]

Rural Communities and War

The Division's regional offices were instructed in late 1943 to make brief intensive studies of village-centered rural communities after two years of war. The interest was (1) in what changes had occurred in the community patterns of organization, and the function of each organization and institution, and (2) which new organizations had come into being, the function performed by each, and the effect on changing old patterns of organization. Twelve communities in as many states were studied, each involving a month or so of field work. Selection was left up to the Division's regional offices with the provision that, if possible, a community be in a county already being used for the Division's Rural Life Trends project, a wartime activity for USDA administrative purposes.[16] The Washington office, with Douglas Ensminger having a major role, provided a set of five schedules with instructions for their use (Taylor 1943). The schedules were for schools, churches, community services, social and economic organizations, and for interviews with a sample of farm and non-farm families.

A review of the reports published on eight of the studies was critical (Hart 1946). The reviewer contended that despite the common outline of types of data to be collected and analyzed, the reports had wide and important differences in content and in what constituted an adequate description and evaluation of processes of social change. Did the changes reported result from differences in the communities or from differences among the researchers in perspective?

The reports contained a wealth of information about the effect of war on many facets of each community, e.g., the economy, the population, the institutions and services. They provided facts on the participation in war programs such as metal scrap salvage and war bond drives. But no summary report was prepared by the Division. The decision was made at the start that each regional office would issue the report for the community it studied. Only eight of the twelve were published, most in mimeo form. They did not carry identification to indicate that each was part of a set, unlike the Rural Life Study series. Only two studies were the basis for publication in a professional journal (Alexander 1944; Neeley 1944). Overall, this set of community studies has received little recognition, in part, it seems, because of the publication procedures followed.

Rural Cultural Regions

By far the most ambitious research project undertaken by the Division was a study of rural regions based on the nation's major types of agricultural production areas. The study was launched in seventy-one "laboratory" counties, each selected from one stratum of counties within type-farming areas. When started in 1944, it was expected that the work would require three to five years to complete. This research held unprecedented promise for building a body of scientific knowledge about rural life in the United States and, at the same time, improving the quality of sociological information useful to farm people and agricultural action agencies. The first phase of this enterprise had not yet been completed when it was brought to an abrupt halt by action of the Congress (see Chapter 4).

The project was a drastic step for the Division. Carl Taylor (1944b) had become convinced that rural social research to date did not add up to a body of understanding that made the application of this research at all imposing. He had been seeking constantly to have the Division's local and emergency studies during the New Deal and early war years fit into the broader fund of research-based knowledge, but this was a frustrating experience. Taylor (1944b) decided to propose that the Division's future research emphasize the analysis and understanding of key geographic and time universes. This would be a way of avoiding the criticisms made of past social research. Regions were one key geographic universe. So, in the midst of wartime demands, Taylor took the Division's research program in a new direction (this had to have had the approval of the BAE Chief, Howard Tolley).

The starting point for this new approach was the major type-of-farming regions prepared as of 1943 by the BAE's Division of Farm Management and Costs. There were seven: the Corn Belt, the Cotton Belt, the dairy areas, the general and self-sufficiency areas, the wheat areas, the range-livestock areas, and the Western speciality crop area, plus an "all other" grouping (Raper and Taylor 1949:330). All of the nation's counties, except for 14 without any rural-farm population, were placed within these eight agriculturally based regions. They were seen as "meaningful regional rural universes" (Raper and Taylor 1949:339). The study conceived of them as modal cultural regions" in the rural life of the United States. The working hypothesis, in effect, was that making a living is one of the major components of the culture of people in any given rural locality; for farm people, type-of-farming is an index of their way of making a living; the type-of-farming is related to material and non-material techniques of production and marketing; and, out of these aspects of rural life, arise many common ideologies, opinions, attitudes, and values (see Raper and Taylor 1949:331–32).

The county was chosen as the primary sampling unit within regions. There were to be seventy-one sample counties, a limit set by administrative considerations. Each region was stratified into groups of relatively homogeneous counties by use of component indexes (Hagood and Bernert 1945). From twelve to fourteen variables chosen from the 1940 Censuses of Agriculture and Population and related sources were used for the indexes. Some variables were common to all regions, others were not. The decision to sample from stratum within regions was based on the assumption that variations internal to each region should be taken into account if the county reports were to be the basis for regional or national reports. The requirement was imposed that each stratum have about the same number of farm people. One "laboratory" county was chosen from each stratum. The selection was not done randomly. Some, but not all, of the counties used for the wartime Rural Life Trends project during 1942–44 were kept for the seventy-one-county sample.

Information collection started with a hurried cultural reconnaissance survey in each county, conducted for the most part by regional office staff. The purpose was to gain a general overview of each county with respect to its culture, social organization, making a living, values, and related matters. Field methods were similar to those for the community stability-instability project. Field workers were provided a detailed outline of the information desired (Taylor 1944a). The workers interviewed local key informants selected to be broadly representative of significant categories of people within the county. Field work required three or four weeks per county.

The original design called for time series on special aspects of rural life such as changes in rural social institutions, change in farm family levels and standards of living, and changes in farmers' attitudes and value systems. The data was to be collected in the sample counties and summarized on a nationwide basis. The series would be updated each five years. None of this time series work got under way. The counties were, however, used for special reports for USDA administrative use, e.g., on current and anticipated rural migration problems and on current problems and postwar prospects; also on veterans adjustments and on farm family use of war-period savings.

The Washington office suggested an outline to be used by the field investigators in preparing their county reconnaissance reports. One was prepared for each county but remained unpublished because of Congressional intervention. The few copies for each county never got beyond administrative use or pre-publication review. The county reports were the basis for regional reports, also unpublished. This work was, however, the foundation for the nine chapters on rural regions by Carl Taylor and associates in *Rural Life in the United State* (1949). The authors considered these chapters "a start toward the development of the cultural anthropology of American rural life" (Taylor et al. 1949:v). The sole exception to the county studies being unpublished was anthropologist Oscar Lewis' *On the Edge of the Black Waxy* (1948), based on his reconnaissance survey in Bell County, Texas.

County Rural Social Organization Studies

When the rural cultural region study was aborted by Congressional man-date, the Division was forced to adjust its locality group research program. It wanted to continue to use the regional type-farming framework and to build on the knowledge already accumulated in the seventy-one counties. At the same time, the research had to be such that it would be unlikely to provoke further political controversy for the BAE and the Division. The decision was made to focus on the rural social organization of and within counties.

The purposes of the revised project were (1) to analyze the types of groups in which rural people are organized; (2) to learn the patterns of group relationships through which they participate in local and non-local programs and services; (3) to analyze the ways in which agencies relate their programs to the existing types of organizations and patterns of rela-tionships; and (4) to compare, by type-of-farming areas, the characteris-tic patterns of organizations and their trends (Alexander and Nelson 1949: Foreword).

From one to five of the seventy-one laboratory counties were selected for study in each of the type-of-farming areas, twenty-four counties in all. The work was generally conducted through cooperative projects with state agricultural experiment stations. This was an adjustment by the Division to the mandated abolition of the BAE's regional offices.

Information for each county was obtained primarily by controlled inter-views with key informants and organization leaders and by observation of rural organizational activities. Field workers were provided an outline of the information to be obtained about a county's rural social organiza-tion (C. Taylor 1946). Reports were issued on some thirteen of the twenty-four study counties, in most cases as agricultural experiment station bulletins. These reports followed a generally uniform outline which cov-ered six types of social organization—the county, spatial groups, institu-tionalized organizations, formally organized groups, informal groups, and public agencies.

After some of the county reports had already appeared, a major refine-ment in locality group classification was devised by a group working under Carl Taylor's leadership (e.g., Alexander and Nelson 1949:10–25). Two scales were developed. One was a quantitative service rating score derived from Dunn and Bradstreet data reported for service centers and from other sources. The second was a group identification rating score. The later was a qualitative measure based on the presence or absence of activities posited to be characteristic of an ideal type of primary neighborhood group. Five gradations were used in the service rating, three in the group identification rating. This method eliminated the sometimes-sticky problem of distinguishing community and neighborhood (Alexander 1952). Some of the reports did, however, use the two ratings to classify spatial groups as communities and neighborhoods (Hay and Polson 1951:12–20).

The thirteen studies carried to publication provided some of the most complete information available on the rural organization in five of the farming areas. But the potential impact of this set of studies was not realized. No summary report was prepared. Separate publication by thirteen agricultural experiment stations, without identification as being part of a common study, weakened the impact they might have had. And by the time these reports appeared, the demand from USDA action agencies for sociological knowledge had virtually vanished. The set of studies was the last locality group research undertaken by the Division.

Other Locality Group Studies

During the Taylor years, there were other studies that used "community" as the object of study or the setting.[17] We will examine one of the most significant of these—Goldschmidt's Arvin-Dinuba study—in our review in Chapter 10 of the research on the sociology of agriculture. Other examples are especially relevant to the practice of sociology, the subject of Chapters 12 and 13. Among these are the studies of the New Deal's subsistence homesteads and resettlement projects; the intensive study by Arthur Raper in Greene County, Georgia, instigated for the USDA's land-use planning program; and the many community and neighborhood delineation activities for the USDA and other agencies.

An illustration of research which used the community as a setting is offered by a study of the rural organization in three Maine towns (Hay et al. 1949). This service project was requested by the University of Maine Extension Service to ascertain the participation of open-country households in rural organizations and extension activities. Division staff designed the research and did most of the analysis for this cooperative venture. Interviews were conducted by twenty-two state and county extension workers.

The Division's locality group research did not stop at the borders of the United States. When Carl Taylor studied the rural life of Argentina at the request of the Department of State, his resulting book (1948a) included chapters on the agricultural and cultural regions and on the rural locality groups within the type-farming areas of that country. He found, for example, a type of locality group existing between the neighborhood and the trade-centered community; this was the cattle or sheep estancia. Former staff members also extended abroad the influence of the Division's locality group research. For example, Olen Leonard's study in Bolivia, similar to Taylor's in Argentina, included a description of the community and rural neighborhood groupings and an analysis of the factors in locality-group solidarity (Leonard 1949; 1952:87–101).

SUMMARY

"Community" has been characterized as not only an important field of study in rural sociology but as "one of the dominant concepts in sociology" (Fear and Schwarzweller 1985:xi–xii). The study of community and other locality groups was a major and continuing core area of the Division's research program. Numerous and significant contributions were made by the work of the Division and its cooperators in this area. The studies made in the 1920s were a basis, in part, for Brunner's assertion, in his review of the first half-century of rural sociological research in the United States, that "community and neighborhood research was the first area in rural sociology in which theoretical considerations began to emerge" (1957:36). The investigations yielded a rich and extensive knowledge base about locality groups in rural America and about ways of studying such groups. Findings, concepts, and some of the methods found widespread application for public purposes.

The full potential for the discipline of sociology was unrealized, however, largely because of factors external to the Division.[18] Most conspicuous of these factors were the outbreak of war and political intervention. The especially promising rural cultural regions research in a national sample of seventy-one counties was stopped by Congressional mandate. The studies of the impact of war on twelve rural communities quickly became fugitive literature, for the most part. The research on the rural social organization of twenty-four counties received little notice. The failure to prepare summary reports, a synthesis, for all the sets of studies completed during the 1940s was a significant barrier to making the impact this research might have had.

The contributions of the Division-conducted and -supported work on the locality group aspects of the social organization of rural society included methods of discovering and delineating spatially based "natural social groups." They included methods of determining the internal structure of neighborhood and community social units. The research was accompanied by conceptual formulations and refinements. Variations empirically discovered in form, structure, and function led to locality-group classification systems. The research went beyond description of cases to hypothesis testing and to lay the basis for comparative analysis. The approaches to locality group study developed by sociologists were, in some research, melded with those of cultural anthropology and social psychology. The research revealed much about the linkage of rural neighborhoods and communities to the larger society, about the structure and functioning of rural society, and about its changes and variations. Finally, this locality group research provided a benchmark for an imposing array of follow-up studies by social scientists, some while the Division was still in existence and others as much as a half-century after the original work.

Notes

1. Briefly, trial boundaries were first established on a county map for each center for the chosen services by interviewing a few key informants such as a banker, leading dry goods merchant, etc. Each was asked "Which are the farm homes, north, south, east, and west, that come the farthest to trade in your village?" A map was then made for each center with its outer limits one mile wider than the trial boundaries. All farm homes were located on a working map for each center and a schedule blank prepared for each farm home. With the package of names and the map, the surveyor visited a key informant for each service to determine which homes were connected with the village institutions and services. Boundaries were drawn to enclose every family using a given service for a center (Galpin 1915:3–6).

2. The five were single service type; limited, simple service type; semi-complete or intermediate type; complete and partially specialized type; and the urban, highly specialized type (Kolb 1923:5–7).

3. In the other two counties, no schedules were obtained from individual families. Instead, service areas for centers were mapped with the assistance of business, professional, and other informed persons.

4. The four primary services were grocery, automobile repair, church, and grange.

5. The use of tabulating machines in sociological research was so new at the time that such use in this study was noted in the summary report (Sanderson 1934:11).

6. One methodological innovation was an exploratory and primitive use of automobile traffic counts as a supplement to family survey data in assessing the patronage of larger villages and towns (Sanderson 1934:87–88).

7. Primary areas in the New York study corresponded to the "general trade" areas used by Kolb; secondary areas resembled the specialized areas in the Wisconsin study (Kolb 1923).

8. The discovery that during the thirty years, several hundred new centers appeared in South Dakota and several hundred disappeared, led to a second study to inquire as to the reasons (Landis 1933). The Division was not a formal cooperator, however, in the follow-up work. By that time it's funding was severely restricted.

9. Nelson resurveyed two of the Utah villages in 1950. The resulting book, *The Mormon Village* (1952), included a reprint from the original reports for all three villages.

10. Summaries of the Dane County and Otsego County restudies were given in Brunner and Kolb's *Rural Social Trends* (1933:326–32) but the data for Dane County was prelimi-

nary. Boone County, Missouri neighborhoods studied in 1924 in a Division cooperative project were also resurveyed in 1931 but without Division participation.

11. There were sufficient differences in the methods of the first and the second studies that Sanderson and Dorn (1934) warned that exact comparisons could not be made in the number of neighborhoods. The investigators noted that in the absence of definite objective criteria or definition of neighborhood, comparisons between two studies could be difficult. Further, lacking unequivocal criteria for neighborhood and community in the Otsego County situation, it was sometimes difficult to decide what was and what was not a neighborhood.

12. The WPA Division of Social Research arranged, through its Plan for Cooperative Rural Research with state agricultural colleges, to have the state cooperators conduct or supervise the field surveys in sixty-nine of the communities (Brunner and Lorge 1937:vii).

13. *FPRLA,* used by itself in a citation, indicates an unsigned article in *Farm Population and Rural Life Activities.*

14. The field manual also suggested that possibly standardized tests, such as the Rundquist-Sletto "Minnesota Scale for the Survey of Opinions" might be used and that detailed family interview schedules might be prepared. The reports do not indicate that such methods were used.

15. El Cerrito has been the subject of no fewer than nine works published subsequent to the original study (Eastman and Krannich 1995:41). Landaff was restudied by Louis Ploch (1989), University of Maine, in the mid-to-late 1980s. Subsequently, rural sociologists at eight state agricultural experiment stations initiated a restudy of all six communities under the aegis of Regional Research Project NE-173 with A. E. Luloff, The Pennsylvania State University, as chair of the project's Technical Committee.

16. The Rural Life Trends project involved periodic surveys in sample counties by regional staff who interviewed key informants. Between 1942 and 1944 as many as seven reports were submitted for each county. The five major fields of interest were agricultural production adjustments, consumer adjustments, community adjustments, war participation, and the manpower situation. We have located only a few of the county reports for this project and have no record of the number of counties surveyed nor the basis for their selection.

17. The research which was the basis for Gessner's (1940) Cornell AES bulletin on selective migration from the Belleville, New York, community included information on social and economic change since the survey made there by Galpin in 1910. This information on what had happened to Belleville as a community as of 1938 has remained unpublished.

18. The community and neighborhood concepts have had their critics. When the rural community concept was being widely applied in the 1940s for federal agricultural programs and for the war effort, Kollmorgen and Harrison (1946), BAE staff members, asserted that there was lack of agreement by rural sociologists on definitions of the rural community and criticized the methods used for discovery. A little later, the rural neighborhood concept came under question as a significant social group in rural America (Slocum and Case 1953) and as a unit for study in rural sociology (Melvin 1954).

8

The Social Organization of Rural Life: Institutions and Services

The Division's research on the non-locality group components of the social organization of rural life was wide-ranging as to topics covered. It lacked the continuity, however, which characterized the work on population, levels and standards of living, and locality groups. Activity in any one area, such as the sociological study of local government or the sociological and psychological aspects of farmer-owned marketing organizations, was generally short-term or episodic. In this chapter, we give primary emphasis to work conducted by Division staff members. The cooperative projects identified were selected because they were pioneers in a research area or made notable contributions to research methods or to concepts.

LOCAL-LEVEL SERVICES AND FACILITIES

The rural reconstruction theme pushed by rural statesmen after World War I was accompanied by numerous efforts at the local level to improve the quality of rural life. Too, country planning was seen "as coming to the front" (Butterfield 1920:6). Secretary Houston's advisory committee urged that the new rural life studies work study the causes of failure and the conditions of success in rural communities in providing facilities and in organizing efforts to better their lives (USDA, Office of the Secretary 1919 6:6). Wayne Nason's study of successful community enterprises respected this admonition.

Nason was transferred to the Division in 1919 from the Bureau of Markets. Until his death in 1934, his work was concentrated on case studies of actual experiences by rural people. These pertained to community buildings, their planning and use; rural hospitals, libraries, and rural community fire departments; and to planning for the social aspects of community life, for recreation, and for villages. The work on rural community buildings (e.g., Nason 1922) was based on 256 cases, asserted to be representative for the nation. The report on fire departments (Nason 1931) was based on a survey of eighty rural fire services. The main reports, eleven in all, were all issued as USDA farmer's bulletins for a general, not a scientific, audience. They offered guidelines, along with real-life examples, to inform rural citizens and agricultural extension service, and other professionals. Over one million copies went out by mail on request (Galpin 1938a:49). The bulletin on planning for the rural village was revised and reissued in 1935. Carl Taylor arranged to have Nason's report on hospitals for rural communities revised (Halbert 1937). More than 10,000 copies were distributed (*FPRLA* 1938:12 [3]:15).

The importance of such institutionalized services as the high school, the library, and the hospital for the farm family's level of living was clearly recognized by pioneering rural sociologists (Kolb 1925:1). The research on these service institutions for town and country, done in a cooperative project led by J. H. Kolb (1925), University of Wisconsin, contrasted with the work by Nason. The report was a companion to an earlier study of town-country service relations (Kolb 1923) in the same eight small towns. Detailed case studies of the three services were made in each town. The feature of the report was setting forth the unit requirements for each of the three services. Thus, it was suggested that a high school should not fall below one hundred pupils. This would require a population base of 1,250 people on the average, and an area of about forty-one square miles for the localities studied. The lower limit for the public library was thirty thousand circulating books. To raise the requisite budget would require the people in about 133 square miles. About thirty beds were considered necessary for a general hospital. To support this unit would require a population of six thousand distributed over about two hundred square miles. Thus, these unit requirements for good services for rural people pointed toward specialization of functions among rural communities and implied that costs must be distributed and equalized over larger units (Kolb 1925:59).

Kolb's study and Nason's early reports were followed by related cooperative projects in sparsely populated rural states. The unit requirement idea in Kolb's Wisconsin study was picked up in South Dakota studies of public libraries (Kumlien 1928) and of high school education for farm youth (Kumlien 1930). Montana reports on rural community halls, rural community clubs, and county public libraries were based on statewide coverage of functioning units (e.g., Berger 1930). Intensive case studies supplemented a quantitative analysis of the factors influencing the distribution and success or failure of community clubs in North Dakota (Willson 1931).

MEDICAL AND HEALTH CARE SERVICES

Health care services for rural people were examined in cooperative projects supported by Galpin. The Ohio research had features similar to work in this subject area a couple of decades or so later (Lively and Beck 1927). It was not until the 1940s that the Division resumed activity in the health care area.

Then there were two major thrusts, each quite different. First, the staff was responsible for the evaluation of seven experimental, federally assisted, voluntary health associations open to all farm families, regardless of income. The Division also did some evaluation of medical and dental care plans which the FSA had organized specifically for its borrowers, all low-income farmers (see Chapter 12).

Second, support was given for two major cooperative projects in Mississippi and New York in the rural health services area, starting in 1949. Funds provided to the Division under the Research and Marketing Act of 1946 made these projects possible. One principal objective for both projects was determining the extent to which rural people used medical and health care resources such as physicians, dentists, hospitals, and public health services. Another was to determine factors associated with differential use of resources. The Mississippi study also sought to determine unmet medical needs of rural people using a medical symptoms technique previously developed with leadership by the Division (Loftin and Galloway 1954:101–13). One purpose of the New York work was developing and testing methods of obtaining data from families on their use of health care resources (Larson and Hay 1951:225). The sample for household interviews for both states was drawn by the BAE, using master sample materials developed in the 1940s. Information on the use of health services during the twelve months preceding interview was obtained for all household members in the sample.[1]

The Mississippi summary report documented, for instance, sharp differences in the use of physicians, dentists, and hospitals by the socioeconomic status of individuals as measured by the short form of the Sewell socioeconomic status scale (Loftin and Galloway 1954). Differences by race in use of these services were pronounced. The New York research tested hypotheses of relationships, of trends, and of methods (Larson and Hay 1951). The available evidence supported, for example, the hypothesis that use of a dentist is one of the most discriminating of the several types of utilization of health resources by rural people.

The rural sociologist researchers had assistance from health care professionals in planning the studies. This helped when it was time to disseminate the research findings to physicians, dentists, and public health educators. Reports on the New York study were published, for example, in the state's Medical Society journal (Larson et al. 1951; Larson and Hay 1952) and in *The Journal of the American Dental Association* (Hay et al. 1953).

Other more limited efforts in the health area in the 1940s included an attempt to measure unmet medical needs (Schuler et al. 1946). The aim was to use non-technical questions on health status and practices to identify individuals having a high degree of probable need for medical care. A field test was made with both white and black rural families representing a good range socioeconomically. There was 79 percent agreement between lay and physician enumerators in the symptoms responses. This symptoms approach was used soon thereafter by Schuler and his colleagues (1949) in at least five rural health studies in Michigan and Peru.

LOCAL GOVERNMENT IN RURAL AREAS

In his Walworth County study in Wisconsin, a state which had the township system below the county level, Galpin (1915) identified local government as a major problem for farm people. Galpin began to suggest, even advocate, a new form of local government, a rural municipality, which would include both farmers and the people in their trade center (Galpin 1918:361–65; 1924a:209–27). The ACLA, at its first annual conference in 1919, received the report of a committee thatdeclared county government the weakest link in American democracy, asserting, among other faults, that it was "expensive, inefficient and wasteful, headless, unorganized and undirected . . . incompetent, irresponsible and lawless" (ACLA *Proceedings* 1919:68–69). The problem received attention at successive annual meetings until, in 1931, rural government was the general theme of the conference.

It was T. B. Manny, however, who among rural sociologists, gave special attention to the study of local government in rural areas. This started as a cooperative project in 1924 to make a nation-wide study using a mail questionnaire. Manny, at the time, was on the faculty of Hendrix-Henderson College in Arkansas. After Galpin brought him on the Division staff, he continued this line of research. Manny's survey was designed to get information about the smallest units of local government within a state, residents' interest in this local unit, complaints, suggestions for more rigid local law enforcement, and opinions about the legal incorporation of rural communities (1930:105–12, 320–22). The questionnaire went through three pretests before a final form was prepared, the last pretest with a mailing to more than one thousand people. Three sub-samples of informants were used for the study—farmers, local government officials, and political science and rural sociology teachers.

The survey results were used in Manny's book, *Rural Municipalities: A Sociological Study of Local Government in the United States* (1930). He saw the local government structure and functions as a barrier to the rural development power needed to aid the enrichment of rural life. The book included a set of proposals for completely reorganizing local government in rural areas. A plan for rural municipalities expanded greatly on the germ of Galpin's idea.

Manny's work on rural municipalities led, for example, to an invitation to sit with the Social Science Research Council's Advisory Committee on Public Administration (*FPRLA* 1932[1]:1–2). It was the basis for an address on modernizing local government at the 1932 New Jersey State Agricultural Convention. Subsequently, Manny made a study of township and school district government in one New Jersey township in cooperation with the New Jersey State Department of Agriculture (*FPRLA* 1935[4]:1). He was one of the BAE participants in a cooperative project with the Kentucky AES to study farm taxes and local government (Manny et al. 1934). Further, he took part in a local government study in Ohio with the BAE's Division of Agricultural Finance and the Ohio AES (*FPRLA* 1935[1]:2).

The Division also cooperated in the early 1930s with a Cornell University study designed to examine the relation between the towns (townships) and the natural socioeconomic areas of New York and the effect of this relationship on services received by the town residents (Wasson and Sanderson 1933:47). The Division's research on local government was phased out by the time of Galpin's retirement. It was not reinstated later.

RURAL RELIGIOUS ORGANIZATION

The relation of religious institutions to farm life problems was on the short list of fields for rural life study suggested by Secretary Houston's advisory committee (USDA, Office of the Secretary 1919b:6). But it turned out that research on the rural church was never a priority for use of the Division's resources. One principal reason during the early Galpin years was the amount of work on the subject by rural sociologists employed by several major Protestant denominational bodies and by the Institute of Social and Religious Research (Brunner 1957:7–9; Nelson 1969:45–48). Later, the surveys made in 1930 for President Hoover's Research Committee on Social Trends provided information on the churches in the national sample of 140 agricultural village communities (Brunner and Kolb 1933:208–41). When the same communities were resurveyed six years later, to ascertain the impacts of the Great Depression, rural religion was one part of the study (Brunner and Lorge 1937:299–328).

Galpin addressed the issue of competitive religion among Protestants in his readable short book *Empty Churches: The Rural-Urban Dilemma* (1925). This was not a research monograph but in it Galpin drew upon the research of the Division and others for his analysis. He used, for example, data from Emily Hoag's (1921) work on migration for the Belleville, New York community. He used data on farm tenancy to make his point that landless rural people were a group the church had detoured around. From his data-based diagnosis, he made a call for community churches in rural areas that would serve people rather than denominations.

A cooperative project with the University of Wisconsin on the rural church was supported in the early 1920s (Kolb and Bornman 1924). The study pertained to all churches in Dane County outside the city of Madison. The boundaries of all parishes were mapped. The relationship between these boundaries and neighborhood locality groups and village trade areas were then examined. The social history of the major religious streams was analyzed. This revealed the association between nationality and religious affiliation. Size of church membership in relation to country or village location of churches was tabulated.

Also, in the cooperative project on rural social and economic areas in central New York, an attempt was made to analyze changes in number of churches and in church membership by size of village, 1900–1928 (Sanderson 1934). Church service areas in the sample counties were mapped and then measured in square miles to compare with the areas of other agencies and services.

During the Taylor years, a small study of the churches in one Virginia county was an outgrowth of the county land-use planning program (Ensminger and Page 1940). A paper on class denominationalism in a California "industrialized" agricultural community was published (Goldschmidt 1944: 348–55). The paper had originally been presented at a regional land tenure conference arranged by the Farm Foundation for the Department of Town and Country Work, Home Missions Council, and the Federal Council of Churches. It was found that in the study community, the older Protestant churches fulfilled the religious needs of the upper class while the evangelical sects served the laboring class. The Catholic church, however, more nearly represented a cross-section of the churchgoers. The Holiness and Pentecostal sects in the Southeastern states were also the subject of a paper (Holt 1940:740–47). A major hypothesis interpreted the growth of these sects as a social movement which was a product of social disorganization and cultural conflict. Generally, however, during the Taylor years aspects of the rural church as a formal institution were one among several components of a study.

The limited extent of the Division's research specifically directed at rural religious organization was not a good indicator of the use of its other research by a wide range of church bodies who were seeking a sociological perspective on rural life and communities. Not only Galpin and Taylor but at least nine other staff members were called upon for presentations to church groups (see "addresses" in *Bibliography*, Larson et al. 1992a:246–75). Thus served were groups as varied as the National Catholic Rural Life Conference, the National Conference of Christians and Jews, the National Conference on the Church and Migratory Labor of the Home Missions Council of North America, the National Convocation on the Church in Town and Country, and the Institute for Missionaries on Agricultural and Rural Development.

VOLUNTARY ASSOCIATIONS

The pioneering studies of the country neighborhood were quickly followed by research on the organized groups in which farm family participation was not limited by locality group boundaries. These were voluntary associations, also referred to as purposive or special interest groups. Leading off in this area of investigation was a cooperative project that resulted in Kolb and Wileden's *Special Interest Groups in Rural Society* (1927).[2]

The researchers spelled out their methodology carefully (Kolb and Wileden 1927:104–9). The unit of analysis was the formal organized or intentional group. To be eligible for the study, a group had to have duly elected officers and rather definite meetings. Other criteria were dropped when found to be nonessential. Religious and fraternal organizations were excluded as, in general, were those located in towns or cities. The area unit for the research was the county. Five counties were selected on the basis of agricultural regions of the state and each county's role in various organization movements, past and present. The results for the five counties were checked by field work in a sixth county, reputedly the most poorly organized in the state. The case method was used for the 351 special interest groups studied. From two to eight persons per organization were interviewed to complete a ten-page schedule about the life history and other aspects of the group. Field interviewers kept a daily diary, one purpose being to assist recall in analysis of the schedule data.

A functional, rather than a structural, classification of the 351 organizations was found to be necessary for the data analysis. Twelve functions or interests were used. These organized interest groups were found to have certain modal characteristics, e.g., the idea to start the group came from outside the local community for about 90 percent (21). A more complete analysis of seven of the twelve special interest classes found each to have certain characteristics, e.g., gender of the officers and length of life of the organization. A distinctive contribution of the research was its treatment of the natural history or life cycle of interest groups (Kolb and Wileden 1927:74–79). A theoretical graph portrayed four stages of the life cycle in relation to time and the intensity of interest. The four stages were stimulation, rise, carrying on, and decline. The characteristics of each stage were given with respect, for example, to outside promotion, local leadership, and conflict.

Charles H. Cooley, in a paper on rural social research at the 1928 ASA annual meeting, praised Kolb and Wileden's use of the case study method (1930:331–39). He found their research a welcome contrast to studies timid about offering nothing unquantitative. Sorokin, Zimmerman, and Galpin, in their discussion of rural social differentiation, cited the Wisconsin special interest group research as one of the most conspicuous examples of a study that recognized the growing replacement of cumulative communities in rural America by special functional groupings (1930:330–32).

Near the end of the Division's life, Wilson Longmore was asked to join in a national study of fifteen service, professional, and other civic clubs (Longmore and Nall 1953:122–46). The focus was on a study of adult education in rural America, supported by the Ford Foundation's Fund for Adult Education and sponsored by the Association of Land Grant Colleges and Universities. The fifteen selected were national organizations with a wide distribution of local units and an integrated hierarchy of levels of administration. Local units in a BAE sample of counties were sent postcard questionnaires. Included was a request for information on the units adult education activities in international understanding for peace, strengthening of democracy, and understanding and strengthening of the economy.

Social Participation

The sociological exploration of rural life included Division support for research by cooperators on participation in voluntary associations. Early efforts gave considerable attention to developing measures of social participation which would permit comparison of individuals, families, and communities (Brunner 1957:107). Although such comparisons could be made within specific studies, the procedures varied so greatly among researchers that only limited comparisons could be made among the studies supported. This was a cost of Galpin's policy of giving cooperators a free hand in exploratory projects.

One of the best of these projects to probe into the organizational behavior of farm people was led by E. L. Kirkpatrick and his associates (1929) at the University of Wisconsin. This project also illustrated the use of the Division's cooperative policy to support cumulative research. In this instance, the work was a follow-up to Kolb and Wileden's special interest group study. The research was done in the same counties they had used. Within the five, twelve rural school districts were chosen to represent localities with high, medium, or low levels of organization as indicated by the number and vitality of their special interest groups. Within each district, participation data for one year for specified types of associations were collected by interview for all families and for all persons ten years of age and over. A participation index was devised for individuals and families. The index was based on the five elements of affiliation, attendance, contributions, committee membership, and leadership roles. The report was a combination of statistical analysis and case studies. The case studies compared high and low organization districts and reported on families selected because they were in one of three affiliation groups, 100 percent, medium, or zero.

Social participation research was not given special attention by the Division after the early 1930s. Lack of funds, at first, and then changing priorities help explain this. Subsequently, in general, social participation was treated and subsumed within projects having a different primary focus, e.g., a study of tenure among Corn Belt and Cotton Belt farmers (Schuler 1938:44–52, 192–215). There was one exception during the Taylor years. Division staff member D. G. Hay (1948)[3] constructed a scale to measure both formal and informal participation by rural households. He used the scale for a comparative analysis of the participation of households (1950) and individuals (1951) in four rural communities in the Northeast. Contemporary statistical procedures were used to determine the discriminate value of participation items and scale validity and reliability.

FARMERS' ORGANIZATIONS

Farmers' organizations constitute a special category of voluntary associations. They received some attention by the Division during much of its life. Galpin had no more than arrived in Washington when he put a clerk to compiling a directory of national and state agricultural organizations (Galpin 1938a:39). Such a directory was a specific recommendation of Secretary Houston's advisory committee. The published list had more than four hundred national and regional organizations and nearly eighteen hundred at the state level (USDA, Office of Farm Management and Farm Economics 1920).[4]

During the agricultural depression of the 1920s, farm leaders and agricultural policy-makers developed a high interest in cooperatives as a means of solving farmers' economic problems. Galpin was impressed that the BAE's research on marketing problems was totally neglecting the psychological factors making for successful cooperatives (1938a:54–55). So, in 1928, the Division joined with the BAE's Division of Cooperative Marketing, created by Congress in the Cooperative Marking Act of 1926, in the first of what proved to be four studies. The emphasis on researching farmer cooperatives was short-term. As the farm problem worsened, interest of agricultural policy-makers shifted to direct government intervention, e.g., production controls and price supports.

T. B. Manny had leadership for the Division for the research on the sociological and psychological aspects of farmer-owned marketing organizations. The first of the four joint studies was about the problems of cooperatives and the experiences of farmers in marketing potatoes in four Eastern Shore counties of Maryland and Virginia (Manny 1929). The second was directed at farmer experiences and opinions with respect to cotton marketing methods during the preceding ten years in Alabama and North Carolina (Manny 1931).[5] Farmer interviews for both studies were limited to those free to make marketing decisions about their crop. This left out tenants and practically all nonwhite farmers. In both studies, members, ex-members, and nonmembers were compared as to characteristics and opinions.[6] In the cotton marketing study, the interviewers rated each respondent as to the person's reaction toward cooperative marketing. The latter found a marked contrast between the small amount of criticism of the marking associations and the small number who marketed through them. In the Eastern Shore, kinship ties were found to contribute to the inefficient assembling of potatoes for the market, a fundamental marketing function.

The third joint study (Manny 1932) was in conjunction with a study of membership of the Ohio Farm Bureau Federation made at the request of the directors of that organization. The interviews with some 1,372 farmers included questions on farmer experience with and opinions about farmer-owned marketing and purchasing cooperatives. Respondents were rated by interviewers into one of four categories of suitability for membership. They were also rated by local informants as to their attitude toward cooperative marketing and purchasing and their ability as a farm operator. In the analysis, members, ex-members, and nonmembers were compared. This study provided information on such matters as farmer satisfaction and dissatisfaction with farmer-owned business organizations, reasons for dropping out or not becoming a member, information sources, and evaluation of accomplishments. Membership in such organizations was found to be distinctly selective in its appeal to farmers. It also appeared that a tie-in between membership in a general farmers' organization and various commodity groups introduced difficult problems both for the general organization and the cooperatives.

Data for the fourth report came from the same survey used for the report described in the previous paragraph. The purpose of this study, in which Ohio State University was also a cooperator, was to get the farmers' view point of the Ohio Farm Bureau Federation (Manny and Smith 1931).[7] Farmers were asked for their perceptions of the Farm Bureau, reasons for joining, reasons for dropping out, opinions as to the organization's accomplishments and related issues. One of the conclusions was that the organization had created some of its bitterest opposition by entering into competition with already established locally owned farmers' cooperative associations. A finding of interest from the interviews with farm men was that 54 percent of the members, 84 percent of the ex-members, and 95 percent of the nonmembers thought that farm women had been of no help to the organization or didn't know of any contribution. Even before Manny started his work, a cooperative project with the Virginia AES made a detailed case study of the Tobacco Growers' Cooperative Association (Garnett 1927:70–108). Later, the resurvey of 140 agricultural communities in 1936 reported on the adjustments to the depression by cooperative purchasing and marketing organizations (Brunner and Lorge 1937:58–64).

Carl Taylor's Work

The most substantial and significant of the Division's work on farmers' organizations, by far, was that done by Carl Taylor. This culminated in his book *The Farmers' Movement, 1620–1920* (1953), intended to be the first of two volumes. The second was never completed.[8]

Taylor's book is a sociological analysis of a social movement. Farmers' organizations are treated within a conceptual framework of the farmers' movement in the United States. The whole spectrum of farmers' organizations in the nation's history up to 1920 are included. Among these are the Farmers' Alliance, farmer-owned cooperatives, and the general farmers' organizations such as the Grange and the Farmers' Union.

Research by Taylor on farmers' organizations was career-long as time and resources permitted. It started before he came to the Division. When at North Carolina State, he had a cooperative project, supported by Galpin, to ascertain the adjustments which national farmers' organizations seek to make (Advisory Committee 1927:67).[9] The book represents a winnowing of a vast amount of "diverse and uneven body of information" (Taylor 1953:494) from farm organization records, newspaper accounts, work in many libraries, interviews with farm organization leaders, and other sources. Taylor (1953:324–26) had some firsthand knowledge of the Farmers' Alliance. When he was growing up on an Iowa farm, his father was a member. He attended meetings of the North Carolina State Farmers' Alliance as a member for five years in the 1920s.

Taylor's concept of a farmers' movement, his theory, and hypotheses evolved over time (Taylor 1953:1–2, 8–12, 492–95). He credits Thorstein Veblen (his teacher at the University of Missouri) and John R. Commons for ideas which helped him frame his concept of a farmers' movement. Veblen emphasized the results of the evolution of the price and market regime in Western society. Commons related the labor movement of the twentieth century to economic conditions and social and political philosophies. These influences brought Taylor to a working hypothesis: "just as the various and varying struggles of laborers arose out of, and have always revolved about, the issues of wages, hours, and working conditions, and just as all these struggles combined constitute the American labor movement, so the various and varying struggles of farmers arose out of, and have always revolved about, the issues of prices, markets, and credits, and all these struggles combined constitute the American Farmers' Movement" (Taylor 1953:493). As research and analysis proceeded, the hypothesis was modified to "the American Farmers' Movement grew out of and has been continued by the more or less organized efforts of farmers either to protect themselves against the impact of the evolving commerical-capitalist economy or to catch step with it" (Taylor 1953:495).

When the Fund for Adult Education supported a study of adult education in rural America, one part pertained to the four major farm organizations. The four were the Grange, the Farmers' Union, the American Farm Bureau Federation, and the National Council of Farmer Cooperatives. This part, like the overall study, had a special interest in programs or activities for adults dealing with three areas, among them international understanding for peace. Taylor, working with Wayne Rohrer of Michigan State College, interviewed national officers and staffs of the four organizations, visited ten state headquarters, and attended local meetings of the three general farm organizations. Quantitative data were obtained by postcard questionnaires mailed to all local units of the four organizations in counties in one of the BAE's general purpose samples. One chapter for the study's overall report described the four organizations with a focus upon the organized channels of communication by which educational processes operated (Taylor and Rohrer 1953:80–99). A second chapter dealt with the content and techniques of the adult education that went through the channels of communication (Rohrer and Taylor 1953:100–121).

OTHER RURAL SOCIAL ORGANIZATION STUDIES

Passage of the Maryland Library Act of 1945 led to a three-way cooperative research project involving the Maryland AES, the Division, and the Prince George's County Memorial Library. As a basis for library planning, the county was delineated into communities and neighborhoods (Galloway et al. 1951:18–24). Library-related institutions and groups in the county, such as white and black public schools, were identified. One year after the system was in operation, all individuals twelve years of age and over in sample households were interviewed. Area sampling techniques were used (Houser et al. 1952:29–31). An eight-item level-of-living index was constructed for the sample families using principal component analysis similar to that previously developed by Hagood in the Division. One analysis compared library acceptors with library rejectors and public library users with nonusers as to levels of living, traits related to library use, and social participation traits (Houser and Galloway 1949). A second analysis pertained to the needs, desires, and preferences of the rural population for reading materials and the relationship between reading habits and levels of living and other factors (Houser et al. 1952). This Maryland study used concepts and methods which contrasted sharply with those of Division-supported library studies in the 1920s.

Two studies on schools done during the Taylor years were quite different in purpose and scope from those for earlier cooperative projects. One was a comparative analysis by size-of-place of the early impact of World

War II on the nation's public schools (Loomis 1942). Statistical data provided by the U.S. Office of Education were used to compare rural with urban schools on such measures as change in number of teachers, the proportion of new teachers and of teachers with emergency certificates, and reasons for teachers leaving the public school system. The second, also made during the war years, reported on farmer opinions about their schools (Raper 1945). The information came from interviews in the thirty-two counties being used at the time for the Division's rural trends project. Farmer support for some school services to the community varied widely by regions. But a majority of those interviewed wanted their schools, after the war, to have farm-machinery repair shops, to operate canneries for the convenience of families, and to expand school libraries to serve adults. The majority wanted the schools to help prepare their children to choose between farm life and off-the-farm life.

Among the other studies, one of the more unique examined the adult education function of six USDA agencies such as the FmHA, the SCS, and the Rural Electrification Administration (Longmore 1953). This, too, was done for the study of adult education commissioned by the Fund for Adult Education. Data came from interviews with agency representatives, official documents, and a mail questionnaire to FmHA and SCS officials in 263 sample counties. Each agency was found to have all the elements necessary to facilitate the educational process but educational objectives tended to be subordinated to the more specific functions for which the agency had been formed.

The Division's work rarely focused directly on the family as a social institution, its structure, and member roles.[10] There were, however, numerous family-related studies. Those on farm family living and on organizational participation are prime examples. The family life cycle concept was applied in the analysis of family living expenditures. Before he came to the Division, Charles Loomis had used the family life cycle concept in a study of North Carolina white farm families. In a paper that identified him with the Division, Loomis (1936) drew on his North Carolina work and that of others to examine the relationship of the stages in the family life cycle to adjustments in the farming enterprise and to the behavior of family members. Two methods of life cycle analysis were distinguished, the historical and the cross-section. Technical difficulties in life cycle analysis were discussed.

Terms such as "social class" and "social status" were seldom highlighted in Division publications. There were exceptions, e.g., *Disadvantaged Classes in American Agriculture* (Taylor et al. 1938) and *Social Status and Farm*

Tenure (Schuler 1938). But a substantial number of studies had the effect of illuminating family and area social differentials in rural America although that was not their direct objective. Examples include the research on farm family living expenditures (Chapter 6) and on the farm tenure structure (Chapter 10).

The Division's research gave much more attention to the family, church, school, and social differentials during the Taylor years than a glance at publication titles would suggest. Field instructions for the comprehensive studies of rural communities and of counties typically called for information on these topics. The analysis, however, was subsumed within an overall report. Thus, the El Cerrito study, in the community stability-instability series, had sections on the school, the church, and the class structure (Leonard and Loomis 1941). In Oscar Lewis's book (1948), based on his cultural reconnaissance survey in Bell County, Texas, separate chapters are devoted to the schools and the churches. The Czech, German, and old-line American families in the county are compared as to behavior and value systems. The twenty-four county rural social organization studies all included an analysis of the institutions of family, church, and school. These studies in a Wheat Belt county in Washington and a general and self-sufficing type-of-farming county in Georgia were used for a comparative rural social organization analysis which included these institutions (Galloway 1948).

SUMMARY

This selective review indicates that the Division's research on the non-locality aspects of social organization was wide-ranging. It dealt in some way at some time with all the major institutional systems, the significant services and facilities, and with indicators of social status differentials in rural America. The emphasis given these several topics was, however, uneven; it was, for most, short-term or episodic.

Wayne Nason's reports on his case studies of successful local experiences in rural community organization and in getting key community services had a wide circulation. T. B. Manny introduced a sociological approach to a nation-wide study of local government. He innovated the sociological and social psychological study of farmer's marketing practices and cooperative marketing organizations. Growing interest in the health services situation in rural areas and available funding led in the postwar period to expanded research in this area. Cooperative projects on such institutions as high schools, libraries, and hospitals were the basis for recommending minimum unit requirements to provide quality services to rural people. Other cooperative projects opened up sociological inquiry into the functional or special interest groups which were modifying the locality group basis of rural society.

One notable exception to the short-term and episodic characterization of the Division's non-locality work in rural social organization was that done by Carl Taylor on farmers' general organizations and cooperatives. This was a long-term, continuing intellectual quest for sociological understanding of the history, origins, and activities of these organizations over the full span of the nation's life. His research made a major contribution to the literature on voluntary associations and social movements.

Notes

1. The Mississippi study asked informants about the use of hospitals and certain health care practices during the five years preceding the survey.

2. An example of closely related work at the time was a cooperative project in North Dakota (Willson 1928). The study was not limited, however, to voluntary associations in the sense used by Kolb and Wileden. Its intent was primarily to portray the organizations, institutions such as schools and churches, agencies, and social facilities available to the farm people of the state. The number and location of each of a score or so of categories of these were reported. There was little analysis.

3. This was a sub-project of cooperative work with Cornell University to study the rural social organization of a county. The sub-project provided the data for Hay's Ph.D. thesis at the University of Minnesota.

4. The published *Directory* gives no indication that it was prepared in Galpin's unit. It is an example of the Division's work that escaped being included in our *Bibliography* (Larson, Moe, and Zimmerman 1992a).

5. Before the cotton-marketing study was published, the Division of Cooperative Marketing was transferred from the BAE to the new Federal Farm Board.

6. The Alabama-North Carolina study included questions on farm production practices, use of services of county agricultural agents, and sources of advice on when to sell the cotton crop (Manny 1931).

7. Manny and Smith also prepared confidential reports on the Farm Bureau situation for each of the fourteen counties in which the survey was made. See Larson et al. (1992a, items 1047–60) for citations to these reports.

8. Carl Taylor was working on the second volume after his retirement when a fire destroyed his home where he had the materials he had been collecting for three decades. Thereafter, he was physically unable to continue his research. The salvageable papers are at Cornell University, as was Taylor's wish, in the Rare and Manuscript Collections, Carl A. Kroch Library, Collection 3230.

9. Taylor (1929) gave a paper, "Farmers' movements as psychosocial phenomena," at the 1928 ASA annual meeting.

10. Galpin (1918), in his book written before coming to the Division, referred to the family as the rural institution *par excellence* and had chapters on the social role of the housewife and of the child.

9

Farm Labor

The social aspects of various types of farm labor and the social aspects of tenancy and landlordism were among the fields of study suggested by Secretary of Agriculture Houston's advisory committee on the establishment of the farm life studies unit which became the Division (USDA, Office of the Secretary 1919 b:7). Galpin promptly initiated cooperative projects on farm tenancy, an area in which he had done research in Wisconsin before going to Washington (Galpin and Hoag 1919). In contrast, the farm labor area turned out to be a late addition to the Division's research activities. Any attention given the subject during the Galpin years was subsumed within studies of farm tenancy and of farm family living.

Galpin had no staff to take the leadership for farm labor research. Soon after Carl Taylor was made Division head by Secretary Wallace, however, the staffing situation began to change. In the Depression 1930s, hired farm laborers and their families came to be recognized as standing at the bottom of the social and economic ladder in American agriculture (Taylor et al. 1938:20). The BAE had a history of using its farmer crop reporting system to collect data regularly on the employment of hired and family workers and on hired worker wage rates (Wallrabenstein and Ducoff 1957:8–14). But the living conditions of farm wage workers were relatively unknown. USDA administrators acted to enable the Division to start filling the knowledge gap.

BAE Chief A. G. Black arranged the transfer from the Division of Land Economics, in late 1935, of J. C. Folsom, a specialist on farm labor. In 1939, when H. R. Tolley was BAE Chief, W. T. Ham and his associates were transferred from the AAA's Program Planning Division along with the work they had been doing in farm labor, tenancy, and rural dependency (FPRLA 1939:13, No. 3, 8). Shortly, farm labor became one of the Division's major and continuing program areas, along with farm and rural population, levels and standards of living, and locality group aspects of rural social organization.

PRE–WORLD WAR II FARM LABOR STUDIES

The Division's initial attention to farm laborers and their families bene-fited from its close working ties with the FSA's social research section, also directed at the time by Carl Taylor. Jointly sponsored interviews with hired farm workers in eleven counties in 1936 inquired as to annual days of work and income, wage rates, and other matters. This WPA-funded proj-ect allowed only three weeks or so for the interviewing done during sum-mer or fall in each county. Interviewers were instructed to reach as many as possible of all the farms hiring labor at the time. Adult hired workers on these farms were to be interviewed with a set schedule. The employers were also interviewed, thus allowing a comparison of employer and worker reports on such matters as wage rates and labor placement methods. This study was not sophisticated in methods by later standards, but it was a start in providing insight into hired farm worker conditions in widely diverse agricultural areas of the nation. We did not locate a summary, how-ever, of the eleven county reports (e.g., Vasey and Folsom 1937a). A spin-off of this series was use of the Louisiana sample parish data by Louisiana State University researchers for a more detailed analysis of the social char-acteristics, employment, wages, earnings, and income of the black cotton plantation workers interviewed (Grigsby and Hoffsommer 1941).

Also coming out of the Division-FSA joint efforts was the chapter on hired farm labor in *Disadvantaged Classes in American Agriculture* (Taylor et al. 1938:19–36) and a study of social status and farm tenure (Schuler 1938b) that included farm laborers in the sample interviewed. The for-mer, based on secondary sources, gave a national overview of what was known from research then available about farm worker living and work-ing conditions. The Schuler study compared hired workers in the Corn Belt and the Cotton Belt with other tenure groups such as renters and own-ers with regard to attitudes and opinions pertaining to farm problems and federal farm programs. They were also compared with respect to levels and standards of living and in other ways.

After Folsom's transfer the Division also prepared a graphic summary of farm labor and population data for the nation on a county and state basis (Folsom and Baker 1937). Some seven thousand copies of this graphic summary, based largely on 1930 and 1935 census reports, were distrib-uted (*FPRLA* 1938:12, No. 3, 15). Also, Folsom immediately joined, with a BAE library staff member, in preparing a comprehensive 493-page anno-tated bibliography on agricultural labor in the United States covering 1915–35 (Colvin and Folsom 1935). He had a hand in keeping this updated periodically as long as the Division existed.

The staff transferred from the AAA were trained in economics. This was reflected in the research problems selected for cooperative projects in Arkansas and South Carolina. There was interest at the time in the effects of agricultural changes underway such as the AAA's crop reduction programs and mechanization. The Arkansas study of cotton farms was designed to determine the effect of changes in the acreage of cotton and other crops and in tractor use on the number and tenure of farm workers (McNeely and Barton 1940). In South Carolina the focus was on changes for wage laborers and sharecroppers in the light of changes in cotton and tobacco acreage (Holcomb and Aull 1940). Both studies made use of AAA records to supplement field interviews. The sharp decline in cotton acreage in 1932–38, attributed to the AAA program, the shift to corn and other crops, and the increase in tractors, reduced labor requirements on the Arkansas farms studied. This decline was accompanied by an increase in the percentage of cotton worked by wage hands rather than sharecroppers and share renters. In South Carolina, despite the cut in cotton and tobacco acreage from 1933 to 1937 in the two counties studied, little change was found in the number and tenure of farm workers. The researchers foresaw, however, changes similar to those already registered in Arkansas. Another feature of the South Carolina work was comparative analysis of the economic status of wage and sharecropper families. A shift from cropper to wage status could bring a sharp decline in the family income from home-use production and perquisites (Holcomb and Aull 1940:59).

When issues of public concern about farm laborers were taken up by congressional committees such as the Senate Committee on Education and Labor in 1940 and 1941, Carl Taylor and no fewer than six other Division staff members testified. They presented statistics on the number, distribution, composition, and employment of the nation's farm workers. They drew on the Division's research on earnings and levels of living and reported on the records kept of strikes of agricultural laborers (see Larson et al. 1992a, items 0035–51 for citations).

In early 1941, the Division identified objectives for farm labor research in general, made up of the following questions (FPRLA 1941:15, No. 2, 1). What changes in farm production and management affect the demand for farm labor and the status of labor on the farm? What are the sources of supply of farm laborers and the factors that affect the rate of movement into and out of the farm labor market? What is the economic and social status of farm laborers, the conditions of their employment, and the place of the farm laborer's family in the community? What are the attitudes of the laborer, of the farmer and his organizations, and of the community, since attitudes condition action? It was acknowledged that definitive information on any of these objectives required painstaking data collection with satisfactory samples. But conditions at the time were rapidly changing and means were limited. So the reconnaissance survey was developed as a shortcut method to get knowledge of labor conditions in an area. Qualified local informants were one resource for such surveys. As a check on these sources, a brief schedule was devised to secure information from a few representative farms on the amount and kind of labor used for each operation in the production of the farm's three major crops or enterprises. This kind of reconnaissance survey was introduced during 1939–40 to serve county land-use planning committees. During the 1940–41 year, surveys were planned for some fifty-two areas.[1] The experience with such shortcut methods of information gathering was applied in meeting the demands placed upon the Division when World War II came.

THE FARM LABOR PROGRAM IN WORLD WAR II

The USDA response, first, to the accelerated defense effort prior to the nation's entry into World War II and, after December 7, 1941, to wartime conditions demanded a reorientation in the Division's farm labor activities.[2] In March, 1941, Secretary of Agriculture Wickard recommended that the state land-use planning committees appoint labor subcommittees to develop plans to deal with any farm labor shortages (*FPRLA* 1941:15, No. 2, 16). Nearly all the states and about half the counties did so. Each of the Division's regional representatives were then given added responsibility as the BAE area leader for farm labor studies. They were to assist the state and county labor committees in appraising alleged labor shortages and in making surveys if needed to develop appropriate action.

On January 1, 1942, the BAE announced a wartime program for all of its Divisions (USDA, BAE 1942). The BAE's efforts to aid in meeting the farmers' labor needs, so they could achieve the nation's agricultural production goals, was to center in the Division headed by Carl Taylor. Major emphasis was projected to be placed upon the compilation, analysis, and interpretation of farm labor data for use by the federal agencies and the state and county committees with policy and program responsibilities for insuring an adequate supply of farm labor. The past years of study of agricultural labor problems gave a base for the Division's revised role in the farm labor area. This reorientation often meant a change in how study results were presented. Publication was deemphasized as a tangible evidence of work accomplished (USDA, BAE, DFPRW 1942:1). Oftentimes, what was intended at the outset was a memo to an action agency or an oral report. The tangible result might be the action taken by a Farm Placement Service office or a farm labor committee. Contributions of individual staff members were often pooled with those of staff from other divisions or agencies with no attempt to disentangle individual contributions.

A few examples suggest the character and range of the Division's farm labor activities just before the war and during its early months (*FPRLA* 1941, 14, No. 4, 1–39; USDA, BAE, DFPRW 1942). Regional offices assisted states to organize farm labor subcommittees and to develop plans for these committees to collect valid information on state and county farm labor situations. Virtually continuous reconnaissance surveys were made of a controversial sugar beet labor situation in three western states to provide timely information to state and federal authorities. A number of projects contributed to programs to shift workers from areas of farm labor surplus to areas of scarcity. In South Dakota, at the request of Selective Service, a questionnaire was developed for use by local draft boards in evaluating agricultural workers for deferment from military service. The effect of new ordnance plants in rural areas on farm employment and wage rates was evaluated at the request of the Office of Agricultural War Relations. A study for use of the U.S. Employment Service constructed a map for the United States which showed counties most in need of farm placement services because they were a source of potential labor supply or an area of high seasonal or year-round labor need. The Division joined with the Division of Farm Management and Costs in analyzing farm labor requirements by states, by crops and livestock, and by separate operations. The Division completed, with FSA cooperation, a 183-page report which assembled in one place the most important facts then available about the highly varied conditions of farm employment (USDA, BAE, and FSA 1942). At the time, employment in nonfarm war industries and entry into the armed forces were expected to be continuing drains on the farm labor force as long as the war lasted.

As the war went on, the Division continued to analyze the farm labor situation for the nation as a whole. In early 1943, for instance, the numerical changes in the rural-farm working force during the preceding three years was reported and an estimate made of the outlook for the agricultural worker supply during the year (Ducoff et al. 1943). The estimates involved specific assumptions, e.g., what would be the effect on farm worker numbers of the newly operative amendment to the Selective Service Act that provided for deferment from military service of farm workers essential to the war effort? How many more women could be brought into the farm working force? The lack of a data source on the number of *different* persons who worked on farms during the course of a year was remedied when arrangements were made with the Bureau of the Census to include questions on farm work in its January 1944 survey for the Monthly Report on the Labor Force. This enumeration of all persons fourteen years of age and over in the national sample of some thirty thousand households was the basis for the Division's estimate of the number of different persons who did any farm work during 1943, either paid or unpaid (Ducoff and Hagood 1944a). These workers were classified by sex, by farm or nonfarm residence, and by number of hours, days, and weeks of farm work done during the year.

As the 1943 crop season drew to a close, the tight farm labor situations experienced made manpower shortages "near the top of the list of favorite topics for discussion" (Taeuber 1943:342). Assumptions and beliefs about the reality of general farm worker shortages were challenged by an analysis presented by Conrad Taeuber at a joint session in September 1943 of the American Farm Economics Association and the Rural Sociological Society. He concluded that there was still a considerable volume of underemployment among farm operators, their family members, and hired workers. Agricultural labor shortages at the time were more a matter of distribution and effective use than of total number of persons available. Among the factors he identified as explaining the persistence of agricultural underemployment were a gradual accommodation in some localities to perennial poverty; geographic, social, and psychological isolation; value-systems; the barriers based on individual characteristics such as health and skin color; legislative restrictions on the free movement of workers outside the home county; and, for farm operators, the characteristics of the farm or the type of farming operation. In the absence of current national data, Taeuber drew on recent surveys by Division and other researchers in Kentucky, North Carolina, and elsewhere and on studies of FSA borrowers.

National-level work was complemented during 1942–44 by quick field studies, seven in all, in at least twenty widely distributed counties. These were sample areas for the Division's rural life trends project initiated to keep abreast of adjustments being made in rural areas to wartime conditions.[3] Farm labor was one of the five areas of interest surveyed.[4] The reports for each county, prepared solely for administrative use, tracked the farm labor adjustments being made by farmers and by local-level agencies. They became the source for special reports prepared by the Washington staff for federal agency administrators on such topics as the shift of males of military age to agricultural work and the wartime use of women in agriculture. The data were incorporated into an analysis which identified cultural factors which were resulting in artificial farm labor shortages and indicated how wartime pressures were breaking down some of the cultural barriers to under-use of farm labor sources (Raper and Forsyth 1943).

Still other examples of the Division's farm labor studies are provided by its work on policy and program issues related to farm wage levels during wartime. These levels were a public policy issue by 1942 because they were rising. This was important because of the perceived relation of wages to inflation and also to stability in the farm labor situation. Early in the war, a Division staff member worked with other BAE staff to assemble in one place the most pertinent data available through October 1942 on farm wages (Brooks et al. 1943). Before a decision was made by the War Food Administrator to apply wage controls to agriculture, as permitted by the Wage Stabilization Act of 1942, the British experience in fixing farm wages was examined to see what lessons it offered to the United States (Ham 1942). Also, material on methods and criteria for determining ceiling wage rates was prepared for administrative use. Soon after the first of ninety-six farm wage ceiling orders was issued, the Division began field studies to analyze and evaluate the farm wage stabilization program. Each wage ceiling order applied to a specific crop, operation, and area. Reports on the first studies were promptly prepared for administrative use, e.g., on the operation in 1943 of the wage ceiling order for harvesting cannery tomatoes in California. These were followed by an analysis of the first two years of farm wage stabilization in California where much of the research was done (Metzler 1946) and by more inclusive analyses (Ducoff 1945:107–13; Ham 1945).[5]

A major exception to the emphasis on service work and evaluation studies for wartime farm labor programs was Louis Ducoff's (1945) USDA technical publication *Wages of Agricultural Labor in the United States*. This comprehensive analysis of wage rates and wages used existing data covering more than thirty years. Among the aspects treated were the course of changes in farm wages when adjusted for changes in living costs, 1910–43; variations in wage rates in relation to size and type of farm; and factors associated with state variations in wage rates. Other topics included the hired laborers' share of national farm income and a comparison of farm wage rates with the hourly earnings of factory and food processing workers. In discussing the implications of the analysis for postwar agricultural wage policy, Ducoff asserted that from the standpoint of public policy, the record over the three decades preceding the war was one of neglect of the interest and welfare of farm laborers (115). The project was conducted in consultation with a BAE committee led by the Division's head, Carl Taylor.

HIRED FARM WORKER WAGES AND WAGE RATES

A new series of farm wage studies was launched before World War II came to an end. In 1944, interagency working groups of technical specialists were organized by Stuart Rice, who headed the Statistical Standards unit in the Bureau of the Budget, to identify the federal government's statistical needs in the postwar conversion period (Martin 1987). One of these groups was concerned with labor data issues. Recommendations of this and other groups were transmitted by the Bureau of the Budget to the Congress. One result was an appropriation to the BAE specifically to collect, analyze, and publish detailed data on agricultural wages and wage rates.

With this special funding, in 1945 the BAE conducted three national surveys on farm wage rates. To catch seasonal variations, one was made in early spring, one in late spring, and one in the fall. These were supplemented by seventy-four local surveys in sixteen states of the wages of harvest workers in special crop areas. This new research was a collective effort within the BAE, an effort in which the Division had a major role. The surveys were planned by a Bureau-wide Wage Project Committee chaired by the Division's Louis Ducoff. Its membership included others from the Division, among them Margaret Hagood. Field operations were conducted with cooperation of the state agricultural statisticians located in each state as a part of the BAE's crop and livestock reporting and estimating system. Division staff, however, authored nearly all of the reports issued on the 1945 national and special wage surveys. Thereafter, the national surveys were continued, but responsibility was shifted to one of the BAE's statistical divisions. This transfer coincided with the drastic cutbacks then being experienced in the Division's budget and staff.

The methods used for the new national farm wage surveys differed greatly from those for the BAE's ongoing farm wage rate series. The data were collected by interviews with a carefully designed sample of farmers rather than by a mail questionnaire to farmers on the BAE's list of crop and livestock reporters. The interviewers inquired as to the wages, time worked, and related matters for each hired worker employed on that farm during the reporting week. Whereas the mail questionnaires called for the average wages in the reporter's locality, the new method permitted wage comparisons among groups of hired workers classified according to variables such as age, gender, race, and duration of employment. This was essential for an analysis of the wage structure in agriculture. A sample of 158 counties was developed specifically for these national surveys (Ducoff and Hagood 1945:52–55). Within counties, the farmers interviewed included all in sample geographic segments selected by the master sample technique that had been newly devised by the Statistical Laboratory, Iowa State College, in cooperation with the BAE and the Bureau of the Census (King and Jessen 1945). The sampling rates for farmers within counties were determined so as to permit publishable estimates not only for the nation but for each of the four major regions into which the states were grouped. About twenty thousand farmers were interviewed for each of the three surveys. Procedures were developed for expanding the data thus obtained into national and regional estimates.

The three surveys provided a wealth of new information pertaining to hired farm workers. They made possible, for the first time, analysis of the seasonal changes in wage rates and wage differentials in agriculture (Ducoff and Reagan 1946). For instance, hourly cash wages increased in all four regions from early spring to fall, but the increase was nearly 30 percent for seasonal workers as compared with 12 percent for regular workers, defined as those expected to be employed by the reporting farmer for six months or more during the year. They also showed seasonal changes in the composition of the hired farm work force. Nearly half of all hired workers were working in crews or gangs in the fall as compared with one-fourth in the early spring. The fall hired work force included five times as many women as in early spring. There were sharp regional differences in wage rates, earnings, and labor force composition. The contrasts were generally greatest between the South and the West.

The same surveys were also the basis for an analysis of the wage structure within each of seven major type-of-farming regions, i.e., Corn Belt, Cotton Belt, general and self-sufficing region, range livestock region, Western Specialty Crop areas, and the wheat region (Reagan 1947). The analysis within regions was with special reference to the type of farm and the type of work done by the hired workers. In the Corn Belt, for instance, the average cost of a day of hired farm labor varied between $2.65 and $5.50 among the farm types. In the Cotton Belt, hourly cash wages were higher for whites than for nonwhites, higher for males than for females. Little information had previously been available on a nation-wide basis to answer questions about the frequency and value of perquisites, i.e., noncash benefits as a part of the hired farm worker's wages or the farmer's labor costs. Accordingly, in the May 1945 survey a special schedule on perquisites was taken for a subsample (Reagan 1946). Perquisites included house or room, meals, food products from the farm, garden space, fuel, and other items. The analysis considered questions such as what proportion of the workers received perquisites, what proportion of the farms furnished them, and how important were the perquisites as a part of the wages?

The sampling for the national wage surveys could miss special crop areas where the harvest season was short and production was highly concentrated geographically. Hence, local surveys were made in 1945 in sixteen states in areas growing such crops as asparagus, cherries, lettuce, and peaches. The special crop areas had high demands for seasonal harvest labor and were important users of migratory farm workers. In these surveys, the wage and related information was usually collected by interviewing growers who reported on harvest workers they had employed during one week, usually at or near the harvest peak. In four states, workers housed in USDA Labor Supply Centers were also interviewed as to their wages for a specified week. The sampling methods were adapted to the local situation, and therefore varied from survey to survey. Information collected included wages of the harvesters of each of the special crops covered, worker characteristics, and certain characteristics of the farms using the workers. Interrelationships of wages with worker and farm characteristics were shown in the reports. The studies provided new information on worker output that could be used in developing estimates of the labor requirements of agriculture. An analysis and statistical summary for thirty-three of the special crop surveys was given in a single report (Ducoff and Persh 1946). The others were usually reported separately. These surveys showed that piece wage rates were more common that time rates for harvest workers. They showed the dependence in many special crop areas on minority races or nationality groups for extra harvest workers and, at that time, use in some areas of prisoners of war and of foreign workers brought in by the federal government under special international agreements (Ducoff and Persh 1946:6–7). Until these national surveys in 1945, no attempt had ever been made to get a national count of migratory farm workers (Ducoff 1951:218). The data from the BAE's national and special crop surveys were used in a paper on such workers for the *Journal of Farm Economics* (Ducoff 1947).

In reviewing the initial reports in this new wage rate series, Paul Taylor (1946:277–80) at the University of California, prominent in the farm labor area, appraised them as substantial studies of agricultural labor. They were executed with "skill and understanding." The reviewer saw the series as "notable," as "a serious effort to bring to agricultural wage labor the protecting coverage of that statistical network which long ago the Department of Agriculture threw over wheat, cotton, hogs, potatoes, and the operators of farms."

THE HIRED FARM WORKING FORCE SERIES

The wage series reports included information on the number and composition of the hired farm workers during the week of the survey. A second new series provided data on those who did any farm work for wages in the course of an entire year. To collect the desired data, the BAE arranged to have the Bureau of the Census add questions in the enumerative surveys for the Monthly Report on the Labor Force (later changed to Current Population Survey). These surveys had a national sample of about twenty-five thousand households, farm and nonfarm. Each person fourteen years of age and over in these households who had done any farm wage work during the survey year was queried as to this employment and the wages received. A definition of farm work was provided enumerators (Ducoff and Hagood 1946a:35–36). The data from the sample were expanded to give national estimates.

The first of the new series covered the 1945 calendar year (Ducoff and Hagood 1946a). The survey showed 3.2 million persons had done some farm work for wages during the year.[6] These were analyzed as to occupation as of the following January, residence, age, gender, household status, World War II veteran's status, days of farm work for wages, number of farms worked on, wages earned for farm work, and other factors. In subsequent surveys, additional topics were included. Thus, although it was known that many hired farm workers also did nonfarm work for wages, information was needed about this overlap. Accordingly, the survey for 1946 added a question for each farm wage worker as to the days of nonfarm work and the year's earnings from such work (Ducoff and Hagood 1947a:20–21). It was found that about one-fourth of the farm workers also had nonfarm work earnings. It appeared, however, that those who shifted between farm and nonfarm labor got only the lowest paid kinds of nonfarm work (7).

In the survey for 1948 a question was asked relating to farm and nonfarm wage work done in each quarter of the year. The reason was the interest in getting an estimate of the number of farm workers who would be covered under the complex terms of a law extending old age and survivors insurance to more regularly employed hired farm workers (Bowles et al. 1950:3–5). This was followed the next year with an inquiry as to the total earnings during the year from farm and from nonfarm work.

The 1949 survey also introduced a question designed to identify migratory farm workers (Ducoff 1950:16–18). Survey enumerators were instructed to report as migratory a farm wage worker who left home to hoe or harvest crops in some other county during the year. The analysis in *Migratory Farm Workers in 1949* provided the first significant comparisons between migratory and other hired farm workers in the nation as to characteristics, employment, and earnings (Ducoff 1950). The sample represented about 420,000 migrant workers aged fourteen and over. Ducoff cautioned, however, that this was probably less than half of all such workers. For example, many Mexican nationals had left before the survey was made in December. The survey for 1952 asked the farthest distance from home the migrants traveled to get work during the year. Three out of five reported they traveled less than 100 miles (Ducoff 1953a). The attention given migrants in the new series coincided with the postwar national attention to the subject which led President Harry S. Truman, in 1950, to establish the President's Commission on Migratory Labor. The BAE loaned the Division's Louis Ducoff to serve as consultant to this Commission.[7] Another response to the public interest in migratory farm laborers was the compilation of an updated annotated bibliography of more than 450 references (Folsom 1953).

Because of the pending coverage of "regular" hired farm workers under old age and survivors insurance, the 1950 survey obtained special information about such persons. They were defined as those who had worked for wages continuously for six months or more on one farm during the year. The regular farm workers were found to be, in general, older than other farm wage workers but younger than nonagricultural workers covered by the insurance program (Ducoff and Birch 1952). Of the estimated 774,000 regular workers, some 95 percent were male. Nearly two-thirds of these were married. And of the then-married or previously married men, 60 percent had children under eighteen years of age, a fact important from the standpoint of insurance benefits in the event of the death or retirement of the insured.

A new feature of the 1951 survey was the collection of information on the number of farmer employers a worker had during the year. This was regarded as an indicator of labor turnover (Ducoff and Birch 1952:2,5). Among those who did twenty-five days or more of farm wage work, more than three-fourths had but one employer during that year.

The series of annual surveys on the nation's hired farm workers, starting in 1945, was essential for the Division to provide correct information as to what was going on with respect to the number, composition, amount of work, and related matters. Thus, the report for 1946, the first full year of peace after World War II, showed a sharp reduction from the preceding year in the number of short-term seasonal workers and of female workers (Ducoff and Hagood 1947:3). These workers were replaced by returning veterans and others who returned to farm work after the war. The impact of defense mobilization for the Korean War on the size and composition of the hired farm working force was discovered in the survey for 1950 (Ducoff and Birch 1952:3). Ducoff drew upon the hired farm working force and other Division research for the chapters on employment in agriculture (1953b) and on wages in agriculture (1953c) he contributed to the Twentieth Century Fund's book on employment and wages in the United States.

In contrast with the national labor force surveys in methods and other respects was an exploratory study in 1948 of the hired farm workers in an area of highly specialized crop production, California's San Joaquin Valley (Metzler and Sayin 1950).[8] The household was the study unit rather than the customary individual worker on the grounds that in such agricultural work the earning unit was usually the family. The research plan called for interviews with a sample of about five hundred households to be drawn from all the hired farm workers in an area 265 miles long by 60 miles wide, taking in parts of nine counties.

Sampling posed difficult problems which required a special design to fit the area's labor situation. Some crops were concentrated in one part, some in another. Different crops ripened at different times. This was a factor in the movement of workers from one harvest job to another. The working force was made up of Anglo Americans, Latin Americans, African Americans, and Filipinos. Local custom and the attitudes of employers and workers had introduced rigidities into the system which influenced the type of worker used in particular harvest operations. (Metzler and Sayin (1950:3–4).

The aim in sampling was to give all of the area's hired farm workers an equal chance to be included. First, fourteen geographic areas were selected, each for its major crop and activity such as apricot picking or cotton picking. Second, each of the fourteen areas was sampled close to the height of its major local harvest and just as interviewing was to start. Third, an attempt was made to draw a sample from each harvest in proportion to the total number of workers employed in it. Workers were usually interviewed at their homes or in their housing quarters at farm labor camps.

A random sample was not easily obtained in every area; adaptations had to be made. With area to area variations in the sampling used to get the 512 households interviewed, no attempt was made to expand the figures from the sample to get totals for the Valley.

The interviewers obtained, among other items, the farm and nonfarm work record for each household member during the past twelve months. Further, information was obtained as to the major occupation prewar, wartime, and postwar. The interviews were also used in the report to provide case experiences which supplemented the quantitative analysis. The study not only provided a wealth of information about the Valley's labor force in 1948 and its variations but, overall, it suggested the complexity of the area's farm labor system.

DEFINITION AND MEASUREMENT

Reliable and valid measurement of the farm labor force, hired and unpaid, required careful technical attention to concepts and definitions. The Division staff in the farm labor area pursued these matters vigorously. For example, an experiment was conducted in 1944 jointly with the Bureau of the Census to test and compare different methods of securing data to estimate the nation's unpaid family workers in agriculture (Ducoff and Bancroft 1945). Such measurement had assumed increased importance during the war. The experiment involved interviews with a subsample of all households in the April 1944 Monthly Labor Report Survey that had a farm operator. Major purposes were to get a complete measurement of all farm work performed by any member of the farm operator's household as well as to explore labor classification problems for the farm population. The research found an estimated 3.3 million persons did one or more hours of unpaid family work during the survey week but who were recorded as nonworkers in the Monthly Labor Report data. Of these, 1.5 million worked at least nineteen hours during the week. This led to a revision by the Bureau of the Census in the Monthly Labor Report survey schedule (Ducoff and Hagood 1947b:26–28). Previously, another cooperative project with the Bureau of the Census had matched a sample of schedules from the 1940 censuses of agriculture and population. Individuals in the farm operator households were identified as to whether they were reported as family workers on the agricultural schedule. This was compared with their labor force classification on the population schedule. The results showed that 2.7 million persons who showed up as family workers on the agricultural schedule were not classified as farm operators or unpaid family workers on the population schedule (Ducoff and Hagood 1947b:25–26). In fact, 1.7 million of these were classified as not in the labor force, among them about one million women.

The definitions used in past studies of migratory farm workers by the BAE, the Bureau of the Census, and others were reviewed as part of a presentation to the Population Association of America (Ducoff 1951). Issues posed by the problem of definition of migratory workers were laid out. For example, in identifying who was a migratory farm worker, should intentions be considered or only the objective record over some defined past period? A case was made for fuller exploration of these issues at both the conceptual level and the level at which concepts are translated into workable definitions for survey use.

Recognition of the special expertise and the experience of the Division staff resulted in their involvement in labor force definition and measurement issues beyond agriculture. Thus, Louis Ducoff and Margaret Hagood were made members of an ongoing interagency Technical Committee on Labor Supply, Employment, and Unemployment Statistics. This was set up in the early 1940s to advise the Bureau of the Census on the Monthly Report on the Labor Force survey (Martin 1987). This survey had been transferred in 1942 from the WPA to the Census Bureau.

When the SSRC Committee on Labor Market Research appointed a working group in the hope of stimulating steps toward conceptual and terminological clarity in labor market studies, Ducoff and Hagood were among the members selected. The subject was important because current labor force data were used by government officials, business, labor, researchers, and others in the analysis of many economic and social problems. Ducoff and Hagood drafted the report *Labor Force Definition and Measurement* (1947b) for the subcommittee chaired by Gladys L. Palmer, University of Pennsylvania. The report dealt primarily with labor force definition and classification problems in current enumerative surveys such as the monthly survey of the labor force by the Census Bureau. Objectives of the report were to increase understanding of the problems relating to adoption of a common set of concepts by the producers or users of labor force statistics, to explain steps in the refinement and improvement of labor force measurement, and to formulate problems in labor force concepts and measurement in need of research.

The emergence of full employment as a national goal for the peacetime economy, as expressed by enactment of the Full Employment Act of 1946, led Division staff to analyze issues in labor force statistics specifically related to that goal. Thus, at the American Statistical Association's annual meeting, Ducoff and Hagood (1946b) discussed, for example, the uses of such statistics for diagnostic and projective purposes with regard to both short-term and long-term change in employment and unemployment. They set forth conceptual and classification additions needed to serve such purposes. The analysis was extended further in a presentation at the ASA's annual meeting (Hagood and Ducoff 1946). In this paper, types of sociological research which could contribute to achieving and maintaining full employment were also considered.

OTHER WORK IN THE FARM LABOR AREA

Still other aspects of farm labor were touched on. For example, an exploratory study developed estimates of farm worker productivity for the United States and geographic divisions and by size of farm enterprise (Ducoff and Hagood 1944b). This study was based on statistical analysis of special sample tabulations from the 1940 Census of Agriculture and on new BAE estimates of farm expenses. The methods of analysis and the assumptions were described in detail (35–54).[9] An index of labor turnover of regular hired workers was developed in a cooperative project in Connecticut (Burnight et al. 1953:32–34). Contributions to knowledge about the structure of American agriculture were a by-product of the analyses of farm labor data. For instance, the wage rate studies in 1945 gave one measure of the extent to which the use of hired labor was distributed among farms (Woytinsky and Ducoff 1953:345). In that year, one percent of the farms accounted for 37 percent of the man-days of hired labor.

Quite in contrast with the quantitative emphasis was the activity related to collective action by farm laborers. Prior to his transfer to the Division, J. C. Folsom (1935) had kept a record of the number and location of strikes of agricultural workers and of organization activities involving them. After his transfer, a file of reference material on the subject continued to be built up as an aid in answering requests for information received by the Division.[10] Distinctly different from any of the other work on farm labor we have cited was the "diary of a farm hand" by Charles Loomis (1940). This record was kept by Loomis when he worked on an Amish farm at the time of the Division's study of the Old Order Amish, a study in which the participant observer method was used (Kollmorgen 1942). It was 1979 before the diary saw publication.

The outbreak of the Korean War in 1950 resulted once more in a wartime need for facts about the current labor situation in agriculture.

This time the Division's capacity to respond was limited by the drastic cutbacks in resources it had suffered since coming under attack. The budget for farm labor studies in 1950 was down to $33,000 (U.S. Congress, House 1951:1973), far less than the annual allocation during World War II. "Defense" funds were, however, secured. These enabled cooperative projects on farm labor supply and use with several state agricultural experiment stations and field studies with the Department of Labor. One study interviewed a sample of truck-crop operators in Maryland's Eastern Shore to appraise the supply and use of seasonal harvest labor during the 1952 season (Rohrer and Motheral 1953). This was an area heavily dependent on Florida-based harvest workers who moved in the Atlantic Coast migratory farm labor stream. Another study was in the High Plains of Texas, a cotton-growing area heavily dependent on Spanish-speaking seasonal workers (Motheral et al. 1953). The area was beginning to use mechanical cotton harvesters. The Texas study sought to appraise the use of seasonal labor during the 1951 season by interviews with a sample of employers selected by the sample segment technique. A principal result was to identify the area's prevailing land tenure system as an institutional barrier to full mechanization of cotton production. In Connecticut research, concern was with regular hired workers on dairy farms (Burnight et al. 1953). One focus was to assess the effect of the Korean War on losses and turnover of these workers on the state's commercial dairy farms, defined as those having twenty or more milk cows. In a survey in seventeen Eastern Kentucky counties, the focus was not on hired farm workers but on all persons fourteen years of age and over in open-country households (Galloway and Beers 1953). Counties within the same area had been surveyed early in World War II to assess the manpower potentially available for war work elsewhere. This was an almost wholly rural area with a high rate of natural increase in population, limited productive farmland, and lack of industrial employment opportunities. Through interviews with a random sample of households, selected by the sample segment technique, data were collected on the characteristics, employment, and past work experience of the survey population. It was concluded that despite extensive out-migration between 1940 and 1950, the area's rural population continued to constitute an underdeveloped manpower resource (48).

SUMMARY

When the Division was started in 1919, the social aspect of farm labor was a field of study recommended for it. Research directly focused on this area was not done, however, until the last half of the 1930s when resources became available. Farm labor then became a major program area; this continued until the BAE was terminated.

The pre–World-War-II research gave particular attention to the living conditions of hired farm workers. It also studied the effects of the AAA's cotton and tobacco acreage reduction measures and of tractor use on the number and tenure of farm workers. Wartime conditions brought a sharp reorientation of the Division's farm labor work and gave it increased importance. The Division had a major role for the BAE in providing and interpreting the farm labor data needed by federal, state, and county data users having responsibilities for an adequate farm labor supply. The wartime situation brought an increase in studies of local situations and in service-type activities along with a de-emphasis on conventional publication of study findings.

In the midst of war, the Division sought to develop continuing statistically sound data collection systems in collaboration with other governmental units. The result was an unprecedented type and quality of information for the nation and regions, not only about the size and composition of the farm labor force, but about such matters for hired workers as employment patterns, migrant status, and old age and survivors' insurance coverage. Numerous farm labor studies were also made in highly specialized crop production areas such as California's San Joaquin Valley.

To improve the quality of farm labor data, significant work was done on problems of definition and measurement of the hired and total farm labor force. The special expertise of the Division staff on these problems was drawn upon by such bodies as the Bureau of the Census, the Social Science Research Council, and the President's Commission on Migratory Labor.

Notes

1. By April 1941 tentative reports had been prepared for the labor reconnaissance surveys in thirty-five areas (FPRLA 1941:15, No. 2, 2). We have not, however, located any of these. The increasing dependence found in some areas on itinerant seasonal farm workers led W. T. Ham (1941) to raise issues concerning employer responsibility to reduce the burden on the community of the workers' seasonal unemployment.

2. A concise overview of the USDA's farm labor program during World War II is given in Baker et al. (1963:308–10).

3. Documentation on the rural life trends project is incomplete. Although we located one or more reports for twenty counties, it is apparent from the Division's regions represented by these counties that there were others in the sample. Report No. 6 for Dallas County, Alabama notes that the material was gathered during six days in the county (Montgomery 1943). The investigator conducted interviews with thirty-three farmers, including eight who were black, from different tenure groups. A set of questions was also asked

of thirty-one other informants such as the county agricultural agents, the FSA supervisor, a War Board member, the Emergency Farm Labor assistant, and a Selective Service Staff person.

4. The other areas surveyed by the rural trends project were agricultural production adjustments, consumer adjustments, community and institutional adjustments, and civilian participation in wartime activities such as War Bond sales and salvage drives.

5. Ham's paper was published after he left the Division to join the War Food Administration staff.

6. The 3.2 million estimate for 1945 excluded persons under fourteen years of age, imported foreign workers, persons who entered the armed forces or died during the year, persons in institutions, and some others who may have done hired farm work during the years. The excluded were estimated to number between 0.8 million and one million persons (Ducoff and Hagood 1946a:1–2).

7. Further recognition of the competence of the Division's achievements in migrant farm labor research was indicated by the selection of former staff member Varden Fuller to be Executive Secretary of the President's Commission on Migratory Labor. Former staff member William Metzler also did work for the Commission.

8. The San Joaquin Valley research was done in cooperation with the Institute of Industrial Relations, University of California. The study was planned to be the first of several in various sections of the state (Metzler and Sayin 1950:17).

9. The Division's plan of work approved for 1949 by the BAE included a project to repeat and expand this analysis of farm worker productivity with data for 1944.

10. Folsom's long-term efforts to collect reference material on strikes and organizational activities of hired agricultural workers were always subsidiary to his primary responsibilities in the farm labor area. In 1949, however, an interest in postwar developments led BAE Chief Oris V. Wells to approve a Division project (line number A-3-2-4) designed to build on and expand Folsom's previous work, The objective was to study recent developments pertaining to employer-employee relations in agriculture, progress of unionization of agricultural workers and of workers in agricultural processing industries, and factors underlying any labor disputes in agriculture. The plan called for secondary source materials to be gathered, as Folsom had done, from the press, from publications of federal and state labor agencies, as well as from private organizations. The project, under the leadership of Louis J. Ducoff, was seen as supplementing the Division's other farm labor research by providing information not amenable to mass statistics-gathering procedures.

10

The Sociology of Agriculture

The Division's research pertaining to the social aspects of agriculture touched upon a wide range of topics that may be placed under the umbrella of "sociology of agriculture," a term not in use during the Division's time. It was not unusual, for instance, to use some aspect of agriculture as a variable in data analysis. Examples are tenure in levels of living comparisons and size of farms in labor studies. We chose to treat in a separate chapter the studies focusing on farm labor to recognize the importance of such work in the Division's program. In this chapter we examine the work in areas as diverse as farm tenancy, culture and agriculture, part-time farming, and agriculture and the community.

FARM TENANCY

The injunction by Secretary Houston's advisory committee that the USDA's new farm life studies unit include the field of farm tenancy in its work reflected the Secretary's assertion that "the increase in farm tenancy has become the subject of deep concern to thoughtful students of rural conditions" (Houston 1920:22). A trend away from owner-operated farms in the United States had been shown since 1880 by the decennial census figures. This was attributed to the virtual exhaustion of the supply of good farmland in the public domain (Spillman and Goldenweiser 1917:321). The concept of "agricultural ladder" came into use about the time of Houston's advisory committee report. This concept considered tenancy as one rung in the ascent from unpaid laborer on the home farm or hired laborer to farm ownership (Spillman 1919).

Galpin wasted no time in getting tenancy studies underway. Staff member Walter Baumgartel (1925), in 1919, initiated a case study of the development, organization, and policies of a large-scale wheat-growing farming corporation in North Dakota which operated with more than sixty tenant holdings.[1] The investigator contended that the study's assessment of the experiences of this large corporate estate offered suggestion for the managers of large land-holdings elsewhere, especially in wheat-growing areas.

Galpin's Cooperative Farm Tenancy Studies

Cooperative projects were promptly initiated, most notably in Missouri (C. Taylor et al. 1920), North Carolina (C. Taylor and Zimmerman 1922), Iowa (von Tungeln 1923), and in Nebraska.[2] The Nebraska work stood out for its comprehensive nature. The BAE's land economics unit, headed by L. C. Gray, joined with the Division to support the research conducted by Nebraska's J. O. Rankin. A socioeconomic survey in 1920 interviewed over 1,100 farm families distributed among ten localities chosen to represent a wide range of conditions in the state. The data analysis included comparisons of owners, part owners, share-cash tenants, share tenants, and cash tenants. For some purposes, managers and hired men were added to the comparisons. More than half a dozen reports on the Nebraska study were issued as agricultural experiment station bulletins. Among the topics included were interrelationships of tenure and the family (Rankin 1923a); living conditions, especially housing and the home grounds (Rankin 1923b); the community phases of tenure (Rankin 1923c); characteristics of the landlords of the tenant-operated land (Rankin 1924); and the steps to farm ownership or the stages of the agricultural ladder experienced by these Nebraska farmers on the way to land ownership (Rankin 1926).

Galpin seemed to see these early cooperative state studies of tenancy as stressing the living conditions of farm tenants (H. Taylor 1924:190). The Missouri study revealed such unsuspected contrasts between the living conditions of landowners and those of tenants and hired men that the Dean of the state's college of agriculture distanced himself from the draft report (see Chapter 4). As a consequence, Galpin was unable to get USDA approval for publication. The North Carolina work was done at the request of the state's Board of Agriculture to study the whole subject of farm tenancy and proposed remedies. Unlike the Missouri study, the North Carolina research included black farmers in the sample. The Iowa study was intended to provide residents in the survey area with information on which to construct a long-term improvement program. It surveyed all 400 open-country families in part of one county.

In his first annual report Galpin stated that the investigations in the social aspects of farm tenancy were "perhaps the most important studies carried on" during the year (H. Taylor 1921:572). Shortly, however, the

Division dropped completely out of the field of farm tenancy. Within the BAE, the organization chart for 1922–23 had land tenure placed in the Division of Land Economics (H. Taylor 1924:137). Galpin later expressed regret about the dropout decision. After retirement he confided to his successor, Carl Taylor, that others seemed to feel that they should have a monopoly on the field. At the time, he did not care to fight. But he had come to conclude that this decision had been a mistake because farm tenancy was a field to which rural sociologists should make their contributions (Taylor 1948c:152). Galpin encouraged Taylor to find ways to again do work on farm tenancy.

Tenure Research Resumed During Depression Years

Soon after Taylor was made Division head in 1935, and also put in charge of the FSA's social research work, he reinstituted farm tenancy studies. By then, about 42 percent of the nation's farms were tenant-operated, and over 200,000 were added between 1930 and 1935 to the tenant numbers. The insecurity of the nation's farm families had been accentuated by the Great Depression and by the droughts of the 1930s. President Roosevelt was moved, in November 1936 to appoint a special committee on farm tenancy. This was chaired by Secretary H. A. Wallace. The committee was to report in less than three months "on a long-term program of action to alleviate the shortcomings of our farm tenancy system" (President's Committee on Farm Tenancy 1937:25).[3]

In this setting of concern at the highest policy-making levels about farm tenancy, Taylor took three actions. First, he included a chapter on farm tenants in *Disadvantaged Classes in American Agriculture* (Taylor et al. 1938:37–70). Second, he had a review made of major existing studies that had quantitative data on the social correlates of farm tenure (*FPRLA* 1936:10, No. 4, 1–2). And third, by late 1936, he had an FSA-Division large-scale interview study in the field which resulted in a report of some 250 pages, *Social Status and Farm Tenure—Attitudes and Social Conditions of Corn Belt and Cotton Belt Farmers* (Schuler 1938b).

The chapter, based on census and available research data, gave an overview nationally of tenure trends since 1880 and the geographic spread of heavily tenanted areas. It showed a vast difference in the characteristics of the Northern and Southern tenant belts. The literature review included about fifty reports[4] on research in twenty-one states. The reports provided data for forty-four items which were analyzed in the context of a social status concept (Schuler 1938a). These quantitative measures pertained to goods and services consumed and to social participation. Measures of other criteria of social status were not available, e.g., prestige held and ideology and class solidarity. The item analysis relied on the consistency of findings among states. The states were divided into Northern and Southern. Schuler concluded by this consistency test that Southern tenants had a lower social status than did Southern owners whereas Northern tenants were not consistently found to have a status below that of their owner neighbors.

Schuler's field investigation, under Carl Taylor's general direction, of over 2,400 farm families was characterized by Taylor as a study in social psychology that dealt with aspects of land tenure for which specific information had not been available. Taylor contended that effective program assistance for those of lower tenure status "should be based as much upon the attitudes and aspirations of the family to be assisted as upon the character of the land or the particular tenure contract" (foreword in Schuler 1938b). This assumption shaped the interview schedule, which had a special focus on attitudes, opinions, and aspirations related to such land tenure matters as the desirability of farm ownership, actions the government should take to check the increase of farm tenancy, personal preferences as to farm size, and landlord-tenant relationships. Among other subjects covered by the wide-ranging inquiry were lifetime experience on the "agricultural ladder," family living goods possessed and desired, and group life.

The families interviewed with a thirteen-page schedule were located in the South's Cotton Belt and flue-cured tobacco area and in the North's Corn Belt. Family selection and data analysis treated these families as comprising three sample populations, white farmers in the South, black farmers in the South, and Northern farmers. The study families lived in fourteen small block sample areas distributed among twelve states. This study predated the sophisticated master sample technique devised in the 1940s with BAE cooperation. This fact helps explain the elaborate procedures used in arriving at the sample and the sample areas (Schuler 1938b:244–49). Among these procedures, which were not uniform for the three sample populations, was reliance on the judgment of agricultural experiment station staff for area selection. One feature of this study was that all interviews with black families were made by blacks who had black supervisors. Another feature was that some areas of inquiry, e.g., family living, were addressed specifically to the "housewife."

Data analysis was designed to compare tenure classes within and between the three racial and regional sample populations. Numerous distinctive differences were found. Evidence is lacking, however, as to how, or if, the findings found action-oriented program use. But from the standpoint of contribution to knowledge, a reviewer asserted that Schuler's study revealed "the psychological, sociological, and economic basis for the class structures in rural farm society in the Cotton and Corn Belts" (Loomis 1938a:200–201). For the first time, the reviewer said, the probe was extensive enough "to determine the structure and rigidity of the American rural farm social and economic hierarchy."

Four years elapsed between Schuler's publication on his interview study of farm tenure and the next published work, a provocative, theoretically oriented paper presented by regional staff member T. G. Standing (1942a) at a Southwestern Social Science Association meeting. Standing argued that it was necessary to go beyond measuring the social correlatives of farm tenure. His purpose was to suggest areas of sociological research that could contribute to understanding the significance of land tenure in influencing the relationships of people and that, as a by-product, could further the development of sociological theory, for example, with respect to social change. Standing's sweeping set of suggestions were made within an overall theoretical framework of land tenancy as a social institution with a structure of supporting symbols, beliefs, and rationalizations. Among the suggestions was a combined sociological-historical approach to the study of the institutional aspects of tenancy, the study of change in tenure relationships, the effect of such crises as depression and war on tenancy, and use of the social process concepts of "conflict" and "competition" in the analysis of relationships among tenure classes.

Trends in Tenure Status in the United States

After Standing's paper, there was no substantial work specific to farm tenancy by the Division until the postwar years. The subject was not among the priority areas for the Division during wartime.[5] But after the war, the first comprehensive analysis of the operation of the "agricultural ladder" in the United States was made by Taylor and his associates, Louis Ducoff and Margaret Hagood (1948). Their *Trends in the Tenure Status of Farm Workers in the United States Since 1880* presented data for each of the forty-eight states, the census regions, and the nation for a sixty-year time span. Estimates were developed of the number of males who were farm owners, farm tenants, and farm laborers (paid and unpaid) per thousand males twenty years of age and over gainfully employed in agriculture. The estimating methods were adaptations of those used by economists John D. Black and R. H. Allen (1937) for their study limited to eight states and the nation as a whole. Data sources were the occupational data from population censuses and data on farm operators from agricultural censuses. Estimates were restricted to males twenty years of age and over to minimize the noncomparabilities from one census to another with respect to completeness of the counts of unpaid family workers.

The analysis showed that farm workers in the United States experienced a general downward shift in tenure status consistently from 1880 to 1940, a trend toward a decreasing proportion of owners and toward an increasing proportion of tenants and laborers. In some areas, the shift was mainly to tenancy, in others it was mainly to farm labor status. The researchers offered an interpretation of the decade by decade tenure shifts which they found.

The report also dealt with the reversal of past trends after 1940, i.e., the drastic decrease in the proportion of tenants among farm operators. Their analysis of the reduction in the tenancy rate after 1940 led them to assert that the change could not be interpreted solely in terms of the traditional agricultural ladder theory (24). They identified causes of the reversal of past trends which were not encompassed within the ladder concept, for example, the relatively heavier outmigration from the farm population of tenants and laborers than of owner-operators (Taylor et al. 1948:23–24).

Tenure Studies in Argentina and Japan

Research by Division staff members on farm land ownership and tenancy issues extended to Argentina and Japan. Carl Taylor was in Argentina for a year, 1942–43 on a special research assignment for the Department of State to make a systematic study of that country's rural life. His report, which approached a textbook in rural sociology for Argentina, included an analysis of the relation of farm people to the land (C. Taylor 1948a: 174–208).

In Japan, after World War II, the Imperial Japanese Government was directed by the Allied Forces to undertake certain agrarian reforms. The most important of these was land reform, an action to abolish what the Allied Forces called a "pernicious land tenure system" (Raper et al. 1950:259). The Natural Resources Section, Supreme Commander for the Allied Forces in Japan, invited Arthur Raper to observe the effects of land and other agrarian reform programs upon the country's rural institutions and organizations. A full report on the research initiated under Raper's leadership was given in the 272-page *The Japanese Village in Transition* (Raper et al. 1950). Papers were also prepared for professional journals for rural sociologists (Raper 1951a) and agricultural economists (Raper 1951b).

The crucial method used by Taylor to acquire knowledge of Argentina's rural life was essentially a national reconnaissance survey. Little detailed empirical information was available. He went to all the major types of farming areas to observe and "to talk to hundreds of farm people on their farms and in their homes" (Taylor 1948a:1). He covered about twenty thousand miles during some hundred days in the field. In this activity, Taylor was assisted by an Argentinean fluent in both English and Spanish. The field observations about land tenure were supplemented by census data for 1914 and 1937 and by historical records.

Taylor found the bulk of farm land ownership to be in the hands of relatively few families (190), a semi-monopoly of the land. The large landholders were the most elite citizens of Argentina, their social status buttressed by their large landholdings (175). Over 44 percent of the farms were reported in 1937 to be tenant-operated. The great extent of farm tenancy was largely the result of hired men moving up the agricultural ladder (192). For most tenants, the agricultural ladder ended there. Taylor concluded that the class structure of hired man, tenant, and owner was quite deeply rooted. At the same time, there was a widespread belief that "a wider distribution of land ownership would help to develop a better and more democratic social order" (174). Taylor contended that the man-land relationships he found could "be understood only in terms of the historic development and institutionalization of land ownership in Argentine culture" (174). His more detailed analysis of field observations and census data was organized around the variables province, type-of-farming, and tenure class.

Raper's research in Japan, like Taylor's in Argentina, had farm tenancy as one component of a more comprehensive study. Raper's work, however, was designed as an evaluation study to provide information about program effectiveness and procedures. It offers one of many examples from the Division's work of the practice of sociology. A major purpose was to determine the changes which resulted in Japan from the five agrarian reform programs required of the Japanese Government by the Allied Forces. One of the five and the most important was land reform, the transfer of land ownership to the families who cultivated the land. A second was the improvement of tenancy practices for the remaining tenants.

Raper led a multidisciplinary team of American and Japanese specialists in sociology, anthropology, agricultural economics, and other areas. He had Signal Corps photographers to visually document life in the villages studied. Two surveys, eighteen months apart, were made of thirteen purposively chosen villages. The first, in May and June 1947, centered on the early administration of the agrarian reforms in relation to rural institutions and organizations, notably family, religion, and land ownership. The second survey, in 1949–50, sought to determine the village-level changes attributed to the required reform program.

The thirteen villages were selected to include one from each major geographic region of Japan and one or more from each major agricultural region. There were also secondary selection criteria, examples being the extent of feudal survivals and the degree of urban influence. For the second survey, a substitution was made to include a farming-fishing village. Village records were the source for data on land ownership, farm tenure, and other items. Personal interviews were held with village leaders and representative households. Also during the second survey one hundred heads of farm households in each village were asked to fill out an opinion questionnaire. The questions pertained to the land reform and associated programs. The sample of heads was selected by a stratified random sampling procedure in each village in such a way as to represent the tenure distribution in 1946 prior to the land reform program (Raper et al. 1950: 246–47). The 1946 tenure status was used in all of the analyses by tenure.

Land ownership had been "the basic background of powerful feudal families throughout Japan" (Raper 1951a:9). The Allied Powers had decided that a prerequisite to launching democratic programs was a breakup of the old feudal system, hence land reform. The study found that in the opinion of the villagers interviewed, land reform was the most significant of the five programs. The researchers concluded that the administration at the village level of the land reform program by an elected commission provided leadership development to tenants and constituted an important adult education experience. In Raper's view, the program had "made a real contribution to the democratization of the Japanese village" (1950a:182).

CULTURE AND AGRICULTURE

The work of the Division took a new turn just before 1940 and for a time thereafter with the addition of cultural anthropologists to the staff. This addition influenced the community studies undertaken at that time and introduced cultural considerations into studies of the New Deal agricultural action programs and into studies of farming methods. This new turn was a specific manifestation of the general interest at the time in the USDA as to the contributions each of the social sciences might make to an integrated approach to the functions and problems of the USDA. This interest was an expression of the intellectual climate fostered by Secretary of Agriculture H. A. Wallace and advocated and led by Under Secretary M. L. Wilson.

On May 17–19, 1939, the BAE sponsored a conference on cultural anthropology. A brief record of this was issued in mimeo form as "Culture and Agriculture: Cultural Anthropology in Relation to Current Agricultural Problems" (Johnstone 1939). This conference was one of a series with representatives of the social science disciplines. The immediate purpose was to acquaint USDA workers with findings in the discipline that might aid the process of agricultural planning and policy-making and the process of efficient administration. Engaged in this anthropology conference dialogue were eminent anthropologists Robert Redfield and Lloyd Warner, both of the University of Chicago; C. M. Arensburg, Massachusetts Institute of Technology; Horace Miner, Wayne University; and Chicago-trained John Provinse. Other social science participants from outside government included black sociologist Charles Johnson from Fisk University; Robert E. Park, sociologist retired from the University of Chicago; and Kimball Young, social psychologist then at the University of Wisconsin. USDA workers attending this conference were drawn from the BAE, the FSA, and other agencies and bureaus in the Department.

Soon after, Miner, Provinse and other anthropologists, and Young were added to the Division staff. The favorable reception within the USDA to cultural anthropology was reinforced by three articles in the USDA's 1940 Yearbook, *Farmers in a Changing World*, planned by a committee chaired by M. L. Wilson. Redfield and Warner wrote "Cultural anthropology and modern agriculture" (1940:983–93). An article on "The cultural setting of American agricultural problems" was prepared by Ralph Turner (1940:1003–32). And in his article "It's beyond economics, building a philosophy of agricultural reform," M. L. Wilson advocated a cultural approach as a guide to the most practical methods of such reform (1940:922–37).

The Division's work soon gave evidence of the addition of cultural anthropologists. Preparation of a bibliography for BAE publication on "Anthropology and Agriculture" was promptly undertaken (MacLeish and Hennefrund 1940). Miner was one of the principal speakers at an October 1939 school for the Washington BAE staff. His topic was "Culture and Agriculture" (Miner 1939:48–56). The purpose of this school, organized by the BAE's Division of Program Study and Discussion, like almost sixty similar schools conducted throughout the United States by that Division, was education for democracy in agriculture.[6] In his presentation Miner used illustrations from his previous work on "peasants" in French Canada and from the field work on the relations between USDA agencies and farmers he had underway for the Division in a Corn Belt county. This is the research reported in his book *Culture and Agriculture* (Miner 1949), the manuscript for which provoked controversy within the USDA when submitted in 1940 for publication (see Chapter 4). Anthropologist Provinse joined with Carl Taylor to address a meeting of the Western Farm Economics Association on "Sociological considerations in a national policy for agriculture" (Provinse and Taylor 1940:109–17). An anthropological influence on the content of this paper was shown by the discussion of the cultural background of the development of American agricultural programs and by the cross-cultural comparisons of American agriculture with agriculture in the "peasant" society of Romania and in an industrialized society, England.

Previously, in Chapter 7, we indicated that the six-community study of community stability and instability was planned by a Division team that included a cultural anthropologist. Further, some of the researchers who did the field work were anthropologists. The influence of this discipline on the project is indicated by the heavy reliance placed upon the participant observation method in the field and by some of the information to be collected. For example, the detailed field manual called for an effort, in repeated and detailed interviews with the sample of informants, "to discuss the attitudes, opinions, and values with respect to . . . cultural patterns having to do with land use, physical and biological phenomena, economic techniques, values as to basic matters such as hard work, thrift, fortitude, and other virtues" (Taylor et al. 1940:4095–ii).

The undergirding for the working hypothesis which was tested in the subsequent seventy-one-county study of rural cultural regions was the assumption of a close relationship between major type-of-farming regions, such as the Cotton Belt, and the conceived rural cultural regions (Raper and Taylor 1949:329–43). The field methods for the cultural reconnaissance survey in each of the seventy-one counties were akin to those for the stability-instability study. The guide for the field interviewers called for the collection of information that included the cultural heritage of the people in the county and value systems with respect to sentimental attachment to the land, the right agricultural techniques to use in the type of agriculture followed, and basic values relating to the use and care of machinery and tools. The unpublished reports on the reconnaissance surveys in these seventy-one counties provided part of the research foundation for a chapter on each of the seven major rural regions and a comparative chapter in *Rural Life in the United States* (C. Taylor et al. 1949). But anthropologist Oscar Lewis, in the book on his reconnaissance survey of Bell County, Texas (1948), did the most detailed analysis of the effects of cultural factors upon types of farming. He compared farmers of Czech and German descent with farmers of old-line American descent with respect to farming customs and value systems related to farming (Lewis 1948:103–5).

Cultural considerations in farming practices were the direct focus of Walter Kollmorgen's (1940) research in which he compared cultural groups in Franklin County, Tennessee. The study compared a "cultural island" group, a German-Swiss community, with three "control" groups of native, traditional, white farmers operating on physically comparable soil. The German-Swiss community was established by immigrants following the Civil War. It was known as a successful agricultural community in the midst of a South with major agricultural problems.

Methods used by Kollmorgen included the field survey which he made of each of the four groups studied and the compilation of detailed statistical data from the original farm schedules of the censuses of 1860, 1930, and 1935. "Cultural considerations" referred to techniques, methods, and attitudes transmitted from generation to generation and reflected in farming practices. The study sustained "the belief that cultural backgrounds are extremely significant in farming enterprises" (Kollmorgen 1940:106). For example, the German-Swiss had shown themselves to be constructive farmers who followed practices to build up and maintain soil fertility and followed a highly diversified form of agriculture, practices which contrasted with the traditional farmers in the control groups.

AGRICULTURE AND COMMUNITY

Locality group studies made or supported by the Division often introduced aspects of agriculture such as type of farming enterprise or scale of operations.[7] In some cases there was simply a descriptive account of the agriculture in the locality group researched, as in some of the early neighborhood and community studies. In other instances the interrelationships of agriculture and the community were pursued. Thus, in Lowry Nelson's original case studies of three Mormon farm-villages (see Chapter 7), all having in common a base in irrigated agriculture along with religious homogeneity, the relatively small size of landholdings, and the low rate of tenancy were interpreted to be, in effect, dependent variables. These agricultural characteristics were seen as associated with the religious orientations, beliefs, and values from the time of first settlement of these communities.

In still other instances, studies were specifically designed so that the type of agricultural system was the organizing theme or the control or independent variable for comparative analysis. The most ambitious effort to use type of farming as the primary frame of reference was the Division's project on rural cultural regions, described in the chapter on locality groups. Type of farming areas were the starting point for selecting the sample of seventy-one "laboratory" counties for comprehensive field research and for the working hypothesis pertaining to the association between type of farming and rural cultural regions. As noted in Chapters 4 and 7, circumstances prevented doing the analysis which would have fully exploited the potential for comparative analysis in the rural regions study and in the subsequent closely linked county rural organization research.

The first notable comparative analysis of communities which specifically used type of agriculture as the control variable was started early in the Division's history. The annual report for the fiscal year ended June 30, 1920, stated "the differences in social life in communities which are founded upon different types of agriculture are being studied in communities of the dairy, grain, and truck type of farming. Whether the people of different types of farming differ, and if so, in what respect they and their institutions differ, are the questions at issue" (H. Taylor 1921:572). The investigator was not named. But we conclude that the study was made by C. E. Lively as one of the cooperative projects encouraged and given some support by Galpin. Lively's paper "Type of agriculture as a conditioning factor in community organization" for an ASA meeting (1928) compared a dairy-farming community in Wisconsin and a grain-farming community in Minnesota. Each was selected to be as "pure" a representative of the type as readily available. Field observations were supplemented by analysis of census data on agriculture and population for ten typical dairy counties in three states and ten typical grain counties in four states. Lively concluded that type of agriculture conditions community life in such ways as density and mobility of the population, seasonal and yearly fluctuation in income, seasonal distribution of labor demands, and seasonal variations in the activity of organizations and some institutions. He reported certain attitudes appeared to be correlated with type of agriculture. Lively cautioned, however, that he was portraying agriculture as a conditioning, rather than the major controlling, factor in the organization of rural community life.

Farm Structure and Community

Walter Goldschmidt's (1944; 1946; 1947) comparative analysis of two California communities, selected because they differed in size of farm, came to be highly influential in the literature and research on the sociology of agriculture and on the sociology of community. This study of Arvin and Dinuba was noted in Chapter 4 because of the political controversy it evoked and the obstacles encountered to publication of the research report. The work was undertaken in response to a request received in the early 1940s by the BAE from the Department of Interior's Bureau of Reclamation. The request was that the BAE join an interagency research program to make studies for the giant reclamation project being developed by the Bureau of Reclamation in California's Central Valley.

The interagency research agenda included some twenty-four problems, one of which was the policy question bearing on size of farm (Goldschmidt 1978a:456). Federal law, dating from 1902, had purposively limited to 160 acres the irrigable land for which any one owner could legally obtain water from a Bureau of Reclamation project. Information was desired as to what ways, if any, agricultural communities with larger scale operations differed economically and socially from those with smaller, predominantly family-size farming units.

Leadership for the research to answer this question was assigned to the Division's regional office in Berkeley. Goldschmidt, an anthropologist who was early in his professional career, was given primary responsibility for designing and conducting the study.[8] Others in the Division, in other units of the BAE, and social scientists outside the BAE, however, also assisted in planning and doing the research (Goldschmidt 1978b:18).

One large-scale and one small farm agricultural community were selected for comparison. Both had a wide range in farm sizes but the average in the large-scale locality was three times larger in "standard acres," a measure converting actual acres to income-producing capacity, and nearly nine times larger in actual acres. An effort was made to have the large and the small farm communities as similar as possible in other factors such as type of agriculture, resource base, and size of center. Both grew high-value crops by intensive irrigation although the type of agricultural production was not identical.

A variety of sociological and anthropological methods were used in the study (Goldschmidt 1944:217). Community boundaries were delineated by a Division staff member, Walter McKain Jr. A 10 percent sample of the families in each community was interviewed. The questionnaire collected

information on families, occupation, and length of residence; on participation in community institutions, activities, and economic life; and items
for a level of living scale. Community leaders were interviewed to get information on the social institutions in each community, historical background,
and evidence on the social structures of the communities. AAA records for
each farm unit and sales tax data were analyzed. The field work in 1944
in each community by Goldschmidt and two others took about four weeks.
This field work was done at a relatively inactive period for agriculture, in
part for the convenience of farmers and in part because of the belief that
the communities would be more stable at that time and the comparisons
more justifiable.

The Arvin-Dinuba study found two major socioeconomic differences
between them. The first difference was in occupational composition.
Compared with the small farm community, the large-scale farming area
had a much higher proportion of its gainfully employed who were agricultural wage and unskilled laborers. It had a much smaller proportion
who were farm operators, professionals, and entrepreneurs. Among farm
operators, there were sharp tenure differences between the two localities
with the small farm area having more than double the percentage of full
owners.

The second major difference was in the indicators of economic and
social life with the comparative advantage resting with the small farm community. The latter had, for instance, a greater number of businesses, a
larger retail sales volume, a greater diversity of social, educational, and
other facilities and institutions, and scored higher on the family level of
living scale. Goldschmidt's interpretation was that the scale of agriculture
strongly influenced the occupational composition which, in turn, contributed to the community difference in the quality of life measures. "The
basic cause of the impoverished social conditions in Arvin as contrasted
with Dinuba" was size of farming operations (Goldschmidt 1944:227).

In 1944, soon after the field work was completed, Goldschmidt presented a preliminary analysis at the annual meeting of the Western Farm
Economics Association. This was his only publication on this research
topic as a Division staff member. When his complete report was deemed
ready for publication by the BAE economist responsible for the Bureau's
Central Valley studies, it was sent to Washington for the usual review prior
to publication. Because of the controversy the project had engendered in
California, the decision eventually was made by the Secretary of Agriculture
(Anderson). He denied approval. Finally, upon appeal to the Secretary by
the Chair of the Senate Special Committee to Study Problems of American

Small Business, the report was released to that committee (Goldschmidt 1946). The condition was that the USDA not be identified in any way with the study. By that time, the author's appointment in the Division had been terminated by order of the Secretary. Soon after, Goldschmidt used the research for his book *As You Sow* (1947).

In time, the Arvin-Dinuba study became one of the best known pieces of research produced in the Division. More than four decades after its initial publication, an assessment of the research in the sociology of agriculture noted the "rediscovery" in the 1970s of Goldschmidt's work (Buttel et al. 1990:145–51). This assessment asserted that his book had become virtually an obligatory citation in research articles on agriculture and the community (146) and had influenced numerous studies in this area in the "new sociology of agriculture" tradition (147).

TECHNOLOGY IN AGRICULTURE

Before the end of the 1930s, social scientists and policymakers in the USDA began to give attention to the rapid increase underway in mechanization and other technological changes in agriculture. The Division's work in this area of the sociology of agriculture thenceforth was occasional and limited. O. E. Baker (1937) included farm machinery and related information in his graphic summary series based largely on the Census of 1930 and 1935. He joined with others in the BAE to prepare the USDA publication *Seedtime and Harvest Today* (Hainsworth et al. 1942). This included graphic presentations as well as photographs of the planting and harvesting methods used for the nation's major crops. Carl Taylor was one of the twenty-five members of an interbureau committee, which produced a major special report, *Technology on the Farm* (Interbureau Committee on Technology 1940). This broad ranging, information providing, policy oriented report reflected the interest in the USDA at the time in identifying technological changes underway in agriculture and their societal consequences.

Among the few studies specific to technology in agriculture that were supported by the Division, two merit special attention here. They offer a sharp contrast in purpose, and scope, methods, and in the nature of their contributions. Both were done with collaborators outside the Division. The first sought to measure the rates of farm technological advance, 1910–45, for the nation and its regions (Ellickson and Brewster 1947).[9] It set out to determine the impact of comparative rates of technological change on the structure of American agriculture with special attention to family farms. The data came from the census and BAE statistical series. Aggregate technological change (i.e., the substitution of tractors for horse and mule power, better plants and animals, and so on) was measured by changes per farm worker in agricultural output for human use. The structure of agriculture was measured by the number and proportion of units in significant groups of farms. The structural analysis excluded all "nominal" farms, tracts so small as to produce less than $400 value of output for home use or sale (at 1939 prices). The remainder, about four million during 1900–1945, were classified into three carefully defined, logically grounded functional groups. These were "family farms," "larger-than-family farms," and "inadequate farms." This classification scheme introduced a new approach to examining the structure of agriculture.

This study found the output per farm worker for human use had more than doubled between 1910 and 1945. The farm structure measure showed an increase between 1900 and 1945 in the number and proportion of family and larger-than-family farms but a marked decline in inadequate farms.[10] This trend in structure tended to be most pronounced in regions where technological advance was most rapid (Ellickson and Brewster 1947:838). This conclusion was reached by observation of the tabulated data rather than by correlation analysis. Ellickson and Brewster went beyond analysis of the data on technological advance and the structure of agriculture to challenge "three fundamental confusions" about the family farm. These were (1) that farm technological advance was necessarily adverse to the family farm; (2) that inadequate farms were identified as being basically the same as family farms; and (3) that the owner-operatership form of land tenure was one of the defining characteristics of the family farm (Ellickson and Brewster 1947:840–45).

The second study, *The Cotton Plantation in Transition*[11] had the accelerated substitution of tractor for mule power during the 1940s, the advent of the mechanical cotton picker, and other technological innovations in cotton production as a backdrop (Pedersen and Raper 1954). The research sought to describe the process of adjustment that was taking place on individual cotton-growing plantations in response to mechanization and labor scarcity.[12] Case studies were made of two plantations in the same Yazoo-Mississippi Delta county. The two were selected as fairly representative of divergent methods of coping with labor scarcity. Each had between two hundred and three hundred people during the year of study. In 1951 "Tractor Plantation" had twenty-one four-row tractors and eight two-row mechanical cotton pickers but only twelve mules, while "Mule Plantation" had nine tractors, only four with cultivator attachments, and forty-eight mules. Plantation owners were interviewed with respect to historical changes in technology use, tenure arrangements, housing for tenants, and other adjustments. Annual "mule records" and AAA crop acreage measurements were also data sources.

The researchers observed that the adjustments made to labor scarcity by introducing labor-saving technology were undergirded by contrasting management philosophies, one aggressive, the other conservative, and by differing assumptions as to the future role of men and machines to do the plantation work (6–8). All workers on Mule Plantation were croppers or some other form of tenant. The workers on Tractor Plantation included 22 tractor drivers who did nothing else along with a few tenants. The cropper tract was the unit of operation on Mule Plantation, the field was the unit on Tractor Plantation. In the first type, housing was associated with the tract and dispersed on the plantation. In the second type, houses had been moved out of the fields and onto main roads. The most distinctive new feature of Tractor Plantation was the new management hierarchy being established to operate and maintain the tractor equipment, thereby breaking the customary line of communication between the individual worker and the plantation owner. These two cases provide examples of the adjustments over several decades in the cotton plantation as a social and economic institution. They identify mechanization and other factors associated with the observed historical changes. This study may also be seen as an early example of research on the diffusion and adoption of farm practices, a topic in which high interest began to develop about this time.

OTHER WORK IN THE SOCIOLOGY OF AGRICULTURE

A variety of additional projects in which the Division engaged from time to time may also be placed under the sociology of agriculture umbrella. Part-time farming was one of the subjects included. The initial contribution in this area was a consequence of the special tabulations on farm residents that Galpin had made for eight counties following the 1920 Census of Population (Galpin and Larson 1924). The tabulations revealed the extent to which farm family members in these counties engaged in off-farm work. This led to inclusion of a question on such work in the 1930 census. This revealed that nearly one in three of the nation's 6 million farm operators in 1929 spent an average of a hundred days off the farm in work under the supervision of someone else (FPRLA 1933: 4, 14–15). Galpin had a brief item in the 1930 *Yearbook of Agriculture* in which he reported on nonfarm work by farm operators studied in southeastern Ohio and in the mountains of Kentucky (1930b:406–7). In the early years of the Great Depression, a study of rural industries was made in Knott County, Kentucky, in cooperation with the Kentucky AES (Nason 1932; Manny and Nason 1934). Also, Theodore Manny participated in a study of part-time farming and industrial employment around Duluth and the Iron Range in Minnesota (*FPRLA* 1933:7, No. 4:12–13). Government attempts in Germany and Russia to change rural life included part-time farming. Charles Loomis' (1935b) report on these efforts was put out in mimeo form by the Division. Near the close of World War II the USDA attempted to develop educational materials about agriculture for the use of returning war veterans. Earl Bell, a cultural anthropologist, joined with an agricultural economist in another BAE unit to prepare a USDA Farmer's Bulletin, *Part-time Farming* (Bell and Scoville 1945). This bulletin was in such demand that after three years it was reissued.

Measurement of the turnover of farm operators was initiated by the leader of the regional office in Berkeley, Walter C. McKain Jr., to meet requests for information received from post-war planning groups. The first test used AAA records to determine farm operator turnover and retirement rates during a year in a California county (McKain and Metzler 1945). This was followed by a study of farm owner and operator turnover on a Bureau of Reclamation irrigation project in Oregon (McKain and Dahlke 1946).

Some research that we treat in "The Practice of Sociology," Chapters 12 and 13, had aspects relating to the sociology of agriculture. For example, the low-income farmer sector had representation in an evaluation of the RA-FSA rural rehabilitation program (Larson 1947a). A study in Greene County, Georgia, selected because it was a USDA "Unified Farm Program" county, was comprehensive in its coverage of all status groups of farmers and farm families (Raper 1943). Likewise, the Division made or joined in special tabulations and analyses of census data which bore on structural and other aspects of American agriculture. One such instance was Galpin's (1930b) set of tables, based on the 1925 Census of Agriculture, which showed the farm population associated with the different size-of-farm categories, with the kind of road on which the farm was located, and other factors. Another instance followed the 1940 Census of Agriculture when the Division joined with the Bureau of the Census in special tabulations of a two percent sample (Roberts and Holmes 1943). These were the basis for previously unavailable information relating farms classified by value of products to farm tenure, farm size, and other variables. There were also tabulations by value of products for black farmers, for Appalachia, and for the South.

Occasionally, during the later Taylor years, informative and interpretive addresses on rural life given by staff members included mechanization and tenure among the topics. These drew on census data and special research. Thus, a paper with special reference to the Southwest that was given at a meeting of the American Association for the Advancement of Science presented general indexes of sociological significance for the recent agricultural adjustments. These included measures of technological change in agriculture and data on changes in land tenure (Standing 1942b). A presentation to the Southern Sociological Society focused directly on the role of agricultural technology in Southern social change (Raper 1946). Also, in a keynote address at the Tuskegee Rural Life Conference, Raper (1950) included mechanization and land tenure in discussing Southern agricultural trends and their effect on black farmers.

SUMMARY

The Division's research related to what has come to be designated as the "sociology of agriculture" was not a major program area. The work lacked the continuity, the concentration, and the resources to be so characterized. Nevertheless, the research resulted in a number of major contributions to knowledge. Topics covered at one time or another included farm tenancy, cultural considerations in agriculture, the interrelationships of agriculture and community, the social aspects of technological advance in agriculture, and part-time farming.

Farm tenancy was originally intended to be one of the important areas for the Division. After a vigorous start through cooperative studies, however, Galpin surrendered this field due to internal BAE circumstances. The work was reinstated in the mid-1930s under Carl Taylor and then continued intermittently.

The influence of cultural anthropology was demonstrated not only in the community stability-instability work discussed in an earlier chapter but in studies of cultural considerations in use of farming practices. Research on the interrelationships of agriculture and community started early in the 1920s with comparative studies of communities with different farming systems. The most renowned work, however, was that which resulted in the book *As You Sow* (Goldschmidt 1947), a comparison of a large-scale agriculture community with a small-scale one.

The work on mechanization on the farm and other technological innovations, mostly done in collaboration with researchers outside the Division, provided factual information on trends, measures of the effect of technological advances on the structure of American agriculture, and insight into the adjustment to mechanization on individual cotton plantations. The limited work on part-time farming was primarily of a sensitizing or service nature.

Notes

1. Charles L. Stewart, of the BAE's land economics unit, later joined in the investigation. He co-authored a preliminary report with Baumgartel and then wrote a separate report, USDA Bulletin No. 1322, on some economic aspects of the study.

2. The unit's annual report for 1919–20 also included Georgia, Maryland, and South Carolina among the states in which investigations of the social aspects of tenancy had been made of 2,500 farms and farm families in twenty different communities. The report also noted that studies of the social aspects of sales of farms had been carried on in five Indiana counties (H. C. Taylor 1921:572). The report for 1921–22 indicated that the study had been extended to include sixteen states (H. C. Taylor 1923:556).

3. The *Report* of the President's Committee on Farm Tenancy acknowledged (30) Carl Taylor's contributions and drew (82–83) on a study by Charles P. Loomis (1935a), of the modern settlement movement in Germany.

4. The studies are listed in Schuler's (1938a) analysis of the data reported.

5. The Division's wartime priorities did not permit participation in an elaborate interdisciplinary tenure project initiated in 1942 by five cooperating Southwestern states. This research pertained to the relationships between the farm family's tenure and its economic and social performance. The project experienced unusual personnel turnover because of World War II conditions (Hoffsommer 1950:vii).

6. Another principal speaker at this school was Kimball Young, the social psychologist who had joined the Division staff. He discussed cultural and psychological factors in the USDA administrator's relation to the farmer and to the research and technical expert (Young 1939:93–103).

7. An inventory and assessment of the rural sociological literature on the social structure and social relations of agriculture concluded that from the early 1900s until the late 1940s and early 1950s the study of the sociology of agriculture was largely coterminous with the sociology of rural communities (Buttel et al. 1990:42). Thus, the Division came to an end about the time that a differentiation developed between sociological research on agriculture and that on rural communities and the social psychological perspective began to dominate rural sociological research on agriculture.

8. Goldschmidt's previous research experience included his study of the Wasco community during 1940–41 for his doctoral dissertation. He included a report on this study, which had Division support, in his *As You Sow* (1947).

9. Division staff member John C. Ellickson was mainly responsible for the technical information used. John M. Brewster, located in another BAE unit, was chiefly responsible for the analysis and writing. Brewster had a doctorate in philosophy but his professional career had turned to agricultural economics.

10. Inadequate farms decreased from 75 to 59 percent of all farms (excluding "nominal") between 1900 and 1945 while family farms increased their share from 25 percent to

39 percent and larger-than-family farms grew from less than 1 percent to 2 percent of the total (Ellickson and Brewster 1947:837).

11. This was a cooperative project between the Mississippi AES, represented by Harold A. Pedersen, and the Division, represented by Arthur F. Raper.

12. Attitudes of plantation operations and plantation workers toward the substitution of machine power for animal power and human labor was the focus of a second phase of the cooperative project with the Mississippi AES (Pederson 1952). Findings were based on interviews with the operators, the head of each resident family and a supplementary schedule for each worker in the family for a sample of thirty-five medium and large cotton plantations in one county. Interval sampling from a list was used to select the large plantations and area samplings were used for the medium plantations.

11

The Division and Black Populations

Yvonne Oliver[1]

Throughout its history, the Division's activities concentrated on building a body of knowledge about and gaining an understanding of rural life. Of approximately 1,000 research citations in the *Bibliography* (Larson, Moe, and Zimmerman 1992a), more than 130 included references to blacks. Other categories of publications, such as "restricted use reports and manuscripts," also included some references to blacks. "Negroes" and "coloreds" are terms found in the citations. Research on blacks was never a priority of the Division. But while black populations were seldom singled out for study by staff of the Division, they were part of the Division's larger view of research needed on rural America. Studies which did target black families and black communities contributed greatly to an understanding of the social history of blacks in the United States, as well as the dynamics of the social relations of the time, especially in the South where blacks in agriculture were concentrated.

The extent to which the Division's research pertained to blacks or included blacks as investigators is the focus of this chapter. This discussion is carried out within the context of some of the major substantive research areas engaged in by the Division. Neither all of the substantive areas nor all the research in a particular substantive area are discussed. Rather, the discussion of selected research is intended to provide an indication of the diversity of the research undertaken that included references to blacks.

DIVISION RESEARCH

During the early 1920s, Galpin initiated cooperative research projects with two historically black colleges and universities (HBCUs), Fisk University and Hampton Normal Institute. It is clear that almost all the research of the Division, including research on blacks, was conducted by white staff. Although the HBCUs were in existence during the period 1919–53, there were few black social scientists engaged in research. There were three major reasons for this: (1) blacks were not significantly represented in the decision-making process at the state level, which resulted in disproportionate allocations of educational resources; (2) the lack of funds to attract scientific and professional expertise, and the inability of these institutions to provide time to do research rather than teaching; and (3) social science scholars did not find their institutions to be particularly receptive to their research interests (Jones 1976:123). These factors combined to result in relatively few social scientists at black institutions who were recognized as having the training to conduct research for the Division or to be investigators for cooperative projects. And not to be overlooked is the sociopolitical climate of the time, when there were few formal relationships of any type between blacks and whites.

At this time, there were few formal relationships between the USDA/BAE and the HBCUs, including the 1890 land-grant institutions. There did exist, however, a number of informal and personal relationships between Division staff and professionals at the HBCUs. Division Head Carl Taylor, for example, had a personal relationship with Charles S. Johnson of Fisk University. Arthur Raper, on the staff during most of the 1940s, worked with Johnson and with Ira de A. Reid of Atlanta University. Frank Alexander was an associate of Lewis W. Jones of Tuskegee Institute. Systematic formula funding for research at the land-grant institutions did not begin until 1967, when the USDA made available $238,000 administered by the Cooperative State Research Service under Public Law 89–106.

The Farm Population

The primary goal of the earliest studies of the farm population was simple—to determine the number and characteristics of the farm population. As indicated in Chapter 5, the first of these was based on special tabulations from the 1920 Census of Population for eight counties (Galpin and Larson 1924; Truesdell 1926). The largest black population was in Wake County, North Carolina,[2] which was also the site of other research that included reference to blacks (Zimmerman and Taylor 1922).

The special tabulations provided detailed data for each of the eight counties by color, tenure, residence, gender, and age, as well as illiteracy, school attendance, and marital status. These tabulations were significant because they represented the first step in including race as a demographic variable in describing the farm population. Special tabulations from the 1920 Census of Population for a sample of rural villages likewise included data for blacks, e.g., the analysis for Southern villages (Fry 1924). The census continued, over time, to be the source for several publications which included blacks in the analysis. Among these was a comprehensive study of net migration to and from farms, 1920–30 (Lively and Taeuber 1939) and one on net migration from the rural-farm population, 1930–40 (Bernert 1944a). Fertility ratios were analyzed on a national basis for 1930 (Lively and Taeuber 1939) and in a study specific to the Mississippi Delta (Taeuber and Taeuber 1940). Replacement rates for rural-farm black males were computed for 1940–50 for every county (Taeuber 1944). An exception to census-based research was a study of population characteristics and recent migration in the upper Mississippi Delta of Louisiana (Hitt 1942; Hitt 1943). By and large, however, most of the publications on farm and rural population did not reference blacks.

FARM LABOR

Throughout the plantation South there was persistent concern with filling labor needs, especially for the cotton, tobacco, and sugar plantations. From a public policy perspective, there was a concern with the wage levels, working, and living conditions of agricultural laborers throughout the nation. Starting in the 1930s, the Division was involved in research on these topics (see also Chapter 9).

Several surveys were conducted on major changes in plantation labor, factors associated with the changes, and effects of the changes, especially in the number of sharecroppers and wage laborers (Barton and McNeely 1939; Holcomb and Aull 1940; Grigsby and Hoffsommmer 1941; Holcomb, et al. 1941). Other studies were undertaken, especially with the advent of World War II, on the number and characteristics of agricultural hired workers. Since black laborers were prominent in the labor force of Southern plantations, they were counted in the surveys. Changes were documented in both the permanent and transient labor force and were compared for whites and nonwhites (African Americans as well as Japanese, Chinese, American Indians, and Mexicans).

During 1936, the Division cooperated with Carl Taylor's social research unit in the FSA, using WPA funds, to conduct surveys of agricultural labor conditions in eleven counties in eleven states. Only two of the areas—Todd County, Kentucky (Vasey and Folsom 1937a) and Concordia Parish, Louisiana (Vasey and Folsom 1937b)—yielded substantial information about black laborers. Data on agricultural laborers were presented by race for tenure, age, education, marital status, dependents, nativity, residence, previous farm experience, reasons for terminating sharecropper status, total income, days worked in agricultural and in mixed employment, piece-work wage rates and average daily earning in picking cotton, and methods of placement of cotton pickers.

Studies of Concordia Parish and Todd County portrayed the labor supply as uneducated, racially distinct, and socially isolated (Vasey and Folsom 1937a:13). Racial differences were found in pay, with blacks being paid lower wage rates than whites. Low earnings, due particularly to low wage rates and intermittent employment, led to increased migration of farm laborers to urban areas in search of improved economic conditions. Consequently, problems of labor scarcity led to various government measures and programs, such as the deferment of agricultural workers from military service, to assure that the farm labor force was adequate to meet the nation's needs relative to the production of food and fiber.

As black men were drawn in military service during World War II, local reactions to this found their way into the Division's research reports. This loss to the military was reputed, in Alabama for example, to give rise to a growing concern locally about the economic independence of black women who received dependency allotments from relatives in the armed services (Jehlik 1943). These women often refused to work during peak periods of the cotton season, and the situation was described as contributing to a tight labor market and, in some instances, heightened racial tensions. Studies of farm labor and wage rates in which blacks were included yielded important information about the structure of agriculture, especially tenure arrangements; racial disparities in pay; migration for economic reasons; and to a lesser extent, social organization and levels of living.

Neighborhoods and Communities

Doggett's (1923) *Three Negro Communities in Tidewater, Virginia* chronicled three rural communities through different states of development. The story was told of how residents worked together to meet their needs, particularly as related to school improvement, economic well-being, health, youth development, and recreation and social life. Considerable emphasis was placed upon providing opportunities for youth to participate in the continued development of the community. As a consequence, Doggett wrote (1923:20): "Families have a lot to lose by leaving. . . . Consequently they do not leave." In each of the communities, progress was slow but was achieved as a result of the efforts of people working together to accomplish common goals.

Zimmerman and Taylor's (1922) study of locality groups in North Carolina was the first of the Division's studies to document the distinct separation of the country neighborhood groupings of blacks and whites within a county. Neighborhood studies confirmed that the concept of "neighborhood" reflected feelings of "belonging" which was sometimes based on locality groups associated with the existence of a church, a grave-yard, a store, or a school. While these factors were often the primary inte-grating factors which determined the existence of a neighborhood, these signs alone were insufficient to constitute the feeling of neighborhood or neighborliness among blacks. Thus, as Sanders and Ensminger (1940:19) noted in the study of Chilton County, Alabama, "The neighborhood exists in the minds of the people although it seldom appears on maps." Despite this, however, on the basis of descriptions provided by community resi-dents, they proceeded to map a total of seventy-six neighborhoods in Chilton County, fifteen of which were black.[3]

Within the community of Chilton, black and white neighborhoods were very distinct. Yet, they followed the same pattern with respect to reasons given for banding together as a neighborhood: social acceptance ("just have always stuck together"), belonging to the same church, kin-ship, loyalty to the local school, and economic ties. While the fifteen black neighborhoods in Chilton were geographically dispersed, each had a school and a cemetery, and all but one had a church. Two of the neigh-borhoods also had fraternal organizations. In Chilton, the sense of com-munity was derived primarily from dependence upon a large, common economic center where residents of both black and white neighborhoods had to go for services that the neighborhood did not provide, such as for major purchases.

Nichols (1941) found in Red River Parish, Louisiana, a plantation sit-uation, that despite the numerical superiority of black families (three to six white families and from 150 to 250 black families), definite neigh-borhoods that were integrated around a church, school, or various other social organizations and trade facilities did not exist. Under the planta-tion system that prevailed in Red River Parish, economic dominance was held by the few whites who essentially governed the social structure. Loyalty to the "furnish" stores or commissaries did not exist as an inte-grating neighborhood factor. Black elementary schools were adminis-tered by whites, and black churches functioned irregularly because of the low financial status of their membership. Thus, the importance of these two institutions as integrating neighborhood forces was signifi-cantly weakened.

Because of the absence of feelings of belonging, the areas could not be accurately described as neighborhoods. Instead, the feeling of belonging was likely to be transferred to the "Big House," and the loyalty which would ordinarily attach to neighborhood institutions was directed to the plantation. An integral part of this loyalty was a strong feeling of dependence upon the "Big House" for economic security. Nichols summarized this phenomenon by saying: "It is debatable whether lack of other strong integrating neighborhood interests, school, church, social organizations, and stores induces the tie to the plantation, or whether loyalty to the plantation and economic dependence upon it are responsible for the failure of normal neighborhood development" (1941:8).

The primary objective of another set of studies of rural communities, collectively known as the *Culture of a Contemporary Rural Community* series, was to determine factors associated with stability or instability of small communities (see also Chapter 7). The communities were chosen to represent points on a continuum from high community stability to great instability. Harmony Community, in Putnam County, Georgia (Wynn 1943), was selected as one of the communities on the stability-instability continuum. It was biracial. The population included twenty white and fifty black families. The majority of whites were descendents of English ancestors who had lived in the area for generations, while the majority of the black population were descendants of slaves. The biracial composition of Harmony led to its being described as two communities with "little in common except the understanding that keeps them apart" (Foreword in Wynn, 1943). To a great extent, social stability in Harmony was tenuous and based on good race relations, which existed as long as blacks "remained in their place." Harmony Community was rated intermediate on the stability-instability continuum.

Levels and Standards of Living

Studies that included levels and standards of living consistently reported that rural blacks were at the bottom in terms of economic and social disadvantageousness, including food, shelter, clothing, and other essentials of healthy living such as medical care (see also Chapter 6). The cumulative work, *The Farmer's Standard of Living* (Kirkpatrick 1929), includes comparative analyses of data for 154 "colored" and 861 white farm families in Kentucky, Tennessee, and Texas. Both material and non-material levels of living were examined based on data for the average value and percentage distribution of goods used during 1919. Among both blacks and whites, the lower the tenure status of the family (cropper, tenant, owner), the lower the total value of all goods consumed. The consumption categories examined were food, clothing, rent, operation (e.g., fuel, other supplies, transportation, power, and household labor), advancement (e.g., education, recreation, reading matter, travel, and participation in clubs and organizations, benevolences, religion, and other interests of a social or spiritual nature), and "other." Findings reported lower levels of living for "coloreds" than whites, regardless of tenure status. For example, the value of all goods used during one year by blacks was $611 compared to $1,436 for whites. Comparative proportions of the value of all goods that were furnished from the farm for both blacks and whites were 39.3 percent and 37.4 percent, respectively. The highest proportions of income spent by both groups were for food, but higher proportions of the value of food was furnished by the farm for white (60.8 percent) than for "colored" (54.7 percent) families. On average, colored families spent 4.6 percent of the total value of expenditures for advancement, compared to 5.9 percent for white families.

The classic report, *Disadvantaged Classes in American Agriculture* included information on income and living levels of the disadvantaged farm population (C. Taylor et al. 1938). The analysis was based largely on secondary sources. It described the situation of farm families nationwide, but references to blacks specifically were almost always limited to discussions of the Southern Cotton Belt. Among the problems highlighted in the study as contributing to extremely low standards of living, particularly among blacks, were those associated with low farm incomes and farm tenancy. Cotton was the main crop in the Southern Cotton Belt, accounting for more than half of the harvested area and an even higher percentage of income from products sold. While returns (incomes) from cotton farming were generally low, tremendous disparities were found in the incomes of black and white families. A study of Greene County, Georgia, for example, revealed that in 1934 the average annual cash income was $300 for whites compared to $150 for blacks (Taylor et al. 1938:15). Primarily because of low incomes from cotton and the predominance of blacks at the lower income levels, the presence of a large black population was viewed as tending to lower the standard of living in the Cotton Belt. The non-material standard of living was described as being even more inadequate than the material standard of living. And this was more true for blacks than for whites. Social participation was extremely limited, educational facilities far below the average for the nation, and illiteracy rates were high.

The 1935–36 Consumer Purchases Study data were used by Schuler (1944) to determine how black families compared with white families, based on three graphic methods devised to analyze levels and standards of living of farm, rural-nonfarm, and urban families. The comparisons were based on a sample of farm families in Georgia and Mississippi and village and small city families in the Southeast. Selected items were categorized as a rarity, a luxury, or a necessity, based upon the proportions of respondents reporting expenditures at low and high income levels. The findings were pretty much predictable. For example, while domestic help was more of a cultural necessity among whites, such help was a rarity among blacks. Similarly, reading material was considered more or less a necessity among whites but was most nearly a luxury for blacks. Dental services were not considered a necessity for any group but were most clearly a rarity among blacks.

The disparate levels of economic and social disadvantageousness of rural black families were major factors precipitating relatively high rates of migration and mobility among them. According to Leonard and Loomis (1939:1), "Some of the country's poorest and most disadvantaged people live on the plantations and farms of the Southern river valleys. This is largely the result of the prevailing agricultural system which accords them their low economic and social status with its accompanying low level of living." Their study of 306 black sharecropper and wage laborer families living in the valleys of the Arkansas, Mississippi, and Red Rivers, found that mobility was often associated with quests for higher standards of living. These moves often proved futile, however, and families with the fewest number of moves were found to have higher standards of living.

Rural Social Organization

Concern with the social structure and organization of rural communities was evident in much of the research conducted or sponsored by the Division. Matters related to social organization were often incorporated in other studies with different foci. Two examples offer a stark contrast in the types of descriptions and approaches to the study of the social organization of blacks in rural areas. For example, Doggett's (1923) study of three black communities conducted during the Galpin years focused on relations among blacks and emphasized the cohesiveness of black communities. In contrast, studies of social organization conducted during the Taylor years often focused on relations between blacks and whites and emphasized how structured inequality limited the opportunities and progress of blacks.

The situation of blacks described in *Three Negro Communities* was significantly different, however, from that of blacks in most of the Division's other studies. For example, in the cultural reconnaissance surveys conducted during 1944 and 1945, one dimension included a special focus on class and status groups. The cultural reconnaissance surveys reported the existence of high levels of stratification and complete social separation between the races even when both races were within the same geographic areas (e.g., a study of Avoyelles Parish, Louisiana, by Pryor 1945). In every instance, blacks had been brought into the plantation South as slaves, and though, particularly after the Emancipation Proclamation, some were able to become farm operators, racial identity functioned to keep blacks relegated to subordinate status. Large black populations were viewed as posing threats to the traditional structure of Southern society.

Many of the studies of rural social organization conducted by the Division were replete with documentation of the existence of taboos and mores through which whites maintained segregation. These included signs indicating "whites only" or "Negroes only," and the exercise of informal and personal control over the black population. The cultural reconnaissance survey of Union County, South Carolina (Montgomery 1945), for example, reported segregation in public carriers, courts, residences, eating and entertainment places, hotels, schools, churches, public offices, and hospitals. And, with few exceptions, blacks were not permitted to vote. In Greene County, Georgia, Raper (1944) reported that the poll tax and white primaries were used to prevent virtually all poor and black people from voting.

In documenting structured inequality based on race, Frank Alexander's (1944) cultural reconnaissance survey of Coahoma County, Mississippi, caused severe problems for the USDA, the BAE, and the Division (see also Chapter 4). In his study, Alexander described the class and status groups in Coahoma County, which were characterized by an absolute division between whites and blacks. The white plantation system dominated the political, social, and economic life of the community. Law enforcement was left to individual plantation owners, and blacks were excluded from voting and office holding. The only county organization to which both blacks and whites were admitted was the Farm Bureau, through black membership in the Farm Bureau was the result of planters enrolling their sharecroppers and charging their membership to the cropper's account. Despite their membership, blacks were allowed no voice in the organization and were not permitted to attend business meetings.

The economic system in the South was based on the production of cotton with most of the labor provided by blacks, most of whom were at the bottom of the ladder in terms of living standards. During World War II, blacks in Coahoma County began to migrate to employment opportunities in the North. As they began to migrate, the remaining black labor became scarce and expensive, resulting in increased racial antagonisms. Alexander's documentation of structured inequality and racial tensions in Coahoma County led to a squelching influence by Congress on the Division's research.

Other Work Undertaken

Other research involving data on blacks included primarily descriptive studies on fertility, migration, and policy-oriented studies related to rural health. There was a small amount of data on fertility. One of the fertility studies by Taeuber and Taeuber (1940) was of a group of counties in the Mississippi Delta, which provided an exception to the generally high fertility of rural blacks of the South. The primary purpose of their research was to determine whether or not real differences existed between these counties and surrounding areas. They found that the differences were real and suggested further field studies to determine the effects of standards of living, the possible effects of contraceptive practices, dietary deficiencies, and other factors in accounting for the differences.

With respect to migration, there were examples of both descriptive and policy-oriented research. For example, a study by Taeuber and Taeuber (1938) examined factors that affected short-distance interstate migration. Limited data on blacks were included. A small amount of data on the migration patterns of blacks was also included in a study by Lively and Taeuber (1939) on the relationships between population movements and such social and economic factors as quality of land, economic status, population growth, unemployment, and the need for public works programs and relief.

A survey of one thousand North Carolina farmers in the early 1920s included black croppers, tenants, operators, and landlords in the sample. They were compared with their white counterparts on such factors as farming practices, farm characteristics, production for home use, and housing (Taylor and Zimmerman 1922). A study of farm tenure in the Cotton Belt during the 1930s included 753 black farmers in the sample along with some farm laborers (Schuler 1938b). These farmers were compared, by tenure status, with the sample of white Southern farmers on numerous questions considered pertinent to farm tenure. Among these were lifetime patterns on the agricultural ladder, opinions about the desirability of farm ownership and about federal government programs for farms, and levels and standards of living.

Greene County, Georgia, underwent intensive study by Division sociologist Arthur Raper for two years after it was selected for the Unified Farm Program promoted by the USDA as part of its land-use planning activities (Raper 1943). More than half of the county's population was black in 1940. Raper's study included the relationship of blacks to the New Deal's agricultural and other programs. He put the Greene County of the early 1940s in historical perspective, drawing, for example, on the stories of four ex-slaves.

Research on the use of health services by rural people in Mississippi resulted in a special report on the health practices of rural blacks in Bolivar County (Galloway and Loftin 1951). The report gave data, for instance, on the use of doctors and dentists, and on insurance for hospital care.

RELATIONSHIPS WITH HISTORICALLY BLACK COLLEGES AND UNIVERSITIES

A strategy developed by Galpin was to initiate collaborative relationships with colleges and universities through cooperative research projects. On occasion, university personnel were also temporarily employed. The Division's records indicate that cooperative projects were initiated with only two historically black colleges—Fisk University in Tennessee and Hampton Normal Institute in Virginia.

There is no evidence that the Fisk project, "Story of the Rise of the 100 Best Negro Farmers in Tennessee," resulted in a research publication (Galpin 1924b:8). Thomas Caruthers was given as the investigator.[4] Of the two cooperative projects with Hampton, one never yielded a research publication.[5] But the other was Doggett's *Three Negro Communities in Tidewater, Virginia* (1923), discussed earlier in this chapter. The cooperative agreement for the latter project called for a $300 budget, $150 from Hampton for Doggett's salary and $150 from the Division for travel. This study was a classic for its time. It provided solid empirical information about three black rural communities and how they functioned. It contributed sociological knowledge about the ethnic and cultural diversity in rural America.

Edward B. Williams

Over the Division's existence, the employment of only one black professional could be verified.[6] This person was Edward B. Williams of Morehouse

College, in Atlanta, Georgia. At the start of World War II Williams was employed by Morehouse, an all-male college in Atlanta, Georgia. Because of declining enrollment imposed by the war, the Morehouse administration encouraged faculty to seek employment elsewhere during this period. About the same time, Ira de A. Reid, Chairman of the Department of Sociology at Atlanta University, was contacted by the BAE/DFPRW regional office in Atlanta. The Division wanted to hire a black member of the staff to work along with the white staff to conduct cultural reconnaissance surveys in selected counties in the Southeast. The Division felt that a black staff member could do a more efficient job of getting information about blacks than a white person. Reid recommended Williams, who worked, on a short-term appointment, as a social science analyst in 1943 and 1944 (Williams 1990).

By his own account,[7] Williams conducted the reconnaissance surveys among blacks in four counties—Coahoma County, Mississippi; Calhoun County, Mississippi; Dallas County, Alabama; and the Union County, South Carolina.[8] Williams' responsibility was to examine the various cultural patterns that existed in black communities and neighborhoods. During the conduct of the reconnaissance surveys, Williams worked with blacks and Division staff members James Montgomery or Frank Alexander worked with whites.

For Williams, his tenure with the Division was characterized by many of the social sanctions and norms of the time. Consider, for example, his description of his experiences gathering data for the reconnaissance surveys.

> In Mississippi, before going on a plantation to make an inquiry about the life of blacks in the community, I first had to get clearance from the plantation owner. So, my first experience in Mississippi, I went to a big plantation owner who had about 300 or more families, the majority of whom were black sharecroppers. The first thing he greeted me with was, 'Boy, what do you want?' So when he said, 'Boy, what do you want?' I pulled my identification card, and said, 'I'm E. B. Williams, and I'm working with the Bureau of Agricultural Economics/Division of Farm Population and Rural Welfare.' I did that very rapidly to let him know my status, and he changed immediately from 'boy' to 'Williams.' From then on he said, 'Williams.' 'Williams,' he said, 'you can go on my plantation and I'm going to give you the name of a man you can talk with and he will give you all the information that you need. But I want to caution you about one thing: Don't tamper with my

labor. Just don't disturb my labor.' I said, 'I'm not going to tamper with your labor, I'm just here to do a little research. . . .'

The head of my Division [in the regional office] said to me one day. . . .'What I think you ought to do when you go into these communities,' he said, 'I think you ought to dress like the people.' He said, 'They'll probably be more responsive to your questions.' I said, 'Frank (Alexander), I don't desire to do that. I want them to see the other side of the black experience.' So I always went with shirt and tie, and sometimes I didn't have my jacket on, but I said, 'I want them to see this part of the black experience.' I said, 'They are familiar with the other part that you mentioned. . . . No, I think that they will respond if I approach them in the proper manner, and I'd like for them to look upon me as a professional trying to get information about the lifestyles.' And I said, 'I prefer not to do that.' But they wanted me to disguise myself.

According to Williams, "It wasn't too difficult to get information from black workers once you let them know what you were about." He described his approach:

I said, 'I'm here to help you to get justice, to get what you deserve. I'm not here to report on you in terms of what you're doing and what you're not doing.' So I developed a pretty good rapport with those who were selected for me as key observers. I had a pretty good relationship with them . . . a lot of interesting things developed and challenged me. I was in one county and was talking with a sharecropper. I said, 'Tell me this.' I said, 'What would you say really governs you in your relationship with these whites and your lifestyle?' And he said, 'I'll tell you Mr. Williams. Us is governed by the seven M's. . . .' I reported this and it went to Washington, and they never got over it. I said, 'Well what are the seven M's?' He said, 'The seven M's is meat, meal, molasses, meet the man at the lot Monday morning!' That was a classic.

In the office:

When I first went to the office, and I've told you about the experience in the restroom . . .[9] well, there was a man in the State [of Georgia] Department of Agriculture . . . a rabid racist . . . the head of my Division in Atlanta, who was Frank Alexander, said to me one day, 'Ed you know, I just don't know how we can handle the situation with (whatever his name was), if he were to come into this office and see you dictating to one of these white secretaries, I just don't know how things would turn out.' So I smiled, and I said, 'Well, Frank, maybe it would be the proper time for him to witness such an event because maybe he isn't accustomed to it, maybe it's a good thing.' They did not build a partition, but what they did was put one of those glass enclosures up and papered it so they could not see inside the office.[10] That did happen. That really happened. (Williams 1990)

Williams left the Bureau in 1944.[11]

The BAE was probably the least racist part of the USDA, and among the least racist in the federal government. Yet, there was a contradictory nature about both the BAE and the Division, especially with respect to social relations. While fairly progressive, as indicated by its professed commitment to helping rural blacks, the BAE was, nonetheless, a product of its time and characterized by some degree of racism, as shown by the experiences of E. B. Williams.

SUMMARY AND CONCLUSIONS

There were many more studies conducted by the Division that referenced blacks than have been included in this chapter. Both the research in which blacks were central and the research in which blacks were only casually referenced contributed significantly to the knowledge base about black people, their institutions, and communities. This research shed light on the dynamics related to the integration of blacks, or the lack thereof, into the larger social structure. Information on this segment of the rural South's population, which was integral to its economy, but which was socially and politically disenfranchised, also helps to put into perspective the racial tensions that became so prominent in the 1950s and 1960s.

There were several themes which pervaded the studies of blacks conducted by the Division. They can be summarized as follows:

1. The cultural heritage of blacks who were brought to the United States as slaves and who never overcame the status of servants and second-class citizens;

2. The historically extreme social, economic, and political disadvantageousness of blacks, and their desire and constant quest for a better
quality of life, which often led to migration in search of economic bet-
terment and greener pastures, often with disappointment;
3. The importance of the non-material quality of life, especially education
and religion, in the lives of blacks;
4. The existence in the 1940s among the Division's professional staff of
"status quo breakers," such as Division Head Carl Taylor, Frank
Alexander, James Montgomery, and Arthur Raper. They documented
social disorganization, structured inequality, and the formal and informal sanctions used to keep blacks "in their place."

Further, we note that implications drawn from a review of the Division's
research that referenced blacks depend upon one's perspective—through
whose eyes one looks. Through the eyes of a black man, Allen B. Doggett
Jr., one sees a proud, struggling people who feared God and valued the
land and education. Through the eyes of another black man, Edward B.
Williams, one sees pride, integrity, and the determination to make sure
that both blacks and whites knew that all blacks were not servants or train
car porters; that many were cultured, well educated, and appreciated social
amenities. Through the eyes of James Montgomery, a white man who took
the time to get to know Williams, one sees empathy and respect. Through
some of the research by the Division, one sees a desire to know, from the
perspective of whites, how blacks were relegated to a servile position based
on the stigmas whites had attached to blacks.

No matter through whose eyes one looks, it is apparent that if the information that was collected and if some of the lessons learned, especially
from the county reconnaissance studies, had become the basis for policy
decisions, some of the racial tensions of later years may have been prevented. Better relations between racial groups might have resulted. Edward
B. Williams (1990) recounted:

> In Coahoma County, Mississippi, and Dallas County, Alabama,
> Negroes were much in the majority. In Coahoma, it was something
> like three to one. And whenever you had blacks in the majority,
> the social sanctions and social controls were very, very rigid. And
> you saw some of that in the Selma march. . . . I spent many days
> in Selma, and I could understand the difficulties they had in Selma
> crossing the Pettis Bridge. I believe that had better use been made

of these studies, it may have alleviated much of the tension that did develop in these counties. (Williams 1990)

Paraphrasing Santayana, "Those who ignore or forget the past are doomed to repeat it." And history teaches us that eventually, slaves rise up against slave masters. Although times have changed, much remains the same as, was revealed by research conducted by the Division about blacks and their relationships with the larger society.

Notes

1. Dr. Oliver is Associate Professor of Sociology at Fort Valley State College, Georgia. She began the work on which this chapter is based in 1988 when she was a visiting professor in the Department of Rural Sociology at Cornell University. This was continued at Fort Valley State College under research project GEOX-2304, "Sociology in the U.S. Department of Agriculture, 1919–53: Relationship to Historically Black Colleges and to the Study of Black Populations."

2. The eight counties were Ostego County, N.Y.; Dane County, Wis.; New Madrid County, Mo.; Scott County, Mo.; Cass County, N.Dak.; Wake County, N.C.; Ellis County, Tex.; and King County, Wash. The largest black population was in Wake County, N.C. (44.2 percent), followed by Ellis, Tex. (25.8 percent), and New Madrid, Mo. (9.4 percent). The majority of persons in King, Wash., who were designated as "coloreds" (11.3 percent) were actually Japanese. Four other counties (Ostego, N.Y.; Dane, Wis.; Scott, Mo.; and Cass, N.Dak.) had negligible "colored" populations of 1.1 percent or less. Essentially the same data are included in both publications. *Farm Population of Selected Counties*, however, includes only tables while *Farm Population of the United States* provides some narrative in addition to the tables, although there is little discussion of "coloreds."

3. Seven additional black neighborhoods were identified, but were not mapped, for a total of twenty-two black neighborhoods in Chilton County.

4. Our October 6, 1989, inquiry to Fisk University elicited the response that a report was not in the Fisk Library collection.

5. The cooperative project at Hampton pertained to farm housing and farm home conditions, particularly farm tenant conditions. The researchers were Allen B. Doggett Jr., and a member of the Virginia Negro Extension Service, J. B. Pierce (Galpin 1924b:8).

6. In addition, in the early 1940s, John Alston, one of E. Franklin Frazier's students at Howard University, held a temporary appointment in a technical position on Olaf F. Larson's rural rehabilitation study funded by WPA.

7. Personal conversation between the author and Dr. Williams at his home on August 3, 1990.

8. Dr. Williams was listed as a co-author of the report on Dallas County, Alabama (Montgomery and Williams 1945). Additionally, a note on the title page read: "In the preparation of this report Edward B. Williams interviewed Negro key observers, wrote the section on 'Current and Anticipated Rural Migration Problems,' reviewed the manuscript, and where necessary made additions and changes which were concerned with the Negro aspects of the culture." The report on Union County, South Carolina (Montgomery 1945), had the following note regarding Dr. Williams' contributions on the title page: "Edward B. Williams did the field work among Negro key observers for this report. In addition he was consulted by the author on a number of topics where intimate knowledge of Negro people was required."

No reference was made to the contributions of Dr. Williams to the reconnaissance surveys conducted in Coahoma or Dallas Counties. Williams asked for copies of the reports when he left the Bureau. He was told that they were "strictly within the Bureau and not for circulation." [None of these reports were published; all were identified by the Division as "for administrative use."] The information Williams collected in the four counties was the basis for his doctoral dissertation, "Negro migration in four selected counties of the Southern region of the United States," submitted in 1953 and directed by Professor Carter Goodrich, Columbia University.

9. During his tenure at the BAE regional office in Atlanta, USDA officials made an offer to build a separate restroom to accommodate Edward B. Williams. He declined the offer.

10. James E. Montgomery, Division staff member in the Atlanta regional office, recalls that in Atlanta in the 1940s sharing an office with a black was taboo. He recollects that placing a large highway map over the glass panel between Williams' office and other offices served to provide the separation demanded by the taboo (Montgomery 1990).

11. When hired by the BAE, it was the understanding that when the employee whose place Edward B. Williams was filling returned from the War, Williams would return to Morehouse College.

1 2

The Practice of Sociology: I[1]

An orientation toward studies that could contribute to the improvement of rural life in the nation was one of the proverbial "red threads" that characterized the Division's work from beginning to end. Such an orientation was in tune with the "charter" set forth for the USDA's new farm life studies unit in 1919 by Secretary Houston's special advisory committee, and implied going beyond doing research to interpreting it, in order to facilitate its use. This thread was closely intertwined with a second, the major goal of adding to the fund of validated knowledge about rural life in the United States. In 1946, in a statement prepared by Division Head Carl Taylor for the Research Committee on Reorganization of the BAE program, the two "red threads" were expressed in a way reflecting the Division's experiences up to that point. He contended that every BAE research activity or project should be measured "in terms of whether its findings will contribute to the improvement of the economic and social status of farm people or to the effective integration of agriculture into the total national economy or assist farm people to effectively participate in the total culture of our society. Every division of the Bureau should strive to serve welfare objectives without apology." At the same time, "valid research methods without equivocation or compromise" should be insisted upon (Taylor 1946c:10).

The focus in this chapter and the next is on the Division's activities in what has been termed the "practice" of sociology, putting it to use, in the federal government setting.[2] This setting had potential users in the form of agricultural action agencies within the USDA; agencies outside of the USDA; an educational system, the extension service; and the Congress, a legislative policymaking body with concerns including agriculture and rural life. The contributions of the Division's practice were as broad as increasing understanding of problems about which policy decisions must be made, on which some action must be taken.[3] They were as narrow as supplying a single piece of research-based data. They included evaluation of agency programs or parts of programs and short-term field research on specific problems or in a particular geographic area. Some contributions were in the form of a concept or a sociological technique which could be applied.

In preceding chapters on the major substantive areas of the Division's research program, such as farm and rural population, locality and other groups, and farm labor, we have made some reference to the origins of requests for sociological assistance received by the Division. We have briefly noted instances of uses made of the unit's research. In this chapter and the next, we relate the Division's research and service to specific federal agencies and programs. We indicate the contrast between the Galpin years and the Taylor years in the Division's practice of sociology. Within the Taylor years, our presentation reveals how two national crises, the Great Depression and resultant New Deal programs and World War II, shaped the Division's research and service.

THE GALPIN YEARS, 1919–1934

Although the committee which advised Secretary Houston to initiate farm life studies on a continuing basis in the USDA clearly had high hopes that the research would benefit the life of people on the land, just who would use the findings and how they would be used was not so clear. At the time there were no policymakers at high levels in the federal government seeking the sociologist's contributions; there were few interventionist action agencies comparable to those initiated later under the New Deal. One potential user was the relatively new Extension Service, a federal-state-local cooperative educational program for farmers, farm homemakers, and farm youth. But sociological research on rural life was in an early phase. The situation permitted the Division and its cooperators to use the meager budget primarily to start building a knowledge base about rural life in the United States. This was the distinctive contribution of the Galpin years.

Galpin vigorously pushed for the dissemination and interpretation of the new knowledge as it became available. Much was published by cooperators in the form of agricultural experiment station bulletins and other university publications. The Division staff had articles regularly in the *Yearbook* of the USDA, issued annually. The audience for speeches by Galpin included not only events for citizens at land-grant colleges, conferences for extension workers but groups as diverse as annual meetings of the National Education Association and a banker's "farm school" in Arkansas. Press releases were issued. Starting in 1928 he gave radio addresses from time to time which were broadcast by stations affiliated with the National Broadcasting Company.

The research and its dissemination and interpretation helped to open up rural social problem issues, to create public awareness as illustrated by the work on farm family living conditions, on the contributions of the population from rural areas to the national society, and by the identification, through special analyses of the 1920 farm population data, of the extent of part-time farming. The research the Division and its cooperators did found local-level applications. For example, the "natural" or "trade center" community concept became the cornerstone in determining boundaries when a rural school centralization program was initiated in the late 1920s in New York. The State Board of Education made approval of a local reorganization plan contingent upon procedures that applied the community concept (Loomis and Loomis 1967: 658–83 n. 10).

In addition to setting about to develop a fund of knowledge about rural life, the Division immediately undertook work intended to encourage and assist rural people, local officials, and local-level agencies to plan and organize needed community services and facilities. Staff member Wayne C. Nason devoted most of his efforts to such work for more than a decade. All of his reports were based on studies of successful rural experiences. There was great interest at the time in having a building that could be the "house" for the entire community. Nason started with a series on community buildings, planning for them, organizational aspects, and uses. One of these, *Plans of Rural Community Buildings* presented the floor plans of a wide variety of community buildings then in successful operation in different parts of the country under different climatic conditions (Nason 1921). The plans were for buildings in five different types of communities ranging from largely farming to farming and small city. He followed with a series on rural planning, one on the social aspects (Nason 1923), one on recreation (Nason 1924), and one on the village (Nason 1925).

Rural areas had striking deficiencies in the availability of rural hospitals, library services, and fire protection. Nason conducted studies of successful experiences in obtaining and maintaining these facilities. Thus, in *Rural Hospitals* the construction and operation of eight different types of rural hospitals, such as county hospitals and southern mountain hospitals, were illustrated by specific cases (Nason 1926). The illustrations were selected because they seemed to be applicable in different political units and in different sections of the country. Rural libraries were advocated as an aid to efficiency in agriculture, through their educational function, and as a means of creating and maintaining a satisfactory farm life. In *Rural Libraries* specific examples were given of seven types of rural library service, among them state extension library agencies, membership fee libraries, and county libraries (Nason 1928).

In all, eleven reports were issued on Nason's studies in the form of USDA farmers' bulletins which were made available upon request at no charge or a cost of perhaps 10 cents per copy. By 1934, it was reported that more than one million copies of Nason's bulletins had been distributed (*FPRLA* 1935; 9[1]:2–3). He also contributed short articles on some of the studies for the USDA annual *Yearbook of Agriculture*.

A Research Start on Farm Policy Issues

Before the 1920s were over the Division made a small start on research pertinent to current farm policy issues. In September 1920, following World War I, the prices of farm products began a drastic decline which persisted (Baker et al. 1963:98). Policymakers and farm organizations entered into prolonged debate over alternative proposals to solve the problem of low prices, falling incomes, and increasing inequality for agriculture (Baker et al. 1963:91–136). How to deal with crop surpluses became a major agricultural issue. Cooperative marketing was vigorously advocated as one solution that did not require price-fixing, production controls, and only limited government intervention. The Capper-Volstead Marketing Act of 1922 was passed to improve the legal status of cooperative associations. The Cooperative Marketing Act of 1926 created a Division of Cooperative Marketing in the BAE for research, advice, and consultation.[4] At the end of the 1920s there was no abatement in farmer economic distress. The Federal Farm Board, created by the Agricultural Marketing Act of 1929, was President Herbert Hoover's response to the pressure to provide federal financial aid to farmers. The Board was charged with encouraging producers to organize effective marketing cooperatives. A $500 million revolving fund was authorized to make loans to cooperatives. The Board was also to aid in preventing and controlling surpluses in any agricultural commodity through orderly production and distribution (Baker et al. 1963:136–38; Rasmussen 1975:2204–13).

About the time of the Cooperative Marketing Act of 1926, Galpin moved the Division into research on cooperatives by supporting projects in Minnesota (Zimmerman and Black 1926) and with Virginia Polytechnic Institute (Garnett 1927). The first of these sought to discover the attitudes of Minnesota farmers toward marketing problems and particularly toward cooperative marketing organizations. Data were collected by interviewing farm operators in nine communities selected to represent the state's important farming systems and the most important social characteristic of Minnesota farmers, their nationality and traditional backgrounds. Some 345 farmers were questioned. The data were analyzed to find the attitudes of the farmers regarding the problems under investigation and to explain

variations among individuals and communities. Among the more fundamental conclusions of the Minnesota study were these observations: "farmers in each community so vary in their attitudes toward the same
phenomenon as to give a distribution often approaching the normal frequency distribution" (49); "communities . . . vary in attitudes toward the
same concept" (50); "an important factor in attitude and behavior variation is the structure of previous experiences and thinking" (50); and "social
distance is a factor behind attitudes" (51). The second of these cooperative projects included descriptive data on Virginia's rural organizations,
among them commodity associations such as milk marketing associations
(Garnett 1927:9–18), but the special feature was a case study of the
Tobacco Growers' Cooperative Association (70–108). This marketing association had members in North Carolina, South Carolina, and Virginia. It
had been chartered in 1922 but went into receivership in June 1926.
Attitudes about this cooperative were sought by interviews with farmer
members and with others in eighteen of the thirty-three tobacco belt counties in the three states.

In 1928 the Division announced (FPRLA 1928:2[3]:12) that jointly
with the BAE's Division of Cooperative Marketing it had undertaken the
first of a new series of research studies focusing upon some of the sociological and psychological problems of cooperative marketing. Galpin
brought T. B. Manny, who had been one of his students in a summer session class at the University of Wisconsin, on to his staff to work in this
specialized area (Galpin 1938a:54–55). The series started with a study
which interviewed 898 farmers and fifty-seven merchants and brokers with
respect to a farmer member-owned potato marketing cooperative and private marketing agencies in a four-county area of Eastern Shore Maryland
and Virginia (Manny 1929). The agricultural experiment stations in the
two states were cooperators in the research. The special achievement of
this study was the analysis of the impact of ingrained habits on farmers'
marketing practices (FPRLA 1929:3[4]:8). Manny (1931) followed with
a survey of farmer opinions and attitudes as to cooperative and other cotton marketing methods in Alabama and North Carolina (see Chapter 8).
Next, with Ohio State University, Manny (1932) reported on the replies
of nearly 1,400 farmers in fourteen selected Ohio counties interviewed
with respect to their experiences with and opinions about farmer-owned
business organizations they had belonged to or patronized since 1920 (see
Chapter 8). The questions were built in to a larger study of membership
relations and farmer attitudes made at the request of the Ohio Farm Bureau
Federation (Manny and Smith 1931; see Chapter 8).

The Ohio study was the last in the series by Manny.[5] In Galpin's words, "the government limelight was turned off cooperative marketing" (1938a: 55). The research on cooperatives is an example of discontinuities in the Division's research program which were caused by a factor external to the Division.

The issue of how government agencies might help farmers adjust became more urgent as the new Federal Farm Board proved unable to cope effectively with agricultural surpluses. In an attempt to answer some questions involved in the problem, Manny (1933) made a yearlong study, *Farmer Opinions and Other Factors Influencing Cotton Production and Acreage Adjustments in the South*. One part of this research edged into USDA agency evaluation by assessing the extent to which economic outlook information prepared by USDA and state agencies was received and used by farmers and by collecting information on the effectiveness of the Extension Service role in providing information on marketing and cooperatives.

In 1931, well before the Roosevelt administration's Agricultural Adjustment Act of 1933 authorized drastic emergency measures to adjust farm production (Rasmussen 1975:2245–78), Manny's enumerators were interviewing 834 farmers in eleven counties chosen to represent three principal cotton-growing areas east of the Mississippi River. Sharecroppers were not questioned; they were not the decision-makers for their production program. The special emphasis in this study was on the reasons farmers gave for adjustments in cotton acreage made during 1926–31, to note the relationship between acreage adjustment and farm and farmer characteristics, to discover the chief sources of resistance to adjustments in the farm business, and to determine information sources used in making farm business adjustments. One feature of the research was the investigator's experimenting with methods to deal with discrepancies between a farmer's expressed opinions and his actions (Manny 1933:3). The report warned that 1931 was not a normal cotton-growing year for the respective areas because of low cotton prices and drought the preceding year and because the labor situation was abnormal due to the return migration from the North of former sharecroppers to their previous location.

The study concluded that there were many hindrances to rapid readjustments in the production of cotton. Some of these obstacles were primarily economic but others were found in the social institutions and habits the farmer psychology had built on long experience with a "cotton civilization." Manny cautioned "all attempts to stimulate more rational planning and management on individual farms must take into account not only the economic factors . . . but the whole social and psychological world in which farm people live" (Manny 1933:41).

Division Bypassed by Early New Deal

The initial years of President Franklin Roosevelt's administration, starting in 1933, marked the low point for the Division during Galpin's headship. The professional staff was reduced to two during part of 1933–35. For the USDA these were the years which Jess Gilbert and Ellen Baker, University of Wisconsin, have referred to as the First Agrarian New Deal (1997:283–84). The centerpiece of the new action programs to solve the farm problem was the Agricultural Adjustment Administration (AAA) with its measures for reducing farm production and increasing farm income. The farmers who benefited most from the AAA measures were those who had farming operations large enough to be helped substantially by higher commodity prices and the government's cash payments.

The Division was literally left out of the action during the First Agrarian New Deal. There was, however, urgent administrative need for current knowledge pertinent to the emergency programs of relief initiated to meet widespread human distress in rural areas. Accordingly, the Federal Emergency Relief Administration (FERA), succeeded in November 1935 by the Works Progress Administration (WPA) quickly moved to set up a new, temporary rural research unit to provide data needed at the national level and to also make detailed analyses of local conditions. The general plan of organization for this research unit followed the model for cooperative research with the states developed by Galpin and the Division. Further, several of the key professionals had close ties with the Division.[6]

The emergency rural research unit originated in August 1933 with a call by Harry L. Hopkins, in charge of the FERA, to University of Wisconsin rural sociologist E. L. Kirkpatrick to be his Rural Relief Advisor (Hobbs et al. 1938:6–12; Nelson, 1969:91–92). Kirkpatrick had been on the Division staff in the 1920s. He brought an initial group of rural sociologists to Washington and quickly worked out temporary cooperative arrangements with state colleges of agriculture to handle the field staffs for rural surveys originating in the Washington office.[7] By July 1934 plans for a more permanent arrangement were in place. There was to be a special Rural Section within the FERA's Division of Research and Statistics.[8] There would be a small central staff responsible for the planning and analysis of rural surveys and studies needed for national purposes.[9] Dwight Sanderson of Cornell University was brought in for a year to be the first Coordinator of Rural Research.[10] In addition, taking the model of cooperative projects instituted by Galpin and the Division, there was a Plan for Cooperative Rural Research. Under this Plan, FERA made special allocations for research to participating state agricultural colleges or other cooperating agencies.

The state cooperators had responsibility for field supervision of the federally initiated surveys but also had the flexibility to independently conduct studies of special interest to a state.[11] In all, forty-one states were included in the Cooperative Plan at some time. The Plan was still operating in twenty states in June 1938 (Hobbs et al. 1938:13) but came to an end within a year as the nation moved into defense activities.

An unprecedented amount of resources were quickly made available for rural social research to provide the information desired for FERA-WPA administrative purposes in policymaking and operating rural relief and rehabilitation programs. Sanderson (1935), without exact expenditure figures available, asserted that in the calendar year 1934 the funds provided for rural research by FERA probably equaled those received by the Division of Farm Population and Rural Life during its first fifteen years existence. Taylor (1948b) stated that the funds allocated to WPA's Rural Research Section ran as high as $500,000 per year.[12]

Until the agrarian part of the Second New Deal was launched in 1935, the Division received no funds for research or service to assist the new action agencies (Gilbert and Baker 1997:284). Nevertheless, the knowledge accumulated by its work was drawn upon by the emergency New Deal programs. Thus, when opportunities arose for rural areas to take advantage of work-relief projects to acquire such facilities as hospitals and community buildings, requests were many for publications on Nason's work done in the 1920s. They were the most satisfactory and available sources of information then available (Manny 1936:13).

Another user of the Division's completed research as New Deal programs got under way was the Division of Subsistence Homesteads organized in August 1933 in the Department of the Interior. The purpose was to construct communities that would combine employment in factories with part-time farming and gardening. During 1930, Nason (1932) had made a study of rural industries in a Kentucky county as part of a survey of economic and social conditions in the Southern Appalachians. Galpin had this expanded during late 1931 and early 1932 to gather data on manufacturing industries, mostly located in places with less than six thousand population or in the open country and scattered over fifteen states east of the Missouri or Mississippi Rivers. The main objectives were to discover the contribution these factories made to the income of farm families and to the general welfare of the rural communities (Manny and Nason 1934). Before the report *Rural Factory Industries* was in print, the results were being used by the Subsistence Homesteads Division administrators in shaping plans for this new venture (*FPRLA* 1934:8[3]:13).

THE SECOND AGRARIAN NEW DEAL AND THE RURAL DISADVANTAGED

By 1935, there was growing recognition that the first Agricultural Adjustment Administration's programs were not of much help to the "lower one-
third" of the nation's farm people. With the depression ongoing and the
Roosevelt New Deal willing to experiment, the administration response
was the initiation of the Second Agrarian New Deal to help the rural disadvantaged (Gilbert and Baker 1997:284–85). This led to a demand for
the Division's help and a dramatic turnaround in its activities and resources.

The Resettlement Administration (RA) was created as an independent
agency on April 30, 1935, by Executive Order of the President. Rexford
G. Tugwell, who was Henry A. Wallace's Undersecretary of Agriculture,
was placed in charge. The new agency was to deal with a host of agriculturally related relief and poverty problems for which neither the simultaneously established WPA work relief program nor the now-abolished FERA
programs were judged to offer suitable solutions (Larson 1947a:32–33).
Rural sociologist Carl C. Taylor was made Assistant Administrator in
charge of the Resettlement Division; this had a project planning section.
Within a few months, the planning section became a Division of Social
Research, staffed almost entirely by sociologists—nearly twenty. This was
continued when the RA was placed within the USDA on January 1, 1937,
and was succeeded by the Farm Security Administration (FSA) on September
1, 1937. A cooperative arrangement provided funds from RA-FSA to the
BAE for work to be done by the Division.[13]

In October 1935, when Taylor was put in charge of the Division of
Farm Population and Rural Life, he relinquished his Assistant Administrator duties in the RA to devote full time to directing the work of the
two research units, one in the RA and the other in the BAE. By design, the
work of the two units was closely integrated.[14] The unit in FSA was discontinued about the time, February 1938, that Taylor became head of the
Division on a full-time basis.

The Division's Cooperative Research with the RA-FSA

One of Taylor's first steps was to have the two research units join with
the rural research group in WPA to prepare WPA-published reports which
examined the social aspects of the severe drought problem in the Great
Plains. The first of these, *Areas of Intense Drought Distress 1930–1936*,
used five measures of drought intensity in 803 Great Plains counties
(Cronin and Beers 1937). A second report, *The People of the Drought*

States, used census data for the same 803 counties to show the population characteristics, document the settlement history of the region, and analyze the volume of migration to and out of the area (Taeuber and Taylor 1937). A third was *Relief and Rehabilitation in the Drought Area* (Link 1937). The two units under Taylor also had a hand in the fieldwork and analysis for a comprehensive study of *Rural Migration in the United States* (Lively and Taeuber 1939) published by the WPA Division of Research. Further, the FSA and the Division jointly issued eleven brief reports (e.g., Vasey and Folsom 1937) on surveys made in 1936 with funds provided by the WPA to the BAE. Each report dealt with agricultural labor conditions in a selected county (see Chapter 9).

During the less than three years that Taylor headed both the RA-FSA's social research unit and the Division, the two jointly published seventeen reports designed to supply administrators with information concerning the problems and conditions with which the agency programs for the rural disadvantaged were concerned. Thus, for example, the Resettlement Administration right at the start was planning a number of resettlement projects. The agency needed available information to guide specific action. When projects were operating, there was a need for analysis of them and for laying the groundwork for evaluation in the future of success and failure. Two of the first reports dealt with the problem of family selection for successful resettlement projects. One of these, *An Analysis of Methods and Criteria Used in Selecting Families for Colonization Projects* drew upon the experiences of past resettlement agencies in the United States and other countries (Holt 1937). It brought together information on procedures, forms, and instructions that had been used in the selection process and analyzed the experiences of persons interviewed who had been in charge of colonization projects. The second report was based on a field study, made in 1936, of a Bureau of Reclamation irrigation project opened in 1927 to 146 homesteaders (Jasny 1938). The study examined the criteria and methods used in selecting families for the project, the relation of the selection measures to family stability and instability on the project over the nine-year period. The study also analyzed the reasons for the success or failure of those who remained on the reclamation project at the end of the period.

Two reports dealt with new resettlement projects started by FERA or the RA and still in the process of development. One, *Standards of Living of the Residents of Seven Resettlement Communities* was designed to establish a "benchmark" against which to gauge the attainment and behavior in the material level of living of the resettled families in the future (Loomis and Davidson 1938). This study anticipated subsequent evaluation research, work which was not done before the resettlement project program was abolished by the Congress. The other, *Social Relationships and Institutions in Seven New Rural Communities* attempted to set a "benchmark" quantitatively as to the extent of social participation among the resettled families (Loomis 1940). The report also depicted the configurations of informal associations by applying sociometric techniques (see Chapter 7).[15] The analysis of small informal groupings proved to be important in helping project administrators understand integration and disintegration in these new resettlement project communities. Three non-resettlement communities and two neighborhoods were also studied for comparative purposes.

A number of other nations had been engaged in land tenure programs and in land resettlement. Accordingly, to mobilize and interpret the experiences of other nations, the report *Tenure of New Agricultural Holdings in Several European Countries* was prepared (Kraemer 1937). This dealt with the nature and results of land-tenure policies adopted in connection with the establishment of new agricultural holdings in England, Scotland, Germany, Denmark, Norway, and Sweden. Another and comprehensive report, *Social Status and Farm Tenure—Attitudes and Social Conditions of Corn Belt and Cotton Belt Farmers* (Schuler 1938b), dealt with aspects of land tenure in the United States for which specific information had not previously been available. This study was based on interviews with over 2,400 farmers, white and "colored," of all tenure categories (see Chapters 6 and 10).

One of the most significant in the set of seventeen jointly issued reports was *Disadvantaged Classes in American Agriculture* (Taylor et al. 1938). This was presented as an impressionistic study derived from U.S. Census and other secondary sources. It gave a sensitizing portrayal of the major factors that tended to reduce about one-third of the farm population to "submarginal standards of living." This work identified the territorial areas in which the rural disadvantaged were concentrated, using data on family income, levels of living, relief and rehabilitation, tenancy, farm laborers, poor land, and migration.

When FERA was inaugurated in late 1933, little differentiation was made between the types of assistance given to needy farm and non-farm families. But, in April 1934, a Rural Rehabilitation Division was added to FERA. This new program provided low-interest loans rather than direct aid for specific farm operating and family living purposes. The procedure for this new FERA rural rehabilitation program was, however, largely determined at the state level. Studies were made by some states of rural relief families and of applicants for rural rehabilitation loans. Later, after the Resettlement Administration was formed in 1935, two RA regions that included three midwestern and three mountain states, compiled information about their rural rehabilitation loan borrowers. The data from these studies provided information on family and farm characteristics. The RA Rural Rehabilitation Division also had schedules completed, from regional office files, for a sample of rural rehabilitation clients in eight widely separated type of farming areas. The research data from these disparate studies were brought together in *Analysis of 70,000 Rural Rehabilitation Families* (Kirkpatrick 1938). Among the implications of the study, pointed out by the investigator, was the need for study of why certain families were rejected for the rural rehabilitation loan program, what happened to those not accepted, and the need for study of families who failed after being accepted.

Other studies made in the joint series included a number on levels of living, especially in rural problem areas, e.g., *Standards of Living in Four Southern Appalachian Mountain Counties* (Loomis and Dodson 1938; see Chapter 6). The work of the Resettlement Administration in one Alabama county provided a unique research opportunity which led to the report *A Basis for Social Planning in Coffee County, Alabama* (Shafer 1937). Before there was an RA, the Alabama State Rural Rehabilitation Corporation had bought more than sixty thousand acres of land in scattered tracts in Coffee county. This gave leverage to reorient the population and the social institutions to the land characteristics. All land in the county had been classified by the Land Use Planning Section of the RA. This was the basis for three land-use areas designated "superior," "intermediate," and "inferior." Shafer related these land-use areas to population numbers and characteristics, farm characteristics, to church life, rural schools, and to singing societies, a form of association important to the people of the county. The report was concluded with specific recommendations for planning and locating community buildings in the county.

Overall, the jointly published set of seventeen reports, the last of which were issued in 1940, and related work was a demonstration to RA-FSA administrators of social science research and service. Some of this action program-related work was sensitizing to major people-oriented rural problems. Some reports were analytical. Others laid the groundwork for program evaluation in the future. And some offered guidelines for agency action in ongoing programs.

DIVISION STUDIES OF FSA PROGRAMS

From the time Carl Taylor assumed duty as head of the Division on a full-time basis in 1938 until after World War II was well underway, the close relationship between the FSA and the Division continued. In fact, the FSA was conspicuous at the time among the USDA's action agencies for the extent to which it called upon the Division for studies and service. Four major studies were made by the Division for the FSA. These were: (1) a national study of the standard rural rehabilitation loan program which covered almost a ten-year time period starting with the forerunners of the program before 1935; (2) a study of an experimental program conducted by the FSA for the USDA between 1938 and 1942 in 10 dispersed counties to develop ways of helping farm families too poor to qualify for the regular standard loan program; (3) a study, requested in 1939, of the FSA's subsistence-homesteads projects, and; (4) after the FSA initiated in 1942, at the behest of the USDA's Inter-bureau Coordinating Committee on Postwar Programs, an experimental tax-assisted health care program through voluntary associations, the Division was called upon to make evaluation studies of the eight experimental county programs established. The Division also joined in a study of the FSA's dental care program.

Another significant area of work related to the specific rehabilitation tools defined as "neighborhood action groups" (study or discussion groups) and "group services" (arrangements to enable small farmers to join together to obtain services or facilities they could not afford to own individually). This area of FSA interest led to studies of neighborhood action groups and group services in seven states, most done by Division staff in one regional office. About the same time, the Division prepared a training publication, issued by the FSA, on the use of neighborhoods and communities in the FSA program. Also, the FSA sought the Division's help in training regional, state, and area personnel in neighborhood and community delineation techniques and in understanding the social processes involved in neighborhood group discussion and organization.

In addition to the above sets of studies, the Division was asked in 1941 to join with the BAE's Division of Farm Management and Costs to provide the FSA's Tenant Purchase Division with information on farm organization and family levels of living on family-type farms in five type-of-farming areas. This was information desired for policy development purposes. Also, in 1943, the Division staff analyzed data collected nationwide by the FSA from its local offices to prepare two reports issued by the FSA.

One, noted in Chapter 5, was on new off-farm work during 1942, the first year of war, by FSA borrower family heads and on migration from farms by low-income families (Jehlik and Larson 1943a). The second was on obstacles to increased food production by low-income farmers (Jehlik and Larson 1943b). Division staff also assisted the FSA in designing a national survey of rural rehabilitation and tenant purchase borrowers to determine their food production in 1941 and 1942 and planned for 1943.

Two Division regional offices worked on studies with their FSA regional counterparts. Thus, in 1941, the Amarillo, Texas, office studied the levels of living on one FSA resettlement project, did an evaluation of the tenant-purchase program in the region, and cooperated with the BAE's Division of Farm Management and Costs in an analysis of FSA borrower farm and home plans and record books for a cotton-growing area in the region. The Lincoln, Nebraska, office cooperated with the FSA to compile data on the housing facilities of FSA borrowers in four northern Great Plains states. In only a single instance did a study for the FSA include agricultural experiment station cooperation. In this case, a study of families who were getting a fresh start as share tenants on new farms in the FSA's Red River Valley resettlement project, the investigator was employed cooperatively with the Rural Sociology Department, North Dakota Agricultural Experiment Station (Johansen 1941).

The Standard Rural Rehabilitation Loan Program

By 1939 the FSA was conducting an array of programs to assist low-income farm and other disadvantaged rural families. These included the standard rural rehabilitation loan program; non-standard loans; grants; assistance to cooperatives through loans, grants, or supervision for a wide variety of activities to benefit FSA borrowers;[17] farm-debt adjustment; tenure improvement; the tenant-purchase program as authorized by Title I of the Bankhead-Jones Farm Act of 1937 (Rasmussen 1975:2120–33); resettlement projects; and migratory labor camps. There were also a number of special programs that had been initiated to cope with problems for a specific locality or to assist a special group or to test rehabilitation methods in a small area. These special programs included, at the time, farm unit reorganization in the Southern Great Plains, the ten-county experiment to reach very low income farm families, a special black neighborhood-community program in eleven areas in the South, a special real estate loan program in a few areas to help farmers who had recently lost or were about to lose their farms through foreclosure, and a water facilities loan program authorized by the Water Facilities Act of 1937 to construct or repair, in seventeen Western states, such facilities as ponds, windmills, irrigation facilities, and farmstead water.[18]

Among this wide-ranging set of FSA programs, the standard rural rehabilitation loan program emerged as the most significant as measured by number of families reached, amount of money involved, or geographic coverage. Some 695,000 families were classified as standard loan borrowers between July 1, 1935, and September 30, 1943 (this excludes farm ownership borrowers and project occupants who may have also had standard loans). These borrower families were dispersed throughout all but a dozen counties of the nation. Between July 1935 and June 1944 a total of 787 million dollars was obligated by the RA-FSA for standard loans to individuals. The chief characteristics of the standard loan program included (1) *credit* for normal farm and home operating expenses to farm families unable to obtain satisfactory financing from any other private or federal source; (2) *supervision,* or advisory assistance, which included help in making farm and home plans and "on the farm" teaching of improved farm and home practices; (3) rehabilitation *in place,* that is without resettlement.

Financial aid was of a "high risk" type from a banking point of view, for the purpose of advancing social welfare objectives. Granting of credit was conditional upon the family's agreement to carry out the farm and home plans developed jointly with the farm and home supervisors. Caseloads for supervisors were usually heavier than the 125 per rural rehabilitation and 200 per home supervisor set by the FSA as desirable. It was the *combination* of credit and supervision that was the unique feature that resulted in the standard loan program's being called a "social invention of high significance" (Black 1945:591–614). This invention evolved from the efforts by FERA-funded state emergency relief programs in a few states in 1933 to experiment with techniques to meet the peculiar problems of farmers on relief as differentiated from the rural destitute who lacked access to land.

Late in 1939, the FSA requested a study of the standard rural rehabilitation loan program. The prime instigator within the FSA for this request was Thomas J. Woofter Jr., a sociologist who was special adviser to FSA administrator C. B. Baldwin. Woofter had been brought on the FSA staff following Carl Taylor's shift to full time in the Division.[19] The intent of this request was that existing records in FSA regional offices be used (1) to ascertain the economic and social characteristics of borrowers at the time of entering the program, their experience during the year before entry, and the trends in the types of borrowers selected; (2) to determine the progress of the borrowers since entering the program; (3) to analyze the action taken by FSA to facilitate rehabilitation; and (4) to analyze the factors associated with progress or failure in rehabilitation.

Data were collected for a sample of 39,295 standard borrowers who entered the program during the period March 1936–February 1939 and who were distributed among the twelve continental FSA regions. This was approximately a 20 percent sample of all borrowers whose first standard loan was authorized within this three-year period.[20] All data came from records in the FSA regional offices. There were no personal interviews with borrowers for this study, no checking back with FSA county personnel. Woofter had arranged $140,000 in funding from the WPA for the transcription and tabulation of the data.[21] The Division's work had the cooperation of all twelve FSA regional offices, the Programs and Reports Division and other units of the FSA in Washington, and the BAE's Divisions of Agricultural Finance, Farm Management and Costs, and Land Economics.

As tabulated data became available on a preliminary basis, the results were prepared for administrative use by the FSA administrator, his special adviser, the director of the rural rehabilitation program, and selected others within the FSA. Between September 1941 and June 1942 some thirty such short special memos and reports were prepared. Each of the twenty-three memos pertained to a specific subject such as the major purposes for which loans were made to borrowers, receipts by borrowers from government benefit payments, size of farm and acres in crops, education of borrowers, and a comparison of white and "colored" borrowers. The seven special reports provided other information gleaned from the available records e.g., actual versus planned cash receipts during a given crop year, the mobility of borrowers, and disabilities of borrowers and their family members. In addition, the director of each of the twelve FSA regions was provided, for administrative use, a set of 123 tables for his region on borrower characteristics, progress of borrowers, and action taken for borrower rehabilitation. The last of the regional reports was submitted in April 1943.

We have no documentation as to how FSA administrators made use of these reports with the extensive data they provided on the borrowers accepted during 1936–39. The research did, however, have unanticipated consequences. When President Roosevelt brought Chester C. Davis into the government as War Food Administrator, outranking the Secretary of Agriculture, Claude R. Wickard, Davis had to decide whether the FSA's contribution to the war effort justified its continuation. To make this important decision, Davis sought the counsel of an advisory group that included

Harvard economist John D. Black. Widely recognized for his work in agricultural policy, Black was no stranger to the USDA; he was frequently called upon for advice. He arranged to have the BAE assign the principal investigator for the standard loan rural rehabilitation loan project, Olaf F. Larson, to assist him in interpreting for Davis the data the FSA was presenting to justify the agency's continuation. Black asked, for example, that a statement be prepared for Davis explaining the sampling procedure and other facts pertinent to assessing the data presented by the FSA on the food production of rural rehabilitation and tenant purchase borrowers (Larson 1943b).[22]

This project took a new turn in 1943. Wartime adjustments in BAE activities had prevented preparation of the planned summary report. In early 1943, FSA representatives asked for an analysis of the accumulated experience with the standard loan rural rehabilitation loan program. This led to a more comprehensive, future-oriented study than originally undertaken.

The purposes of the report on this revised study were (1) to record the significant experience accumulated in the United States in conducting rehabilitation "in place," i.e., to trace the development of program policies and of rehabilitation tools and techniques associated with the standard rural rehabilitation loan program; and (2) to evaluate this experience in terms that would be useful for any continuing or new programs. Evaluation meant (1) stating the basic lessons learned with respect to the principles of rehabilitation of disadvantaged farm families and in regard to the use of rehabilitation tools and techniques; and (2) stating and clarifying the major issues involved in rural rehabilitation from the standpoint of public policy. Further, because it was thought that the experiences in the United States with this program might have value for the rural reconstruction and rehabilitation efforts of war-ravaged and poverty-stricken countries, the report treated administrative procedures and some of the rehabilitation techniques in more detail than would otherwise be necessary.

The report on the revised project did make extensive use of the statistical data for the sample of 39,295 borrowers accepted during 1936–39. Additionally, use was made of the FSA's published summaries of the annual family progress reports of standard borrowers for the years 1937–43, periodic and special reports prepared by the FSA for internal use, and special compilations requested of the FSA. Administrative procedural documents, congressional hearings, and interviews and field observations at all administrative levels were used to supplement and interpret the statistics. The findings of more localized studies by the state agricultural experiment stations and the BAE were also freely drawn upon in the attempt to summarize existing research in this field. The USDA Library prepared a bibliography on rehabilitation of low-income farmers as an aid in identifying the published studies available (McNeil 1943).

Release of the completed study was delayed for a year after the manuscript was submitted for the BAE's customary review and approval procedure. This was despite the best efforts of Division head Carl Taylor.[23] The 433-page report, *Ten Years of Rural Rehabilitation in the United States,*[24] sketched the genesis of the rehabilitation idea and its legislative and administrative history (Larson 1947a). It stated the program's objectives, both explicit and inferred, for borrower families, for agriculture, and for the general welfare of the nation, and it indicated how these objectives were realigned in response to changing economic and political conditions, shifts in FSA administrative personnel, and the coming of war. Likewise, the organizational structure for conducting the rural rehabilitation program and how it functioned was described. An analysis was made of the personal characteristics of the borrowers, of their before-acceptance level of living, income, assets, and of their land and other farming resources. While there was a wide range of characteristics and resources on the part of borrowers coming on the program within each FSA region, there were central tendencies which set individual regions and groups of regions apart. The average borrower accepted in some regions would have to make tremendous progress to be as well off as were the borrowers in others, even before they received rehabilitation assistance.

The report described and analyzed each of the rehabilitation tools and techniques such as supervision, credit, grants, and group services. Problems and issues with respect to each of the tools and techniques were stated, thereby raising questions for future public policy as well as questions for rural poverty research. Quantitative measures of progress toward rehabilitation objectives for families were limited to selected groups of borrowers who had not repaid their loans as yet. It was concluded that there was improvement for many of these families in such observed items as health, tenure status, production of food for family use, household facilities and equipment, income, net worth, working capital, land resources, and leasing arrangements. Changes, however, in such significant factors as attitudes, morale and work habits had not been adequately measured for even active borrowers. What gains were made while on the program by families who had paid up their loans or who had been dropped was largely an open question. A general assessment was made of the progress toward the various objectives of the rehabilitation program for agriculture and the general welfare of the nation.

In a chapter on the rehabilitation process, the diverse factors that condition the efforts to help families with a wide range of characteristics and problems were analyzed (331–45). The conclusion was reached that the real meaning of rehabilitation (or habilitation) is the attainment of the *cluster* of interrelated economic and social goals which may be defined in terms of the program objectives for the individual families. The content of these goals may be expressed in terms of practices, behavior patterns, attitudes, and material possessions. It was asserted that an understanding of the process whereby a family achieves the cluster of goals defined as constituting rehabilitation was one of the most important lessons to be learned from the FERA-RA-FSA experience. It was categorically stated that the speed of the rehabilitation process is conditioned by (1) family characteristics and physical and economic resources; (2) rehabilitation aids; (3) the culture—especially as expressed by attitudes, social values, class structure, social and economic institutions and facilities—within which the relationships of the family and the program are conducted; and (4) more or less impersonal forces such as depression or natural calamities outside the control of family or program agency.

The final chapter "A Look Ahead" stated noteworthy lessons learned from the nation's experience in rehabilitating lower-income farm families with the help of the standard loan program (346–52). It raised the issue as to the role to be played by a standard loan-type activity as a national publicly financed program. And it set forth hard facts to be faced by agriculture and rural society as a whole if the chosen role was as a program to be a positive instrument of social and economic improvement on behalf of the lower-income segment in American agriculture.

A reviewer of *Ten Years of Rural Rehabilitation in the United States* for the journal *Rural Sociology* observed that this was a case where "through painstaking search many valuable data were obtained and assembled, particularly information about the early years of the program, that might not have been available a few years hence. Their preservation in this report will make it a valuable source book" (Smith 1947:431–33). He went on to say, "The analysis of this 'new social invention of major significance' should be of practical value today not only to those responsible for carrying out the rural rehabilitation program in our own country but to those who are dealing with problems of rural reconstruction in war-devastated and other impoverished countries all over the world." Four years later, in India, the research secretary of the Indian Society of Agricultural Economics, B. S. Mavinkurve, prepared an abridged summary of the report which was published under the same title in both hard and paper cover by the Indian Society (Larson 1951). Included was a preface which applied the study of the American experience with rural rehabilitation to the conditions in India.[25]

An Experiment in Rural Rehabilitation

By 1938 experience had demonstrated that for many reasons, including the expectation that loans be repaid, the RA-FSA standard loan rural rehabilitation program was increasingly selecting the "better risks" among the rural poor. This led to a decision in the USDA to initiate an experimental program to develop ways of helping toward self-support those rural families too poor to qualify for the regular program. The only barriers to admission into this new experimental approach were to be mental or physical disabilities that precluded rehabilitation. The FSA was assigned major responsibility for conducting the experiment, sometimes referred to as the "noncommercial" program, under the general sponsorship of a USDA interagency committee that included administrators from the Extension Service, the Bureau of Home Economics, the FSA, the BAE, and the AAA. The Division was to make evaluation studies.

The experiment lasted about four years. It was initiated in late 1938 and terminated, because of the war, at the end of 1942. The experimental program was to differ from the regular program in two ways. First, there was to be more intensive supervision of the families; this would be possible because of smaller case loads for the farm and home management supervisors assigned to the program. Second, the rehabilitation tools and techniques were to be used differently; in particular, the supervisors were to have more leeway in the use of grant and loan funds than under the standard program. Some 606 families located in ten widely dispersed counties were accepted in the program.[26] The families and the counties presented a wide range of low-income farm family situations, e.g., black sharecroppers in one Georgia county, white sharecroppers in another Georgia county, a Spanish-American area in New Mexico, one of the poorest sections of the Southern Appalachians, and part-time farming families who had settled on cutover land in Washington.

A Division staff member, Rachel Rowe (Swiger), working first with Conrad Taeuber and subsequently with Olaf F. Larson, was assigned to the evaluation work. Annual reports of the farm and home management supervisors were analyzed. Over the four-year trial period, visits were made to the ten counties to observe and to meet with the supervisors and some of the participant families. Six reports were issued on this study. Because of wartime conditions, all were in mimeo form with a limited number of copies. Those reports quickly became "fugitive" literature. First of the six was *Five Hundred Families Rehabilitate Themselves* (Taeuber and Rowe 1941). The concluding report and summary appraisal of the experiment was *Climbing Toward Security* (Swiger and Larson 1944).[27] In addition, Division staff member Charles P. Loomis took the lead in an independent analysis of the experimental effort in the one Spanish-American situation. This was published in *Applied Anthropology* (Loomis and Grisham 1943).

The final report noted that the full potential of the rehabilitation approach as originally conceived was not realized because of obstacles to maintaining experimental conditions within the project areas. For example, there was turnover and reduction of supervisory personnel, some mistakes in selection of supervisors, administrative failures to instruct supervisors fully as to the objectives and methods of the experiment. In most counties, as the FSA made wartime adjustments, the experimental program tended to merge more and more with the regular standard loan program (Swiger and Larson 1944:IV).

Despite such obstacles to maintaining the planned experimental conditions, the final assessment of the four-year trial was that this experiment with rural families at the very bottom of the socioeconomic ladder had demonstrated that there was hope many such families could better their condition and maintain the improvement if society would provide the opportunity. A public policy decision would be called for, the researchers stated, balancing the short and long run costs of this experimental approach to rehabilitation against the expense of maintaining families on relief, wasted manpower, and other considerations (Swiger and Larson 1944:40).

The final report identified ten definite and useful lessons learned from the experiment. It pointed out certain factors which appeared to condition the relative success in the rehabilitation of families with individualized characteristics, resources and capacities. The report described in some detail the adaptation of rural rehabilitation tools, techniques, and methods devised by the farm and home management supervisors to improve the depressed economic, health, social, and emotional conditions prevalent among the families at the program's start. Case studies illustrated problems encountered in working with families on the program and coping methods used by supervisors. Indicators of the progress of the families was documented quantitatively and described in such respects as production of food for home use and for sale, housing and sanitary facilities, medical and dental care, construction and repair of farm and home equipment, farm management practices, leasing arrangements for renters and sharecroppers, and financial status.

Among the lessons learned from this experiment with severely disadvantaged families was that good results required a highly individualized approach in each case and supervisors who, in addition to technical farm and home management knowledge, had sufficient understanding of human behavior to meet the social and personal problems of families. And, "perhaps most of all the experiment revealed the importance of small, common-sense things when helping people help themselves" (Swiger and Larson 1944:40). For example, training in simple farm and home tasks was an important part of helping these families.

Looking ahead to the postwar years, the summary report suggested that the activities and experiences of these 606 families were not unlike those that would have to be planned for in the realization of "Freedom from Want" on a world-wide basis. On reading *Climbing Toward Security,* rural sociologist George H. Hill, filling an administrative post in the USDA's wartime farm labor program, wrote to Division head Carl Taylor. He stated that he was impressed with it as "a rare sociological contribution" in the field of rural rehabilitation research, "outstanding in comparison" with much of the research in this area by sociologists in the past decade (Hill 1945).

Subsistence Homesteads Projects

When the FSA was set up in 1937 as successor to the Resettlement Administration, it inherited nearly seventy "subsistence-homesteads" projects to include in its program. These had been initiated by the Department of Interior's Subsistence Homesteads Division, operating under authorization of Section 208 of the National Industrial Recovery Act of 1933 and by FERA. The projects were experimental efforts intended, in part, to relocate workers left stranded by shifts in industry and farmers who were on definitely submarginal agricultural land. The first director of Interior's Subsistence Homesteads Division was M. L. Wilson; one of his right-hand staff members was Carl Taylor.

In 1939 the FSA requested a study of its subsistence-homesteads. The purpose was to procure information that would be valuable in the administration of subsistence homesteads projects. The FSA wanted to know what things had worked, what things had not worked, what social, psychological, and economic factors were responsible for certain project developments not easily explainable. The resulting research had the aid and guidance of an Interbureau Coordinating Committee chaired by Raymond C. Smith, in the office of the BAE Chief.

Nine of the thirty-three projects established by the Interior's Division of Subsistence Homesteads were selected for study. The aim was to select projects representing a range of characteristics and conditions, among them success and failure, rural settings, and in or near metropolitan areas. In all, ten members of the Division's professional staff had major roles in the research. Six were the field investigators who, under the direction of Charles P. Loomis, were sent into the project communities to live with the homesteaders. The participant-observer technique was used. There were no questionnaires but the interviews and observations had as guides thirteen "points of observation," with definitions and instructions all thoroughly explored in repeated conferences. Opinions about the projects were also gathered from local business and newspaper persons, original local sponsors, and other citizens. More than a thousand interviews were recorded. The projects record books were examined and their history documented. There was, however, no analysis of costs or of project administration nor was any elaborate statistical treatment of data attempted. Field investigators were told that their task was to find out and to report, as objectively as possible, what was going on with respect to these subsistence-homesteads projects and why. These investigators submitted reports to the program administrators.

The original purpose of the study was altered when the second draft of the manuscript for the report had already been completed. The approach of World War II altered the purpose and changed the anticipated users. It appeared that the study findings would be of value not only in the administration of the ongoing subsistence homesteads and resettlement projects but in the formulation of war and postwar programs. Officials, for example, were already talking of war housing programs, of industrial decentralization during the war, and of the role of housing projects in a postwar public works program. At that point, the study was reoriented, the projects were rechecked, and new emphasis was given to elements of the study that might apply to conditions and needs generated by the war.

The result of the reoriented research was the book-length *A Place on Earth: A Critical Appraisal of Subsistence Homesteads,* issued in mimeo form (Lord and Johnstone, eds. 1942). The publication, completed in October 1941, gave an historical account, prepared by two historians then on the Division's staff, of the subsistence homesteads idea, the back-to-the-land movement, of legislative developments and of the administration of the subsistence homesteads program. A chapter was devoted to each of the nine projects studied. A summary was given of the lessons learned from this study about subsistence homesteads. The conclusions, many tentative, were based on a fifteen-question memorandum sent in September 1941 to all the researchers who had participated.

Experimental Health Program

Soon after the rural rehabilitation program was started, it was recognized that many of these low-income families were handicapped by poor health. Major problems underlying this health situation appeared to be a lack of health care personnel and facilities in rural areas, lack of families' ability to pay for medical service, lack of preventive health care services, and poor nutrition and sanitation. The RA stated, in its first annual report in 1936, that the most urgent and complex problem confronting the Resettlement Administration was providing adequate medical, hospital, and dental care for fees that people could afford. Among all the pioneering efforts organized in the 1930s to improve health services for rural people, the work of the RA-FSA was the most extensive. In January 1936 the RA established a Public Health Section headed by a medical officer assigned by the U.S. Public Health Service. The health program conducted under the leadership of the Chief Medical Officer included the organization of local prepaid medical and dental care services for borrowers. On June 30, 1941, the FSA reported about seven hundred active medical care units, mostly on a county basis, with some 104,000 borrower families participating.[28] About one-third of these units were informal, unincorporated associations; the others had a "trustee" who administered the medical care fund.

In November 1941 the accelerating concern with the rural health services situation in the immediate pre–World War II period prompted the USDA's Interbureau Committee on Post Defense Planning (soon changed to Committee on Postwar Programs) to announce it would sponsor experimental health associations in a few counties. These would be voluntary prepaid plans intended to serve all farm families in the selected counties, not just low-income families. Member contributions to meet the cost of health care services would be based on ability to pay. Some federal funds would be available to assist in covering costs of services. The FSA, because of its experience with health associations for its borrowers, was designated to administer this experimental program. The Interbureau Committee involved regional, state, and selected county agricultural planning committees in determining the counties for the experiment. Six counties were originally chosen but a seventh was added.[29] Health associations were started in all seven counties between July and November 1942.

The Division was subsequently asked to study this experiment in health care for rural people. The research was a collective effort with the field investigations done by seven regional office staff members under the direction of Washington-based Douglas Ensminger. The stated objectives of the study were to appraise the organizational setup and method of operation in each experimental county "in order to provide information for the development of (a) postwar rural health programs, and (b) immediate health programs to meet the needs of rural people now faced with a shortage of medical facilities" (USDA, BAE, DFPRW 1943:1). Procedures called for discussions, prior to any fieldwork in a county, with the chairman of the USDA regional postwar planning committee, the regional FSA director, and the chairman of the state rural health committee (if there was one). In each county, the Board of Directors of the health association was to be asked to sponsor the study. Fieldworkers were given about five pages of questions to be answered by their research. Each county association manager placed local records at the disposal of the researchers. All physicians and dentists in these seven counties provided information. As an illustration of methods used, in one county, Newton, Mississippi, the Division researcher lived in the county for four weeks. Information was secured from the association manager and his records; members of the board of directors; all participating physicians, dentists, and druggists; agricultural and other agency leaders; bankers, industrialists, and the local newspaper; and members and non-members of the association. Using interview guides, information was obtained (a) from a 3 percent random sample of members as to opinions of the association, medical and dental services received the year prior to the association and during its first year of operation, and participation in developing and directing the association; (b) from dropouts and non-members as to reasons for not renewing membership or not joining; (c) from physicians, dentists, and county leaders; and (d) members of the board of directors.

Some reports covered only the 1942–43 operations, others covered the 1942–44 period. All reports were in a mimeo series. At the time these reports were being completed, a Senate Subcommittee on Wartime Health and Education, chaired by Senator Claude Pepper of Florida, was studying the distribution and use of health personnel, facilities, and services in the United States. It had become increasingly aware of the shortage of doctors and hospitals in many rural areas and of the great health needs, generally, of rural people. It had a special interest in methods of prepaying medical expenses. Learning of the USDA's experimental health program and of the Division's studies, Senator Pepper, on July 17, 1945, requested of Secretary of Agriculture Clinton O. Anderson a summary presentation of the studies. About three months later, on October 25, 1945, Secretary Anderson transmitted to the Senator the report prepared by the Division. This report was printed in a 166-page Subcommittee monograph (U.S. Congress, Senate 1946).

The summary report for the Senate Subcommittee was prepared by T. Wilson Longmore, who had co-authored two of the county reports, under the leadership of Carl Taylor and Douglas Ensminger. In preparing the final report, assistance was given by the medical, dental, and statistical staffs of the FSA's Health Services Division. Further, for two counties the preparers had access to unpublished reports of field studies made by an FSA medical consultant, Franz Goldman, M.D., Yale University School of Medicine.

After a concise description of the seven tax-assisted voluntary health associations, the Division's evaluation was presented. This included such aspects as the unique character of the associations, attitudes of health care professionals, program coverage, and patterns of health care before and after the health associations began. Conclusions were plainly stated. The main element of strength was the provision for supplementing family contributions through federal grant funds; without this outside assistance none of the associations could have operated (37). Most weak points came under two heads: (1) incomplete population coverage; and (2) inadequate scope and quality of care. Steps that might improve the program were suggested and the wider implications for any broad program of health insurance were stated. The report then gave detailed accounts of three of the associations studied, each representing a different method of paying for the services of health practitioners, i.e., fees for service rendered to individuals according to a predetermined schedule, capitation based on families rather than individuals, and salary, full- or part-time. The report was buttressed with fifty-nine tables of data dispersed through the text. To assist groups looking forward to developing their own health association, the report included important documents, such as a charter of incorporation, and the step-by-step highlights in the planning and operation of one of the experimental associations were given. The preparers of three of the county reports also used their studies as the basis for articles in the journal *Rural Sociology* (Matthews 1946; Montgomery 1945; Vaughan and Pryor 1946).[30]

Independently of the studies of the experimental health programs described above, Charles Loomis also made a study of the Taos County,

New Mexico, experiment. At the time, he was jointly employed by the Division and the USDA's Office of Foreign Agricultural Relations. Most of the travel costs for his visits to the county in 1942, 1943, and 1944 were paid by the Carnegie Corporation. Loomis's findings were published in the *American Sociological Review* (1945). His evaluation of the results of the experiment in Taos County was preceded by an analysis of the acculturation process going on in the area, where over 95 percent of the people had Spanish as their mother tongue, and an analysis of the relation of this process to the emerging class structures and to the primitive beliefs concerning medicine and healing. Among other factors in the culture and social organization identified as important factors for the health association, the village pattern of settlement was ranked second in importance only to the acculturation process and its relationships.

The FSA's Dental Care Program

The FSA's first dental care programs for its borrowers were of an emergency nature, offered in combination with medical care. Soon, however, it was often found more practical to organize a separate dental unit for a county. These plans were limited to FSA borrowers; no government subsidy was involved. These county dental programs operated, however, with only limited supervision and investigation by the FSA's Washington Office. Little was known about the dental program, e.g., how close was it approaching its objectives in dental care for different age and income groups?

The Division was asked to join with the FSA's dental officer in a study. Available resources prohibited a detailed study of even a sample of the units. The decision was made to make an intensive study of one county, Randolph, Georgia. The fieldwork was undertaken in May 1945. The study aimed to answer three large questions: (1) had the dental programs achieved their purpose in dental care; (2) what factors assisted or prevented the full functioning of the program; and (3) what suggestions and recommendations could be made regarding future policies for the dental care program.

To determine present dental conditions, services received, and attitudes toward the FSA dental program, over one-half of the currently participating families were selected on the basis of size of family, race, and income along with a "control" group of families who had never been participants. The families were visited in their homes by a dentist and an interviewer. The dentist examined and recorded the dental condition of the members of all these sample families. The interviewer had a questionnaire guide that was used in an informal way. Responses were recorded after the visit. Meanwhile, a third member of the study team obtained background cultural data and information on the program's administration.

The researchers concluded that the current dental care program in this Georgia county had some strong elements but was weak or only adequate in others (Lantis et al. 1945). The program did include all available dental personnel and facilities in the county (there were only two dentists) and provided minimum dental care to some who would not receive it if not in the plan. The organization and administration of the plan, however, was judged to be a weakness; there was no written agreement between dentists and the association. Record-keeping was poor. A most important point made by the researchers was that the FSA's Randolph County program had made no changes in dental personnel, facilities, schedule of fees, or in habits or concepts of dental care. The report stated four difficulties in existing rural dental care, at least in the Southeast, to be considered in future planning and administrative changes with respect to dental health care. Among these were transportation and related problems of distribution of dental services, and misunderstanding and inadequate education about dental health.

Studies of Rehabilitation Tools

Among the tools used by supervisors in the rural rehabilitation program were "group services" and "neighborhood action groups." The group services were a form of mutual aid, the formalization of a practice among farmers to join together in the acquisition and use of items they could not afford individually, e.g., a piece of equipment such as a tractor or a better herd sire. The use of this tool started during the first year of the RA by loans to "joint owners" or, less often, to a "master owner" who provided a service to his neighbors. The participants in the group service to which the RA-FSA made loans and assisted were not all agency borrowers or even other low-income farmers. By June 30, 1942, nearly twenty-five thousand of these simple cooperatives had been started. Neighborhood action groups were a tool adapted from the experiences of the agricultural extension service, the Ohio Farm Bureau, and other farm organizations. Such groups were generally made up of six or eight families who met in each others' homes to discuss common problems. Members elected a chairperson and called the meetings. The supervisor's role was to be an advisor, attending meetings by invitation. The term "action" was used by the FSA to denote the intention that out of discussions a decision for joint action might result. The first use of neighborhood action groups by the FSA was about 1939, in its region headquartered in Lincoln, Nebraska. In 1941, the tool was introduced to all FSA regions. During 1944, the number active was estimated at four thousand, the greater part of them in the FSA region headquartered in Little Rock, Arkansas.

The Division made firsthand studies of these rehabilitation tools in a dozen counties located in seven states—Arkansas, Illinois, Kentucky, Louisiana, Oklahoma, Oregon, and Texas.[31] Three of the twelve reports prepared included both group services and neighborhood action groups. Three were limited to group services and six pertained to neighborhood action groups. The distribution of five of the reports was limited to administration circles within the USDA. The remainder were issued in mimeo form with only a few copies. Eight of the reports were prepared in the Division's regional office in Little Rock, Arkansas, the rest in the Washington office.

The observations suggested that weaknesses in the FSA's use of group services included administrative pressures on county staff to go out and organize such groups, setting "quotas," and the practice of organizing without regard to the felt need of the participants arrived at by free and full discussion. Other problems faced by some of the groups studied were identified along with factors that contributed to making these simple cooperatives function effectively. One report set forth criteria that might apply in an evaluation of such groups (Standing and Pryor 1943:10).

Understanding of neighborhood action groups was enhanced by the almost verbatim reports of the observed meetings of a dozen such groups in Oklahoma (Longmore 1943a) and in Texas (Longmore 1943b). Observation of these groups during the early stages of their organization indicated the soundness of basic principles the FSA recommended in their organization and servicing to achieve full effectiveness. Observations of other groups not more than a year after they started pointed up some of the problems encountered in the early experiences with this rehabilitation tool and provided the basis for suggestions by the researchers as to how the problems could be met.

Family Living Needs for Tenant Purchase Borrowers

Growing concern with the increase in the proportion of farmers who did not own the land they farmed led Congress in 1937 to adopt legislation, the Bankhead-Jones Tenant Purchase Act to initiate a modest program that would attempt to counter this trend (Rasmussen 1975:2120–33). Responsibility for administering the funds appropriated rested with the

Farm Security Administration which set up a Tenant Purchase Division. Funds could be loaned to tenants and others to help them obtain family-sized farms that would produce enough income to cover family living expenses, farm operating expenses and maintenance, interest on the debt to the FSA, and amortization of the loan. By 1941 the program was operating in over 1,800 counties. Restrictions imposed by Congress on size of loan and size of farm raised nagging questions, however, for the FSA.

Following several conferences between members of the BAE and FSA staff as to FSA research needs that the BAE could meet, the Tenant Purchase Division requested a study whose purpose would be to supply the FSA with farm plans showing income expectancy on different types of family farms that would aid in appraising their program and in explaining the reasons for certain actions that would have to be taken in order that the families could pay for the farms they purchased and still maintain a satisfactory level of living. The Division of Farm Management and Costs was assigned primary responsibility for providing the FSA with these plans. Farm Population and Rural Life had secondary responsibility. The information requested by the FSA was needed first for the South, the Corn Belt, and the Great Plains. It was anticipated that the same type of information would be needed in the future for other sections of the country. The project was expected to be a continuing one.

In early March 1941 memoranda went out from the Washington office of the Division of Farm Management and Costs and of the Division to five of their respective regional offices instructing them to jointly prepare by June 1 a first report. After the Farm Management staff had made its contribution in each of the five regions, the Division staff in the region was to evaluate the income expectancy of the farm plans in terms of the levels of living that could be provided. The time frame permitted no new field projects to secure answers. This first report had to be prepared on the basis of data available. This meant that the quantity and adequacy of available data varied greatly from region to region. Each of the five regions prepared its report independently to explore, at this stage, alternative approaches to the problem posed by the FSA. Thus, for example, one report suggested the importance of planning for different types of families rather than a single type. Another showed the desirability of working out plans for a long period in the family's life cycle, twenty years in this case. And another started with a measure of family satisfaction with what they presently had and worked back into the quantitative and monetary measures of level of living.

A preliminary summary of the five regional reports was drafted by December 1941 and circulated in the BAE and FSA for review.[32] By March 1942 the final report was ready (Rush and Larson 1942). This was reviewed and discussed by the Washington-based researchers, one an economist, the other a sociologist, in a session with the director of the FSA's Tenant Purchase Program. The summary report and the five regional analyses were issued by the BAE in mimeo form. In this instance the responses to the FSA's request was completed in a year's time.

Clearly, the Second Agrarian New Deal with its focus on the rural disadvantaged and its action programs, the Resettlement Administration and its successor agency, the Farm Security Administration, had major inport for the Division. For a number of years starting in 1935 and well into the World War II years, the RA and FSA were major users of the Division's research and services. But when the Congress replaced the FSA with the Farmers' Home Administration in 1946, the new agency did not turn to the Division for studies.

Notes

1. This chapter and the next one are a major revision of Olaf F. Larson and Edward O. Moe, "Pioneering in the development and practice of sociology by the USDA's Division of Farm Population and Rural Life: A dialogue," presented at the 1990 annual meeting of the American Sociological Association. Parts of the chapter were used in Olaf F. Larson and Julie N. Zimmerman, "The USDA's Bureau of Agricultural Economics and sociological studies of rural life and agricultural issues, 1919–1953," presented at the Eightieth Anniversary Symposium of the Agricultural History Society in 1999 at Mississippi State University.

2. "The Uses of Sociology" was the theme of the 1962 annual meeting of the American Sociological Association. The papers presented at that meeting, and other material, were used by Paul F. Lazarsfeld, William H. Sewell, and Harold L. Wilensky in their edited book, The Uses of Sociology (1967). See especially, the "Introduction," (IX–XXXIII) for a paradigm for understanding the uses of sociology and Chapter 24 "Rural Sociology" by Charles P. Loomis and Zona Kemp Loomis.

3. The term "understanding" was used by Donald Young (1955) in discussing the relationships of sociology to the practicing professions.

4. The BAE's Division of Cooperative Marketing was transferred to the Federal Farm Board on October 1, 1929 (Baker et al. 1963:137).

5. Later, the Division cooperated in a survey of 140 village-centered agricultural communities which tracked rural trends during the depression years 1930–36. The depression-period adjustments by cooperative purchasing and marketing organizations in these communities received some attention (Brunner and Lorge 1937:58–64).

6. The Division, through its quarterly publication Farm Population and Rural Life Activities, reported periodically on the staff, the research program, and organizational changes of the rural research unit in FERA and WPA, e.g., 8(1):7; 8(4):7–9; 10(2):5–9.

7. During 1933 and the early part of 1934 much of the cooperative work in the states

involved the use of the short-lived Civil Works Administration (Hobbs, Link, and Winston, 1938:7).

8. The Rural Section of the Division of Research and Statistics, FERA, later became the Rural Unit of the Research Section, Division of Research, Statistics, and Finance, FERA. When WPA replaced FERA, on November 29, 1935, the rural research unit became the Rural Research Section of the Division of Social Research, WPA and, later, the Rural Surveys Section.

9. In Fall 1934, the Washington staff of the Rural Section was comprised of nine professional staff members and a consultant (FPRLA 8[4]:7).

10. Prior to Sanderson's arrival, E. D. Tetreau of Ohio State University was temporarily in charge of research pertaining to rural relief, under E. L. Kirkpatrick, the Rural Relief Advisor. After Sanderson returned to Cornell, T. C. McCormick, already on the staff, was Acting Coordinator until J. H. Kolb, University of Wisconsin, came to fill the position for a few months. When Kolb returned to Wisconsin in fall, 1935, T. J. Woofter Jr., of the University of North Carolina, became Coordinator of Rural Research and served until the Cooperative Plan was terminated in 1939 (Nelson, 1969:92). All of these men were sociologists.

11. Under the Cooperative Plan, each cooperating state had a State Supervisor of Rural Research—usually a rural sociologist, selected with the approval of the agricultural experiment station director—who served in this position part-time in addition to regular duties as college faculty member. The FERA-WPA funding usually also provided for a full-time Assistant State Supervisor of Rural Research, not normally a regular member of the college or experiment station staff but employed specifically for this temporary position.

12. The FERA-WPA Rural Section staff, in some instances with cooperators in other federal agencies, published some 20 research monographs (Hobbs et al. 1938:18; Nelson, 1969:92–95). The Plan for Cooperative Rural Research resulted in the publication by cooperating states of approximately 200 printed or mimeographed bulletins as of the June 30, 1938, cutoff date for the inventory taken by Hobbs et al. (1938:32–56).

13. By Taylor's (1939) account, $40,000 was allocated to the Division during the second half of fiscal year 1935–36, $143,000 during 1936–37, $28,733 during 1937–38, and $2,970 during 1938–39. Additionally, during 1936–37 some $60,000 was provided by the RA to several of its regional offices for social research supervised by the Division.

14. The work of the Division in the BAE and of Taylor's research unit in the RA-FSA was so integrated that some former staff members we interviewed for this study said that even though they worked side by side, they were not sure which payroll their fellow workers were on. Several RA-FSA staff members held "collaborator" appointments in the Division.

15. The application of sociometric methods in studying the informal relationships, such as visiting among resettlement project families, is discussed by Loomis and Davidson in "Sociometrics and the study of new rural communities" (1939a).

16. In the spring of 1943, the House created a Select Committee of the House Committee on Agriculture to investigate the activities of the FSA. This committee held extensive hearings during 1943 and 1944.

17. Cooperative association activities assisted by the FSA included not only purchasing and marketing, but medical, dental, and hospital care, agricultural processing and facilities such as creameries and cotton gins, land leasing, livestock insurance, life insurance, veterinary service, small water facilities in the arid and semi-arid states, and other purposes.

18. Other special programs were added by FSA after 1939. Among these was an experimental farming program to find new ways of farming in low-income areas. This never got beyond ten farmers in one Georgia county because of World War II. Also a farm and home improvement loan program was started in 1942 and a number of "special area" programs were started in 1941 and early 1942, e.g., Aroostock County, Maine; a four-county

light soil area in central Wisconsin; a ten-county area in New Mexico; and a seven-county area in Missouri's "bootheel."

19. Just prior to taking the advisory position with the FSA, Woofter had been Coordinator of Rural Research in the WPA and, before that, had been a member of the University of North Carolina faculty.

20. Details on the sampling, the FSA records consulted, the data transcribed, and the completeness of the FSA records for the sample cases are given in Larson (1947a:425–27).

21. Woofter was the principal liaison with the FSA in the early phase of the requested study, working closely with the project's principal investigator, Olaf F. Larson. The WPA funds were used to pay for the clerical workers selected from WPA rolls who transcribed data in eleven regional FSA offices and who tabulated data in the project's Washington office. These WPA workers numbered about three hundred at the peak of the operations in 1940 and 1941. All tabulations for the 39,295 cases were done manually. The WPA funds also paid for up to five supervisory personnel employed temporarily for the project by the Division. The clerical workers in each regional FSA office were under the immediate supervision of an FSA staff member.

22. Preparation of the statement for the War Food Administrator was facilitated by the fact that Larson had assisted FSA personnel in planning the procedures for the survey used as a source of the production figures in question.

23. Shortage of paper and of publication funds were asserted to be factors complicating publication of the complete report (Larson 1947c). Taylor rejected the suggestion of the BAE's Division of Economic Information that the manuscript be greatly curtailed in length in order to issue a printed or multi-lithed report. Finally, a compromise was reached whereby a few copies of the full report would be made available in mimeographed form to administrators, interested research workers, and some libraries. As noted in Chapter 4, the then-head of the BAE personally reviewed the manuscript.

24. A summary of this report was presented at the 1946 meeting of the Rural Sociological Society. See Olaf F. Larson "Rural Rehabilitation-Theory and Practice," *Rural Sociology* 12(3):223–37.

25. For a review of the abridged version see Edmund deS. Brunner in *Rural Sociology* 17(4):396–97.

26. The ten counties were Laurens and Oglethorpe, Georgia; Mercer, West Virginia; Knox, Kentucky; Grayson, Virginia; Reynolds, Missouri; Beltrami, Minnesota; Orange, Vermont; San Miguel, New Mexico; and Thurston, Washington. Plans for an experimental program in Grundy County, Missouri did not materialize.

27. A condensed summary analysis of the experimental program prepared by Rachel Rowe Swiger was included in *Ten Years of Rural Rehabilitation in the United States* (Larson 1947a:285–91).

28. Health Services for rural rehabilitation borrowers are discussed and evaluated in *Ten Years of Rural Rehabilitation* (Larson 1947a:230–51).

29. The counties chosen were Cass County, Texas; Hamilton County, Nebraska; Nevada County, Arkansas; Newton County, Mississippi; Taos County, New Mexico; Walton County, Georgia; and Wheeler County, Texas. Taos County was not in the group originally selected; its inclusion was an outgrowth of an association established in 1941 with the help of a Carnegie Corporation-funded University of New Mexico project. This association, in turn, developed out of a small FSA-sponsored plan of medical and dental care for FSA borrowers started in 1940 (Loomis 1945:154).

30. It is likely that it was because of James E. Montgomery's participation in the study of the FSA's experimental health program that he was invited to attend the June 25–27, 1946, Southern Rural Heath Conference and serve on the committee which prepared a report on prepayment medical care plans. This was included in the conference report *The South's*

Health: A Picture with Promise (U.S. Congress, House 1947). The conference sponsors included the Steering Committee for Postwar Studies of the Cotton Belt, the Farm Foundation, and the Southern Rural Health Conference Planning Committee. The report was reprinted from hearings held July 7 and 8, 1947, before a House Special Subcommittee on Cotton of the Committee on Agriculture.

31. The studies of group services and neighborhood action groups were drawn upon in the preparation of the sections on these rehabilitation tools in *Ten Years of Rural Rehabilitation in the United States* (Larson 1947a:194–208).

32. One reviewer, chief of the Home Management Section in the FSA's Rural Rehabilitation Division, commented that the study brought out "very important information related to the family-sized farm and which will be most helpful to Farm Security Administration employees." However, she believed "that the family living material shows the need for a person trained in the field of family economics" (Ogle 1942).

13

The Practice of Sociology: II

In this chapter we continue our examination of the Division's experiences during the Taylor years in the practice of sociology in the federal government. The Division's opportunities and organizational structure began to take a new turn when the Secretary of Agriculture assigned administrative responsibility to the BAE for the USDA's land utilization program. We note the effect on the Division of this new BAE responsibility. We give major attention to two unique sets of experiences afforded the Division in the area of practice. One was related to the innovative land-use (agricultural) planning program which was a prime component of the USDA reorganization in 1938, which made the BAE the economic and social program planning agency for the whole USDA. The second set of experiences emerged from the national crisis precipitated by the December 7, 1941, attack on Pearl Harbor and the ensuing years of war. This chapter also looks at assistance to the Soil Conservation Service, the Division's activities in postwar planning and in a significant public policy area, social security for farm people. This chapter also relates the Division's extensive contributions to the investigations that went into planning the vast Columbia River Basin irrigation project, which was to be constructed by the Department of Interior's Bureau of Reclamation. We conclude the chapter with identifying the lessons that the Division thought it had learned from its experiences and with some observations about putting sociology to work during the Taylor years.

THE DIVISION AND THE BAE'S LAND UTILIZATION PROGRAM

The Division's ties to the BAE's land utilization program turned out to be brief, lasting less than a year. This program traced back to 1934 when the AAA started a submarginal land purchase program with $25 million provided by the FERA (Wooten 1965:5).[1] At the time, the proposal was to acquire about ten million acres of land in forty-five states, primarily to withdraw submarginal land from cultivation and convert it to other uses such as grazing, forests, or recreation. In May 1935 responsibility for the program was transferred from the AAA to the RA. Title III of the Bankhead-Jones Tenant Purchase Act of 1937 gave the land utilization program a more permanent status. On September 1, 1937, the Secretary of Agriculture transferred the program to the BAE, allowing until July 1, 1938, for the actual transition to take place. During 1938, the BAE made Bankhead-Jones Act funds available to enable the Division to employ five sociologists, one to be located in each of five out of the BAE's seven land utilization program's regional offices.[2] These sociologists were barely in place when in October 1938, the Secretary of Agriculture transferred responsibility for this land program to the Soil Conservation Service. The transfer was a part of the BAE reorganization, which ushered in the USDA's Third New Deal.

Prior to the sociologists arrival in the regional offices, Carl Taylor prepared a statement for use at a meeting in Washington of the regional directors.[3] It concerned the sociological research to be done in relation to the land program. Taylor listed three topics that seemed to him to be the most generic to all phases of the land program and that probably should be given priority. They were (1) population analysis of areas; (2) standard of living analyses of areas for which the program planned activities; and (3) a study of the natural cultural history of areas or what might be called an area case history. Taylor indicated to the land program directors that the Division's Washington staff would be prepared to assist the sociologists in the regions in these analyses. He left room for flexibility, stating that he recognized each director might find it desirable to have the regional sociologist assist in a number of other things than the three he listed.

The limited research published by the regional sociologists as a result of work undertaken during their brief association with the BAE's land utilization program reflects more the regional directors' desires than Taylor's list. They dealt, for example, with the families displaced by the land purchase program (e.g., Cronin 1939), the social effects of government land purchase (Nichols and King 1943), and the uses made of the land purchased, e.g., recreational sites in Maine (Niederfrank and Draper 1940).

THE DIVISION AND THE USDA'S PLANNING, 1938–1945

The Second Agrarian New Deal, started in 1935, which had revitalized the Division's fortunes so much, was followed three years later by the short-lived Third Agrarian New Deal. This was Secretary of Agriculture Henry A. Wallace's reorganization in 1938 of the USDA. The new development had direct and immediate consequences for the Division's activities, its organizational structure, and brought a sharp increase in its resources.

The reorganization had two major components. First, in October 1938, the BAE was designated as the central planning agency for the USDA, an addition to its economic and social research functions. This arrangement lasted until January 1, 1946, when then-Secretary Clinton P. Anderson removed the planning function from the BAE and restored it to the Secretary's Office.

The second major component, and the more important one for the Division, established an organizational system for what was called "land-use planning," in reality an agricultural planning system that could go far beyond issues of agricultural land use and reach out broadly to the "human side" of agricultural problems. This system was built upon an agreement reached between representatives of the land-grant colleges and the USDA on July 8, 1938, at a conference at Mount Weather, Virginia. This was a cooperative approach involving county and community committees, the majority of whose members were farmers; the land-grant colleges, primarily through the Extension Service at the state and county levels; and the USDA, all agencies but especially the BAE and the Extension Service. The main purposes of this land-use planning setup were (1) to improve coordination at the local level of the several New Deal agricultural action and other programs; (2) to have farmers involved in a democratic planning process to build USDA farm programs on farmer recommendations so they better fit local needs and conditions; and (3) to improve federal-state working relations in agency agricultural activities. These purposes and the setup were an outgrowth of experiences to date with the operations of New Deal farm programs at the local and state level. They were a reflection of the commitment of Secretary Wallace and his close associate, M. L. Wilson, to participatory democracy.

The county and community land-use planning committees were the base of the new planning system. But the machinery included the establishment within the BAE of a Division of State and Local Planning to take the lead in directing this federal-county planning effort. A BAE representative was placed in most states. Within states there was a State Land-Use Planning Committee, which received the county reports and handled broader types of planning concerns. In Washington, the USDA established an Agricultural Planning Board to review plans and programs before they were approved by the Secretary.

This planning setup was ended when Congress forbid the BAE to use any funds for this purpose after June 30, 1942. But before it came to an end, there were land-use planning committees in two-thirds of the nation's agricultural counties, in forty-seven states. The membership of county, community, and state planning committees in early 1942 was put at almost 200,000 men and women (Tolley 1943:138).

The USDA reorganization of 1938 and the BAE's central role in the planning process opened wide the doors of opportunity for the Division to provide sociological knowledge to be put to use. Shortly, in a review of the work of the Division published in *Rural Sociology*, Taylor stated that "the demand from the new agricultural agencies, the new agricultural planning system, and others had his staff swamped almost to the point of confusion in attempting the render requested service far beyond its personnel and financial resources" (1939:225). Little more than two years into the reorganization, Taylor (1941a) observed at an annual meeting of the Southern Sociological Society "that attempting to do research while operating under the white heat of imminent and imperative action is a hectic and sometimes precarious undertaking. Administrators can't wait." We note that out of the twenty-four documented instances in which Division staff had an opportunity to provide information to Congressional Committees through direct testimony or submit a requested report, 18 were during 1940 and 1941.

The increased reliance by the USDA on the Division's assistance, as a result of the 1938 reorganization, brought increased resources. During 1939–40 the professional staff numbered fifty-seven, the life-history high point. By 1939 the Division had professional staff in all seven of the BAE's regional offices. These were located in Amarillo, Texas; Atlanta, Georgia; Berkeley, California; Lincoln, Nebraska; Little Rock, Arkansas; Milwaukee, Wisconsin; and Upper Darby, Pennsylvania. These regional offices were successors to those started by the BAE's land utilization program. Each office also had a representative from the Division of State and Local Planning and professional staff from the BAE's Division of Farm Management and Costs and Division of Land Economics. The Division's regional offices carried the major load of assisting the county land-use planning program. The BAE's regional offices were abolished effective July 1, 1946, by Congressional action. Even before the county planning program was abolished in 1942, the war was bringing a shift in priorities to farm labor and other areas of service and research.

The County Land-Use Planning Program[4]

The county-level land-use or agricultural planning process had three stages. The first stage was getting organized and discussing the philosophy of democratic planning. The second stage was "intensive," starting with the preparation of land-use classification maps and moving from there to economic and social analysis and then to goals for short-term and long-run adjustments and plans to guide action agencies. The third stage was the "unified" program, getting the county planning committee's recommendations implemented.

The Division developed educational materials to assist in the organizational stage of county planning. It provided technical assistance and training and even did service research for this stage. The expertise of the division in the area of locality groups—the concepts and the methods of identifying and delineating communities and neighborhoods—had special relevance for getting representative participation on the committees for the democratic approach so vigorously pushed. Thus, it took part in the preparation by the BAE and cooperating USDA agencies of some of the fifteen widely disseminated. "County Planning Series" pamphlets, the first of which was issued in March, 1940. Clearly, for instance, the seven-page non-technical pamphlet on *Communities and Neighborhoods in Land Use Planning* (USDA, BAE 1940) was the Division's work.

The land-use planning program generated numerous requests for assistance in community and neighborhood delineation. In a paper presented at the Southern Sociological Society annual meeting in April, 1941, Taylor stated that during the last two years, with the assistance of farm people and their leaders, some 1,250 communities and 7,500 neighborhoods had been mapped in 125 counties in twenty-six states (1941:157). In a paper published late in 1941, other Division staff members reported assistance in response to local requests had been given in thirty-two states (Loomis et al. 1941:339). Further, by early in 1942 it was expected that the delineation of all the communities and neighborhoods would be completed in seven of these states: Alabama, Arkansas, Kentucky, Mississippi, Missouri, North Carolina, and Virginia. In a few instances, the Division's locality group identification studies resulted in a publication. Thus, reports in mimeo form were issued during 1940 and 1941 on the communities and neighborhoods in one county in each of eight states: Alabama, Kansas, Louisiana, Mississippi, North Carolina, Oklahoma, South Dakota, and Tennessee. An example is the study in Nemaha County, Kansas (Longmore et al. 1940).

In the second or "intensive" stage of land-use planning, the county committees mapped local land-use areas but were expected to go beyond that. They were to decide on adjustments in land use needed in each area, analyze the economic and social constraints of land use, and develop recommendations to guide government agencies help achieve the desired adjustment goals. In anticipation of requests for help from the committees in the "intensive" stage, the Division's outline of prospective work for fiscal year 1939–40 identified four subject matter areas in which it could assist (*FPRLA* 1939[3]:2–3). The four were population analyses, social organization analyses, tenure and other class structure of the population, and standard or levels of living analyses. The work plan stated that the Washington office could compile data on the number, distribution, composition, and trends of the population for all counties in the intensive or unified stages of planning. Work that would have to be done in the field included mapping the population in place within minor civil divisions and the analyses of family composition. Local data sources were suggested for accomplishing such work. Except for the population data that the Washington office could compile, the guidance, technical assistance, and service research for committees on all the other topics would fall to the Division's regional office staffs. A Division-prepared mimeo statement, "Significant Social Facts for County and Community Planning Committees to Know About Their County" (c. 1940), was also a resource for Division staff and others engaged in supporting the county planning program.

The regional staffs did meet numerous requests from county committees, typically channeled through the state BAE representatives, for some type of technical help in the study of problems such as population, rural youth, school situations, farm family levels of living, and health conditions and services. In rare instances the Division's service research led to a mimeo publication, e.g., "A Study of Churches of Culpeper County, Virginia" (Ensminger and Page 1940) put out by the Division with the county land-use planning committee cooperating.

The Division hoped to develop a nationwide study of the land-use planning program (Beers et al. 1941:preface).[5] The extent of research in this area turned out to be limited, however, in part because America's entry into World War II drastically reshaped the Division's program and, in part, because of the ending of the land-use planning program in 1942 by Congressional action. Field investigations were completed in only three states for major publications before this line of research was cut off. Two of these were the result of cooperative research for which University of Kentucky sociologists Howard W. Beers and Robin M. Williams Jr. were the lead investigators. The fieldwork for this research was started in 1939, the first year of the land-use planning program in Kentucky, and completed in summer, 1940. The two publications were issued by the Kentucky Agricultural Experiment Station. The first was *Community Land-Use Planning Committees: Organization, Leadership, and Attitudes, Garrard*

County, Kentucky, 1939 (Beers et al. 1941). One major purpose of this study was to find out whether in this county the neighborhood or community areas were distinct from any other subareas, whether discovery of them would require technical investigation, and whether knowledge of the locality groups would suggest any alterations in the nine "trial" areas used when the planning program was begun in the county (145). A further purpose was to analyze the characteristics and activity of the community land-use planning committee members originally selected, to compare them with an equal number of randomly selected persons who were not committee members. This analysis was an effort to explain differences among the communities and among individuals in their interest in land-use planning tasks. Additionally the Garrard County study moved into relatively unexplored areas of rural social psychology by seeking opinions of committee members and of nonmembers about issues relevant to planning. The study of the locality groups revealed the presence of several unintentionally unrepresented groups in the original county land-use planning organization and other groups which were inadequately represented. The original selection of committee members proved to be persons who differed in significant ways from the randomly selected sample of neighbors. Also, the committee members selected differed in general in attitude and opinion from their neighbors with respect to conservation practices, evaluation of extension work and of the Agricultural Adjustment Program and most other areas queried. A commendable feature of this report was the detail given about field procedures and methods, especially in collecting data concerning opinions, and the reasons for the methods used in interviewing this group of Kentucky farmers.

The second Kentucky report, *Farmers on Local Planning Committees in Three Kentucky Counties, 1939–1940* (Williams and Beers 1943) extended the study of land-use planning committees into two additional counties. One of these, Hopkins, had been designated as the "unified" planning county for the state. As in the first study, the socioeconomic characteristics and selected opinions of the committee members were compared with a random sample of farmer neighbors. Further, pairings of eight characteristics and seven opinions were made for both committee members and non-committee members to examine the relationships (16–17, 32–33). This analysis was supplemented by study, using a form of contingency analysis, of the relations of the opinions held such as opinions on adjustment and planning programs and opinions on education, rural living, and satisfaction (17–22, 34–35). A feature of this study was the examination of the relationship between the opinions and the actions of this group of farmers (23–26). Behavior records for activity in land-use planning committees and participation in AAA programs over a period of years permitted the opinion-action comparison. Among the findings of this study were the definite interrelations among opinions concerning various aspects of land-use planning, county-agent work, and programs of agricultural adjustment and the correspondence of opinion and behavior with respect to both land-use planning and agricultural adjustment programs.

The most comprehensive study of the land-use planning program for any county was that during 1940–42 in Greene County, Georgia by Division staff member Arthur F. Raper.[6] This was published in the 403-page book *Tenants of the Almighty* (1943) lucidly written, free of technical terminology, and without sophisticated statistical analysis. A determination was made in early 1939 that a county-wide Unified Farm Program would be developed in Greene County as a demonstration area in which federal, state, and local agencies would work together in a new way. The choice of county originated with the Georgia State Land-Use Planning Committee but the idea met with the approval of the agricultural agencies and the county leaders (Raper 1943:203).

Raper arrived in September 1940 to start his task. He expected to stay ten months to study the Unified Farm Program. In trying to understand why different people felt as they did about the program, he was led into a full study of what had happened to people over the county's history. He ended up staying in the county, living there with his wife and three children, for two years. By the time Raper completed his study, World War II was making its effects felt in Greene County and the USDA had been required to discontinue the land-use planning program. Raper and Greene County were not strangers to each other. He had made a study there in 1927 and 1928 for his 1931 Ph.D. dissertation at the University of North Carolina. A second study was made there in 1934 and 1935 for the Commission on Interracial Cooperation in Atlanta directed by W. W. Alexander, later the first administrator of the FSA.

The county's 1940 population of 13,700 was about equally divided between white and black. The segregated pattern of living was suggested by the locality group delineation done by Lee Coleman of the Division's Atlanta office. He found twenty-six white neighborhoods, eight white communities, thirty-seven black neighborhoods, and eleven or twelve weak black communities (Raper 1943:380–82). Of the 1,337 farm operators in 1940, over two-thirds did not own the land they farmed.

Raper found that "things began to happen in Greene county when the Unified Farm Program was begun early 1939. . . . The programs of well-established agencies were revitalized, new programs were launched" (207). The Unified Farm Program was made possible by many local, state, and federal agencies working together. "Most important of all have been the various agencies of the Department of Agriculture" (211). In his effort to understand the Program as a whole, Raper was led to examine what was done agency by agency, how they responded to the suggestions and recommendations made by farmer committee members. His report included the USDA action agencies—the Agricultural Adjustment Administration, the Farm Security Administration, the Soil Conservation Service, and also the Forest Service. The report for the FSA was far more comprehensive (233–93) than for any other agency. This reflected the scope of the FSA's program in the county. When the United Farm Program was launched, the number of families assisted by the FSA was increased from 146 to 535 and the professional staff was increased from one supervisor to twelve along with two engineers and two nurses. The work of the Extension Service with farmers, women, and youth was documented. The report covered non-USDA federal agencies involved in the Program. These were the Civilian Conservation Corps (until it was discontinued in July 1942 by Congress), the National Youth Administration, and the Work Projects Administration. And the actions of each local government agency that cooperated in the intensive Program were noted. These included the County Board of Health (295–303), the County Board of Education (304–10), and the County Welfare Board (313–14). The agency-by-agency analysis gave comparative data for the participation of the black and the white population.

In view of the numerous accomplishments of the Unified Farm Program in areas as diverse as farming practices, lengthened tenure of farm tenants, farm housing, school buildings, better-trained teachers, and health services, Raper concluded that "A world of things have been done in the past four years" although "A larger world of things still remain to be done" (209). Further, in Raper's view, most of the Unified Farm Program "represented not a new approach, but the expanding of services already begun on a small scale" (295).

In his study of the Greene County program, Raper relied heavily on participant observation, a method in which he was skilled. But he and the staff assisting him also interviewed "scores" of families with a thirteen-page schedule and, with the cooperation of school teachers, obtained information from the oldest child in school from about nine hundred families. Additional data were compiled from agency records.

Readers of *Tenants of the Almighty* were introduced to the county by seventy-eight photographs of its people and places taken by Jack Delano of the Historical Division of the FSA in Washington. The portion of the book dealing with Raper's study of the Unified Farm Program was given a context by a lengthy account of the county's historical development through the coming of the New Deal programs. This historical section was based on such sources as newspaper files, old county records, and interviews with the elderly, among them ex-slaves. The book concluded with the coming of World War II and its first effects on the county.

A feature of the procedures used by Raper was publication of a draft of his manuscript in installments, prior to book publication, in the local newspaper. This served as a report to the people of Greene County on the study. But this was also a means of eliciting suggestions from the residents which he considered in the final that.

Greene County Locality Groups and USDA Action Agencies

Lee Coleman's report (1942) on his delineation of Greene County's neighborhoods and communities included a series of maps which enabled a comparison of the boundaries of these "natural" social groupings with the geographic areas created by the AAA, the FSA, and the SCS for the local administration of their programs. Similarly, comparisons were made for the areas used by the Agricultural Extension Service. Also, the geographic location of the committee members for the agricultural agencies was mapped. This part of the study was extended to the members of the agricultural planning board.

Two Division senior staff members drew on Coleman's work for their paper "Governmental administration and informal local groups" published in *Applied Anthropology* (Loomis and Ensminger 1942:1[2]:41–59). They demonstrated that each of the agricultural agencies studied had a different number of local administrative areas, that the agency local areas did not coincide with each other, and the areas did not coincide with the natural communities and neighborhoods. At the time of Coleman's study, the agricultural planning board lacked representation from two of the county's communities. Further, nearly half of all the land-use planning committee positions were held by residents of the county seat community. Communities and neighborhoods with the highest social and economic status tended to have the most representatives on the committees of the agricultural agencies examined (51). Low-income families tended to be most prevalent in the unrepresented locality groups.

Assistance to the Soil Conservation Service and Other USDA Action Agencies

A section labeled "assistance to action agencies" was included in the Division's outline of prospective work for 1939–40 (*FPRLA* 1939[3]:3–4). This suggested topics for studies that might be made for the Agricultural Adjustment Administration, the Soil Conservation Service, the Farm Security Administration, and the Forest Service. Subsequently, however, unlike the proposals for assisting the land-use planning program, little came of the action agency proposals except for the FSA. At the time, the county planning program was a high priority activity for the USDA and the BAE. The program's demands on the Division's resources were heavy. And, shortly, the approach and then the coming of war reshaped priorities.

Loomis and Ensminger stated that in a number of counties in Virginia and Maryland and in some other areas, agency administrative areas within counties were being based on natural neighborhood and community groups (1942:48, 59). But they did not elaborate or name specific USDA agencies. Presumably, such steps by the agencies were a consequence of the locality group delineation work for the land-use planning program that the Division did or in which it assisted.

The one well-documented research for a USDA action agency was for the SCS. This work was carried out during 1945–46 by Lee Coleman (1947) in a single Illinois county. As high-lighted by Carl Taylor (1947b:4) in his presidential address to the American Sociological Society, the problem posed to the Division by SCS was "why is it that two Soil Conservation Districts located in the same locality and type-of-farming area, staffed by equally competent technicians, and composed of people of the same nationality composition, behave so differently. In one district our program is an outstanding success, in the other we must admit a high degree of failure." The SCS called for sociological assistance in analyzing both districts.

Facts were obtained about the people in these localities, their background, beliefs, customs, and value systems, and how these influenced their attitudes and activities in soil conservation. Case histories were obtained from 110 farmers who had conservation plans or who had adopted contour farming practices. Interviews conducted with farmers were designed to obtain leads which would help develop methods and suggest appeals to use in working with farmers in soil conservation.

This research uncovered the attitudes and values of the farmer participants in soil conservation practices and of the nonparticipants, identified the accepted and trusted folk leaders, and revealed to the action agency and its technicians factors that were causing the difference in the soil conservation behavior of the two areas compared in detail (Taylor 1947b:4). Coleman's report organized his findings regarding the interest and motivations of the Illinois county's people in soil conservation in four categories. They were: how farmers get interested in and sold on soil conservation; motivations that caused farmers to become conservationists; reasons why farmers had not yet accepted conservation; and how the acceptance of soil conservation varied between areas and groups and the factors responsible for the variance. Then the report went on to interpret the research findings by offering sixteen detailed suggestions as to methods which Soil Conservation Service technicians could use in their conservation education and in getting farmers to adopt conservation practices. Among these were further emphasis on group methods, developing and using farmers as demonstrators and promoters of conservation practices, and finding "natural" leaders as neighborhood demonstrators.

The SCS in the Upper Mississippi Valley Region promptly followed up on Coleman's research report. It developed and tested training material for in-service use to improve the effectiveness of its technicians in carrying on conservation work with farmers. The material was based on principles, techniques, and procedures flowing from the Division's research. These principles and techniques were reviewed with several rural sociologists and others in the region. And the procedures presented in the training guide were field-tested by the SCS.

IN SUPPORT OF THE WAR EFFORT

Well before December 7, 1941, the nation's growing defense activities began to shape what the Division did. The USDA perceived that the national defense program would call for an unprecedented expansion to provide the materials of war. It further perceived that modern aerial warfare made it desirable to minimize the concentration of the needed industrial development in centralized areas. Numbers of them might better be placed in rural and semi-rural areas, especially in areas of extensive unemployment and underemployment. USDA representatives discussed their conclusions with officials of the various defense agencies (Tolley 1943:165). By late 1940, plants were being built in rural areas; these included several munitions plants. Concurrently, at the county and state levels, land-use planning committees began to deal with national defense issues as they came to rural America (Tolley 1943:160–62).

As a consequence of the top-level USDA defense agencies' discussions, requests came to the Division for help. For example, the National Defense Advisory Commission wanted data for determining the location of defense industries. The Office of Production Management asked for surveys to ascertain the quantity of unskilled labor that might be drawn from agricultural areas around new defense plants without harming farm operations. Reports, solely for administrative use, were prepared in 1941 on the effect of ordnance plants in Iowa, Indiana, and Ohio on the local rural labor situation. In the same year, one staff member presented a paper on agricultural labor in relation to agricultural planning for national defense (Fuller 1941). Another prepared an article on defense and decentralization for the BAE periodical *Land Policy Review* (Danhof 1941:4[1]:3–10). In the same year Division-head Taylor referred to studying the experiences of farm families forced to move because their land was purchased for defense projects (1941:156). He noted the Division was studying the impact of the defense program on farmers and farm laborers. The latter instances are illustrations of requests for information which came from county and state land-use planning committees.

The events of December 7, 1941, and the entry of the United States into World War II marked the start of the second great national societal crisis experienced by the Division.[7] On January 1, 1942, the BAE announced the immediate wartime work program for the Bureau as a whole and for each of its eleven divisions (USDA, BAE 1942). The BAE had begun its preparations for the possibility of war in the months before Pearl Harbor. Bureau Chief Howard Tolley had put three *ad hoc* interdivisional committees to work. One was to develop recommendations for the BAE's program in the event of war. A second was to make recommendations for postwar reseach, and the third was to focus on the BAE's research program in the event that there was not war. The third report was presented after the staff group assembled in Tolley's office had listened on the radio to President Roosevelt ask Congress for a declaration of war.

The BAE's January 1, 1942, statement of its immediate wartime program redefined priorities. For the Division, farm labor was given first priority. The BAE's efforts to aid in meeting the farmers' labor needs were to center in the Division. A second high priority area assigned the Division was the application of its expertise in rural social organization to assist the Extension Service, the Office of Civil Defense, and others in organizing rural communities for wartime activities. While all lines of work that made significant contributions to winning the war had highest priority for the BAE, the January 1, 1942, statement gave second priority to work that had the promise of making a practical contribution to the solution of major problems of the immediate postwar period. For the Division, this led to participation in the USDA's postwar planning committees and to numerous special studies.

Farm Labor Work in Wartime

In Chapter 7 we discussed the Division's farm labor program during World War II. We noted that often this work was of a service nature to an agency with responsibilities for recruiting or placing farm labor or for one of the many local farm labor committees encouraged by the USDA. We stated that the results of much of this service work never saw publication. Sometimes a few copies of a written report were distributed in typed or mimeo form for administrative use within the government. Here we present, in more detail, as an illustration, an account of one such service activity.

In fall 1942 some areas of Ohio were reporting a labor shortage for their dairy farming operations. At the same time, it was known that a large reservoir of unproductively used workers remained in eastern Kentucky. The FSA was considering initiating a small-scale experimental program to recruit manpower from eastern Kentucky for placement on Ohio dairy farms. Two Division staff members conducted quick reconnaissance work in both states for the purpose of learning of data available pertinent to the dairy farm labor and supply situation in the two states and to do field spot-checking that might help the FSA in determining procedures and policies for an initial dairy labor program experiment.[8] This work included a two-day conference at the University of Kentucky, a two-day conference at Ohio State University, and fieldwork in the Ohio county proposed for the initial placement of workers recruited in Kentucky.

The conference at the University of Kentucky was attended by members of a farm labor committee of agricultural experiment station staff who reported on the preliminary work they had already done on the state's labor requirements and labor supply and related matters. The conference was also attended by three FSA staff representatives and by two BAE Atlanta regional office staff members. The result of this conference was agreement that there was no question as to an adequate supply of workers who could be recruited in the numbers anticipated for the proposed experimental program. The Kentucky staff cautioned, however, as to possible local opposition, including political, that such a recruitment activity might encounter.

At the meeting at Ohio State University, staff working under the direction of the head of the Department of Rural Economics and Sociology reported on their study of farm labor in seventeen counties that had been completed during the preceding two weeks. The conference was also attended by six FSA representatives and by a staff member from the BAE's regional office in Milwaukee. At this meeting it was recommended that the FSA start its experimental program in Medina County if the demand for labor was found to be sufficient. Five additional counties were identified for expansion of the program in a sequence specified. The reports from the Ohio fieldwork indicated quite a lack of enthusiasm had been found among farmer-employers for eastern Kentucky workers.

The session at Ohio State University was followed by a visit to Medina County by the two Division staff members. There the visit started with a joint meeting with the FSA supervisor and the county agent, both of whom had been advised by their respective state offices of the purpose of the visit. A farmer member of the county farm labor committee participated in this meeting to decide specifically what would be done during the visit to the county. The county agent then called a meeting of eleven farmers, all with local leadership roles, to discuss the farm labor situation in the county and to make suggestions relative to the proposed experimental program. This meeting was chaired by a farmer member of the county farm labor board. Next, some fourteen additional farmers, all prospective employers of hired workers, were interviewed at their farms in the company of the FSA supervisor. Other persons contacted during the visit to Medina County included members of the County War Board and the U.S. Employment Service representative.

The ten-page report (Larson 1942) on the October 20–27 reconnaissance work was completed two days later. It was written for administrative use only.[9] The principal features of the report were the conclusions reached from the fieldwork in Medina County and a set of ten recommendations as to policies and procedures to be considered if the proposed experimental program was initiated. The conclusions included an appraisal of the demand for hired men as judged by the interviews with twenty-five farmers; findings as to working conditions for hired workers (wage rates, perquisites, and hours of work); and major obstacles to the proposed program which had been identified. Obstacles included a lack of housing for married farm workers and farmer attitudes. Many farmers were skeptical as to whether the Kentuckians would stay even if trained and placed with government assistance and doubtful that if they stayed they would be good workers. Further, in a predominantly Republican county, some farmers were critical of government programs which could be labeled "New Deal." A favorable response was found to the idea of a two or three week practical orientation at Ohio State University for the recruited Kentuckians to become acquainted with Ohio dairy farm equipment, e.g., milking machines, and practices. Information was also given as to the operations of the U.S. Employment Service in the county with respect to farm labor.

The report recommended that specific beginning wage rates be established for dairy workers recruited and placed under the FSA experimental program and proposed procedures for establishing the rates. An aggressive orientation program was advocated for both Ohio farmers and Kentucky workers. Placement procedures within the county were suggested. The need for an understanding between FSA and the U.S. Employment Service, especially within the county, was identified along with suggestions for the steps to be taken in obtaining the first job orders. Among other recommendations was that home management personnel be available within the county to ascertain housing conditions before placement and to work with farm labor families after placement.

Subsequently, the FSA decided to proceed with an experimental farm labor program which included orientation training at Ohio State University for the workers recruited in Kentucky prior to their placement on dairy farms.

Assistance in Wartime Rural Organization

The war brought a need for the Extension Service to develop a form of organization that could deal with the many national campaigns that were being directed to local areas, e.g., promotion of War Bond sales and scrap metal drives. Not only the Extension Service but the Office of Civilian Defense, Nutrition Committees, and others were all carrying on programs intended to reach all farm families. The Division's sociologists, assisted by rural sociologists at land-grant colleges, aided the Extension Service in developing a plan for action. This plan was based on the concepts already used in the county land-use planning program, i.e., neighborhood, community, "natural" leader, and the techniques for identifying them in rural situations (Taeuber 1945:169–70; Tolley 1943:133, 160). Division staff then had a role in providing research-based material useful to the administrators involved. As the outline was transformed into an acting field organization, they conducted demonstrations of identification techniques, they served as advisors as the plan of organization proceeded (Taeuber 1945:170).

The need for studying the plans for mobilization for the war effort were soon evident, as well as the need to assess the structure and its functioning with respect to wartime needs. Numerous quick surveys were made, largely to serve immediate administrative needs. However, fifteen or so of these studies of civilian mobilization in support of the war effort or of civilian participation in the various wartime programs were made available to the general public. Typically, a study pertained to a single county. All of these reports were issued by regional offices of the Division. The first appeared in 1942, the last in 1944. Examples of such studies are: a study in San Joaquin County, California of the methods of mobilizing rural people for war purposes (Goldschmidt and Page 1942); a study in three Louisiana parishes of civilian participation in wartime programs (Standing et al. 1943); and a report on the neighborhood group approach in the war effort (Anderson 1943).

The conservation and use of food was a concern for the war effort. Four members of the Division staff worked with the Nutrition and Food Conservation Branch of the Food Distribution Administration to prepare material on organizing for face-to-face nutrition education (Ensminger et al. 1943). Studies of specified food programs were made or assisted. For instance, a report on the Share the Meat Program in Rhode Island described the organization used in the program and analyzed the program's results (McKain 1943). The Rhode Island work was done in cooperation with the Office of Defense Health and Welfare Services of the Federal Security Agency and the state's Nutrition Council. In another case, the Division joined with the War Food Administration's Office of Distribution in an evaluation of the effectiveness of experiments conducted in two localities to minimize consumer food waste (Cottam 1944).

Other War-Related Work

Among the Division's other war-related activities, the Rural Life Trends project was by far the most ambitious. This was initiated to provide information as to the current situation in rural areas that would serve USDA administrative purposes. Information about this project is, however, incomplete. Thirty-five widely dispersed counties were selected to provide national coverage.[10] Regional office staff made visits to the counties periodically to interview key observers chosen to represent groups classified by categories such as income, farm tenure, and race. Each visit to each county covered a uniform set of topics. Seven reports in all were prepared for each county over a two-year period from the start of the project until its termination in 1944. Few of these reports, all for administrative use, have survived. In our search, we located only numbers 3, 4, 5, and 7. The project had five major fields of interest: farm manpower adjustments,

agricultural production, farmers' use of income, participation in war programs, and changes in community and institutional life. As an example,
in the fifth report for Pittsylvania County, Virginia,[11] prepared in September,
1943, the section on farm manpower adjustments dealt in detail with the
nature of the farm outlook for the peak-work period, as well as farm wages
and the availability of farm labor, women as farm workers, high school
and college students, the use of employed townspeople as farm workers,
and the use of factory workers with rural backgrounds. The section on
community and institutional life described the effect of wartime developments on the county's schools and churches.

The thirty-five-county rural life trends reports were, in turn, used by
the Division's Washington staff to prepare reports for the information of
federal government administrators. Each such report was limited to a specific topic. For example, the reports in 1943 included farmers' views on
farm labor, shifts of males of military age to agricultural work during 1942
and 1943, shifts in rural medical facilities, and how farmers were spend-
ing their increased incomes. When the Rural Life Trends Project was
replaced by the seventy-one-county rural cultural regions study in 1944,
the fieldwork included questions on new topics used for special reports
for administrative use within the USDA. The topics included current and
anticipated rural migration problems, veterans' adjustments,[12] opinions
about current problems and postwar prospects, and farm-family use of
war-period savings.

Associated with the Rural Life Trends Project was a study to ascertain
the effect of the war to date in twelve rural communities located in twelve
of the thirty-five sample counties (see Chapter 7). The fieldwork, conducted by the regional office staffs, used a set of schedules prepared by
the Washington office to interview a sample of farm and nonfarm people
and to collect information about the wartime changes for each community's schools, churches, community services, and social and economic
organizations. Although the instructions for the regional offices for these
brief, intensive studies were sent in late 1943, most of the reports were
not available until 1945. Only eight of the twelve were released for general use, e.g., Alexander's (1945) study of a Georgia community.

The Division's other wartime related work also included some small-
scale studies on subjects of quite a different nature than those already mentioned. One such was based on an analysis, directed by Carl Taylor, of a
sample of rural newspapers during the first three months of 1943. The
purpose was to discover the attitudes and activities about farm production these newspapers recorded. Walter McKain, in the Division's regional

office in Berkeley, prepared a report, in 1944, on "When the Japanese return to California" and another, in 1945, on an "anti-Jap" meeting held in the Imperial Valley. All these reports were labeled "for administrative use only."

The effect of the war on rural youth was the focus of work in Illinois and Indiana for which the Division's cooperation was enlisted. The work in both states was intended primarily for use by the Extension Service within the states. The Illinois project was limited to one county (Lindstrom et al. 1942, Lindstrom 1943). In Indiana, material on wartime adjustments of rural youth in the state was prepared for a rural youth leadership training school.

POSTWAR PLANNING

With the war well underway, the USDA established an Interbureau Committee on Postwar Programs. This committee set up numerous working groups, each pertaining to a specific major area of agriculture or rural life.[13] The working groups identified problems or issues anticipated in the transition from war to peace and in the postwar years. They recommended policies and programs to deal with the problems. On September 5, 1945, all the working groups submitted summary reports of their postwar recommendations.

Division staff in Washington were assigned to thirteen of the working groups. Carl Taylor was "national activity leader" for the group on farm laborers and for the group on social security for farm people. He was also a member of the groups on land tenure and on rural education. Earl Bell served on four working groups, the distribution of surplus war property for which he chaired a subcommittee on medical and hospital equipment and supplies, farming opportunities (also known as the land settlement work group), industrialization of rural areas and agricultural-industrial relations, and rural public works programs.[14] Louis Ducoff was appointed to the group on farm laborers and the one on maintaining full employment. John Ellickson served on the rural housing and farm buildings group and the social security group, as well as the one on rural electrification. Douglas Ensminger was designated to be a member of the group on cooperatives, the one on rural education, and the one on social security. Josiah Folsom was made a member of the farm laborers group and the social security group. Rural health and sanitation was the group with which T. Wilson Longmore was placed.

We give some examples of recommendations made by these interbureau working groups, of publications they prepared for public use, and of other activities. When social security legislation was enacted in 1935, farm operators and hired farm workers were excluded from coverage for old-age and survivor's insurance. The first recommendation of the working group on social security, led by Taylor, was that the Social Security Act be amended to include farmers and farm laborers. Another recommendation was that unemployment compensation and insurance against temporary disability be extended to cover hired laborers on large farms. Over a two-year period, the BAE issued at least fifteen committee reports and releases relating to the extension of social security to agricultural workers. These included radio addresses by Taylor on the National Farm and Home Hour, speeches by Taylor and other Division staff members about social security for farm people, and a compilation of a list of references on the topic (Folsom 1944). In addition, the Social Security Board, which was represented on the working group, issued at least as many fact sheets, bulletins, and other materials providing information about social security for farm people.

The working group on farm laborers, which was also led by Taylor, was not initiated until March, 1945. But, by the time a summary report was submitted in September to the Interbureau Committee on Postwar Programs, a dozen recommendations were ready. This working group also placed the extension of social security to all persons gainfully employed in agriculture at the top of its list. Among the other recommendations were that farm laborers no longer be excluded from the application of labor standards set by state or federal laws, that provisions of child labor laws be made applicable to all children working for wages in agriculture, and that a single agency be made responsible for the recruitment and placement of farm laborers. Other recommendations pertained to training and educational services, housing standards and housing availability, safeguarding the health of farm laborers, and a program of rural public works in periods of heavy unemployment.

The analysis and recommendations in the 129-page report of the land settlement work group (USDA, Interbureau Committee on Postwar Programs, Land Settlement Work Group 1945) had especially in mind the interests of returning veterans. Sample surveys of men in the Army had indicated that possibly 900,000 to 1,000,000 were interested in full-time farming, and another 500,000 were thinking of part-time farming. These numbers far exceeded the number of farms estimated to be available from the sale or lease of existing farms, created by new land development work such as irrigation, or resulting from the sale of land used for military purposes. The report dealt with the outlook for farming, estimates of the extent of farming opportunities, experiences with land settlement including current programs in the United States to aid veterans, and public policies directly related to farming opportunities. The group made recommendations with respect to the establishment of returning veterans and other qualified persons in farming. These included federal and state legislative and other action. The anticipated interest of veterans in part-time farming led to the preparation of a USDA Farmers' Bulletin on the topic prepared by the Division's Earl Bell and an agricultural economist (Bell and Scoville 1945).

The Division's participation in the working groups set up by the Inter-bureau Committee on Postwar Programs exemplifies how staff members were expected to work with other disciplines and on an inter-division, inter-agency basis as the situation required. Thus, Earl Bell served on the land settlement work group with six persons from other divisions within the BAE and representatives from six USDA agencies outside the BAE.

Veterans

Some attention was given to returning veterans in addition to active participation in the USDA's postwar planning working groups. Some of this additional work was, in fact, published by education and information units of the armed forces. The Information and Education Division Headquarters, Army Service Forces included a report on soldier's plans for farming after leaving the army in its series on Postwar Plans of the Soldier (Schuler et al. 1944). The United States Armed Forces Institute included a chapter on part-time farming in a publication, *What is Farming* (Bell 1944). The *Bulletin of National Association of Secondary-School Principals* published a paper on counseling and education for the veteran in rural communities (Schuler and Ensminger 1945). Other papers were for more general audiences than veterans or their counselors. Thus, an article in *The Annals of the American Academy of Political and Social Sciences* provided an overview of the availability of farms for returning veterans and of postwar agricultural prospects (Taylor 1945 [238]:48–55).

Use was also made by the Division of ongoing research on rural regions and farm population to collect information about veterans. In 1945 most of the regional offices prepared reports, in mimeo form, on postwar rural trends in their region. These reports, based on the seventy-one-county rural regions study field observations, included a section on veterans (e.g.,

Niederfrank 1946). Also in 1946, the questions to collect data for the annual estimates of farm population elicited information about veterans who had returned to farms. After the findings had been presented in a report for administrative use, a summary was made available in an article "Million Veterans on Farms of U.S." in the BAE's periodical publication *Agricultural Situation* (Hagood and Ducoff 1946[30]8:13).

SOCIAL SECURITY FOR FARM PEOPLE

Under the original Social Security Act, passed in 1935, the only farm people who had the opportunity to contribute so as to later receive old-age and survivors insurance benefits were those who worked in covered employment off the farm. The efforts of the USDA's postwar planning group on social security, under the strong leadership of Carl Taylor, furthered the movement toward the eventual inclusion of both farm operators and hired farm workers in the old-age insurance program. Concurrently with his time as leader of the working group on social security, starting in 1943, and later, into 1949, Taylor not only prepared material about social security for farm people for administrative use within the USDA, he also prepared material for wider use and spoke on the topic to the USDA and other audiences. In these materials and addresses he performed an educational function, providing information about the provisions of the existing social security law, and about principal proposals before Congress. He discussed problems and issues in getting social security coverage for farm people. He argued that none of the difficulties in administering a social security program for them were insurmountable. He was a vigorous advocate for changing the Social Security Act so that farm people were not left out.

An annotated bibliography on social security and related insurance for farm people, published by the USDA Library, provided an updated guide to information related to social security for farm people (Folsom 1949). Starting in 1946, the nationwide enumerative surveys, conducted for the BAE's hired farm working force series (see Chapter 9), were used to collect information about the nonfarm work earnings of hired farm workers (Ducoff and Hagood 1947a:20–21; Bowles et al. 1950:3–5). Data on the number of farm employers a farm worker had during the year were obtained in the survey of the hired farm working force of 1951 which also secured special information on regular workers in 1950 (Ducoff and Birch 1952). Such types of information contributed over time to developing legislative proposals and administrative procedures. In 1950, the Social

Security Act was amended to give hired farm workers old-age and survivors insurance coverage.

With farm operators still left out, in 1951 the Division undertook a cooperative study with the University of Wisconsin AES to ascertain the extent to which farm operators had the basis for economic security in old age, what plans they had for retirement or curtailment of farming operations when they reached retirement age, and what their opinions were toward Old Age and Survivors Insurance as a plan for protecting their livelihood in old age (Sewell et al. 1953:3).[15] Parallel cooperative research was conducted the same year with the Connecticut AES (McKain et al. 1953) and the following year with the Texas AES (e.g., Adkins and Motheral 1953).

The Wisconsin study interviewed some 658 farm operators in two economic areas with contrasting characteristics, one a good farming area and the other a relatively poor area for farming (Sewell et al. 1953:8). An area sampling technique was used to select the farmers interviewed. Five age classifications, ranging from under thirty-five to sixty-five and over, were used in the analysis of farmer responses.

Overall, the responses in this carefully designed Wisconsin study indicated that many of the farmers in both the good and the poor farming areas were uncertain of their ability to plan adequately and provide for their economic security in old age. It was clear that most farmers were in general agreement that farm operators needed the protection of an old age insurance program (Sewell et al. 1953:22–23). There were differences in some respects in the farmer responses when the two areas were compared but not in other respects. For example, a larger percentage of all age classifications in the good farming area estimated their net worth at $20,000 and over. But among operators aged 55 and over, there was little difference between areas in the percentage with fairly definite plans for retirement or who were confident they would have sufficient income to be self-supporting when they reached retirement age.

In 1954 the Social Security Act was changed to include farm operators in the Old Age and Survivors Insurance Program. The work of the Division was important in achieving this result.

PLANNING FOR THE COLUMBIA RIVER BASIN IRRIGATION PROJECT

In 1939 the Bureau of Reclamation in the U.S. Department of the Interior started the "Columbia Basin Irrigation Project Joint Investigations" (Torbert

1941:3–9). This project was to be the largest and most complex irrigation project in the history of the nation. The project included some two and one-half million acres, currently used mostly for large dry land wheat farms, in south-central Washington. The suitable land would be opened to irrigation farming, watered by the Grand Coulee Dam to be constructed. When fully developed, the project area would increase its rural and town population many-fold; new towns and some cities would emerge. In view of the complexity and magnitude of this irrigation project, the Bureau of Reclamation decided to draw on the specialized competence of federal, state, regional, and local agencies and organizations to assist in the investigations needed (U.S. Department of the Interior, Bureau of Reclamation 1941:2). The object of these investigations was to provide a general plan for the development and settlement of the Columbia Basin area as a whole and detailed plans for the parts to be irrigated relatively soon.

The USDA was among the agencies requested to assist in the joint investigations. Marion Clawson, a BAE staff member, was designated by the Secretary of Agriculture to be the USDA's field representative for the joint investigations. Shortly, the Division had a unique opportunity in the practice of sociology.[16] It accepted "heavy responsibilities" in this planning activity (Taylor 1941a:156).

While the physical problems in converting the area from its present uses, the economic problems, and the social problems were recognized as interrelated, to facilitate the detailed investigations essential to analysis, twenty-eight separate problems were identified (U.S. Department of the Interior, Bureau of Reclamation 1941:7–29; Taylor 1946a:322). Each problem had an investigating committee with between three and twenty-two experts assigned. Specialists such as irrigation engineers and agricultural economists brought to their tasks a greater body of validated knowledge than was possible for the sociologists (Taylor 1946a:322–23). But the investigation committee assignments opened opportunities for the sociologists to make their contributions. This was done not only through the research and analysis the Division staff participants did as members of specific committees but through participation at the conferences at which all investigating committees reported and at conferences of investigators working on related problems.

The Division was a contributor to the reports submitted by eight of the twenty-eight committees. Taylor chaired two committees, one on the problem of settlement patterns and one on the problem of location of sites for service centers. Special research by the Division staff made major contributions to the report on levels of living, for which the problem was stated as "What feasible means could be adopted or created to help insure an adequate level of living and to minimize the financial commitments of needy settlers in providing suitable and essential improvements?" (see Chapter 6). The other five committees in which the Division had membership as investigator or adviser dealt with the problems of part-time farms and laborers' allotments, financing needy settlers, planning for the orderly development of existing cities and villages, rural parks and recreational grounds, and the pattern of local government units.

Planning for Rural Settlement Patterns

Problem 10 was stated as "What advantages, economic and social, and what disadvantages, if any, in farm layout and farm work might result from the concentration of settlers in small communities or nuclear hamlets? Should experiments be made on some of the earlier project units with such farm community centers?" (Taylor 1946a:326). The committee chaired by Taylor recognized that its recommendations for the pattern of settlement had to be made within the boundaries set by the legal limit on the size of farm holdings (eighty acres), the location of the main irrigation canals, which would be largely determined by topography, and by the fact that in some areas the wells for domestic water supply might cost as much as $3,000 each because they would need to be seven hundred feet deep. It was assumed that farm family residence locations should be determined by criteria of convenience to community services, trade centers, public utilities, and settler desires as well as convenience to farm work. The committee did not confine itself to a choice between "nuclear hamlets" and isolated farmsteads (Taylor 1946a:326).

Fieldwork was done by Division staff in studies of ten Mormon village irrigated farming communities, ten FSA resettlement projects, and of two other irrigation projects. Few of the findings from these studies were quantitative. For example, in the Mormon communities an attempt was made to ascertain ideas and attitudes about village settlement, to discover trends toward or away from locating farm residences in villages during the past fifteen years, and to determine the differential availability of utilities in different patterns of settlement.

The first of seven final recommendations made by this committee under Taylor's leadership was that, insofar as conditions permitted, the line pattern of settlement should be established throughout the Columbia Basin project. Specific suggestions were made as to means of achieving this end, e.g., farm units should be rectangular with the short axis paralleling the service road and all roadways should be determined prior to settlement. Another recommendation was that groups of settlers, no fewer than twenty or more than sixty in number, should have the privilege of establishing a farm village in an area before the installation of the water system. However, such types of settlement should not be coerced by the administrative agency dealing with settlers (Taylor 1946a:328; see also U.S. Department of the Interior, Bureau of Reclamation 1947).

Planning the Location of Sites for Community Services

The charge to the committee for Problem 27 was "to plan the location (first for the northern and southernmost parts of the area), and, insofar as practical, the improvement of sites for rural schools, churches, community halls, market centers, athletic fields . . . and the like. Selections might well be made of more sites than are likely to be utilized, with the idea that some of them will be released as unneeded after the settlement of the sections involved" (Taylor 1946a:329). The committee's report was largely the work of the Division (U.S. Department of the Interior, Bureau of Reclamation and USDA, BAE 1946). Carl Taylor chaired the seven-member investigating committee. He drew on the competence of five Division staff members to conduct the desired field research and to prepare major portions of the report.

In developing its recommendations, the Problem 27 committee assumed that the recommendations of certain other committees would be carried out. For instance, the recommendations of committees concerned with type and size of farm and part-time farms had a bearing on the distribution and density of the rural population. Also, the number and location of existing centers in the area, railroads, highways, and topography had to be taken into account.

The committee rejected a utopian approach to their planning for the Columbia Basin project. Rather, it took a social trends approach. The assumption was that the recommendations should be largely guided by an analysis of the accumulated research by rural sociologists and others in the United States on trends in the location of schools, churches, stores, and recreational and cultural activity centers. The analysis of the findings of this past research was a major part of the committee's report. In addition, field studies as to the trends in the location of community services was made in two established irrigation projects similar to the Columbia Basin.

The research analysis concluded that for a number of decades the trend, in the United States, in the location of schools, churches, and recreational and cultural services had been away from the open country, hamlets, and small villages toward towns. The trends research suggested a minimum and maximum size to be an adequate social service center and to perform useful trade functions. Towns from 1,500 to 3,000 in population approached an ideal size. Efficient town-centered rural communities had total populations ranging from 3,000 to 5,000, divided about equally between farm and nonfarm. The study of the two resettlement projects found that settlers rapidly telescoped the trends which had occurred more slowly in older established communities.

The committee set forth research-based criteria and principles essential to planning service centers, which it contended were objective and practical. However, the committee went beyond the criteria and principles to propose nineteen communities and service centers for the Columbia Basin. The service areas were mapped. Estimates of the number of farms, the farm population, the rural nonfarm population, and the town population when fully developed were made for each service area. In Taylor's view, for planning purposes the mapped service areas were "as geographically precise as farm layout or road designs" (1946a:329).

LESSONS AND OBSERVATIONS

The high point in the Division's practice of sociology in the federal government setting, as gauged by requests received for assistance, activities, and resources, extended from the launching of the Second Agrarian New Deal, with its programs for the rural disadvantaged, through World War II until about 1946.[17] The requests came from administrators and staff of the USDA and other action agencies, from the Extension Service, from Congressional committees, and from others. The subject matter of some requests was squarely in areas in which sociologists had been developing a high level of competence, e.g., farm and rural population characteristics, trends, and migration; farm family levels and standards of living; farm labor; and rural locality groups. Other requests dealt with previously unexplored areas of sociological inquiry, e.g., rural rehabilitation, rural health resources, and social security for farm people.

The Division met the many and varied requests as best it could by drawing on the existing fund of sociological knowledge, by conducting major evaluation studies, by quick spot studies in the field of special problems and situations, by training professional staff of action agencies and the Extension Service in the application of relevant concepts and shortcut research techniques, and by instructing local leaders in the collection and analysis of data desired to serve local-level planning purposes. Information from the existing knowledge base and from the new special studies was provided administrators, agency staff, and policymakers by whatever means was appropriate to the situation at the time, e.g., a telephone call, an office conference, a memo, a special report for internal administrative use, testimony before a Congressional committee, or a report with unrestricted distribution.

For a decade the Division was afforded an unprecedented opportunity to put sociology to the test of meeting information needs of action agencies and for policy purposes. It was not the practice, however, to make any systematic follow-up of the uses made of the information provided. In some instances, the uses were direct and immediate as in the case of community and neighborhood delineation for the land-use planning program or natural leader identification for organizing civilian defense work during World War II. Clearly, the Division's work in the area of social security for farm laborers and farm operators contributed to getting the Social Security Act amended so they gained the protection of old age and survivors insurance. But, typically, the Division's input was one among several, even many, which entered into an administrative or policy decision.

Lessons

What lessons did the Division believe had been learned from its experience in the practice of sociology as a unit within the USDA's Bureau of Agricultural Economics? On a number of occasions, when he was Division head, Carl Taylor made statements that we interpret here as "lessons." For instance, with the benefit of thirteen years as a sociologist in the federal government, he published a paper "The social responsibilities of the social sciences—the national level," in the *American Sociological Review* (1946b:384–92). The paper discussed areas at the national level to which the sociological sciences could make definite contributions by objective analysis. One of these areas was "federal government administration as social organization." Nowhere does the paper make reference to the Division. Nevertheless, the excerpts that follow reflect Taylor's view of the government setting as a whole in which the Division operated. "The Federal Government administrative organization is different in both structure and functioning" than large industries or the army—"The only two others of sufficient magnitude and scope to warrant comparison" (388).

"[T]he administrative organization of the Federal Government is almost as complex as American Society" (388). "The constant turnover in top personnel [above the level of Bureau chiefs] is far greater than in any other type of large administrative group" (389). The regulations by which government workers are made to function "are prescribed more by administrators than by law" (389). "It is not the sole or even the primary function of Government to conduct research. Its primary function is to assist the people of the United States to fulfill their ideals and hopes, many of which are more aptly represented by politicians and pressure groups than by the cold delineation of facts" (391). "The unevenness with which the . . . acceptance of social science exists among the various levels of people (in government) dictates that there shall be conflict between people on these levels concerning its value. . . . very little of the body of knowledge called sociological knowledge is . . . accepted and used in Government" (391).

In other writings, we identify lessons specific to the Division's experience.[18]

1. Writing for a Southern Sociological Society annual meeting in 1941, at a time when the Division was "on the spot" coping with the demands placed on it by the Second and Third Agrarian New Deals, Taylor stated: "Let us admit or recognize that practical administrators will pose foolish or impossible questions . . . will expect us to furnish easy answers to questions which we know are exceedingly difficult" (1941a:159).

2. "[A]ttempting to do research while operating under the white heat of imminent and imperative action is a hectic and sometimes precarious undertaking. Administrators can't wait. . . . The research worker is, therefore, asked for judgments of which he is not sure, is called into conferences which absorb time he would like to spend on research. . . . But if our science has a body of knowledge and understanding, built up over years of development, all that knowledge can and should be brought to bear on a moment's notice" (Taylor 1941a:159). In the same vein, Conrad Taeuber reported that during World War II statistics relating to agricultural employment and farm population were among the facts that required greater speed and precision so that administrators would have a basis for decisions in the rapidly changing wartime situation (1945:170).

3. In his Rural Sociological Society presidential address, Taylor commented that in many cases USDA action agencies had not properly conceived social problems because they had assumed they were residuals rather than concomitants of physical and economic problems (1940:17–31). The action agencies often assumed "that the social elements in the

situation operate in universes confined by physical and economic boundaries" (31). Consequently, in such cases, the first necessary step in undertaking research to attack the problem raised by the administrator was to redefine the problem, to formulate a clearly stated frame of reference for the research (25–26).

4. At the time the BAE was readjusting to the transfer of the economic and social planning function for the USDA back to the Secretary's Office, Taylor (1946c) prepared a Division statement for use by an *ad hoc* Research Committee on Reorganization of the BAE Program. This statement reflected his convictions growing out of the Division's experiences during the New Deal and war years. Taylor asserted that "most of the work of the Division is better done if it is inter-divisional. If done adequately a great deal of it requires inter-agency cooperation" (1). This assertion was based, in part, on the structural context within which the Division operated. It was a unit with a relatively specialized professional staff of social scientists, most of them sociologists. But Taylor emphasized the point that cooperation was necessary because the social facts which the Division researched were "the social aspects of facts which also have physical, biological or economic aspects" (1).

5. A corollary of the preceding point was Taylor's conclusion, based on the past few years of experience, that it was impossible for any one BAE division to make its full contribution, even in the fields of its own special competence, without the type of inter-divisional cooperation which could "be had only if planned and somewhat directed at a Bureau level" (Taylor 1946c:13). The Division, Taylor stated, "was convinced that its contributions . . . depend upon a higher degree of integration in the whole Bureau program than has ever existed" (15).

6. Experience had demonstrated the importance of systematic research to build a fund of knowledge which the Division could draw on to help meet the repeated requests which came from agencies and individuals for assistance. Taylor stressed, in his statement for the *ad hoc* BAE committee, that "it should be evident to everyone that each individual's request for information or assistance cannot be met by a special research project" (Taylor 1946c:13–14). To at least partially supply the frequently requested "cafeteria" services,[19] what was needed was systematic research "so conducted as to yield the best possible answers at any given moment" (13). He suggested that such research be organized around fairly generalized subjects and be conducted with projects in sample areas across the nation or on type situations.

Observations on the Division's Practice of Sociology

With the perspective of nearly fifty years which have passed since the Division of Farm Population and Rural Life was abolished, we offer some observations on the Division's practice of sociology in government.

1. The societal setting and its changing issues and problems clearly influenced the extent and nature of the opportunities afforded the Division in the area of practice to assist federal agencies and policymakers. Two contrasting periods of national crisis, the Great Depression of the 1930s with its array of New Deal programs, and World War II with the resulting priorities in support of the war effort, offer numerous examples of impact on the Division's assistance through service and research.

2. The New Deal's experimental, innovative action programs for agriculture and rural people were especially conducive, given the intellectual climate which prevailed in the USDA at the time, to opening opportunities for the Division to contribute by drawing on existing research-based knowledge and through new research.

3. The Division's experience clearly demonstrated the importance, for such a subordinate research unit in the USDA organizational structure, of the support of key decision-makers in positions of power in the organizational hierarchy, persons from the Bureau and agency head level to the Secretary. These decision-makers were political appointees who rarely had a social science background.

4. The important role played by Carl Taylor, during his tenure as Division head, in gaining support from administrators for putting sociology to use should not be overlooked. He came to his position with the insights gained by firsthand high-level action agency experience. Taylor was a distinguished sociologist. He was convinced that sociology had factual information, techniques of study, and points of view that would be of material service to action agencies. A good speaker, Taylor was a vigorous advocate for sociology in his interactions with administrators.

5. Time and again the requests for "cafeteria" service required drawing on the existing fund of accumulated research knowledge. Typically, the testimony of Division staff members before Congressional committees on topics such as farm population trends, rural manpower, and rural problem areas was based on such accumulated knowledge rather than on new special studies. As another example, the report on the location of service centers prepared for the Columbia River Basin irrigation project relied heavily on past sociological research on rural trade centers

and communities. However, it was a constant challenge, with always limited resources and the pressures for timely response, to serve the immediate demands of practice and, concurrently, organize and conduct systematic research on the basic aspects of the structure and functioning of the nation's rural life and how it was changing.

Notes

1. Within the AAA, the administration of the land purchase and other parts of the land utilization program was the immediate responsibility of the Land Policy Section (Wooten 1965:5). In 1934–35, Carl Taylor was regional director, in Raleigh, North Carolina, of the AAA's Land Policy Section.

2. At the time, these appointments, like many others in the federal government, were excepted from the civil service. Such USDA agency appointments were subject to a personnel political clearance procedure and required the formal approval of Special Assistant to the Secretary Julien L. Friant, who was the representative in the USDA of the Democratic National Committee (Hardin 1954:220–21). Subsequently, such employees were brought into the civil service system by the Ramspack Act of 1940.

3. Taylor's statement was typed and undated. We found a copy in the collection of his papers in the Carl A. Krouch Library, Cornell University.

4. An account of land-use planning in its early phases is given by two BAE participants, Foster and Vogel (1940). For a sociological analysis of the four years of agricultural planning, some fifty years later, see papers by Jess Gilbert, University of Wisconsin, e.g., "Democratic planning in agriculture policy: the federal-county agricultural planning program, 1938–1942" (1996) and "Participatory democracy and democratic planning in the work of Carl C. Taylor, New Deal sociologist" (1997). Numerous examples of the operations and achievements of county planning committees are offered in Howard R. Tolley's *The Farmer Citizen at War* (1943:134–75), written when Tolley was BAE chief.

5. In his April 4, 1941, address to the Southern Sociological Society's annual meeting, Taylor (1941a:156) stated that the Division was "studying the planning process in seven so-called unified counties." He did not name the counties.

6. In addition to the county studies in Georgia and Kentucky, there was also a published report on planning in Eddy County, New Mexico (Johansen and Rossoff 1942). Also, a study of the visiting and kinship patterns in one neighborhood delineated for land-use planning in a Maryland county was published (Loomis et al. 1941:339–41).

7. A summary characterization of the Division during World War II is given in Chapter 1.

8. One staff member who did this reconnaissance was William T. Ham, a specialist in farm labor policy and other farm labor areas, who at the time was in charge of the Division's farm labor section. The other was Olaf F. Larson who, when most of the FSA's Washington staff was decentralized to Cincinnati, Ohio early in the war, was transferred to the same location to facilitate his work with the FSA.

9. More than fifty copies of this report for administrative use were distributed. About half of these went to a special list prepared by the Division head. This number was substantially more than was typically the case for such material prepared for internal use.

10. We lack information about the basis for selecting the thirty-five counties. However, Margaret J. Hagood, in 1943, prepared a statement for restricted distribution on the possible uses of the "master sample" by the Division in the Rural Life Trends project. We also know that the seventy-one-county study of rural regions, started in 1944, built on the thirty-five-county project.

11. The Pittsylvania County report was prepared by U. T. Miller Summers. A copy was made available to us by courtesy of her daughter, Mary Summers, at Yale University.

12. Veterans' adjustments was a topic included in the surveys made during October–December 1945 in the seventy-one-county rural cultural regions sample. In the four counties in the Pacific Northwest, arrangements were made with State Selective Service headquarters and local Selective Service Boards to compile data on all Selective Service Board registrants who, at the time, were or had been in military service. The analysis showed the extent to which the armed forces drew off manpower from rural areas and revealed characteristics of the veterans that might bear on the likelihood of their return to farming after their military service. The BAE approved use of this analysis for publication in *Rural Sociology* (Larson 1946:270–74).

13. There were also regional USDA Postwar Planning Working Groups on some topics but our information on this is sketchy. The Association of Land-grant Colleges and Universities had a committee on postwar agricultural policy whose report was issued in October, 1944.

14. There is little to suggest that Division staff in the regional offices was involved to any extent in the work of the USDA's Interbureau Committee on Postwar Programs. However, in 1944, John Page of the Berkeley office prepared a report for administrative use on plans for using demountable defense houses for postwar rural housing in California.

15. Louis J. Ducoff, then Assistant Head of the Division, co-authored the report on the Wisconsin study. The Social Security Administration provided technical assistance in planning the study and the tabulations and also assisted in the fieldwork. Division staff member Josiah C. Folsom also assisted in the fieldwork.

16. The Division also participated in studies for the Bureau of Reclamation's Central Valley irrigation project in California but on a much more limited basis. Two staff members in the regional office in Berkeley were on a nine-person BAE committee, which drafted a report as to the effect of this project on the agricultural and industrial economy and on the social character of California (U.S. Department of the Interior, Bureau of Reclamation 1949). The draft report was dated March 1945 but was not published until 1949. A brief section on the rural community in California referred to ongoing studies of two agricultural communities, Arvin and Dinuba. It was these studies by Walter Goldschmidt, eventually used in his book *As You Sow*, which evoked so much controversy (see Chapter 4; also see the section on "Farm Structure and Community" in Chapter 10).

17. Although the Division's professional staff was always comprised predominantly of sociologists, during the highpoint in its practice of sociology the staff included some cultural anthropologists, social psychologists, and other social scientists. Carl Taylor sometimes noted that he was including anthropologists and social psychologists in the group of sociological sciences (Taylor 1946b:384).

18. Some of the "lessons" we identify from the Division's experience in "practice" are strikingly similar to the observations about the experience of the United States Army's Research Branch, Information and Education Division made by Robin M. Williams Jr. (1946:573–77), despite the sharp differences in organizational context. The Army's Research Branch was charged with the study of the "attitudes" and "morale" of soldiers during World War II with "service" research directed toward immediate administrative problems. Among Williams' observations: "In many instances . . . concrete problems represented the interlacing of technical, economic, political and psychological or sociological problems. . . . In such a social climate, interdisciplinary cooperation in some sense becomes a practical necessity" (573); "group research of this type requires frequent conferences and much discussion" (575). The research technicians are "continually under pressure to deliver immediately usable, specific results quickly" (575). And (as a hypothesis) "research findings are not utilized to the extent warranted by their intrinsic merit if sole reliance is placed upon dissemination by the printed page. . . . The best immediate results in translating research into action came through repeated contacts with persons in positions of authority and influence" (577).

19. Taylor reported that the most frequently repeated requests for "cafeteria" service were in the fields of assistance in organization, especially in the effective local organization of farm people; understanding, knowledge and analysis of farmer thinking and attitudes; information on items in farmer's levels of living, most often on health and next most often on housing, followed by information on reading materials in farm homes; information on population numbers and changes; information on the farm labor force and farm wages; and information on customs, traditions and attitudes which condition the adoption of new farm and home practices (1946c:13).

14

Some Other Areas of Research

Not all of the Division's wide-ranging research and related activities could be fitted neatly into the preceding chapters dealing with the major substantive areas of study or with the practice of sociology. But some of this other work cannot be overlooked in a systematic examination of the Division's lifetime record despite its episodic nature or the subordinate place the subject had in the Division's program as a whole. In this chapter we consider a disparate selection from the Division's other areas of research. We give primary emphasis to the Division's studies of farm women, to a set of studies of rural youth that were almost exclusively made through cooperative projects with agricultural experiment stations, and to the research on farmer attitudes and opinions.

THE DIVISION AND STUDIES OF WOMEN

In the early 1900s, those interested in inproving rural welfare saw the importance of women to rural life. President Theodore Roosevelt's Commission on Country Life appointed in 1908 "made special effort to ascertain the condition of women on the farm" (*Report* 1944:103). The Commission's inquiry led it to include "woman's work on the farm" as one of the six main special deficiencies of country life at the time. This concern was later picked up in the 1913 annual report of the U.S. Department of Agriculture when Secretary Houston reported on some of the needs of women on the farm (Houston 1914:9–74). The secretary had sent out fifty-five thousand open 'letters of inquiry' to farm women across the country. About the same time, home economics was a growing field. The 1914 Smith-Lever Act had, for example, not only named home economics but, by providing funds for extension work, granted formal recognition of home economics as the parallel to agricultural education. The 1917 Smith-Hughes Act also included home economics. And, with World War I, both the funds and the reach of home economics and extension work grew.

When Secretary Houston formed an advisory committee on establishing a rural life studies unit in the USDA, seven of the twenty-eight members were women. They undoubtedly were an important influence in the committee's decision to lead off the ten suggested topics for study with rural home life, including the farmer's wife, the boy, the girl, and the farmhouse (USDA, Office of the Secretary 1919b:6). This suggestion was quickly implemented by Galpin in the form of research on farm family levels and standards of living. Two of the women on Houston's advisory committee were on the staff of the USDA's Office of Extension Work and in charge of home demonstration work for women nationally. The advisory committee's report had been submitted to the Secretary barely a month when one of these women, Florence Ward, in charge of extension work with women in the North and West, had a survey of more than ten thousand farm women under way (Ward 1920:437–57). The purpose was to provide evidence of living and working conditions of farm women. This evidence would be used to guide the Extension Service in extending practical and acceptable assistance to farm women in the solution of these problems.

The impacts of the growing field of home economics were felt in the new Division. This is in part illustrated by an address by Charles J. Galpin to the twelfth annual meeting of the American Home Economics Association. In this, he outlined the nature of research on the farm home to be conducted by what would become the Division. Specifically, he stated what would and would not be covered in this research. "Farm Life Studies will not undertake to explore the technical aspects of food, dietetics, clothing, household equipment, household work, or household management of the farm home" (Galpin 1920:159). Instead, the areas the Division would be examining included the relationship of the farm home to neighborhoods and communities, "social elements in the farm home situation," the "family cycle which is a little larger than the unit usually associated with the home" as the farm passes from one generation to the next, and the "use and distribution of leisure on the part of members of the farm home" (Galpin 1920:159–60). While Galpin clearly delineated the differences between the two fields, he also sought cooperative relationships with home economics as illustrated in the involvement of USDA and land-grant college home economists in numerous levels of living studies, especially during the 1920s.

Within a few months of his arrival in Washington, Galpin recruited two of his former graduate students at the University of Wisconsin, Emily Hoag Sawtelle and Veda Larson Turner to join him. Larson Turner shared in the pioneering work on farm population done in the Division before she left in 1925. The annual report for the year ending June 30, 1922, had a terse listing of rural life studies projects completed or well along toward completion. One of these was described as "the story of one hundred farm women. Fieldwork completed and text of three bulletins in preparation" (H. Taylor 1923:556). Presumably, this referred to work done by Emily Hoag Sawtelle. In any case, she was the author of the one piece of Division research devoted solely to farm women. This was a study of the attitudes of farm women toward farm life.

Sawtelle's mimeographed report (1924) "The Advantages of Farm Life: A Study by Correspondence and Interviews with Eight Thousand Farm Women" carried the subtitle "Digest of an unpublished manuscript." The unpublished manuscript was based on Sawtelle's visits with farm women in their homes, a reading of letters volunteered by farm women in response to an article "The women God forgot" published in the September 1920 issue of *Farm and Home* put out by the Phelps Publishing Company in Springfield, Massachusetts, as well as the reading and analysis of seven thousand letters of farm women written in response to the question, "Do you want your daughter to marry a farmer?," which appeared in the January 1922 issue of *The Farmer's Wife,* a publication of the Webb Publishing Company, St. Paul, Minnesota.

Sawtelle used three major categories in her analysis of the responses of farm women; these were the work side, the social side, and the home side. Each of these categories had sub-categories. The "work side" had satisfaction in good farming, partnership on the farm, the work habit for farm children, and effacement of drudgery. Under "the social side" category was "the stage of modern organization," (meaning that American country life had reached its third movement with improved transportation and the trend to trade center communities), "native social advantages in farm life," "possibilities open to country life," and "experiments in rural organization." The "home side" had sections on the physical setting and the farm home. Some of the sub-categories were further subdivided to convey a theme found in the interviews and letters.

Sawtelle supported her analysis with numerous direct quotations from the interviews and letters. She started with the belief that contemporary popular conceptions of farm life were "one-sided," and focused on the undesirable phases of country life. In her interviews and examination of the correspondence, Sawtelle found in women's own voices a view that emphasized the possibilities of farm life. The emphasis in her report was consistent with Galpin's interest in the early years of the Division in identifying some of the good aspects of rural life, the success stories.

Beyond Sawtelle's one study, women were not considered as a subject in and of itself for Division study. They might be one small component of a larger study as in the case of the rural organization research. For example, the guide for the interviews in the reconnaissance survey of the seventy-one counties in the rural cultural regional study (see Chapter 7) called for collecting information on the division of labor by gender and age within the family, on women's leadership in different categories of organizations, and on the expected role of the mother by status and ethnic groups. The published use of this information was limited. Most typically, women were a variable in the analysis of quantitative data in the farm labor and wage and wage rates studies initiated in the 1940s (see Chapter 9) such as those by Louis Ducoff and Barbara Reagan (1946). In these studies, women were included insofar as the data were disaggregated by gender.

While women rarely formed the sole focus of research emanating from the Division, many women worked on its professional staff, even at a time when scholarly opportunities for women were limited. Of the 145 professionals employed at some time on the Division staff, twenty-seven, or almost 20 percent, were women (see Appendix for names). By contrast, from its inception in 1938 until the year the Division was abolished, membership by women in the Rural Sociological Society averaged only about 12 percent (Willits et al. 1988:135).

In the end, only a few areas of research in the Division included women and then only as part of the larger landscape of rural life. This could have been in part due to the fact that women's work on the farm extended beyond gender definitions for women. It could also be in part attributable to the rise of home economics, which defined women's work as that within the home itself. And finally, the demands of the New Deal period and of World War II set different priorities for use of the Division's resources. Still, women formed an important part of the professional staff of the Division, even at a time when opportunities for women were limited. And some of the most notable women in the field formed an integral part of the Division's history.

RESEARCH ON RURAL YOUTH

Rural youth studies began to be included in the Division's program during the Galpin years, but this area was pursued only episodically. The timing of the first such research, started in 1926 (Kirkpatrick 1927), was associated with a recommendation to the state agricultural experiment stations by a joint land-grant-college–USDA committee that they include rural youth among the high priority areas for sociological investigations funded under the Purnell Act of 1925 (Joint Committee 1925:23–25). The priority given youth studies reflected concerns about farm young people growing out of the pronounced farm-to-city shift during the past few years. This was a shift revealed by the Division's annual estimates of farm population.

Shortly, Galpin had E. L. Kirkpatrick engaged in a large-scale study that had the active cooperation of the Extension Service and other youth-serving agencies. Extension interest centered largely on ascertaining whether rural youth were contented to live on the farm and the factors that might account for their attitudes toward farm life. Among the latter was the influence of 4-H Club work. Although nearly eight thousand usable questionnaires were obtained from youth, most of whom were inferred to be between ten and twenty years of age, the sample was such a mixed one that Kirkpatrick warned that conclusions from the study might not be typical of all farm boys and girls (1927:50). He concluded that "by and large, the problems of farm youth of these ages exist primarily in the minds of the adult workers interested in the welfare of the youth they are striving to serve" (Kirkpatrick 1927:51).

Except for Kirkpatrick's study, during the Galpin years the Division's involvement in youth studies was limited to support of cooperative projects with the AESs in Missouri (Morgan and Burt 1927), New York (Beers 1933),[1] Pennsylvania (Dennis 1931), and Virginia (Garnett 1930). The four had little commonality in their purposes and methods. They reflected efforts to provide information about youth desired in each state along with the interests of the AES investigators. This is reflected in the titles of the respective agricultural experiment station bulletins which was the form of publication. The Missouri report was *Community Relations of Rural Young People*. The New York report was *The Income, Savings and Work of Boys and Girls on Farms in New York, 1930*. The Pennsylvania study was issued as *Organizations Affecting Farm Youth in Locust Township, Columbia County, Pennsylvania*. The title of the Virginia AES bulletin, *Young People's Organizations in Relation to Rural Life in Virginia—with Special Reference to 4-H Clubs,* was suggestive of the fact that this was largely a general survey of the state's organizations found to be contributing most to the specialized training of rural youth for country life.

After these early studies, the Division gave relatively little attention specifically to the rural youth area. The exceptions were O. E. Baker's extension-related work[2] in the mid-1930s, assistance to a few studies which originated with county land-use planning committees, and cooperative projects in North Dakota (Hay et al. 1940)[3] and Massachusetts (Meldrum and Sherburne 1941).[4]

The North Dakota research, initiated in 1938, clearly reflected concerns in the state about the situation for rural youth in an agricultural area impacted by the twin forces of economic depression and drouth. The age group 15–29 was selected for study to include the final years in school, the years of adaptation into life work, and participation in adult group activities (Hay et al. 1940:6). The investigation gave particular emphasis to the economic status of rural youth and to the interaction of this status with educational attainment, employment, participation in social organizations, and interest in community life. The intent of the study was to provide information useful for developing effective programs to aid in the adjustment of rural youth. The Massachusetts work was done at the request of rural policy committees in the state. The first purpose was to provide information as to the resources, problems, and opportunities of the state's rural youth. The second purpose was to create interest among the young people in recognizing and solving their problems. Most of the fieldwork for the study was done by volunteers who were 4-H club members.

RURAL SOCIAL PSYCHOLOGY—ATTITUDES AND OPINIONS

Galpin had plans to include rural social psychological studies among the Division's major research areas when, in 1927, he added T. B. Manny to the staff. Some twenty years later, however, when Taylor (1948b) reviewed the development of rural sociological research in the Division during the Galpin years, he could only say "a start" had been made "in the field of attitude studies." This was in contrast to the major contributions in farm population, levels and standards of living, and rural organization. The "start" Taylor was referring to was, of course, Manny's research on attitudes and opinions included in his investigations of cooperative marketing and other subjects (see Chapter 12). All such studies were among those which the Division had to abruptly drop when funds were drastically curtailed in the early 1930s.

Despite Carl Taylor's strong interest in social psychology dating back to his time as a graduate student, he did not move immediately when he became Division head in 1935 to reinstate social psychology as a major program area.[5] During the time when he also headed the social research unit in the RA-FSA, one major joint project included a social psychological emphasis. This was Schuler's (1938b) field investigation of land tenure in the Corn Belt and the South, a study that had such a focus on attitudes, opinions, and aspirations that Taylor characterized it as a study in social psychology (see Chapter 10). About the same time, the Division made two small-scale exploratory ventures into the attitude and opinion area. One of these sought to analyze comments volunteered by farmers who responded to the annual farm population estimates mail questionnaires. The comments for the 1933 and 1937 responses were used to obtain some indication of what the nation's farmers were thinking in the depression year of 1933 and three years later when economic stress had lessened (Loomis et al. 1938). The second had a twofold objective: (1) to test a technique of measuring opinions quantitatively; and (2) to compare the opinions of a sample of leading agricultural economists and rural sociologists with respect to twenty-four statements pertaining to broad theories or philosophies of agriculture and rural life (Taylor and Loomis 1939).[6]

The most distinctive use by the Division of the field of social psychology during Taylor's seventeen years as head was associated with the coming of the Third Agrarian New Deal. At that time he was requested to include social psychologists, along with cultural anthropologists, on the staff. This request reflected the pronounced interest in these social sciences on the part of then Undersecretary of Agriculture M. L. Wilson and the BAE Chief, Howard Tolley. Taylor promptly recruited a succession of prominent social psychologists from universities for short-term appointments on the Washington staff. About this time, when the Division staff was at its peak and the Washington research staff was grouped into informal sections, one such section was designated "social psychology."[7] This arrangement and the inclusion of social psychologists on the staff was, however, a short-term arrangement.

First to join the staff was Kimball Young who later was ASA president. Young and J. E. Hulett Jr. were the social psychologists on the multidisciplinary team, which planned and conducted the community stability-instability studies, thereby insuring that this work had an important social psychological component (see Chapter 7).

Following this was research devoted solely to farmer attitudes in one South Carolina county (Matthews et al. 1942). Washington staff member Raymond F. Sletto, on leave from Ohio State University, was co-investigator for this cooperative project started in 1940.[8] This carefully designed study, made at the request of the farmer members of the Edgefield County Agricultural Planning Committee, analyzed attitudes and values of farmers in relation to a group of agricultural programs and proposals. Farmer attitudes were obtained on fourteen program topics selected with the help of planning committee representatives, local action agencies, and Clemson College staff in agricultural economics and rural sociology. Because nearly all farmers in the county were AAA cooperators, the AAA list of farm units was used to get a 10 percent random sample. During interviews, fieldworkers made a record of attitudes toward each program or proposal, using a five-point scale from "strongly disapprove" through "undecided" to "strongly approve," and the reasons for attitudes. Before field interviews were started, extensive tests were made to determine the reliability of the sample. Tests were also conducted to ensure that the two interviewers were rating attitudes objectively (Matthews et al. 1942:8–9).

The recorded attitudes and reasons were analyzed by race (white and black), tenure, and farm size for each program or proposal. Among all farmers, approval ratings for the fourteen programs and proposals ranged from 31 to 94 percent. The quantitative treatment of attitude data was supplemented by a qualitative analysis of the reasons for the attitudes, a feature that provided insights and a richness unusual in a databased report of this type.

Quite different in method and scope than any of the preceding work by the Division was Taylor's attempt, in the midst of World War II, to answer the question of whether farmers were more "isolationist" than other Americans.[9] The backdrop for the question was the concern about the nation's postwar international arrangements and relations. For data, Taylor turned to the Gallup and *Fortune* public opinion polls, national election records, voting behavior in Congress of representatives from farming areas, and the resolutions passed by large general farmers' organizations. These data sources proved to have major limitations for answering the question. For instance, when polling data did not segregate responses of farmers as an occupational group, selected regions were used as surrogates best representing farmer opinion. The study was published as "Attitudes of American farmers-international and provincial" in the *American Sociological Review* (Taylor 1944c:657–64). Taylor stated that the information he was able to obtain did not justify a sure answer to the question posed. He did, however, offer seven conclusions about farmers' attitudes and opinions, the first of which was that "when responses to all questions on international relations, including those related to the present war, are considered, farming areas and farmers' responses are less favorable than are those for the nation as a whole" (Taylor 1944c:663). Taylor ended his paper with an interpretation of the significance of the study conclusions for those who would be responsible for handling the nation's international affairs at the end of the war.

BOOKS, DEMOCRACY, AND THE WORLD OVERSEAS

To give a reasonably complete view of the full range of the Division's activities three additional areas need to be mentioned. The first of these pertains to books. Most of the books published by Division staff or with the unit's support, fewer than twenty over the Division's thirty-four-year life, were research-based. Most of these have been noted in earlier chapters. One exception to a research-based book was the edited three-volume work *A Systematic Source Book in Rural Sociology* (Sorokin et al. 1930–32), made possible by BAE funding as reported in Chapter 3. The main objective of the *Source Book*, with its 212 readings, was to give a survey of the knowledge in the main fields of rural sociology. It was intended to be a complete encyclopedia, a reference work, a substantial systematic treatise to give an adequate and up-to-date knowledge of European, Asiatic, and American scientific literature (Sorokin et al. 1930: viii–ix). The *Source Book* provided evidence from many countries which was used by Pitirim Sorokin and Carle C. Zimmerman for a rural sociology text, *Principles of Rural-Urban Sociology* (1929).

The other was Charles P. Loomis' translation of *Fundamental Concepts of Sociology (Gemeinschaft und Gesellschaft)* by Ferdinand Tonnies (1940c). Loomis made the translation from the German text and wrote an analytical supplementation. This effort increased the availability of an important work on sociological theory. The project was done by Loomis as a Division staff member, but he also had some assistance from an SSRC grant-in-aid. The fact that this book was published reflected the interest of Carl Taylor and Loomis in the nature of social relations in understanding the basis of social disorganization (Loomis 1990). It also reflected the breadth of interests which social scientists were free to pursue within the USDA at that time.

Democracy as a Theme

The Division did not do research on democracy per se. We detect democracy as a recurring theme, however, during Carl Taylor's tenure as head.[10] The times were conducive for a variety of expressions of this theme. The theme was consistent with the philosophical views of such top-level USDA administrators as Secretary of Agriculture Henry A. Wallace, M. L. Wilson, the secretary's close associate, and BAE Chief Howard Tolley (1943). They were advocates of "economic democracy" and "democratic planning." The theme was consistent with the increased articulation of the importance of democracy that accompanied the approach and then the entry of the nation into World War II. The democracy theme was expressed by the Division in such ways as the community-neighborhood delineation and other work in support of the land-use planning program initiated by the Third Agrarian New Deal (see Chapter 13) and in speeches by Taylor and other staff members.[11] Also, there were instances in which the implications for democracy of research findings were interpreted as Taylor (1948a) did with respect to the land tenure situation he found in Argentina.

The Division and the World Overseas

We conclude this chapter with a review of the Division's relation to other countries. The outbreak of World War II increased the extent to which the Division was engaged in some way with countries outside the borders of the United States and greatly changed the purpose and nature of the activities related to other countries. When Galpin was Division head, he had the opportunity to visit thirteen European countries in 1926 on official assignment. Charles Loomis and Conrad Taeuber, among the first added to the professional staff by Carl Taylor, both had prior experience in Germany as graduate students. Taeuber (1936) drew on his research there for a paper on the German population registration system as a data source for internal migration. Loomis used his work to prepare Division-issued publications on the modern settlement movement in Germany (1935a) and on attempts to change rural life in Germany and Russia. While Taylor headed both the RA-FSA's social research unit and the Division he had one staff member prepare a report on the tenure of new agricultural holdings in European countries (Kraemer 1937).

With the outbreak of the war, South America and the Caribbean area assumed a new strategic importance for the United States (Nelson 1969:142–43). Both the State Department and the USDA's Office of Foreign Agricultural Relations (OFAR) engaged rural sociologists to obtain a better understanding of these areas. Carl Taylor was employed by the State Department in 1942 for a temporary assignment in Argentina. A major result was his book *Rural Life in Argentina* (1948).

By 1943 the OFAR was recruiting a small group of rural sociologists, mostly from the Division, whose work was done in cooperation with the State Department. One reason for the interest in South America was that locations now occupied by the Japanese had been a major source of strategic agricultural products, such as cinchona bark, from which quinine is derived, derris, from which rotenone is produced, pyrethrum, rubber, and certain fiber crops; many of these were native to South American countries (Loomis 1943). The USDA was expected to assist these countries in developing dependable supplies of the needed agricultural materials. Yet the North Americans had little reliable knowledge about the rural areas where production of these crops might be encouraged.

Olen Leonard, Glenn Taggart, and Theo Vaughan shifted from the Division to OFAR at some point. Loomis, for a period in 1943, was working in Peru, El Salvador, and Mexico for the Division, OFAR, and the Society for Applied Anthropology (*Rural Sociology* 9[1]:95). Out of this and other work with OFAR came a series of articles by Loomis on extension work, rural development and agricultural production in Latin America, most of which were published in *Applied Anthropology* (e.g., Loomis 1943).

As the end of the war was in sight, some Division staff members became increasingly involved in the problems that would be faced overseas in the rehabilitation and reconstruction of war-torn countries and, by extension, with the problems of the less developed countries. Thus, Douglas Ensminger was general chairman of a conference held in 1944 in Washington to develop a report on the contribution of extension methods and techniques toward the rehabilitation of the war-torn countries (USDA, Extension Service and Office of Foreign Agricultural Relations 1945).[12] Other Division staff members served on some of the ten committees constituted to lay the substantive groundwork for the conference; these were organized around such areas of the world as Western Europe, India, Eastern Asia and Southeastern Asia. A spin-off of this conference was the book *Farmers of the World: The Development of Agricultural Extension* (Brunner et al. 1945) to which Ensminger and Loomis contributed. Five years later, in 1949, Ensminger was also chair of a conference, again sponsored by the USDA, Extension Service, and the OFAR which resulted in a *Conference Report on Extension Experiences Around the World* (Ensminger 1951).

After the war was over several Division staff members accepted foreign assignments with public or private international agencies where their specialized knowledge and analytical skills were used in rural development and related areas. Earl Bell left in 1947 to head the United Nations International Emergency Children's Fund Mission in Poland. Douglas Ensminger was recruited by the Ford Foundation to be its representative in India and Nepal. He worked closely with the government of India in shaping its rural development programs. There he brought T. Wilson Longmore to assist him and arranged for Carl Taylor and Helen W. Johnson to undertake a sociological analysis of India's experience in planned development (Taylor et al. 1965). Taylor also had other consultant roles on rural development. Following Arthur Raper's lead role in a postwar study of Japanese villages and an evaluation of the land reform program mandated for Japan by the Allied Powers (Raper et al. 1950), he became Social Science Advisor for the U.S. Mutual Security Agency in Taiwan.

Notes

1. Beers' report identified T. B. Manny as the Division staff member who assisted materially.

2. O. E. Baker, who was added to the Division staff in 1936 after Carl Taylor became head, was much in demand as a speaker to extension and other audiences. Youth was often the subject of his addresses. In his talks he drew extensively on demographic and related data from the Division's studies and the census. In October 1936 his appointment called for one-fourth time with the Extension Service.

3. Conrad Taeuber, in the Division's Washington office, assisted in planning the North Dakota study and in the selection of survey areas. The WPA cooperated by paying for workers who tabulated data and drafted charts for the report. Bruce L. Melvin, in the WPA's rural research unit, also advised on study plans.

4. O. E. Baker of the Division's Washington office was credited with assisting in planning and guiding the Massachusetts project, as were Walter C. McKain and C. R. Draper of the Division's regional office for the Northeast.

5. In an assessment made in 1937–38 by an RSS-BAE committee of past rural sociological research, social psychology was one of the categories included. The committee reported that "although much has been done on the structure of rural society, we have had but little research . . . on the social psychology of rural behavior" (Joint Committee 1938:12). The Division's record of activity in social psychology, as of that time, was consistent with the record for rural sociology generally.

6. Degree of agreement with a statement was scored from one to five. Degree of disagreement was similarly scored (Taylor and Loomis 1939:7–8).

7. It was about this time that the Division announced plans for increased work on studies of rural attitudes and opinions in cooperation with the Division of program Surveys, a new unit created in the BAE (FPRLA 1939[3]:8).

8. Concurrently a Division staff member in the Milwaukee regional office constructed and standardized a twenty-two-item scale, using the Likert method, to measure the degree of pro-rural or pro-urban sentiment (Forsyth 1941).

9. We noted in Chapter 13 that during the war, the Division used the thirty-five-county Rural Life Trends Project and, later, the seventy-one-county rural cultural regions study to obtain farmers' opinions on topics of current interest to federal government administrators. An example is a report, for administrative use, prepared in 1944 by Arthur F. Raper and others on farmers' opinions about postwar conditions.

10. In a 1997 paper, sociologist Jess Gilbert asserted that a radical-reformist concept of democracy was essential to Carl Taylor for his work in the USDA, especially in connection with the land-use-planning program. Gilbert also discussed democratic theory in relation to Taylor's vision for rural sociology and rural America.

11. Examples of Taylor's speeches, which had a democracy theme, include one on "the issues of democracy" at a Virginia Social Science Association meeting (1938) and one on "democracy in the face of crisis" given to an Iowa Farm and Home Week audience (1941c).

12. M. L. Wilson, who had moved in 1940 from the Secretary of Agriculture's office to be Director of Extension, and the USDA's Office of Foreign Agricultural Relations jointly called the conference.

15

The Division and the Social Science Research System

The Division contributed to the development, strengthening, and maintenance of the social science research system in ways that one might not expect of a small, subordinate research unit in the U.S. Department of Agriculture. This account of the Division would not be complete without mentioning these contributions. Examples include helping to get rural sociological research underway in colleges and universities during the 1920s, assisting in upgrading the methodological competence of land-grant college sociologists during the 1920s and 1930s, taking an important role in periodic evaluations of the status of rural sociological research in the United States and in framing research priorities, and active involvement in the development and support of sociologists' professional associations.

COOPERATIVE RESEARCH AGREEMENTS

Little sociological research on rural life was being done by colleges and universities when Galpin was brought to Washington in 1919 to head what became the Division. By design, Galpin tested and developed a policy of cooperative research agreements to encourage the initiation and expansion of sociological studies by investigators who were on the staff of colleges and universities (see Chapter 3). The general idea of this strategy for planting the "seed of rural sociology" was clarified for Galpin on his first tour of state colleges of agriculture after he came to Washington (Galpin 1938a:39). His thought was that "each college of agriculture should have a man and finally a staff whose business was to come to know more and more perfectly the farm life of his state. . . . These key rural-life men in the states would be the eyes, fingers, and ears of the Federal unit of rural-life research" (Galpin 1938a:39).

The cooperative plan was tried out with six land-grant institutions in 1920. A few more were added each year until, in 1924, the Division was ready to lay out a formal policy on such agreements whereby it paid part of the cost for study of a specific rural life problem (Galpin 1924). By the time of Galpin's retirement in 1934, the Division had entered into cooperative agreements with forty-eight institutions in thirty-seven states (Galpin 1934a:2). The small grants provided under these agreements supported rural social research in liberal arts and teachers colleges in addition to agricultural colleges (Brunner 1957:6). The joint research projects initiated by Galpin's policy were an early form of federal-university cooperation in social science research. Brunner's assessment in his *The Growth of a Science* was that the grants stimulated much of the "pre-Purnell" rural sociological research done in the United States (1957:6).

THE DIVISION AND THE PURNELL ACT OF 1925

Prior to passage by Congress of the Purnell Act of 1925, few state agricultural experiment station directors were willing to approve the use for sociological research of federal funds that came to them annually under the terms of the Hatch Act of 1887 and the Adams Act of 1906. Not only were most skeptical of the value of such research, but they could claim the provisions of the two acts gave them no authority to use these federal funds for social science research (Nelson 1969:86). The Purnell Act, however, was a breakthrough. It authorized annual appropriations to each state agricultural experiment station which could be used for purposes including "such economic and sociological investigations as have for their purpose the development and improvement of the rural home and rural life." The federal funds authorized for each state amounted to $20,000 for the fiscal year ending June 30, 1926; an increase of $10,000 each year through June 30, 1930; and for $60,000 for each fiscal year thereafter.[1]

The Purnell Act established rural sociology as a legitimate research discipline in the agricultural experiment stations. It provided for a stable source of funds which, if the station director was favorable, permitted initiating rural social research for more poorly financed stations and for planning projects on a longer-term basis.

Congress passed the Purnell Act of February 24, 1925, in accord with a recommendation made by the National Agricultural Conference (Baker et al. 1963:128). This was one of scores of recommendations made by the Conference which met January 23 to 27, 1922, at the call of Secretary of Agriculture Henry C. Wallace (Davis 1940:300–302).[2]

The Purnell Act funds distributed to the states were administered by the USDA's Office of Experiment Stations. Its annual reports recorded the progress of what was classified as rural sociological research. In 1924–25, the year before the Act, there were thirty-four active projects at the state agricultural experiment stations (Jardine 1935:8). Five years later, in 1929–30, there were forty-six. And in 1933–34 the reports showed sixty active projects in twenty-six state stations. Six of these twenty-six had separate rural sociological research divisions and, in all, the state AESs had a total of about forty research staff members under employment as rural sociologists. The Chief of the Office of Experiment Stations stated that the feeling in his Office was that rural sociology had made, in many respects, "extraordinary progress in the nine years which have elapsed since the approval of the Purnell Act" (Jardine 1935:9).

The Division had a hand in the Purnell Act coming into being in the sense that the advocates for the legislation could use the examples generated by Galpin's cooperative research agreements to illustrate what might be accomplished for the improvement of rural life if funds were made available to the states for sociological studies on a continuing basis. The Division also had a hand in establishing guidelines for use of the new money. Galpin was made one of the six members of a special USDA–land-grant-college committee which recommended the research areas to be given priority by the agricultural experiment stations. The three major areas already a part of the Division's program were reaffirmed for the states; rural youth was a recommended addition (see Chapter 4).

RESEARCH WORKERS — INCREASING THE NUMBER AND COMPETENCE

When Galpin started his plan of small grants for cooperative research agreements, colleges and universities had few competent social science researchers available. This professional resource problem increased with the new funds made available to state AESs by the Purnell Act.

In the pre-Purnell period, Galpin is said to have viewed the cooperative research agreements as a way of developing competent researchers for rural sociology (Brunner 1957:6). Following passage of the Purnell Act, the Social Science Research Council, at the urging of its Committee on Social and Economic Research in Agriculture, made a grant in 1928 to establish a series of fellowships in agricultural economics and rural sociology (Schultz 1941:307). These were spread over a five-year period. Of the 106 appointments, seventeen were for training in rural sociology (Schultz 1941:311–16). Galpin was a member of the selection committee for five years which annually picked "young men to spend a year or more at some university in graduate study in rural sociology." (Galpin 1938a:59).

The Purnell Act was soon followed by the first Institute on Research Methods in Rural Sociology. This five-day training session held at Purdue

University was organized by the Committee on Rural Social Organization and Agencies, a land-grant-college–USDA Committee of which Galpin was a member. This Institute was attended by twenty-three Purnell-funded researchers in rural sociology. They came from twenty AESs. Researchers from other colleges and from social agencies also attended. The program involved discussion of current projects in rural sociology and recommendations on projects and procedures made by committees for such areas as population and rural groups. The emphasis, however, was on formal presentations on research methods having special application to the field of rural sociology (Committee on Rural Social Organization and Agencies 1927). Among the topics were the use and limitation of statistical methods, scientific methods, and research methods employed by the Institute of Social and Religious Research in its study of 177 agricultural villages.

A second Institute on methods, jointly sponsored by the BAE and the AESs, was held December 31, 1929, to January 4, 1930, in Washington. The summary report was issued by the Division (USDA, BAE 1930). Featured were presentations by notables Stuart A. Rice and Gordon W. Allport on measurements of social attitudes and public opinion and by Ernest W. Burgess on the case study method. There were other presentations which included U.S. Census procedures in population statistics, methods of obtaining vital statistics, the use of statistics in analysis, graphic analysis and presentation, the use of a newly invented tabulating machine, and a demonstration of procedures of editing and coding field schedules for tabulation. Participants in this second Institute numbered fifty-seven from twenty-six states; fifteen of the fifty-seven came from institutions such as Columbia University, Harvard, Oberlin College, and private agencies. There were also two from Canada and one from China.

The Division also joined with the University of Missouri's College of Agriculture in sponsoring the first Mid-Western Conference on Rural Population Research (University of Missouri 1937). Researchers from twelve Colleges of Agriculture attended the two-day conference along with staff from federal agencies. The discussions covered rural population migration, population composition, and regional population research (FPRLA 1937[3]:22).

ASSESSING THE STATUS OF RURAL SOCIOLOGICAL RESEARCH

The Division had an important part in periodic major efforts during its lifetime to assess the status of rural sociological research. Thus, Galpin chaired the committee appointed to report on the status of the research in the field during 1926–27, the first full year of operations under the Purnell Act. This committee worked under the direction of the Social Science Research Council's Advisory Committee on Social and Economic Research in Agriculture. The preliminary report (Galpin et al. 1927) was followed by *Rural Sociological Research in the United States* issued by the Social Science Research Council as a social science research monograph (Galpin et al. 1928). These reports analyzed the rural sociological research underway as reported by universities and private agencies in twenty-seven states. The analysis included problems studied, types of methods, expenditures from all sources, the academic degrees of the persons doing the research work, and publications issued. The scope of the ongoing research was indicated and a suggested bibliography on methodology was provided.[3]

A second major appraisal of rural sociology was made a decade later by a committee appointed by Carl C. Taylor as an outgrowth of the Midwestern Conference on Population Research, which Taylor had chaired. The committee was comprised of C. E. Lively of Ohio State University, Lowry Nelson of the University of Minnesota, and Dwight Sanderson of Cornell University. The report had three major parts. The first examined the more important accomplishments in rural sociology from the scientific point of view and from the extension view. The second part presented the current research emphasis in rural sociology based upon information supplied by twenty-five researchers in twenty-two states and the District of Columbia. The third part was future-oriented, asking what areas for research were timely in the immediate future? The committee's report was intended to be the basis for discussion at a session at the forthcoming annual meeting of the Rural Sociology Section of the ASA. However, to better prepare participants for the discussion, the Division published in advance the complete report in its quarterly publication, *Farm Population and Rural Life Activities* (1938[1]:1–32).

In December 1948 at its annual meeting the Rural Sociological Society passed a resolution authorizing its executive committee to set up a society-wide research committee of fifteen members "to appraise the whole field of rural sociology over two or more years, and make recommendations for its more orderly and systematic development." Carl Taylor agreed to chair this ad hoc committee. At its initial meetings, the committee members had various interpretations as to the charge given to it (Sewell 1950:115).[4] It was finally agreed that the major task was to examine the field to determine needed areas of research and to outline the basic research to be undertaken with its theoretical connections and methodological requisites (Sewell 1950:116). Two lists of needed research were developed. One list identified nine areas of public concern in which rural sociology could make a fundamental contribution, e.g., agricultural policy. The second list specified twenty-two areas of greatest significance to rural sociology as a scientific discipline and in which the professional interests of rural sociologists were greatest, e.g., "dynamics of rural population and its distribution" and "methodology." Taylor then sought a chair for a subcommittee for each of the thirty-one research topics. The subcommittee chairs, in turn, had the responsibility to select others for their committee and to come up with a well-outlined project for basic research. Taylor, through correspondence, sought to give general guidelines to the subcommittees and to encourage them to complete their work. Progress reports were made by some subcommittees at annual meetings of the RSS from 1949 through 1953. Taylor's hope that the subcommittee's would ultimately produce a document worthy of publication was realized in only a few instances, e.g., a paper "Problems of theory and method in the study of social stratification in rural society" (Kaufman et al. 1953:12–34).[5]

COMMUNICATION AND CLEARING HOUSE ACTIVITIES

The Division came to have a central position in a communication network among social scientists interested in rural life. It served as something of a clearing house among the agencies doing rural social research and between the field of rural social research and other research related to agriculture.

Especially important for the communication function was the quarterly *Farm Population and Rural Life Activities*. This was started in March, 1927. It was discontinued after the January 1942 issue because the war forced a redirection of efforts. This publication was a major means, at the time, of informing social scientists about rural sociological research planned and completed by the Division and cooperating institutions and agencies. Each issue listed federal, state, and other research publications received. It was also a source of information about activities of rural sociologists and of pertinent conferences and meetings in the United States and abroad.

In addition, from 1928 to 1936 the Division issued lists from time to time of publications relating to farm population and rural life such as those released at the various state colleges of agriculture. A further service was the publication, starting in 1930, of directories of personnel in the United States in rural sociology. These were put out almost annually from 1930 through 1941 and again in 1949. The directories usually identified the personnel listed according to function—teaching, research, extension.

Both Galpin and Taylor were committed to reaching non-sociologist audiences to provide and interpret sociological knowledge. This was generally about rural life, but they did not limit themselves to this area. Thus, use was made, as judged appropriate, of speeches, radio, press releases and brief articles written for the non-professional reader. In Galpin's summary account of his fifteen years with the Division, he reported that he had given 160 formal addresses at various institutions, other staff members had given 31 (*FPRLA* 1934[2]:1–3). Many of Taylor's speeches were published. But we also identified 170 unpublished speeches he made in his role as Division head. During the same time we found a record of nearly 40 unpublished addresses made by other Division staff members (Larson et al. 1992a:251–75).

THE DIVISION AND PROFESSIONAL SOCIAL SCIENCE ASSOCIATIONS

Throughout its life the Division had a close relationship with major professional social science associations. This took a number of forms. Thus, Division staff held elected positions. Galpin, in 1932, was vice-president of the ASA. Taylor was ASA president in 1946 and Margaret Hagood vice-president in 1950. Taylor was president of the RSS in 1939, the second person to hold that office.

Division staff held appointed positions that involved important activities on behalf of associations. For example, Taylor was made chair of the ASA Committee on Sociology in Latin American Countries appointed in 1942 by ASA president Dwight Sanderson. Both Taylor and Conrad Taeuber were members of an RSS committee appointed in 1943 on postwar recruitment and training of rural sociologists. Taeuber was allowed time to serve as secretary-treasurer of the Population Association of America.[6] Charles Loomis served as associate editor for Latin America for the journal published by the Society for Applied Anthropology.

The Division had a hand in fostering the developments that led to the initiation of the journal *Rural Sociology* in March 1936, and the formation of the Rural Sociological Society in December 1937. Galpin, who had been active in the ASA prior to going to Washington, continued to have an active role after becoming Division head. Prior to the 1921 ASA annual meeting, he supplied a list of 250 persons to Dwight Sanderson of Cornell University, who was chair of an informal group on rural sociology. These persons were invited to join the ASA (Holik and Hassinger 1986:235). In

1922, a Rural Sociology Section was formed within the ASA, the first such section to be organized. During 1924, Galpin was a member of two sub-committees on the future policy of the rural section. At its 1935 meeting the Section decided to publish a journal, *Rural Sociology*. Taylor was made a contributing editor. At the 1935 Section meeting, Taylor was one of the members appointed to a "Committee on Better Organization for Rural Sociologists." The outcome was the organization, at the December 1937 Section meeting, of the Rural Sociological Society of America. Taylor was elected to the first executive committee.

The first issue of *Rural Sociology* announced that each issue would have a summary and discussion of bulletins on sociological topics published by AESs and other research agencies in America and abroad. This was a task performed by Division staff from the first issue until the Division was ended.

Clearly, the Division of Farm Population and Rural Life had a role in creating greater capacity in the total social science research system. It had a part in strengthening social science research. And, during its existence, it was central to the development of the specialized area of rural sociology in the United States. These contributions may be credited to the vision and the determination of Charles J. Galpin and Carl C. Taylor, to the influence they earned, and to their willingness to be advocates for sociology.

Notes

1. Subsequently, the Bankhead-Jones Act of 1935 and the Agricultural Research and Marketing Act of 1946 further increased funds to the experiment stations and did so on the basis of rural population rather than by fixed grants to all states. In 1955 the Hatch Act was amended to combine all the previous authorizations into one law but retained much of the language of the Purnell Act (Nelson 1969:89–90).

2. Nearly 400 representatives of agricultural and related industries attended the National Agricultural Conference (Davis 1940:301).

3. Galpin also chaired a committee, under SSRC auspices, which prepared a report, *Rural Sociological Adult Education in the United States* (Galpin et al. 1929). This report dealt with extension uses of rural sociology research.

4. William H. Sewell, a member of the ad hoc Research Committee and chair of two subcommittees, prepared an insightful and critical account and analysis of the initial discussions of the fifteen-member group (1950:115–30).

5. Subcommittee work also resulted in journal publication of papers on the dynamics of rural population (Ad Hoc Subcommittee on Population of the Rural Sociological Society 1954), on the rural sociocultural area as a field for research (Lively and Gregory 1954), and on sociological research on farmers' organizations and agricultural cooperatives (Wakeley 1957).

6. After leaving the Division but while still in the BAE, Taeuber was also asked to serve as secretary-treasurer of the ASA. At the time, that also meant being managing editor for *The American Sociological Review*.

16

Retrospect and Reflections

The Division of Farm Population and Rural Life, located in the Bureau of Agricultural Economics within the U.S. Department of Agriculture for thirty-four years, from 1919–53, holds a unique place in the history of American sociology. It was central to establishing and shaping the specialized field of rural sociology. Its influence in building a body of knowledge about rural life and on developing methods of social research persists. The Division had a pioneering role in the practice of sociology in the federal government setting. In that role it developed one model for the interface of sociology with government.

When sociology finds a place within a society, some form of interface inevitably develops between the discipline, the profession, and the national government. The Division may be seen as one among several models which have emerged over time in the United States (Larson et al. 1992b:6). We identify four distinguishing features of the Division model. They are: (1) it was a subordinate unit within a larger unit in the administrative hierarchy of the executive branch; (2) it was located in a research agency; (3) it had the capacity to do research funded by other federal units; and (4) it had a cooperative research network extending beyond the federal government.

Being within the USDA's BAE had several consequences. For example, the hierarchy filtered appropriation requests to the Congress, could channel Division-provided research knowledge to Congress, and stood between the Division and external influences, be they positive or negative. The BAE was predominantly a research agency, not an "action," regulatory, or educational agency. It was a research agency with a broad mission, not one just to meet information needs of the USDA or the administration. The Division, therefore, operated in a research-oriented intellectual environment that permitted it to develop a fund of basic knowledge about rural life. The intent, it is true, was that the knowledge be put to use for the welfare of rural people. This was quite different than existing solely to serve the needs of agency administrators.

The Division could receive funds, through the BAE, from any federal agency to do agreed-upon research. This capacity increased the amount and scope of the Division's research. Invariably, this work for other agencies was policy or program-oriented. The cooperative research arrangements with universities had a multiplying effect upon the quantity of research. It also diffused accountability and responsibility for the research between the Division and the cooperator. Simultaneously, it opened the possibility of societal influences and the political process being brought to bear on the Division from the state level.

This interface model with the government represented by the Division stands in contrast with other models for a sociological interface developed by design or happenstance. One alternative is "in-house" research, whereby an agency, e.g., "action," has sociologists on its own staff solely to do studies to serve the agency administration. A second alternative is the "formula" grants funding arrangement whereby federal monies are distributed through a government agency to all states on a formula basis as illustrated by the Hatch Act funds. The money goes to the state agricultural experiment stations where an investigator works with station administrators to decide on the specific research. This is done under general federal legislative guidelines and national government oversight. A third alternative, among others, is the competitive grant model illustrated by the National Science Foundation (Larsen 1992). Here funds appropriated by Congress are awarded by the agency for research on broadly defined problems. Award-making involves open competition by investigators and a peer review procedure for award decisions.

The administrative context was important for the Division's resources, its program, and even for its survival. The immediate administrative context was provided by the Bureau of Agricultural Economics within which it was one small unit, the only one within the USDA devoted to sociological research. The BAE was primarily an economic research agency. It had a history of engendering controversy with powerful agricultural interests. The experience of the Division argues for a pluralistic social science research system as in the best interest not only of the social sciences but of society.

CLOSING COMMENTS

The history of the Division furnishes an essential window into the history of sociology as an intellectual enterprise in America and an aperture through which to interpret broader societal trends. For example, the epistemological and methodological development of our discipline is evident in this history of the Division as the discipline moved from a qualitative information gathering endeavor to one espousing a positivist, predictive stance. The actors, debates, and larger social changes which played a role in this transition left tangible footprints in the Division's history.

The Division's research which never got beyond administrative use or never got beyond preliminary reports remains underutilized. It remains available for exploration by the social historians of rural life, a source which has potential for adding new insights into America's rural past and its changes.

Epilogue

Neither the name "Farm Population and Rural Life" nor most of the former Division's research program disappeared with the breakup of the Bureau of Agricultural Economics ordered by Secretary of Agriculture Ezra Benson effective November 2, 1953. What had been a "Division" was, however, down-graded in the organizational hierarchy to "Branch" status. The Branch was in the Agricultural Economics Division of a new agency, the Agricultural Marketing Service. Subsequently, in 1961, another USDA reorganization replaced the AMS with the Economic Research Service. The 1961 change was under Secretary Orville Freeman at the start of the President John F. Kennedy administration.

Benson was the first Republican Secretary of Agriculture in twenty years. He came to his post determined to change agricultural policy (Rosenbaum 1965:3). If his viewpoint was to prevail, he believed that a reorganization of the USDA was essential. The abolishment of the BAE was but one part of the reorganization ordered by Benson. He made O. V. Wells, who had been BAE Chief since 1946, Administrator of the AMS. Well aware of the controversies provoked by the Division's Arvin-Dinuba and Coahoma County studies (see Chapter 4), Wells' appointment insured that the resulting caution in the USDA lingered on in research approved within the AMS.

Prior to the BAE breakup, the Division's staff was down to fewer than twenty professionals. This number dwindled further after 1953. Just before Benson's order, the work still ongoing in rural organization, including locality-group studies, was being phased out. The influence of cultural anthropology and social psychology, so strong for a time, disappeared even before the BAE breakup. The Division's current main lines of research in farm population, farm labor, and rural levels and standards of living were continued in the Farm Population and Rural Life Branch except that the aspects of farm labor closely related to farm management were transferred to another new agency, the Agricultural Research Service.

Margaret Hagood, who had been made Head of the Division in 1952, was named to head the Branch. She continued to do so until her resignation in 1962 for health reasons. During her time as Head of the Branch, Hagood was elected president of the Population Association of America (1954–55) and of the Rural Sociological Society (1955–56). Previously, in

1950, she was vice-president of the ASA. Louis J. Ducoff was Hagood's immediate successor as Branch head. Two Branch staff members who had served in the Division were early recipients of the RSS' Distinguished Rural Sociologist Award soon after it was established, Calvin L. Beale in 1983 and, in 1984, Gladys K. Bowles.

One example of the continuity of core areas of work is provided by the annual estimates of farm population. This long-running series, started in 1923 by Charles J. Galpin, was continued through 1991. The series was discontinued then, in part because so many farm families were living away from their farms and, in part, for budgetary reasons. Another long-standing annual series on farm employment, hired farm worker characteristics, and wage rates continued until 1987 when it, too, succumbed to rising costs.

The Branch, like the former Division, responded to information needs for public purposes generated by an ever-changing set of researchable issues. The resulting publications of the Branch and its cooperators through 1959 may be found in a bibliography compiled by staff member Vera Banks (1960). Work pertaining specifically to minority groups is included in a listing for all of ERS (Banks et al. 1966). In addition to the continuing work in farm population, farm labor, and levels of living, these sources show that research by the Branch included rural development, low-income areas and populations, minority groups, the impacts of industrialization in rural areas, the social and economic effects of social security on farmers, the availability and use of health services in rural areas, the use of health insurance by rural people, and the rural elderly.

The legacy of the Division has continued in a succession of organizational forms within the USDA's Economic Research Service. But the successors have never come close to having the research resources once achieved by the Division. Over time the scope of research activities has shifted more to themes dealing with social and economic issues in rural and small town America as a whole and less to farm questions. The successor units continued to be recognized as an authoritative source of research-based knowledge about rural America, its changes, and its problems of public concern.

Appendix:

Persons on the Professional Staff of the Division of Farm Population and Rural Life, Bureau of Agricultural Economics, U.S. Department of Agriculture, 1919–1953.

Aaronson, Franklin M.
Alexander, Frank D.
Allen, William
Almack, Ronald B.
Anderson, Anton H.
Anderson, Olaf C.
Asch (Gruen), Berta*
Ashby, Richard
Babcock, James
Baker, O. E.
Barton, Glen T.
Baumgartel, Walter
Beale, Calvin L.
Bell, Bernard R.
Bell, Earl H.
Bernert (Sheldon), Eleanor
Birch, Eleanor M.
Bowles, Gladys K.
Bradshaw, Nettie P.
Brown, James S.
Camp, Miriam
Cates, Joseph R.
Christensen, Harold T.
Clowes, Harry G.
Coleman, A. Lee
Cronin, Francis D.
Dahlke, H. Otto
Danhof, Ralph H.
Davidson, Dwight M.
DeHart, William A.
Dodson, Linden S.
Draper, Charles R.
Ducoff, Louis J.
Ellickson, John C.
Ensminger, Douglas
Eselun, Mary P. B.

Forsyth, F. Howard
Frame, Nat T.
Fuller, Varden
Galloway, Robert E.
Galpin, Charles J.
Goldschmidt, Walter R.
Goodwin, Dorothy C.
Green, Arnold
Greiner, Harold L.
Grigsby, S. Earl
Hagood, Margaret J.
Ham, William T.
Hamilton, C. Horace
Hanger, Michael R.
Hay, Donald G.
Hitt, Homer L.
Hoag (Sawtelle), Emily F.
Hoffman, Charles S.
Hoffsommer, Harold C.
Holcomb, Ernest J.
Holley, Wilaim C.
Holt, John B.
Houser, Paul M.
Hulett, Edward, Jr.
Janow, Seymour J.
Jasny, Marie Philippi*
Jehlik, Paul J.
Johansen, John P.
(Johnson), Helen Wheeler
Johnstone, Paul H.
Jones, Ronald E.
Kirkpatrick, E. L.
Kollmorgen, Water M.
Kraemer, Erich*
Lacy, Frances S.
Larson, Olaf F.

Fisher, Lloyd H.
Flagg, Grace L.
Folsom, Josiah C.
Lister, Joseph J.*
Longmore, T. Wilson
Loomis, Charles P.
Losey, J. Edwin
Lyall, Lawrence B.
MacLeish, Kenneth
Manny, Elsie S.
Manny, Theodore B.
Martin, Virginia C.
Matthews, M. Taylor
McCamman, Dorothy F.
McEntire, W. Davis
McKain, Walter C., Jr.
McKean, Eugene C.
McMurray, J. Donald
McNamara, Robert L.
McNeeley, John
Meldrum, Gilbert S.
Metzler, William H.
Miles, Sarah
Moe, Edward O.
Molyneaux, J. Lambert
Montgomery, James E.
Montgomery (Clawson), Mary
Motheral, Joe R.
Nason, Wayne C.
Neeley, Wayne
Nelson, Lowry*
Nichols, Ralph R.
Niederfrank, E. J.
Page, John S.
Parmalee, Maurice
Persh, Louis
Provinse, John H.

Larson (Turner), Veda B.
Leonard, Olen E.
Lewis, Oscar
Pryor, Herbert
Raper, Arthur F.
Reagan, Barbara B.
Reuss, Carl
Reynolds, Charles N.
Riecken, Henry W.
Roberts, Roy L.
Robinson, C. Aubrey
Rossoff, Milton R.
Sanders, Irwin T.
Shafer, Karl A.
Schloesser (Taylor), Pauline
Schuler, Edgar A.
Shea, John P.
Sletto, Raymond F.
Sower, Christopher
Standing, Theodore G.
Summers, U. T. Miller
Swiger, Rachel Rowe
Taeuber, Conrad
Taggart, Glenn L.
Taylor, Carl C.
Taylor, Mary Splawn
Udell, Jolley
Vasey, Tom*
Vaughan, Theo L.
Wakefield, Richard
Whetten, Nathan L.
White, Harold B.
White, Helen R.
Williams, Edward B.
Woolley, Jane
Wynne, Waller, Jr.
Young, Kimball

* The asterisk identifies persons who worked under Carl C. Taylor in the Division of Social Research, Farm Security Administration. While their work was closely integrated with that of the DFPRL, their appointment status in the DFPRL is uncertain except for Jasny and Nelson, who had collaborator appointments.

Notes on Sources

The above list is intended to include all persons who had a professional social scientist role during all or part of their period of appointment on the staff of the Division of Farm Population and Rural Life. A few persons changed from a non-professional to a professional status during the time of their employment with the Division.

The names for 1919 to June 30, 1934 were given in: (1) Charles J. Galpin's *My Drift into Rural Sociology* (1938), and (2) a November 24, 1941 letter from Carl C. Taylor to Henry C. Taylor which gave a year-by-year listing of the professional staff. The list for July 1934 to 1953 was constructed from multiple sources. Thus, for the period July 1934–July 1941, a "Division Notes" section in the quarterly issues of *Farm Population and Rural Life Activities* identified appointments and departures of professional staff as well as their location if in a regional office. A partially complete list of former professional employees of the Division between 1942 and 1952 was given in a typed list prepared by Ralph R. Nichols (a senior Division staff member) in June 1953. Information on the Division's professional staff was also published in *Rural Sociology*. The March 1945 issue gave a complete listing of current staff as of January 5, 1945. A listing as a February 1, 1946, appeared in the June 1946 issue. The "News Notes" section of *Rural Sociology* also provided information on staff in the issues of March 1943, June 1943 and December 1946.

In developing the list, correspondence, telephone calls, and interviews were undertaken with a number of former staff members of the Division whose personal knowledge encompassed the period 1936–53. The Advisory Panel, all of whom had served on the Division staff, reviewed successive drafts of the list and provided leads to a number of names.

As a working principle in the absence of Division-originated documentation or the personal knowledge of our resource persons, any individual known to be on the Division staff who was also named in the Division-prepared "Directory of personnel in rural sociology," who was a member of the Rural Sociological Society, or who authored or co-authored a publication, was classified as a professional for the purposes of this list.

References

Ad Hoc Subcommittee on Population of the Rural Sociological Society. 1954. "Dynamics of the Rural Population." "Part I: Levels and Trends in Rural Fertility," Margaret Jarman Hagood. "Part II: Levels and Trends in Rural Mortality," Homer L. Hitt, J. Allan Beegle, and John N. Burrus. "Part III: Levels and Trends in Rural Migration," T. Lynn Smith. *Rural Sociology* 19(2):73–82.

Adkins, William G., and Joe R. Motheral. 1953. "Attitudes toward the Old-Age and Survivors Insurance Program: Wharton County, Texas, Farm Operators, 1952." Mimeo. College Station: Texas A&M College System, Texas AES. USDA, BAE [DFPRL] cooperating.

Alexander, Frank D. 1944a. "Cultural Reconnaissance Survey of Coahoma County, Mississippi: For administrative use." Dittoed. Atlanta: USDA, BAE [DFPRW].

———. 1944b. "Some Effects of Two Years of War on a Rural Community." *Social Forces* 23(2):196–201.

———. 1945. "A Rural Community in Time of War: The Valley Community in Rabun County, Georgia." Mimeo. Atlanta: USDA, BAE [DFPRW].

———. 1952. "The Problem of Locality-Group Classification." *Rural Sociology* 17(3):236–44.

Alexander, Frank D., and Lowry Nelson. 1949. *Rural Social Organization: Goodhue County.* University Farm, St. Paul, Minn.: University of Minnesota AES, Bulletin 401. USDA, BAE [DFPRL], and University of Minnesota AES, Division of Rural Sociology cooperating.

Allen, E. W. 1910. "Editorial." *Experiment Station Record* 23(5):401–9.

American Country Life Association. Various years. *Proceedings.* Chicago: University of Chicago Press.

Anderson, Anton H. 1943. "The Neighborhood Group Approach in the War Effort." Mimeo. Lincoln, Nebr.: USDA, BAE [DFPRW].

———. 1946. "Some Practical Implications of Farm-population Density in the Northern Great Plains." Mimeo. Lincoln, Nebr.: USDA, BAE [DFPRW].

———. 1950. "Space as a Social Cost: An Approach toward Community Design in the Sparsely Populated Areas of the Great Plains." *Journal of Farm Economics* 32(3):411–30.

Baker, Gladys L., and Wayne D. Rasmussen. 1975. "Economic Research in the Department of Agriculture: A Historical Perspective." *Agricultural Economics Research* 27(3–4):53–72.

Baker, Gladys L., Wayne D. Rasmussen, Vivian Wiser, and Jane M. Porter. 1963. *Century of Service: The First 100 Years of the United States Department of Agriculture.* Washington, D.C.: USDA, Centennial Committee.

Baker, Oliver E. 1937. *A Graphic Summary of Farm Machinery, Facilities, Roads, and Expenditures* (Based largely on the Census of 1930 and 1935). Washington, D.C.: USDA. Misc. Publication 264.

Banks, Vera J., compiler. 1960. "Bibliography of Publications of the Farm Population and Rural Life Branch, 1950–59." Mimeo. Washington, D.C.: USDA, AMS.

Banks, Vera J., and Calvin L. Beale. 1973. *Farm Population Estimates 1910–70.* Washington, D.C.: USDA, Rural Development Service. Statistical Bulletin 523.

Banks, Vera J., Elsie S. Manny, and Nelson L. LeRay, compilers. 1966. *Research Data on Minority Groups: An Annotated Bibliography of Economic Research Service Reports: 1955–1965.* Washington, D.C.: USDA, ERS. Misc. Publication 1046.

Barton, Glen T., and J. G. McNeely. 1939. "Recent Changes in Farm Labor Organization in Three Arkansas Plantation Counties: Preliminary report." Mimeo. Fayetteville: University of Arkansas, College of Agriculture AES, Department of Rural Economics and Sociology. USDA, Agricultural Adjustment Administration, Division of Program Planning, and BAE [DFPRW] cooperating.

Baumgartel, Walter H. 1923. *A Social Study of Ravalli County, Montana.* Bozeman: University of Montana AES Bulletin 160. USDA, Office of Farm Management and Farm Economics, Division of Farm Life Studies, cooperating.

———. 1925. *Centralized Management of a Large Corporate Estate Operated by Tenants in the Wheat Belt.* Washington, D.C.: USDA. Circular 351. Contributed by BAE, Division of Land Economics [and DFPRL].

Beall, Robert T. 1940. "Rural Electrification." *Yearbook of Agriculture, 1940,* 790–809. Washington, D.C.: GPO.

Beers, Howard W. 1933. *The Income, Savings, and Work of Boys and Girls on Farms in New York, 1930.* Ithaca: Cornell University AES. Bulletin 560. USDA, BAE [DFPRL] cooperating.

Beers, Howard W., Robin M. Williams Jr., John S. Page, and Douglas Ensminger. 1941. *Community Land-Use Planning Committees: Organization, Leadership, and Attitudes, Garrard County, Kentucky, 1939.* Lexington: University of Kentucky AES. Bulletin 417. USDA, BAE [DFPRW].

Bell, Earl H. 1942. *Culture of a Contemporary Rural Community: Sublette, Kansas.* Washington, D.C.: USDA, BAE [DFPRW]. Rural Life Studies 2.

———. 1944. "Part-Time Farming," in *What is Farming?* Madison: Armed Forces Institute.

Bell, Earl H., and Orlin Scoville. 1945. *Part-Time Farming.* Washington, D.C.: USDA. Farmers' Bulletin 1966. Revised and reissued July 1948 with same authors and title.

Bercaw, Louise O., compiler. 1931. *Rural Standards of Living: A Selected Bibliography.* Washington, D.C.: USDA. Misc. Publication 116.

Bernert, Eleanor H. 1944a. "Volume and Composition of Net Migration from the Rural-Farm Population, 1930–40, for the United States, Major Geographic Divisions and States." Mimeo. Washington, D.C.: USDA, BAE [DFPRW].

———. 1944b. "County Variation in Net Migration from the Rural-Farm Population, 1930–40." Mimeo. Washington, D.C.: USDA, BAE [DFPRW].

Black, John D. 1945. "Agricultural Credit Policy in the United States, 1945." *Journal of Farm Economics* 27(3):591–614.

———. 1947. "The Bureau of Agricultural Economics: The Years in Between." *Journal of Farm Economics* 29 (4, part II):1027–42.

Black, John D., and R. H. Allen. 1937. "The Growth of Farm Tenancy in the United States." *Quarterly Journal of Economics* 51(3):393–425.

Bogue, Donald J., and Margaret Jarman Hagood. 1953. *Subregional Migration in the United States, 1935–40. Volume 2: Differential Migration in the Corn and Cotton Belts: A Pilot Study of the Selectivity of Intrastate Migration to Cities from Nonmetropolitan Areas.* Oxford, Ohio: Miami University, Scripps Foundation. Scripps Foundation Studies in Population Distribution 6.

Bowles, Gladys K., Louis J. Ducoff, and Margaret J. Hagood. 1950. "The Hired Farm Working Force, 1948 and 1949, with Special Reference to Coverage of Hired Farm Workers under Old-Age and Survivors Insurance." Mimeo. Washington, D.C.: USDA, BAE [DFPRL].

Bradley, Frances Sage, and Margaretta A. Williamson. 1918. *Rural Children in Selected Counties of North Carolina.* Washington, D.C.: GPO. U.S. Dept. of Labor, Children's Bureau Publication 33.

Brooks, E. M., L. J. Ducoff, C. A. Gibbons, and Wylie D. Goodsell. 1943. "Farm Wage Rates, Farm Employment, and Related Data." Mimeo. Washingtion, D.C.: USDA, BAE.

Brunner, Edmund deS. 1952. "Review of *Ten Years of Rural Rehabilitation:* An Abridgement." *Rural Sociology* 17(4):396.

———. 1957. *The Growth of a Science: A Half-Century of Rural Sociological Research in the United States.* New York: Harper & Brothers.

———. 1968. *As Now Remembered: The Interesting Life of an Average Man.* Private printing.

Brunner, Edmund deS., and J. H. Kolb. 1933. *Rural Social Trends.* New York: McGraw-Hill.

Brunner, Edmund deS., and Irving Lorge. 1937. *Rural Trends in Depression Years: A Survey of Village-Centered Agricultural Communities, 1930–1936.* New York: Columbia University Press. USDA, BAE [DFPRL], and the Columbia University Council for Research in the Social Sciences cooperating.

Brunner, Edmund deS., Irwin T. Sanders, and Douglas Ensminger, eds. 1945. *Farmers of the World: The Development of Agricultural Extension.* New York: Columbia University Press.

Burnight, Robert G., Walter C. McKain Jr., and Paul L. Putnam. 1953. *Regular Hired Workers on Commercial Dairy Farms in Connecticut, April 1950–April 1952.* Storrs: University of Connecticut, College of Agriculture, Storrs AES, Bulletin 267. USDA, BAE [DFPRL] cooperating.

Buttel, Frederick H., Olaf F. Larson, and Gilbert W. Gillespie Jr. 1990. *The Sociology of Agriculture.* New York: Greenwood Press.

Carney, Mabel. 1912. *Country Life and the Country School.* Chicago: Row, Peterson, and Company.

Carver, Thomas N. 1905. *Sociology and Social Progress: A Handbook for Students of Sociology.* Boston: Ginn and Company.

———. 1911. *Principles of Rural Economics.* Boston: Ginn and Company.

———. 1915. "The Organization of a Rural Community." *Yearbook of Agriculture, 1914,* 89–138. Washington, D.C.: GPO.

Carver, Thomas N., and Henry B. Hall. 1923. *Human Relations: An Introduction to Sociology*. Boston: D. C. Heath and Company.

Claghorn, Kate Holladay. 1918. *Juvenile Delinquency in Rural New York*. Washington, D.C.: GPO. U.S. Dept. of Labor, Children's Bureau Publication 32.

Clawson, Marion. 1946. "Discussion." *American Sociological Review* 11(3): 330–32.

———. 1987. *From Sagebrush to Sage: The Making of a Natural Resource Economist*. Washington, D.C.: ANA Publications.

Coleman, A. Lee. 1942. "Community Organization and Agricultural Planning, Greene County, Georgia." Mimeo. Atlanta: USDA, BAE [DFPRW].

———. 1947. "Some Aspects of Human Relations in Soil Conservation." Abstract: Appendix A in "Group Action in Soil conservation: Upper Mississippi: Valley, Region III." Mimeo. Milwaukee: USDA, Soil Conservation Service.

Colvin, Esther M., and Josiah Folson, compilers. 1935. "Agricultural Labor in the United States, 1915–1935: A Selected List of References." Mimeo. Washington, D.C.: USDA, BAE. Agricultural Economics Bibliography 64.

Commission on Country Life. 1909. *Report*. Reprint 1944. Chapel Hill: University of North Carolina Press.

Committee of the Rural Sociological Society of America and the Bureau of Agricultural Economics. 1938. *The Field of Research in Rural Sociology*. Washington, D.C.: USDA, BAE.

Committee on Rural Social Organization and Agencies, Subcommittee of Joint Committee on Projects and Correlation of Research, Association of Land-grant Colleges and U.S. Department of Agriculture. 1927. "Institute on Research Methods in Rural Sociology." Conference, April 4–8, 1927, Purdue University. Mimeo. Washington, D.C.: Association of Land-grant Colleges and USDA, BAE [DFPRL].

Conkin, Paul K. 1959. *Tomorrow a New World: The New Deal Community Program*. Ithaca: Cornell University Press.

Cooley, Charles Horton. 1918. *Social Organization: A Study of the Larger Mind*. New York: Charles Scribner's Sons.

———. 1930. *Sociological Theory and Social Research: Selected Papers*. New York: Henry Holt.

Cottam, Howard R., with the assistance of E. L. Kirkpatrick, Arnold Green, Jane Woolley, and Miriam Sadagursky. 1944. *Effectiveness of Campaigns in Minimizing Consumer Food Waste: A Report of Experiments Conducted in Elmira, New York, and New Kensington, Pennsylvania, 1943*. Washington, D.C.: War Food Administration, Office of Distribution. USDA, BAE [DFPRW], and the Nutrition Committees of Elmira, N.Y., and New Kensington, Pa., cooperating.

Cronin, Francis D. 1939. "Displaced Families in the Land Utilization Program." *Southwestern Social Science Quarterly* 20(1):43–57.

Cronin, Francis D., and Howard W. Beers. 1937. *Areas of Intense Drought Distress, 1930–1936*. Washington, D.C.: Works Progress Administration. Research Bulletin Series 5, 1.

Culver, John C. 1996. *Seeds and Science: Henry A. Wallace on Agriculture and Human Progress*. Washington, D.C.: Carnegie Institution of Washington.

Dadisman, Andrew J. 1921. *French Creek as a Rural Community*. Morgantown: West Virginia University, College of Agriculture AES. Bulletin 176. USDA, Office of Farm Management and Farm Economics cooperating.

Danhof, Ralph H. 1941. "Defense and Decentralization." *Land Policy Review* 4(1):3–10.

Davidson, Dwight M., Jr., and B. L. Hummel. 1940. *Standards of Living in Six Virginia Counties*. Washintgon, D.C.: USDA, Farm Security Administration. Social Research Report 15. BAE [DFPRW], Work Projects Administration, and Virginia Polytechnic Institute cooperating.

Davis, Chester C. 1940. "The Development of Agricultural Policy since the End of the World War." *Yearbook of Agriculture, 1940*, 297–326. Washington, D.C.: GPO.

Dennis, W. V. 1931. *Organizations Affecting Farm Youth in Locust Township, Columbia County [Pennsylvania]*. State College: Pennsylvania State College, School of Agriculture and Experiment Station. Bulletin 265. USDA, BAE [DFPRL] cooperating.

Dodson, Linden S. 1937. *Living Conditions and Population Migration in Four Appalachian Counties*. Washington, D.C.: USDA, Farm Security Administration. Social Research Report 3. BAE [DFPRL] cooperating.

Doggett, Allen B., Jr. 1923. *Three Negro Communities in Tidewater Virginia*. Hampton, Va.: Hampton Normal and Agricultural Institute. Bulletin 19:4. Contributed by School of Agriculture. USDA, BAE [DFPRL] cooperating.

Du Bois, W. E. B. 1968. *The Autobiography of W. E. B. Du Bois: A Soliloquy on Viewing My Life from the Last Decade of Its First Century*. New York: International Publishers.

Ducoff, Louis J. 1945. *Wages of Agricultural Labor in the United States*. Washington, D.C.: USDA, Technical Bulletin 895.

———. 1947. "Migratory Farm Workers in the United States." *Journal of Farm Economics* 29(3):711–22.

———. 1950. *Migratory Farm Workers in 1949*. Washington, D.C.: USDA, BAE. Agriculture Information Bulletin 25.

———. 1951. "Migratory Farm Workers: A Problem in Migration Analysis." *Rural Sociology* 16(3):217–24.

———. 1953a. "The Hired Farm Working Force of 1952, with Special Information on Migratory Workers." Mimeo. Washington, D.C.: USDA, BAE [DFPRL].

———. 1953b. "Employment in Agriculture." W. S. Woytinsky and Associates, *Employment and Wages in the United States*, 367–82. New York: The Twentieth Century Fund.

———. 1953c. "Wages in Agriculture." W. S. Woytinsky and Associates, *Employment and Wages in the United States*, 482–92. New York: The Twentieth Century Fund.

Ducoff, Louis J., and Gertrude Bancroft. 1945. "Experiment in the Measurement of Unpaid Family Labor in Agriculture." *Journal of the American Statistical Association* 40(230):205–13.

Ducoff, Louis J., and Eleanor M. Birch. 1952. "The Hired Farm Working Force in 1951, with Special Information on Regular Workers in 1950." Mimeo. Washington, D.C.: USDA, BAE [DFPRL].

Ducoff, Louis J., and Margaret J. Hagood. 1944a. "The Farm Working Force of 1943." Mimeo. Washington, D.C.: USDA, BAE [DFPRW].

——. 1944b. "Differentials in Productivity and in Farm Income of Agricultural Workers by Size of Enterprise and by Regions." Mimeo. Washington, D.C.: USDA, BAE [DFPRW].

——. 1945. "Wages and Wage Rates of Hired Farm Workers, United States and Major Regions, March 18–24, 1945." Mimeo. Washington, D.C.: USDA, BAE. Surveys of Wages and Wage Rates in Agriculture, Report 4.

——. 1946a. "Employment and Wages of the Hired Farm Working Force in 1945, with Special Reference to its Population Composition." Mimeo. Washington, D.C.: USDA, BAE [DFPRW].

——. 1946b. "Objectives, Uses, and Types of Labor Force Data in Relation to Economic Policy." *Journal of the American Statistical Association* 41(235): 293–302.

——. 1947a. "Farm and Nonfarm Wage Income of the Hired Farm Working Force in 1946." Mimeo. Washington, D.C.: USDA, BAE [DFPRW].

——. 1947b. *Labor Force Definition and Measurement: Recent Experience in the United States.* New York: Social Science Research Council, Bulletin 56.

Ducoff, Louis J., Margaret J. Hagood, and Conrad Taeuber. 1943. "Effects of the War on the Agricultural Working Force and on the Rural-Farm Population." *Social Forces* 21(4):406–12.

Ducoff, Louis J., and Louis Persh. 1946. "Wages and Wage Rates of Harvesters of Special Crops in Selected Areas of Thirteen States, 1945: A Statistical Summary." Mimeo. Washington, D.C.: USDA, BAE. Surveys of Wages and Wage Rates in Agriculture, Report 17.

Ducoff, Louis J., and Barbara B. Reagan. 1946. "Wages and Wage Rates of Hired Farm Workers, United States and Major Regions, September 1945." Mimeo. Washington, D.C.: USDA, BAE. Surveys of Wages and Wage Rates in Agriculture, Report 16.

Duncan, Otis Durant. 1941. "Contemporary Sociological Research in Farm Family Living." *Rural Sociology* 6(4):300–310.

Eastman, Clyde, and Richard S. Krannick. 1995. "Community Change and Persistence: The Case of El Cerrito, New Mexico." *Journal of the Community Development Society* 26(1):41–51.

Edwards, Allen D. 1939. *Influence of Drought and Depression on a Rural Community: A Case Study in Haskell County, Kansas.* Washington, D.C.: USDA, Farm Security Administration. Social Research Report 7. BAE [DFPRL] cooperating.

Ellickson, J. C., and John M. Brewster. 1947. "Technological Advance and the Structure of American Agriculture." *Journal of Farm Economics* 29(4) Part 1:827–47.

Elliott, F. F. 1940. "The Farmer's Changing World." *Yearbook of Agriculture, 1940,* 103–10. Washington, D.C.: GPO.

Ensminger, Douglas, Chairman, Conference Overall Committee. 1945. *Conference Report on the Contribution of Extension Methods and Techniques Toward the Rehabilitation of War-Torn Countries.* September 19–22, 1944. Washington, D.C.: USDA, Extension Service and Office of Foreign Agricultural Relations.

Ensminger, Douglas, Conference Chairman. 1951. "Summary of the Conference." *Conference Report on Extension Experiences Around the World*, 200–207. May 16–20, 1949. Washington, D.C.: USDA, Extension Service and Office of Foreign Agricultural Relations.

Ensminger, Douglas, Ronald B. Almack, Olen E. Leonard, and Walter C. McKain Jr. 1943. "Organizing for Face-to-Face Nutrition Education." Mimeo. Washington, D.C.: USDA, BAE, Food Distribution Administration, Nutrition and Food Conservation Branch.

Ensminger, Douglas, and Robert A. Polson. 1946. "The Concept of the Community." *Rural Sociology* 11(1):43–51.

Evans, Anne M. 1918. *Women's Rural Organizations and Their Activities*. Washington, D.C.: USDA. Bulletin 719.

Fear, Frank A., and Harry K. Schwarzweller, eds. 1985. *Research in Rural Sociology and Development: Focus on Community*. Research Annual Vol. 2. Greenwich, Conn.: JAI Press.

Fisher, Lloyd H. 1943. "What is a Minimum Adequate Farm Income?" *Journal of Farm Economics* 25(3):662–70.

———. 1947. "Standards of Levels of Living of Prospective Settlers on New Irrigation Projects." U.S. Department of the Interior, Bureau of Reclamation, Columbia Basin Joint Investigations, *Standards and Levels of Living. Studies by the USDA for Problem 9*, 1–27. Washington, D.C.: GPO.

Flagg, Grace L., and T. Wilson Longmore. 1949. *Trends in Rural and Urban Levels of Living*. Washington, D.C.: USDA, BAE. Agriculture Information Bulletin 11.

———. 1952. *Trends in Selected Facilities Available to Farm Families*. Washington, D.C.: USDA, BAE. Agriculture Information Bulletin 87.

Folsom, Josiah C. 1935. "Farm Laborers in United States Turn to Collective Action." *Yearbook of Agriculture, 1935*, 188–91. Washington, D.C.: GPO.

———. 1953. *Migratory Agricultural Labor in the United States: An Annotated Bibliography of Selected References*. Washington, D.C.: USDA, Library. Library List 59.

———. 1944. "Social Security for Farm People: A List of References." Dittoed. Washington, D.C.: USDA, BAE [DFPRW].

———. 1949. *Social Security and Related Insurance for Farm People: An Annotated Bibliography of Selected References*. Washington, D.C.: USDA, Library. Library List 50.

Folsom, Josiah C., and O. E. Baker. 1937. *A Graphic Summary of Farm Labor and Population* (Based largely on the Census of 1930 and 1935). Washington, D.C.: USDA. Misc. Publication 265.

Forsyth, F. Howard. 1941. "Measuring Attitudes Toward Rural and Urban Life." *Rural Sociology* 6(3):234–41.

Foster, Ellery A., and Harold A. Vogel. 1940. "Cooperative Land Use Planning: A New Development in Democracy." *Yearbook of Agriculture, 1940*, 1138–56. Washington, D.C.: GPO.

FPRLA (Farm Population and Rural Life Activities.) 1927–42. Various issues.

———. 1941. "Farm Labor Reconnaissance Surveys." 15(1):1–7.

———. Annual Report. Division of Farm Population and Rural Welfare, July 1, 1940–June 30, 1941. 15(4):1–39.

Fry, C. Luther. 1924. *A Census Analysis of Southern Villages*. Mimeo. New York: Institute of Social and Religious Research. U.S. Bureau of the Census and the USDA, BAE [DFPRL] cooperating.

———. 1925. *A Census Analysis of American Villages—Being a Study of the 1920 Census Data for 177 Villages Scattered over the United States*. New York: Institute of Social and Religious Research. U.S. Bureau of the Census and USDA, BAE [DFPRL] cooperating.

Fuller, Varden. 1941. "Agricultural Labor in Relation to Agricultural Planning for National Defense." *Proceedings of the 14th Annual Meeting of the Western Farm Economics Association*, 120–28. June 25–27, Salt Lake City, Utah.

Fuller, Varden, and Seymour J. Janow. 1940. "The Migrants: IV. Jobs on Farms in California." *Land Policy Review* 3(2):34–43.

Galloway, Robert E., and Howard W. Beers. 1953. *Utilization of Rural Manpower in Eastern Kentucky: A Study of Economic Area Eight*. Lexington: University of Kentucky, Kentucky AES, Department of Rural Sociology. USDA, BAE [DFPRL] cooperating.

Galloway, Robert E., and Marion T. Loftin. 1951. *Health Practices of Rural Negroes in Bolivar County*. State College: Mississippi State College AES. Sociology and Rural Life Series 3. USDA, BAE [DFPRL] cooperating.

Galpin, Charles J. 1911. "The Social Agencies in a Rural Community." *First Wisconsin Country Life Conference*, 12–18. Madison: Bulletin of the University of Wisconsin. Serial No. 472, General Series No. 38.

———. 1915. *The Social Anatomy of an Agricultural Community*. Madison: University of Wisconsin AES. Research Bulletin 34.

———. 1918. *Rural Life*. New York: Century.

———. 1920. "Farm Life Studies and their Relation to Home Economics Work." *Journal of Home Economics* 12(4):159–61.

———. 1924a. *Rural Social Problems*. New York: Century.

———. 1924b. "The Division of Farm Population and Rural Life: An Outline of its Establishment, Staff, Cooperative Policy, Research Problems, Publications." Mimeo. Washington, D.C.: USDA, BAE [DFPRL].

———. 1925. *Empty Churches: The Rural-Urban Dilemma*. New York: Century.

———. 1927a. "Population Flow from Farms to Cities Declines." *Yearbook of Agriculture, 1926*, 591–92. Washington, D.C.: GPO.

———. 1927b. "Analysis of Migration of Population to and from Farms. Part 1: Study of 2,745 Farm Operators Who Have Left Farming for City, Town, or Village. Part 2: Study of 1,167 Persons Who Have Left City, Town, or Village for the Farm." Mimeo. Washington, D.C.: USDA, BAE [DFPRL]

———. 1929. "The Standard of Living of the Farm Population." *Recent Economic Changes in the United States: Report of the Committee on Recent Economic Changes of the President's Conference on Unemployment, including the Reports of a Special Staff of the National Bureau of Economic Research*, Volume 1, 70–76. National Bureau of Economic Research. New York: McGraw-Hill.

———. 1930a. "Part-time Farming is Common in Alliance with Rural Industries." *Yearbook of Agriculture, 1930*, 406–7. Washington, D.C.: GPO.

———. 1930b. "Farm Population Associated with Size of Farms; With Value of

Farm Land and Buildings; With Mortgaged Owner-operated Farms; With Location of Farms on Kind of Road: Based on the 1925 Census of Agriculture." Mimeo. Washington, D.C.: USDA, BAE [DFPRL].

———. 1934a. "Fifteen Years of Research." *Farm Population and Rural Life Activities* 8(2):1–3.

———. 1934b. "To Our Cooperators." *Farm Population and Rural Life Activities* 8(3):1.

———. 1938a. *My Drift Into Rural Sociology.* Baton Rouge: Louisiana State University Press.

———. 1938b. "The Development of the Science and Philosophy of American Rural Society." *Agricultural History* 12(3):195–208.

Galpin, Charles J., and Alonzo B. Cox. 1919. *Rural Social and Economic Problems of the United States.* Madison: Office of the Secretary of the Association for Agricultural Legislation. Bulletin 3.

Galpin, Charles J., and Emily F. Hoag. 1919. *Farm Tenancy: An Analysis of the Occupancy of 500 Farms.* Madison: University of Wisconsin AES. Research Bulletin 44.

Galpin, Charles J., B. L. Hummel, C. E. Lively, and C. C. Zimmerman. 1929. *Rural Sociological Adult Education in the United States.* New York: Social Science Research Council. Prepared under the direction of the Advisory Committee on Social and Economic Research in Agriculture.

Galpin, Charles J., J. H. Kolb, Dwight Sanderson, and Carl C. Taylor. 1927. *Preliminary Report on Rural Sociological Research in the United States during the Year July 1, 1926–June 30, 1927.* Mimeo. New York: Social Science Research Council. Prepared under the direction of the Advisory Committee on Social and Economic Research in Agriculture of the Social Science Research Council.

Galpin, Charles J., J. H. Kolb, Dwight Sanderson, and Carl C. Taylor. 1928. *Rural Sociological Research in the United States.* New York: Social Science Research Council. Prepared under the direction of the Advisory Committee on Social and Economic Research in Agriculture of the Social Science Research Council.

Galpin, Charles J., and Veda B. Larson. 1924. *Farm Population of Selected Counties: Composition, Characteristics, and Occupations in Detail for Eight Counties, Comprising Otsego County, NY; Dane County, WI; New Madrid and Scott Counties, MO; Cass County, ND; Wake County, NC; Ellis County, TX; and King County, WA.* Washington, D.C.: Department of Commerce, Bureau of the Census. USDA, BAE [DFPRL] cooperating. Reprinted 1926 in Leon E. Truesdell, *Farm Population of the United States: An Analysis of the 1920 Farm Population Figures, Especially in Comparison with a Study of the Main Economic Factors Affecting the Farm Population,* 319–536. Census Monographs VI. Washington, D.C.: Bureau of the Census.

Galpin, Charles J., and T. B. Manny. 1932. "Farm Population Now Increasing." *Agricultural Situation* 16(11):2–5.

———. 1934. *Interstate Migrations Among the Native White Population as Indicated by Differences Between State of Birth and State of Residence: A Series of Maps Based on the Census 1870–1930.* Washington, D.C.: USDA, BAE [DFPRL].

Garkovich, Lorraine. 1989. *Population and Community in Rural America*. New York: Greenwood Press.

Garnett, William E. 1927. *Rural Organizations in Relation to Rural Life in Virginia: With Special Reference to Organizational Attitudes*. Blacksburg, Va.: Virginia Polytechnic Institute, Virginia AES. Bulletin 256. USDA, BAE [DFPRL] cooperating.

Garnett, William E. 1930. *Young People's Organizations in Relation to Rural Life in Virginia: with Special Reference to 4-H Clubs*. Blacksburg, Va.: Virginia Polytechnic Institute, Virginia AES. Bulletin 274. USDA, BAE [DFPRL] cooperating.

Gaus, John M., and Leon O. Wolcott. 1940. *Public Administration and the United States Department of Agriculture*. Chicago: Public Administration Service.

Genung, A. B. 1940. "Agriculture in the World War Period." *Yearbook of Agriculture, 1940*, 277–96. Washington, D.C.: GPO.

Gessner, Amy A. 1940. *Selective Factors in Migration from a New York Rural Community*. Ithaca: Cornell University AES. Bulletin 736. USDA, BAE [DFPRW] cooperating.

Gilbert, Jess. 1996. "Democratic Planning in Agricultural Policy: The Federal-County Land-use Planning Program, 1938–1942." *Agricultural History* 70(2):233–50.

———. 1997. "Participatory Democracy and Democratic Planning in the Work of Carl C. Taylor, New Deal Sociologist." Presentation, Rural Sociological Society annual meeting. Toronto, Canada.

Gilbert, Jess, and Ellen Baker. 1997. "Wisconsin Economists and New Deal Agricultural Policy: The legacy of Progressive Professors." *Wisconsin Magazine of History* 80(4):281–312.

Gilbert, Jess, and Carolyn Howe. 1991. "Beyond State vs. Society: Theories of the State and New Deal Agricultural Policies. *American Sociological Review* 56(2):204–20.

Goldschmidt, Walter R. 1944. "Large Farms or Small: The Social Side." *Proceedings of the 17th Annual Conference of the Western Farm Economics Association*, 216–27.

———. 1946. *Small Business and the Community: A Study in Central Valley of California on Effects of Scale of Farm Operations [Comparative Study of Arvin and Dinuba, California.]* U.S. Congress, Senate Report of the Special Committee to Study Problems of American Small Business, 79th Congress, second session. Washington, D.C.: GPO. Senate Committee Print 13.

———. 1947. *As You Sow*. New York: Harcourt, Brace & Co.

———. 1972. "Statement Prepared for the Subcommittee on Monopoly of the Select Committee on Small Business." *Farmworkers in Rural America, 1971–1972*. Hearings before the Subcommittee on Migratory Labor of the Committee on Labor and Public Welfare U.S. Senate, 92nd Congress, 1st and 2d sessions. Appendix, part 5A, 3306–54.

———. 1978a. *As You Sow: Three Studies in the Social Consequences of Agribusiness*. Montclair, N.J.: Allanheld, Osmun and Co.

———. 1978b. "Reflections on Arvin and Dinuba." *Newsline* 6(5):10–19.

Goldschmidt, Walter R., and John S. Page. 1942. "A Study of the Methods of

Mobilizing Rural People for War Emergencies, San Joaquin County."
Preliminary. Dittoed. Berkeley: USDA, BAE [DFPRW].

Goodrich, Carter, Bushrod W. Allin, and Marion Hayes. 1935. *Migration and Planes of Living, 1920–1934*. Philadelphia: University of Pennsylvania Press.

Goodrich, Carter, et al. 1936. *Migration and Economic Opportunity: The Report of the Study of Population Redistribution*. Philadelphia: University of Pennsylvania Press.

Grigsby, S. Earl, and Harold Hoffsommer. 1941. *Cotton Plantation Laborers: A Socio-Economic Study of Laborers on Cotton Plantations in Concordia Parish, Louisiana*. Baton Rouge: Louisiana State University and Agricultural and Mechanical College AES. Bulletin 328.

Hagood, Margaret J. 1939. *Mothers of the South*. Chapel Hill: University of North Carolina Press.

———. 1941. *Statistics for Sociologists*. Revised with Daniel O. Price 1952. New York: Henry Holt & Company.

———. 1943a. "Development of a 1940 Rural-Farm Level of Living Index for Counties." *Rural Sociology* 8(2):171–80.

———. 1943b. "Rural Level of Living Indexes for Counties of the United States, 1940." Mimeo. Washington, D.C.: USDA, BAE [DFPRW].

———. 1946. "Farm-Population Adjustments Following the End of the War." Mimeo. Washington, D.C.: USDA, BAE [DFPRW].

———. 1949. "Big Baby Crop, Low Death Rates Boost Farm Population." *Agricultural Situation* 33(8):9.

———. 1952. "Farm-operator Family Level-of-Living Indexes for Counties of the United States: 1930, 1940, 1945, and 1950." Mimeo. Washington, D.C.: USDA, BAE [DFPRL].

Hagood, Margaret J., and Eleanor H. Bernert. 1945. "Component Indexes as a Basis for Stratification in Sampling." *Journal of the American Statistical Association* 40(231):330–41.

Hagood, Margaret J., and Gladys K. Bowles. 1957a. "Farm Population Estimates." *Major Statistical Series of the U.S. Department of Agriculture*. Vol. 7: *Farm Population, Employment and Levels of Living*, 1–7. Washington, D.C.: GPO. Agriculture Handbook 118.

———. 1957b. "Farm-operator Family Level-of-Living Indexes for the United States." *Major Statistical Series of the U.S. Department of Agriculture*, 15–23. Washington, D.C.: GPO. Agriculture Handbook 118.

Hagood, Margaret J., and Louis J. Ducoff. 1946. "Million Veterans on Farms of U.S." *Agricultural Situation* 30(8):1–3.

Hagood, Margaret J., and Emmit F. Sharp. 1951. *Rural-Urban Migration in Wisconsin, 1940–1950*. Madison: University of Wisconsin AES. Research Bulletin 176.

Hagood, Margaret J., and Jacob S. Siegel. 1951. "Projections of the Regional Distribution of the Population of the United States to 1975." *Agricultural Economics Research* 3(2):41–52.

———. 1952. "Population Projections for Sales Forecasting." *Journal of the American Statistical Association* 47(259):524–40.

Hainsworth, Reginald G., Oliver E. Baker, and Albert P. Brodell. 1942. *Seedtime and Harvest Today*. Washington, D.C.: USDA. Misc. Publication 485.

Halbert, Blanche. 1937. *Hospitals for Rural Communities*. Washington, D.C.: USDA. Farmers' Bulletin 1792.

Hall, Tom G. 1983. "Professionalism, Policy, and Farm Economists: Comment." *Agricultural History* 57(1):83–89.

Ham, William T. 1940a. "The Impact of Industrial, Labor, and Agricultural Control Policies upon Farm Labor." *Rural Sociology* 5(1):46–58.

———. 1940b. "Farm Labor in an Era of Change." *Farmers in a Changing World: The Yearbook of Agriculture*, 907–21. Washington, D.C.: USDA. Reprinted 1940 as USDA Yearbook Separate 1767.

———. 1941. "The Management of Seasonal Labor." *Land Policy Review* 4(9):29–34.

———. 1942. "To Fix or Not to Fix Farm Wage Rates." *Land Policy Review* 5(7):35–39.

———. 1945. "Wage Stabilization in Agriculture." *Journal of Farm Economics* 27(1):104–20.

Hamilton, C. Horace. 1944. "Current Bulletin Reviews." *Rural Sociology* 9(2): 184–87.

Hamilton, David E. 1991. *From New Day to New Deal: American Farm Policy from Hoover to Roosevelt, 1928–1933*. Chapel Hill: University of North Carolina Press.

Hane, A. Paul. 1979. "Moreno, Jacob L." In David L. Sills, ed. *Intergenerational Encyclopedia of the Social Sciences: Bibliographical Supplement*, 537–41. New York: The Free Press.

Hanson, Herbert C. 1939. "Ecology in Agriculture." *Ecology* 20(2):111–17.

Hardin, Charles M. 1946. "The Bureau of Agricultural Economics under Fire: A Study in Evaluation Conflicts." *Journal of Farm Economists* 28(3):638–68.

———. 1954. "The Republican Department of Agriculture." *Journal of Farm Economics* 36(2):210–27.

———. 1955. *Freedom in Agricultural Education*. Chicago: University of Chicago Press.

Harding, T. Swann. 1951. *Some Landmarks in the History of the Department of Agriculture*. Washington, D.C.: USDA. Agricultural History Series 2.

Hart, Clyde W. 1946. "Rural Communities in Time of War." *Rural Sociology* 11(2):159–160.

Hay, Donald G. 1940. "Rural Population Migration in the Northern Great Plains." Testimony: September 16. U.S. Congress, House, Select Committee to Investigate the Interstate Migration of Destitute Citizens. Part 4, Lincoln Hearings, 1384–97. Lincoln Nebr.: USDA, BAE [DFPRW].

———. 1941. "Relationship of National Defense Activity to Migration in Nebraska and the Dakotas." Testimony: November 25. U.S. Congress, House, Select Committee Investigating National Defense Migration, 77th Congress. Part 22, Omaha Hearings, 8598–600. Washington, D.C.: GPO.

Hay, Donald G., Douglas Ensminger, Stacy R. Miller, and Edmond J. Lebrun. 1949. *Rural Organizations in Three Maine Towns*. Orono: University of Maine. Maine Extension Bulletin 391.

Hay, Donald G., James P. Greenlaw, and Lawrence E. Boyle. 1940. *Problems of*

Rural Youth in Selected Areas of North Dakota. Fargo: North Dakota Agricultural College AES. Bulletin 293. USDA, BAE [DFPRW] cooperating.

Hay, Donald G., and Robert A. Polson. 1951. *Rural Organizations in Oneida County, New York*. Ithaca: Cornell University, New York State College of Agriculture AES Bulletin 871. USDA, BAE [DFPRL] cooperating.

Hill, George W. 1945. Memorandum to Carl C. Taylor, January 6, 1945.

Hitt, Homer L. 1942. "A Comparative Analysis of the People on New Ground Farms, Plantations, and Old Family Farms in the Upper Mississippi Delta of Louisiana." *Rural Sociology* 7(4):404–14.

———. 1943. *Recent Migration Into and Within the Upper Mississippi Delta of Louisiana*. Baton Rouge: State University and Agricultural and Mechanical College AES. Louisiana Bulletin 364. USDA, BAE [DFPRL] cooperating.

Hoag, Emily F. 1921. *The National Influence of a Single Farm Community: A Story of the Flow into National Life of Migration from the Farms*. Washington, D.C.: USDA. Department Bulletin 984.

Hobbs, S. H., Jr., Irene Link, and Ellen Winston. 1938. "Plan for Cooperative Rural Research: Organization-Scope-Results." Mimeo. Washington, D.C.: Works Progress Administration, Division of Social Research. Series II: 17.

Hoffsommer, Harold, ed. 1950. *The Social and Economic Significance of Land Tenure in the Southwestern United States: A Report of the Regional Land Tenure Research Project*. Chapel Hill: The University of North Carolina Press.

Holcomb, Ernest J., and G. H. Aull. 1940. *Sharecroppers and Wage Laborers on Selected Farms in Two Counties in South Carolina*. Clemson: Clemson Agricultural College, South Carolina AES. Bulletin 328. USDA, BAE cooperating.

Holcomb, Ernest J., G. McMurray, J. C. Folsom, and H. A. Turner. 1941. "Farm Labor and Tenancy in Southeast Missouri." Testimony: November 26–27. U.S. Congress, House, Select Committee Investigating National Defense Migration, Part 23, 9302–47. Washington, D.C.: GPO.

Holik, John S., and Edward W. Hassinger. 1986. "The Rural Sociological Society: The Beginning." *The Rural Sociologist* 6(5):331–40.

Holmes, George K. 1915. "Movement from City and Town to Farms." *Yearbook of the United States Department of Agriculture, 1914*, 257–74. Washington, D.C.: GPO.

Holt, John B. 1937. *An Analysis of Methods and Criteria used in Selecting Families for Colonization Projects*. Washington, D.C.: USDA, Farm Security Administration. Social Research Report 1. BAE [DFPRL] cooperating.

Houston, David F. 1914. "Report of the Secretary." *Yearbook of the United States Department of Agriculture, 1913*, 9–74. Washington, D.C.: GPO.

———. 1920. "Report of the Secretary of Agriculture." *Annual Reports of the Department of Agriculture for the Year Ended June 30, 1919*, 3–46. Washington, D.C.: GPO.

———. 1926. *Eight Years with Wilson's Cabinet: 1913 to 1920*. Vol. 1. New York: Doubleday, Page & Company.

Inter-bureau Committee on Technology. 1940. *Technology on the Farm*. A special report by an inter-bureau committee and the Bureau of Agricultural Economics of the United States Department of Agriculture. Washington, D.C.: GPO.

Isabell, Eleanor C., and Dorothy S. Thomas. 1938. "Annotated Bibliography of American and English Contributions." Dorothy Swaine Thomas, *Research Memorandum on Migration Differentials*, 175–268. New York: Social Science Research Council. Bulletin 43.

Jardine, James T. 1935. "The Development of Rural Sociological Research." *Rural America* 13(8):8–11.

Jasny, Marie. 1938. *Family Selection on a Federal Reclamation Project: Tule Lake Division of the Klamath Irrigation Project, Oregon-California*. Washington, D.C.: USDA, Farm Security Administration. Social Research Report 5. BAE [DFPRL] cooperating.

Jehlik, Paul J. 1943. "Rural Life Trends Report 5: Dallas County, Alabama." Dittoed. Washington, D.C.: USDA, BAE [DFPRW].

Jehlik, Paul J., and Olaf F. Larson. 1943a. *Movement from Farms: A Report on New Off-farm Work by FSA Family Heads and Migration from Farms by FSA and Other Low-income Families, 1942*. Cincinnati: USDA, FSA, Program and Reports Division. 1942 Family Progress Report, Release No. 2. BAE [DFPRW] cooperating.

———. 1943b. *Obstacles to Increased War-food Production by Low-income Farmers: A Summary of Reports Made by FSA County Supervisors*. Cincinnati: USDA, FSA, Program and Reports Division. 1942 Family Progress Report, Release No. 3. BAE [DFPRW] cooperating.

Johansen, John P. 1941. *One Hundred New Homesteads in the Red River Valley, North Dakota: A Study of the Resettlement and Rehabilitation of Farm Families*. Fargo: North Dakota Agricultural College AES. Bulletin 204. Contributed by Department of Rural Sociology. FSA cooperating.

Johansen, Sigurd, and Milton Rossoff. 1942. *Community Planning in Eddy County, New Mexico*. State College, N.M.: New Mexico College of Agriculture and Mechanic Arts AES. Bulletin 297. USDA, BAE [DFPRW] cooperating.

Johnstone, Paul H. 1939. "Culture and Agriculture: Cultural Anthropology in Relation to Current Agricultural Problems." Mimeo. Washington, D.C.: USDA, BAE.

Joint Committee on Projects and Correlation of Research, Association Land-grant Colleges and U.S. Department of Agriculture. 1925. "Report of Subcommittee on Rural Social Organizations and Agencies." Mimeo. Washington, D.C.: Association of Land-grant Colleges and USDA.

Jones, Clyde C. 1958. "Henry C. Taylor: Father of Agricultural Economics." *Agricultural History* 32(3):196–97.

Jones, Lewis W. 1976. "Rural Development Research." In B. D. Mayberry, ed., *Development of Research at Historically Black Land-Grant Institutions*, 123–30. Tuskegee Institute, Ala.: Association of Research Coordinators, Land Grant 1890 Colleges and Universities.

Kaufman, Harold F., Otis Dudley Duncan, Neal Gross, and William H. Sewell. 1953. "Problems of Theory and Method in the Study of Social Stratification in Rural Society." *Rural Sociology* 18(1):12–34.

King, A. J., and R. J. Jessen. 1945. "The Master Sample of Agriculture. I: Development and Use. II: Design." *Journal of the American Statistical Association* 40(229):38–56.

Kirkendall, Richard S. 1964. "Social Sciences in the Central Valley of California: An Episode." *California Historical Society Quarterly* 43(3):195–218.

———. 1966. *Social Scientists and Farm Politics in the Age of Roosevelt.* Columbia: University of Missouri Press.

Kirkpatrick, Ellis L. 1923. *The Standard of Life in a Typical Section of Diversified Farming.* Ithaca: Cornell University AES, Bulletin 423. USDA, BAE [DFPRL] cooperating.

———. 1926. *The Farmer's Standard of Living: A Socio-Economic Study of 2886 White Farm Families of Selected Localities in 11 States.* Washington, D.C.: USDA. Department Bulletin 1466.

———. 1927. "Attitudes and Problems of Farm Youth." Mimeo. Washington, D.C.: USDA, Extension Service, Office of Cooperative Extension Work, Circular 46.

———. 1929. *The Farmer's Standard of Living.* New York: Century.

———. 1930. *Standards of Living: Let's Live While We Work.* Madison: Extension Service of the College of Agriculture, University of Wisconsin and the American County Life Association. Circular 241.

———. 1938. *Analysis of 70,000 Rural Rehabilitation Families.* Washington, D.C.: USDA, Farm Security Administration, Social Research Report 9. BAE [DFPRL] cooperating.

Kirkpatrick, Ellis L., and H. W. Hawthorne. 1928. "Family Living among Poorer Farm People Studied Statistically." *Yearbook of Agriculture, 1927,* 293–95. Washington, D.C.: GPO.

Kirkpatrik, Ellis L., P. E. McNall, and May L. Cowles. 1933. *Farm Family Living in Wisconsin.* Madison: University of Wisconsin AES. Research Bulletin 114. Contributed by University Departments of Rural Sociology, Agricultural Economics, and Home Economics. USDA, BAE [DFPRL] and Farm Management and Costs cooperating.

Kirkpatrick, Ellis L., and J. T. Sanders. 1925. "The Cost of Living among Colored Farm Families of Selected Localities of Kentucky, Tennessee, and Texas: A Preliminary Report." Mimeo. Washington, D.C.: USDA, BAE [DFPRL]. University of Kentucky, Kentucky AES, and the University of Tennessee AES cooperating.

———. 1926. *The Relation Between the Ability to Pay and the Standard of Living Among Farmers: A Socioeconomic Study of 861 White Farm Families of Kentucky, Tennessee, and Texas.* Washington, D.C.: USDA. Department Bulletin 1382.

Kirkpatrick, Ellis L., Rosalind Tough, and May L. Cowles. 1934. *The Life Cycle of the Farm Family: In Relation to its Standards of Living and Ability to Provide.* Madison: University of Wisconsin AES. Research Bulletin 121. Contributed by University Departments of Rural Sociology and Home Economics. USDA, BAE [DFPRL], and Farm Management and Costs cooperating.

Kolb, J. H. 1921. *Rural Primary Groups: A Study of Agricultural Neighborhoods.* Madison: University of Wisconsin AES. Research Bulletin 51. USDA, Office of Farm Management and Farm Economics cooperating.

———. 1923. *Service Relations of Town and Country: The Service Organization of Town and Country.* Madison: University of Wisconsin AES. Research Bulletin 58. USDA, BAE [DFPRL] cooperating.

————. 1933. *Trends of Country Neighborhoods: A Restudy of Rural Primary Groups, 1921–1931*. Madison: University of Wisconsin AES. Research Bulletin 120. USDA.

Kolb, J. H., and Edmund deS. Brunner. 1935. *A Study of Rural Society: Its Organization and Changes*. Boston: Houghton Mifflin Company.

Kolb, J. H., and R. A. Polson. 1933. *Trends in Town-Country Relations*. Madison: University of Wisconsin AES. Research Bulletin 117. USDA, BAE [DFPRL], and the President's Committee for the Study of Recent Social Trends cooperating.

Kollmorgen, Walter M. 1940. *The German-Swiss in Franklin County, Tennessee: A Study of the Significance of Cultural Considerations in Farming Enterprises*. Washington, D.C.: USDA, BAE [DFPRW].

————. 1942. *Culture of a Contemporary Rural Community: The Old Order Amish of Lancaster County, Pennsylvania*. Rural Life Studies 4. Washington, D.C.: USDA, BAE [DFPRW].

Kollmorgen, Walter M., and Robert W. Harrison. 1946. "The Search for the Rural Community." *Agricultural History* 19(3):1–7.

Kraemer, Erich. 1937. *Tenure of New Agricultural Holdings in Several European Countries*. Social Research Report 2. Washington, D.C.: USDA, Farm Security Administration. BAE [DFPRL] cooperating.

Kumlien, W. F., Charles P. Loomis, Zetta E. Bankert, Edmund deS. Brunner, and Robert L. McNamara. 1938. *The Standard of Living of Farm and Village Families in Six South Dakota Counties, 1935*. Brookings: South Dakota State College of Agriculture and Mechanic Arts AES. Bulletin 320. Works Progress Administration, Social Research Division; USDA, FSA, Social Research Section; and USDA, BAE [DFPRL] cooperating.

Kumlien, W. F., Robert L. McNamara, and Zetta E. Bankert. 1938. *Rural Population Mobility in South Dakota (1928–1935)*. Brookings: South Dakota State College of Agriculture and Mechanic Arts AES. Bulletin 315. Contributed by Department of Rural Sociology. Works Progress Administration, Division of Social Research, and USDA, BAE [DFPRL] cooperating.

Lachman, David, and Jess Gilbert. 1992. "Democratic Ideology and Agricultural Policy: The U.S. Department of Agriculture's Farmer Discussion Groups and Schools of Philosophy, 1934–1946." Presentation, Rural Sociological Society annual meeting. Pennsylvania State University.

Landis, Paul H. 1932. *South Dakota Town-Country Trade Relations 1901–1931*. Brookings: South Dakota State College of Agriculture and Mechanic Arts AES. Bulletin 274. Contributed by College Department of Rural Sociology. USDA, BAE [DFPRL] cooperating.

————. 1933. *The Growth and Decline of South Dakota Trade Centers 1901–1933*. Brookings: South Dakota State College of Agriculture and Mechanic Arts AES. Bulletin 279.

Lantis, Margaret, M. R. Hanger, and Philip W. Woods, under the general direction of Douglas Ensminger. 1945. *The Farm Security Administration Dental Program of Randolf County, Georgia*. Washington, D.C.: USDA, Farm Security Administration, Health Services Division, and BAE [DFPRL]. Rural Health Report 8.

Larsen, Otto N. 1992. *Milestones and Millstones: Social Science at the National Science Foundation, 1945–1991*. New Brunswick, N.J.: Transaction Publishers.

Larson, Olaf F. 1942. "Report on Reconnaissance Work in Ohio and Kentucky for Pilot Project on Mobilizing Unproductively Used Rural Manpower, with Special Reference to a Dairy Labor Program." Preliminary. Washington, D.C.: USDA, BAE [DFPRW].

———. 1943a. "Wartime Migration and the Manpower Reserve on Farms in Eastern Kentucky." *Rural Sociology* 8(2):148–61.

———. 1943b. Statement to Chester C. Davis, Administrator, War Food Administration, on production reported for Farm Security Administration borrowers. May 8, 1943.

———. 1946. "Farm Veterans in the Pacific Northwest." *Rural Sociology* 11(3): 270–74.

———. 1947a. "Ten Years of Rural Rehabilitation in the United States." Mimeo. Washington, D.C.: USDA, BAE [DFPRW].

———. 1947b. "Rural Rehabilitation: Theory and Practice." *Rural Sociology* 12(3):223–37.

———. 1947c. Personal correspondence with Paul J. Jehlik. January 22.

———. 1951. *Ten Years of Rural Rehabilitation in the United States: Summary of a Report.* Abridged, Sri B. S. Mavinkurve. Bombay, India: Indian Society of Agricultural Economics.

———. 1989. "Determinants of Research Priorities and Programs: Continuities and Discontinuities: The Case of the USDA's Division of Farm Population and Rural Life." *The Rural Sociologist* 9(4):18–23.

———. 1990. Interview with Charles P. Loomis. Las Cruces, New Mexico, April 20.

———. 1999. "Taylor, Carl Cleveland." In *American National Biography*, Vol. 21, 355–56. Ed. John A. Garraty and Mark C. Carnes. New York: Oxford University Press.

Larson, Olaf F., and James C. Downing. 1943. "Manpower for War Work: Eastern Kentucky." Mimeo. Washington, D.C.: USDA, BAE.

Larson, Olaf F., and Edward O. Moe. 1990. "Pioneering in the Development and Practice of Sociology by the USDA's Division of Farm Population and Rural Life: A Dialogue." Presentation, American Sociological Association annual meeting. Washington, D.C.

Larson, Olaf F., Edward O. Moe, and Julie N. Zimmerman, eds. 1992a. *Sociology in Government: A Bibliography of the Work of the Division of Farm Population and Rural Life, U.S. Department of Agriculture, 1919–1953.* Boulder, Colo.: Westview Press.

———. 1992b. "Sociology and Government: The case of Rural Sociology in the U.S. Department of Agriculture, 1919–1953." Presentation, World Congress for Rural Sociology. Pennsylvania State University.

Larson, Olaf F., Robin M. Williams Jr., and Ronald C. Wimberley. 1999. "Dismissal of a Sociologist: The AAUP Report on Carl C. Taylor." *Rural Sociology* 64(4): 533–53.

Larson, Olaf F., and Julie N. Zimmerman. 1999. "The USDA's Bureau of Agricultural Economics and Sociological Studies of Rural Life and Agricultural Issues, 1919–1953." Presentation, Eightieth Anniversary Symposium of the Agricultural History Society. Mississippi State University, Starkville, Miss.

Lazarsfeld, Paul F., William H. Sewell, and Harold L. Wilsensky, eds. 1967. *The Uses of Sociology.* New York: Basic Books.

Leonard, Olen E. 1944. "Some Efforts of Rural Sociology in the Present War." *Rural Sociology* 9(2):142–51.

———. 1949. "Locality Group Structure in Bolivia." *Rural Sociology* 14(3): 250–60.

———. 1952. *Bolivia: Land, People, and Institutions*. Washington, D.C.: The Scarecrow Press.

Leonard, Olen E., and Charles P. Loomis. 1939. "A Study of Mobility and Levels of Living among Negro Sharecropper and Wage-Laborer Families of the Arkansas River Valleys." *Farm Population and Rural Life Activities* 13(2): 1–11.

———. 1941. *Culture of a Contemporary Rural Community: El Cerrito, New Mexico*. Washington, D.C.: USDA, BAE [DFPRW]. Rural Life Studies 1.

Lewis, Oscar. 1948. *On the Edge of the Black Waxy: A Cultural Survey of Bell County, Texas*. St. Louis: Washington University Studies: Social and Philosophical Sciences 7.

Lindstrom, D. E. 1943. "Wartime Movement of Rural Youth: A Study of Randolph County, Illinois." Mimeo. Urbana, Ill.: University of Illinois AES, Department of Agricultural Economics. USDA, BAE [DFPRW]; University of Illinois, Extension Service in Agriculture and Home Economics; and Randolph County Farm Adviser cooperating.

Lindstrom, D. E., E. G. Mosbacher, R. B. McKenzie, O. E. Baker, N. T. Frame, and E. C. Secor, assisted by L. L. Colvis and G. T. Hudson. 1942. "Rural youth in Wartime Illinois: Randolph County." Urbana, Ill.: University of Illinois AES. USDA, BAE [DFPRW] cooperating.

Link, Irene. 1937. *Relief and Rehabilitation in the Drought Area*. Washington, D.C.: Works Progress Administration, Division of Social Research. Series 5, No. 3.

Lively, Charles E. 1928. "Type of Agriculture as a Conditioning Factor in Community Organizations." *Publications of the American Sociological Society* 23:35–50.

Lively, Charles E., and Cecil L. Gregory. 1954. "The Rural Sociocultural Area as a Field for Research." *Rural Sociology* 19(1):21–31.

Lively, Charles E., and Conrad Taeuber. 1939. *Rural Migration in the United States*. Washington, D.C.: Works Progress Administration, Division of Research. Research Monograph 19.

Longmore, T. Wilson. 1943a. "Neighborhood Discussion Groups among Low-Income Farm Families in Oklahoma." Mimeo. Little Rock: USDA, BAE [DFPRW].

———. 1943b. "Neighborhood Discussion Groups among Low-Income Farm Families in Texas." Mimeo. Little Rock: USDA, BAE [DFPRW].

Longmore, T. Wilson, Milton Rossoff, T. G. Standing, and Merton Otto. "Kansas Rural Communities: A Study of Nemaha County." T. G. Standing, ed., in consultation with Douglas Ensminger (DFPRW), Roger Stewart (BAE), and Randall C. Hill (Kansas State College). 1940. Mimeo. Amarillo, Tex.: USDA, BAE [DFPRW]. Kansas AES cooperating.

Longmore, T. Wilson, and Carl C. Taylor. 1951. "Elasticities of Expenditures for Farm Family Living, Farm Production, and Savings, United States, 1946." *Journal of Farm Economics* 33(1):1–19.

Loomis, Charles P. 1935a. "The Modern Settlement Movement in Germany: I, Rural; II, Suburban." Washington, D.C.: USDA, BAE [DFPRL]. Social Science Research Council cooperating.

———. 1935b. "Some Attempts to Change Rural Life: I, German; II, Russian." Mimeo. Washington, D.C.: USDA, BAE [DFPRL].

———. 1940a. *Social Relationships and Institutions in Seven New Rural Communities.* Washington, D.C.: USDA, Farm Security Administration. Social Research Report 18. BAE [DFPRW] cooperating.

———. 1940b. "A Farmhand's Diary." Washington, D.C.: USDA, BAE [DFPRW]. Also published 1979 in the *Mennonite Quarterly* 53(3):235–56.

———. 1942. "Wartime Migration from the Rural Spanish Speaking Villages of New Mexico." *Rural Sociology* 7(4):384–95.

———. 1943. "Applied Anthropology in Latin America: Developing a Permanent and Stable Supply of Needed Agricultural Materials." *Applied Anthropology* 2(4):15–17.

———. 1945. "A Cooperative Health Association in Spanish speaking Villages, or the Organization of the Taos County Cooperative Health Association." *American Sociological Review* 10(2):149–57.

———. 1960. *Social Systems: Essays on their Persistence and Change.* Princeton: D. Van Nostrand Company.

———, ed. 1938. "Land Tenure and Utilization." *Rural Sociology* 3(2):200–202.

———, trans. 1940c. *Fundamental Concepts of Sociology (Gemeinschaft und Gesellschaft), by Ferdinand Tonnies.* New York: American Book Company.

Loomis, Charles P., and J. Allan Beegle. 1950. *Rural Social Systems.* New York: Prentice-Hall.

Loomis, Charles P., and Dwight M. Davidson Jr. 1938. *Standards of Living of the Residents of Seven Rural Resettlement Communities.* Washington, D.C.: USDA, Farm Security Administration. Social Research Report 11. BAE [DFPRL] cooperating.

———. 1939a. "Sociometrics and the Study of New Rural Communities." *Sociometry* 2(1):56–76.

———. 1939b. "Measurement of the Dissolution of In-Groups in the Integration of a Rural Settlement Project." *Sociometry* 2(2):84–94.

Loomis, Charles P., E. deS. Brunner, and D. M. Davidson Jr. 1938. "What the Farmer is Thinking About." *Rural Sociology* 3(1):84–88.

Loomis, Charles P., and L. S. Dodson. 1938. *Standards of Living in Four Southern Appalachian Mountain Counties.* Washington, D.C.: USDA, Farm Security Administration. Social Research Report 10. BAE [DFPRL] cooperating.

Loomis, Charles P., and Douglas Ensminger. 1942. "Governmental Administration and Informal Local Groups." *Applied Anthropology* 1(2):41–62.

Loomis, Charles P., Douglas Ensminger, and Jane Woolley. 1941. "Neighborhoods and Communities in County Planning." *Rural Sociology* 6(4):339–41.

Loomis, Charles P., and Glen Grisham. 1943. "The New Mexican Experiment in Village Rehabilitation." *Applied Anthropology* 2(3):12–37.

Loomis, Charles P., Joseph L. Lister, and Dwight M. Davidson Jr. 1938. *Standards of Living in the Great Lakes Cut-over Area.* Washington, D.C.: USDA, Farm Security Administration. Social Research Report 13. BAE [DFPRL] cooperating.

Loomis, Charles P., and Olen E. Leonard. 1938. *Standards of Living in an Indian-Mexican Village and on a Reclamation Project.* Washington, D.C.: USDA, Farm Security Administration. Social Research Report 14. BAE [DFPRL] cooperating.

Loomis, Charles P., and Zona Kemp Loomis. 1967. "Rural Sociology." In Paul F. Lazarsfeld, William H. Sewell, and Harold L. Wilensky, eds. *The Uses of Sociology.* 655–91. New York: Basic Books.

Lord, Russell, and Paul H. Johnstone, eds. 1942. *A Place on Earth: A Critical Appraisal of Subsistence Homesteads.* Washington, D.C.: USDA, BAE [DFPRW].

Losey, J. Edwin, Lynn Robertson, and Irma Windleblack. 1944. "Wartime Adjustments of Indiana Rural Youth: Tentative Summary for Leadership Training School for Indiana Rural Youth." Dittoed. Lafayette, Ind.: Purdue University, Department of Agricultural Extension.

Lowitt, Richard, ed. 1980. *Journal of a Tamed Bureaucrat: Nils A. Olsen and the BAE, 1925–1935.* Ames, Iowa: Iowa State University Press.

Lundquist, Gustav A., and T. N. Carver. 1927. *Principles of Rural Sociology.* Boston: Ginn and Company.

MacLeish, Kenneth, and Helen E. Hennefrund, compilers. 1940. "Anthropology and Agriculture: Selected References on Agriculture in Primitive Cultures." Mimeo. Washington, D.C.: USDA, BAE. Agricultural Economics Bibliography 89.

MacLeish, Kenneth, and Kimball Young. 1942. *Culture of a Contemporary Rural Community: Landaff, New Hampshire.* Washington, D.C.: USDA, BAE [DFPRW]. Rural Life Studies 3.

Manny, Theodore B. 1929. *Problems in Cooperation and Experiences of Farmers in Marketing Potatoes.* Washington, D.C.: USDA. Circular 87. Contributed by BAE [DFPRL and Cooperative Marketing]. Maryland AES and Virginia AES cooperating.

———. 1930. *Rural Municipalities: A Sociological Study of Local Government in the United States.* New York: Century.

———. 1931. *Farmers' Experiences and Opinions as Factors Influencing Their Cotton-Marketing Methods.* Washington, D.C.: USDA. Circular 144. Contributed by BAE [DFPRL]. Division of Cooperative Marketing cooperating.

———. 1932. *What Ohio Farmers Think of Farmer-Owned Business Organizations in That State.* Washington, D.C.: USDA. Circular 240. Contributed by BAE [DFPRL]. Ohio State University and the Federal Farm Board cooperating.

———. 1933. *Farmer Opinions and Other Factors Influencing Cotton Production and Acreage Adjustments in the South.* Washington, D.C.: USDA. Circular 258.

———. 1935. "Population Distribution and Changes." In *Economic and Social Problems and Conditions of the Southern Appalachians,* 120–36. Bureau of Agricultural Economics, Bureau of Home Economics, and Forest Service. Washington, D.C.: USDA. Misc. Publication 205. Office of Education, U.S. Department of the Interior, and Agricultural Experiment Stations of Tennessee, Virginia, West Virginia, and Kentucky cooperating.

Manny, Theodore B., and Wayne C. Nason. 1934. *Rural Factory Industries.* Washington, D.C.: USDA. Circular 312.

Manny, Theodore B., and R. C. Smith. 1931. "The Ohio Farm Bureau Federation from the Farmers' Viewpoint: A Preliminary Report." Mimeo. Washington,

D.C.: USDA, BAE [DFPRL]. The Federal Farm Board and Ohio State University [Department of Rural Economics] cooperating.

Martin, Margaret E. 1987. Personal correspondence with Olaf F. Larson. November 7.

Matthews, M. Taylor. 1946. "The Wheeler County, Texas, Rural Health Services Association." *Rural Sociology* 11(2):128–37.

Matthews, M. Taylor, David R. Jenkins, and Raymond F. Sletto. 1942. *Attitudes of Edgefield County Farmers Toward Farm Practices and Rural Programs.* Clemson: Clemson Agricultural College, South Carolina AES. Bulletin 339. USDA, BAE [DFPRW].

Mayo, Selz C. 1983. "A History of Sociology at North Carolina State University, 1920–1981." Manuscript. Raleigh: North Carolina State University, Department of Sociology, Anthropology, and Social Work.

McDean, Harry C. 1983. "Professionalism, Policy, and Farm Economists in the Early Bureau of Agricultural Economics." *Agricultural History* 57(1):64–82.

McEntire, Davis, and N. L. Whetten. 1939. "The Migrants: Recent Migration to the Pacific coast." *Land Policy Review* 2(5):7–17.

McKain, Walter C., Jr. 1939. "The Concept of Plane of Living and the Construction of a Plane of Living Index." *Rural Sociology* 4(3):337–43.

McKain, Walter C., Jr., Elmer D. Baldwin, and Louis J. Ducoff. 1953. *Old Age and Retirement in Rural Connecticut: Economic Security of Farm Operators and Farm Laborers.* Storrs: University of Connecticut, College of Agriculture, Storrs AES. Bulletin 299. USDA, BAE [DFPRL] cooperating.

McKain, Walter C., Jr., and H. Otto Dahlke. 1946. *Turn-Over of Farm Owners and Operators, Vale and Owyhee Irrigation Projects.* Berkeley: USDA, BAE [DFPRW].

McKain, Walter C., Jr., and Grace L. Flagg. 1948. "Differences Between Rural and Urban Levels of living: Part I: Nationwide Comparisons. Part II: Regional Comparisons." Mimeo. Washington, D.C.: USDA, BAE [DFPRL].

McKain, Walter C., Jr., and William H. Metzler. 1945. "Measurements of Turnover and Retirement of Farm Owners and Operators." *Rural Sociology* 10(1): 73–76.

McNeely, J. G., and Glen T. Barton. 1940. *Land Tenure in Arkansas: Change in Labor Organization on Cotton Farms.* Fayetteville: University of Arkansas, College of Agriculture AES. Bulletin 397.

McNeil, John M., compiler. 1943. "Rehabilitation of Low-Income Farmers: A List of References." Introduction by Olaf F. Larson. Mimeo. Washington, D.C.: USDA Library. Library List 6.

Meldrum, Gilbert, and Ruth Sherburne. 1941. *Rural Youth in Massachusetts.* Amherst: Massachusetts State College, Massachusetts AES. Bulletin 386.

Melvin, Bruce L. 1929. *Village Service Agencies, New York, 1925.* Ithaca: Cornell University AES. Bulletin 493. USDA, BAE [DFPRL] cooperating.

———. 1954. "The Rural Neighborhood Concept." *Rural Sociology* 19(4):371–76.

Metzler, William H. 1946. *Two Years of Farm Wage Stabilzation in California.* Berkeley: USDA, BAE [DFPRW].

Metzler, William H., and Afife F. Sayin. 1950. "The Agricultural Labor Force in the San Joaquin Valley, California: Characteristics, Employment, Mobility, 1948." Mimeo. Washington, D.C.: USDA, BAE [DFPRL]. University of California Institute of Industrial Relations cooperating.

Miner, Horace. 1939. "Culture and Agriculture." In *Standards of Value for Program Planning and Building: Proceedings of School for Washington Staff of BAE, October 17–20, 48–56*. Mimeo. Washington, D.C.: USDA, BAE.

———. 1949. *Culture and Agriculture: An Anthropological Study of a Corn Belt County*. Ann Arbor: University of Michigan Press.

Moe, Edward O., and Carl C. Taylor. 1942. *Culture of a Contemporary Rural Community: Irwin, Iowa*. Washington, D.C.: USDA, BAE [DFPRW]. Rural Life Studies 5.

Montgomery, James E. 1943. "Rural Life Trends: Dallas County, Alabama. Report 6. For administrative use." Mimeo. Atlanta: USDA, BAE [DFPRW].

———. 1945. "Reconnaissance Survey of Union County, South Carolina: Summary. For administrative use." Mimeo. Atlanta: USDA, BAE [DFPRW].

———. 1945. "Experimenting in Rural Health Organizations." *Rural Sociology* 10(3):296–308.

———. 1990. Personal correspondence with Olaf F. Larson. March 17.

Montgomery, James E., and Edward B. Williams. 1945. "Reconnaissance Survey of Dallas County, Alabama. For administrative use." Attached are "Current and Anticipated Rural Migration Problems" and "A Summary of Current Problems and Post-War Prospects: Dallas County, Alabama." Mimeo. Atlanta: USDA, BAE [DFPRW].

Moore, Elizabeth. 1917. *Maternity and Infant Care in a Rural County in Kansas*. Washington, D.C.: GPO, U.S. Dept. of Labor, Children's Bureau Publication 6.

Moran, J. Sterling. 1917. *The Community Fair*. Washington, D.C.: USDA. Farmers' Bulletin 870.

Morgan, E. L., and Henry J. Burt. 1927. *Community Relations of Rural Young People*. Columbia: University of Missouri, College of Agriculture AES. Research Bulletin 110. USDA, BAE [DFPRL] cooperating.

Morgan, E. L., and Owen Howells. 1925. *Rural Population Groups*. Columbia: University of Missouri AES. Research Bulletin 74. USDA, BAE [DFPRL] cooperating.

Motheral, Joe R., William H. Metzler, and Louis J. Ducoff. 1953. *Cotton and Manpower: Texas High Plains*. College Station: Texas Agricultural and Mechanical College System, Texas AES. Bulletin 762. USDA, BAE [DFPRL] cooperating.

Nason, Wayne C. 1921. *Plans of Rural Community Buildings*. Washington, D.C.: USDA. Farmers' Bulletin 1173.

———. 1922. *Uses of Rural Community Buildings*. Washington, D.C.: USDA. Farmers' Bulletin 1274.

———. 1923. *Rural Planning: The Social Aspects*. Washington, D.C.: USDA. Farmers' Bulletin 1325.

———. 1924. *Rural Planning: The Social Aspects of Recreation Places*. Washington, D.C.: USDA. Farmers' Bulletin 1388.

———. 1925. *Rural Planning: The Village*. Washington, D.C.: USDA. Farmers' Bulletin 1441. Revised in August 1935 and reissued under the same title and bulletin number.

———. 1926. *Rural Hospitals*. Washington, D.C.: USDA. Farmers' Bulletin 1485.

———. 1928. *Rural Libraries*. Washington, D.C.: USDA. Farmers' Bulletin 1559.

———. 1931. *Rural Community Fire Departments*. Washington, D.C.: USDA. Farmers' Bulletin 1667.

———. 1932. "Rural Industries in Knott County, Kentucky: A Preliminary Report." Mimeo. Washington, D.C.: USDA, BAE [DFPRL], Kentucky AES cooperating.

Nason, W. C., and C. W. Thompson. 1920. *Rural Community Buildings in the United States*. Washington, D.C.: USDA. Department Bulletin 825.

National Country Life Association. 1919. *Proceedings of the First National Country Life Conference: Baltimore, 1919*. Ithaca: National Country Life Association.

Neeley, Wayne C. 1944. "The Impact of War on a Mid-West Urban Community." *Rural Sociology* 9(4):327–40.

Nelson, Lowry. 1925. *A Social Survey of Escalante, Utah*. Provo, Utah: Brigham Young University Studies 1. Contributed by University Division of Research. USDA, BAE [DFPRL] cooperating.

———. 1928. *The Utah Farm Village of Ephraim*. Provo, Utah: Brigham Young University Studies 2. Contributed by University Division of Research USDA, BAE [DFPRL] cooperating.

———. 1933. *Some Special and Economic Features of American Fork, Utah*. Provo, Utah: Brigham Young University Studies 4. Contributed by University Division of Research. USDA, BAE [DFPRL] cooperating.

———. 1952. *The Mormon Village: A Pattern and Technique of Land Settlement*. Salt Lake City: University of Utah Press.

———. 1969. *Rural Sociology: Its Origins and Growth in the United States*. Minneapolis: University of Minnesota Press.

Nichols, Ralph R. 1941. "Locating Neighborhoods and Communities in Red River Parish, Louisiana." Mimeo. Baton Rouge: Louisiana State University. USDA, BAE [DFPRW], and Louisiana State Extension Service cooperating.

———. 1955. "Notes on History of Division of Farm Population and Rural Life." Typed manuscript. Prepared for submission by Margaret J. Hagood to Oris V. Wells, Administrator, Agricultural Marketing Service, U.S. Department of Agriculture.

Nichols, Ralph R., and Morton B. King Jr. 1943. *Social Effects of Government Land Purchase*. State College: Mississippi State College AES. Bulletin 390.

Niederfrank, E. J., and C. R. Draper. 1940. *Use of Recreation Sites Developed on Federal Submarginal Land-Purchase Areas in Maine*. Orono: Unviersity of Maine, College of Agriculture AES. Bulletin 280. USDA, BAE [DFPRW] cooperating.

Niederfrank, E. J., Donald G. Hay, Henry W. Riecken Jr., and Ralph R. Nichols. 1946. "Some Postwar Social Trends in the Rural Northeast." Mimeo. Upper Darby, Pa.: USDA, BAE [DFPRW].

Odum, Howard W. 1951. *American Sociology: The Story of Sociology in the United States Through 1950*. New York: Longmann, Green & Co.

Ogle, Lelia C. 1942. Memorandum to Donald R. Rush. February 14.

Paradise, Viola I. 1919. *Maternity Care and the Welfare of Young Children in a Homesteading County in Montana*. Washington, D.C.: GPO, U.S. Department of Labor, Children's Bureau Publication 34.

Pedersen, Harald A. 1952. "Attitudes Relating to Mechanization and Farm Labor Changes in the Yazoo-Missippi Delta." *Land Economics* 28(4):353–61.

Pedersen, Harald A., and Arthur F. Raper. 1954. *The Cotton Plantation in Transition: The Case Studies of a Mechanized and an Unmechanized Cotton Plantation in the Yazoo-Mississippi Delta*. State College: Mississippi State College AES. Bulletin 508. USDA, BAE [DFPRL] cooperating.

Ploch, Louis A. 1989. *Landaff: Then and Now*. Orono: University of Maine AES. Bulletin 828.

President's Committee on Farm Tenancy. 1937. *Farm Tenancy: Report of the President's Committee*. Washington, D.C.: GPO.

Provinse, John H., and Carl C. Taylor. 1940. "Sociological Considerations in a National Policy for Agriculture." In *Proceedings of the 13th Annual Meeting of the Western Farm Economics Association*, 109–17 . Pullman, Wash.

Pryor, Herbert. 1945. "Cultural Reconnaissance: Avoyelles Parish, Louisiana. For administrative use." Dittoed. Little Rock: USDA, BAE [DFPRW].

Rankin, J. O. 1923a. *The Nebraska Farm Family: Some Land Tenure Phases*. Lincoln: University of Nebraska AES. Bulletin 185. USDA, Office of Farm Management and Farm Economics cooperating.

———. 1923b. *The Nebraska Farm Family: Some Land Tenure Phases*. Lincoln: University of Nebraska AES. Bulletin 185. USDA, Office of Farm Management and Farm Economics cooperating.

———. 1923c. *Nebraska Farm Tenancy: Some Community Phases*. Lincoln: University of Nebraska AES. Bulletin 196. USDA, BAE cooperating.

———. 1924. *Landlords of Nebraska Farms*. Lincoln: University of Nebraska AES. Bulletin 202. USDA, BAE [DFPRL] cooperating.

———. 1926. *Steps to Nebraska Farm Ownership*. Lincoln: University of Nebraska AES. Bulletin 210. USDA, BAE [DFPRL] cooperating.

Raper, Arthur F. 1943. *Tenants of the Almighty*. New York: Macmillan.

———. 1944. "Cultural Reconnaissance: Greene County, Georgia. For administrative use." Dittoed. Washington, D.C.: USDA, BAE [DFPRW]. {NAL}.

———. 1946. "The Role of Agricultural Technology in Southern Social Change." *Social Forces* 25 (1):21–30.

———. 1950. "Southern Agricultural Trends and their Effect on Negro Farmers." In *The Changing Status of the Negro in Southern Agriculture*, 12–36. Proceedings of the Tuskegee Rural Life Conference, ed. Lewis W. Jones. Tuskegee Institute, Rural Life Council, Rural Life Information Series, Bulletin 3.

———. 1951a. "Some Recent Changes in Japanese Village Life." *Rural Sociology* 16(1):3–16.

———. 1951b. "Some Effects of Land Reform in 13 Japanese Villages." *Journal of Farm Economics* 33(2):177–82.

Raper, Arthur F., and F. Howard Forsyth. 1943. "Cultural Factors Which Result in Artificial Farm Labor Shortages." *Rural Sociology* 8(1):3–14.

Raper, Arthur F., and Carl C. Taylor. 1949. "Rural Culture." In Carl C. Taylor et al., *Rural Life in the United States*, 329–43. New York: Alfred A. Knopf.

Raper, Arthur F., Tamie Tsuchiyama, Herbert Passin, and David L. Sills. 1950. *The Japanese Village in Transition*. Tokyo: Supreme Commander for the Allied Powers, General Headquarters. Report 136.

Rasmussen, Wayne D. 1975. *Agriculture in the United States: A Documentary History*. New York: Random House.

Rasmussen, Wayne D., and Gladys L. Baker. 1972. *The Department of Agriculture.* New York: Praeger Publishers.

Reagan, Barbara B. 1947. "Wages by Type of Farm and Type of Farm Work: United States and Major Regions, 1945." Mimeo. Washington, D.C.: USDA, BAE. Surveys of Wages and Wage Rates in Agriculture, Report 19.

Redfield, Robert, and W. Lloyd Warner. 1940. "Cultural Anthropology and Modern Agriculture." In *Yearbook of Agriculture, 1940,* 983–93. Washington, D.C.: GPO.

Reuss, Carl F., and Lloyd H. Fisher. 1941. *The Adjustment of New Settlers in the Yakima Valley, Washington.* Pullman: State College of Washington AES. Bulletin 397. Division of Rural Sociology and the USDA, BAE [DFPRW] cooperating. Also published as *New Settlers in Yakima Valley, Washington.* Washington, D.C.: USDA, BAE [DFPRW], Migration and Settlement on the Pacific Coast, Report 8. Washington AES, cooperating, 1941.

Rhoades, Lawrence J. 1980. "Sociologists Form Separate Independent Society." *Footnotes* 8(1):1,7.

Roberts, Roy L., and Irwin Holmes. 1943. *Analysis of Specified Farm Characteristics for Farms Classified by Total Value of Products.* Washington, D.C.: U.S. Department of Commerce, Bureau of the Census, and USDA, BAE and Farm Security Administration, cooperating. Technical Monograph based on a 2% sample from the 1940 Census of Agriculture. Parts issued separately in Technical Releases 1–9.

Rohrer, Wayne C., and Joe R. Motheral. 1953. *Labor Use in the Eastern Shore Truck Crop Harvest.* College Park: University of Maryland, Maryland AES. Misc. Publication 174.

Rohrer, Wayne C., and Carl C. Taylor. 1953. "Adult Educational Programs and Activities of the Feneral Farmers' Organizations and Cooperatives." In Charles P. Loomis et al., *Rural Social Systems and Adult Education,* 100–127. East Lansing: Michigan State College Press.

Rosenbaum, Walter A. 1965. *The Burning of the Farm Population Estimates.* Inter-University Case Program Series 83. Indianapolis: The Bobbs-Merrill Company.

Rush, Donald R., and Olaf F. Larson. 1942. "Farm Resources and Farming Systems Needed to Meet Living Needs of Farm Families in Five Type-of-Farming Areas: Part I: Summary." Mimeo. Washington, D.C.: USDA, BAE.

Ruttan, Vernon W. 1954. "The Relationship Between the BAE Level-of-Living Indexes and the Average Income of Farm Operators." *Journal of Farm Economics* 36(1):44–51.

Sanders, Irwin T. 1950. *Making Good Communities Better: A Handbook for Civic-Minded Men and Women.* Lexington: University of Kentucky Press. Revised 1953.

———. 1990. Personal correspondence with Olaf F. Larson. December 10.

Sanders, Irwin T., and Douglas Ensminger. 1940. *Alabama Rural Communities: A Study of Chilton County.* Montevevallo: Alabama College. Bulletin 136 (Vol. 33, No. 1A). USDA, BAE [DFPRW] cooperating.

Sanderson, Dwight. 1917. "The Teaching of Rural Sociology: Particularly in the Land-Grant Colleges and Universities. *American Journal of Sociology* 22(4):433–60.

———. 1934. *Rural Social and Economic Areas in Central New York.* Ithaca:

Cornell University AES. Bulletin 614. USDA, BAE [DFPRL] cooperating.
———. 1935. "Status and Prospects for Research in Rural Life under the New Deal." *American Journal of Sociology* 41(2):180–93.
———. 1939. "The Beginnings of Rural Social Studies in the United States Department of Agriculture." *Rural Sociology* 4(2):219–21.
———. 1942. *Rural Sociology and Rural Social Organization*. New York: John Wiley & Sons.
Sanderson, Dwight, and Harold F. Dorn. 1934. "The Rural Neighborhoods of Otsego County, New York, 1931." Ithaca: Cornell University AES (Department of Rural Social Organization). Mimeo. Bulletin 2. USDA, BAE [DFPRL] cooperating.]
Sanderson, Dwight, and Warren S. Thompson. 1923. *Social Areas of Otsego County*. Ithaca: Cornell University AES. Bulletin 422. USDA, BAE [DFPRL] cooperating.
Sawtelle, Emily H. 1924. "The Advantages of Farm Life: A Study by Correspondence and Interviews with Eight Thousand Farm Women: Digest of an Unpublished Manuscript." Mimeo. Washington, D.C.: USDA, BAE [DFPRL].
Schuler, Edgar A. 1938a. "The Present Social Status of American Farm Tenants." *Rural Sociology* 3(1):20–33.
———. 1938b. *Social Status and Farm Tenure: Attitudes and Social Conditions of Corn Belt and Cotton Belt Farmers*. Washington, D.C.: USDA, Farm Security Administration. Social Research Report 4. BAE [DFPRL] cooperating.
———. 1944. "Some Regional Variations in Levels and Standards of Living." *Rural Sociology* 9(2):122–41.
Schuler, Edgar A., et al. 1944. "Soldiers' Plans for Farming after They Leave the Army." Mimeo. Washington, D.C.: Army Service Forces, Information and Education Division Headquarters. Postwar Plans of the Soldier Series Report B-131.
Schuler, Edgar A., and Douglas Ensminger. 1945. "Counseling and Education for the Veteran in Rural Communities." *Bulletin of National Association of Secondary School Principals* 29(129):24–28.
Schuler, Edgar A., and Rachel Rowe Swiger. 1946. "Trends in Farm Family Levels and Standards of Living." Dittoed. Mimeo. Washington, D.C.: USDA, BAE [DFPRW]. Revised 1947 by Walter C. McKain Jr.
———. 1947. "Farm Family Levels and Standards of Living in the Plains and the Northwest." In U.S. Department of the Interior, Bureau of Reclamation, Columbia Basin Joint Investigations, *Standards and Levels of Living. Studies by the USDA for Problem 9*, 29–48. Washington, D.C.: GPO.
Schultz, Theodore W. 1941. *Training and Recruiting of Personnel in the Rural Social Studies*. Washington, D.C.: American Council on Educaiton.
Sewell, William H. 1950. "Needed Research in Rural Sociology: A Review of the Initial Discussions of the Research Committee of Fifteen," *Rural Sociology* 15(2):115–30.
Sewell, William H., Charles E. Ramsey, and Louis S. Ducoff. 1953. *Farmers' Conceptions and Plans for Economic Security in Old Age*. Madison: University of Wisconsin AES. Research Bulletin 182. USDA, BAE [DFPRL] cooperating.
Shafer, Karl. 1937. *A Basis for Social Planning in Coffee County, Alabama*.

Washington, D.C.: USDA, Farm Security Administration. Social Research Report 6. BAE [DFPRL] cooperating.

Sherbon, Florence Brown, and Elizabeth Moore. 1919. *Maternity and Infant Care in Two Rural Counties in Wisconsin*. Washington, D.C.: GPO, U.S. Dept. of Labor, Children's Bureau Publication 46.

Sherman, Caroline B. 1934. "Rural Factories Play a Part." *Rural America* 12(5): 6–8.

Slocum, Walter L., and Herman M. Case. 1953. "Are Neighborhoods Meaningful Social Groups throughout Rural America?" *Rural Sociology* 18(1):52–59.

Smick, A. A., and F. R. Yoder. 1929. *A Study of Farm Migration in Selected Communities in the State of Washington*. Pullman: State College of Washington AES. Bulletin 233. Contributed by College Division of Farm Management and Agricultural Economics. USDA, BAE [DFPRL] cooperating.

Smith, Elliott D. 1919. "Community Councils: Their Present Work, Their Future Opportunity." In *Proceedings of the First National Country Life Conference*, 36–46, 223–38. Ithaca: National Country Life Association.

Smith, Raymond C. 1947. "Review of *Ten Years of Rural Rehabilitation in the United States*." *Rural Sociology* 12(4):431–33.

Smith, T. Lynn. 1975. "Carl Cleveland Taylor, 1884–1975." *Footnotes* 3(6):21.

Sorokin, Pitirim A., and Carle C. Zimmerman. 1929. *Principles of Rural-Urban Sociology*. New York: Henry Holt and Company.

Sorokin, Pitirim A., Carle C. Zimmerman, and Charles J. Galpin, eds. 1930–32. *A Systematic Source Book in Rural Sociology*, 3 vols. Minneapolis: University of Minnesota.

Spillman, W. J. 1919. "The Agricultural Ladder." *American Economic Review* 9. Supplement, 170–79.

Spillman, W. J., and E. A. Goldenweiser. 1917. "Farm Tenancy in the United States." In *Yearbook of the United States Department of Agriculture, 1916*, 321–46. Washington, D.C.: GPO.

Standing, T. G. 1942a. "The Sociological Aspects of Farm Tenure." *Southwestern Social Science Quarterly* 23(3):264–74.

———. 1942b. "Some Recent Changes in Agriculture, with Particular Reference to the Southwest." *Southwestern Social Science Quarterly* 22(4):273–86.

Standing, T. G., T. Wilson Longmore, and Herbert Pryor. 1943. "Civilian Participation in War Programs, Louisiana, 1943. Part 1: An Analysis of Wartime Programs in St. Landry, Madison, and Lincoln Parishes." Mimeo. Little Rock: USDA, BAE [DFPRW].

Standing, T. G., and Herbert Pryor. 1943. "Community and Cooperative Services and Discussion Groups, West Carroll Parish, Louisiana. For administrative use." Mimeo. Little Rock: USDA, BAE [DFPRW].

Steiner, Jesse F. 1919. "Home Service of the Red Cross: Its Significance as an Experiment in Rural Social Work." In *Proceedings of the First National Country Life Conference*, 30–35. Ithaca: National Country Life Association.

Swiger, Rachel R., and Olaf F. Larson. 1944. "Climbing Toward Security." Mimeo. Washington, D.C.: USDA, BAE [DFPRW]. Reprinted 1966 in *A Ten-County Program Experiment with 606 Low-income Rural Families*, 9–58. Ithaca: Cornell University, New York State College of Agriculture, Department of Rural Sociology Bulletin 68.

Swiger, Rachael Rowe, and Edgar A. Schuler. 1947. "Farm Family Levels and Standards of Living in the Plains and the Northwest." In U.S. Department of the Interior, Bureau of Reclamation, Columbia Basin Joint Investigations, *Standards and Levels of Living. Studies by the USDA for Problem 9*, 29–48. Washington, D.C.: GPO.

Taeuber, Conrad. 1936. "A Registration System as a Source of Data Concerning Internal Migration." *Rural Sociology* 1(4):441–51.

———. 1938. "Changes in Farm Population." *Agricultural Situation* 22(6):11–12.

———. 1940. "Statement on Farm Population Trends." Testimony, May 8. U.S. Congress, Senate, Committee on Education and Labor. *Violations of Free Speech and Rights of Labor: Hearings before a subcommittee*, 76th Congress, Third Session Part 1. In *Supplementary Hearings: National Farm Labor Problem*. 1941, 89–110. Washington, D.C.:GPO.

———. 1942. "Rural Manpower and War Production." Testimony, February 13. U.S. Congress, House, Select Committee Investigating National Defense Migration, 77th Congress, Second Session. *The Manpower of the Nation in War Production*, Book II, Part 28. Washington, D.C.: GPO.

———. 1943. "Agricultural Underemployment." *Rural Sociology* 8(4):342–55.

———. 1944. "Replacement Rates for Rural-Farm Males Aged 25–69 Years, by Counties, 1940–1950." Mimeo. Washington, D.C.: USDA, BAE [DFPRW].

———. 1945. "Some Recent Developments in Sociological Work in the Department of Agriculture." *American Sociological Review* 10(2):169–75.

———. 1975. "Carl Cleveland Taylor, 1884–1975." *Newsline* 3(2):1–3.

Taeuber, Conrad, and Rachel Rowe. 1941. *Five Hundred Families Rehabilitate Themselves: Summarized from Annual Reports of Twenty-two Farm Security Administration Farm and Home Supervisors*. Washington, D.C.: USDA, BAE [DFPRW], and Farm Security Administration cooperating.

Taeuber, Conrad, and Carl C. Taylor. 1937. *The People of the Drought States*. Washington, D.C.: Works Progress Administration, Division of Social Research, Series 5 No. 2.

Taeuber, Conrad, and Irene B. Taeuber. 1938. "Short Distance Interstate Migrations." *Social Forces* 16(4):503–6.

———. 1940. "Negro Rural Fertility Ratios in the Mississippi Delta." *Southwestern Social Science Quarterly* 21(3):210–20.

———. 1942. "A Research Memorandum on Internal Migration Resulting from the War Effort." New York: Social Science Research Council Committee on Research on Social Aspects of the War.

Taeusch, Carl. 1940. "Schools of Philosophy for Farmers." In *Yearbook of Agriculture, 1940*, 1111–24. Washington, D.C.: GPO.

Taylor, Anne Dewees, compiler. 1958. "A Bibliographic Guide to the Writings of Henry C. Taylor, Agricultural Economist, Covering the Years 1893–1957." *Agricultural History* 32(3): Supplement, 1–28.

Taylor, Carl C. 1919. *The Social Survey: Its History and Methods*. Columbia: University of Missouri. The University of Missouri: Bulletin 20(28). Social Science Series 3.

———. 1926, 1933. *Rural Sociology*. New York: Harper & Brothers.

———. 1929. "Farmers' Movements as Psychosocial Phenomena." *Publications of the American Sociological Society* 23:153–62.

———. 1938. "What is Rural Youth's Interest?" Presentation, American Farm Bureau Federation. December 12, New Orleans. Typed. Washington, D.C.: USDA, BAE [DFPRL].

———. 1939. "The Work of the Division of Farm Population and Rural Life of the Bureau of Agricultural Economics, U.S. Department of Agriculture." *Rural Sociology* 4(2):221–28.

———. 1940. "Social Theory and Social Action." *Rural Sociology* 5(1):17–31.

———. 1941a. "Social Science and Social Action in Agriculture." *Social Forces* 20(2):154–59

———. 1941b. Personal correspondence with Henry C. Taylor. November 24.

———. 1941c. "Democracy in the Face of Crisis." Presentation, Iowa Farm and Home Week. February 10, Ames, Iowa. Mimeo. Washington, D.C.: USDA, BAE [DFPRW].

———. 1943. "General Instructions for Schedules Used in Study of Rural Community in Wartime (Bureau of the Budget No. 40-43194): Schools Survey, Family Survey, Community Services Survey, Social and Economic Organizations Survey. For administrative use." Dittoed. Washington, D.C.: USDA, BAE [DFPRW].

———. 1944a. "Guide for Reconnaissance Survey of Sample Countries. For administrative use." Dittoed. Washington, D.C.: USDA, BAE [DFPRW].

———. 1944b. "Notes on Measuring the Long Time Culture Changes in Rural Communities. For administrative use." Dittoed. Washington, D.C.: USDA, BAE [DFPRW].

———. 1944c. "Attitudes of American Farmers: International and Provincial." *American Sociological Review* 9(6):657–64.

———. 1945. "The Veteran in Agriculture." *Annals of the American Academy of Political and Social Science* 238:48–55.

———. 1946a. "Outline and Instructions for Studies of Rural Organizations Within Counties." Washington, D.C.: USDA, BAE [DFPRW].

———. 1946b. "The Sociologists' Part in Planning the Columbia Basin." *American Sociological Review* 11(3):321–30.

———. 1946c. "The Social Responsibilities of the Social Sciences: The National Level." *American Sociological Review* 11(4):384–92.

———. 1946d. "BAE Research Program. Memo to regional leaders." Washington, D.C.: USDA, BAE [DFPRW].

———. 1947a. "Foreword." In U.S. Department of Interior, Bureau of Reclamation, Columbia Basin Joint Investigations, *Standards and Levels of Living. Studies by the USDA for Problem 9*, iv–v. Washington, D.C.: GPO.

———. 1947b. "Sociology and Common Sense." Presidential address, annual meeting of the American Sociological Society, December 28–30, Chicago, Ill. *American Sociological Review* 12(1):1–9.

———. 1948a. *Rural Life in Argentina*. Baton Rouge: Louisiana State University Press.

———. 1948b. "The Status of Rural Sociological Research in the Department of Agriculture." Presentation, Rural Sociological Society annual meeting. Chicago, Ill.

———. 1948c. "Dr. Galpin at Washington." *Rural Sociology* 13(2):145–55.

———. 1953. *The Farmers' Movement, 1620–1920*. New York: American Book Company.

————. 1964. "In Memoriam: Margaret J. Hagood (1907–1963)." *Rural Sociology* 29(1):97–98.

Taylor, Carl C., Louis J. Ducoff, and Margaret J. Hagood. 1948. *Trends in the Tenure Status of Farm Workers in the United States Since 1880.* Washington, D.C.: USDA, BAE [DFPRL].

Taylor, Carl C., Douglas Ensminger, Helen W. Johnson, and Jean Joyce. 1965. *India's Roots of Democracy: A Sociological Analysis of Rural India's Experience in Planned Development Since Independence.* Bombay: Orient Longmans Ltd.

Taylor, Carl C., and Charles P. Loomis. 1938. "The American rural culture of the future: What the rural sociologists and agricultural economists think it should and will be." *Farm Population and Rural Life Activities* 12(4):1–14.

Taylor, Carl C., Charles P, Loomis, John Provinse, J. E. Hulett Jr., and Kimball Young. 1940. "Cultural, Structural, and Social-Psychological Study of Selected American Farm Communities. Field manual. Preliminary and confidential. For administrative use." Mimeo. Washington, D.C.: USDA, BAE [DFPRW].

Taylor, Carl C., Arthur F. Raper, Douglas Ensminger, Margaret Jarman Hagood, T. Wilson Longmore, Walter C. McKain Jr., Louis J. Ducoff, and Edgar A. Schuler. 1949. *Rural Life in the United States.* New York: Alfred A. Knopf.

Taylor, Carl C., and Wayne C. Rohrer. 1953. "General Farmers' Organizations and Cooperatives." In Charles P. Loomis et al., *Rural Social Systems and Adult Education,* 80–99. East Lansing: Michigan State College Press.

Taylor, Carl C., Helen W. Wheeler, and E. L. Kirkpatrick. 1938. *Disadvantaged Classes in American Agriculture.* Washington, D.C.: USDA, Farm Security Administration. Social Research Report 8. BAE [DFPRL] cooperating.

Taylor, Carl C., Fred R. Yoder, and Carle C. Zimmerman. 1920. "Tenants on Reclaimed Land in Southeastern Missouri: Living Conditions of Farm Residents in the White Sections of the Upper Mississippi Delta." Typed. Washington, D.C.: USDA, Division of Farm Management and Farm Economics, Section of Farm Life Studies. University of Missouri AES cooperating.

Taylor, Carl C., and Carle C. Zimmerman. 1922. *Economic and Social Conditions of North Carolina Farmers: Based on a Survey of 1,000 North Carolina Farmers in Three Typical Counties of the State.* Raleigh: North Carolina State College of Agriculture. USDA, BAE [DFPRL] cooperating.

Taylor, Edward A., and F. R. Yoder. 1926. *Rural Social Organization in Whitman County.* Pullman: State College of Washington AES. Bulletin 203. Contributed by College Division of Farm Management and Agricultural Economics. USDA, BAE [DFPRL] cooperating.

Taylor, Henry C. 1921. "Report of the Chief of the Office of Farm Management and Farm Economics." In *Annual Reports of the Department of Agriculture in the Year Ended June 30, 1920,* 569–75. Washington, D.C.: GPO.

————. 1923. "Report of the Chief of the Office of Farm Management and Farm Economics." In *Annual Reports of the Department of Agriculture for the Year Ended June 30, 1922,* 545–66. Washington, D.C.: GPO.

————. 1924. "Report of the Chief of the Bureau of Agricultural Economics." In *Annual Reports of the Department of Agriculture for the Year Ended June 30, 1923,* 131–97. Washington, D.C.: GPO.

————. 1939. "A Century of Agricultural Statistics." *Journal of Farm Economics* 21(4):697–734.

———. 1948. "Galpin Undertakes the Study of Rural Life." *Rural Sociology* 13(2):119–29.

———. 1992. *A Farm Economist in Washington 1919–1925*. Madison: University of Wisconsin, Madison, Department of Agricultural Economics.

Taylor, Henry C., and Anne Dewees Taylor. 1952. *The Story of Agricultural Economics in the United States, 1840–1932*. Ames, Iowa: Iowa State College Press.

Taylor, Paul S. 1946. "Survey of Wages and Wage Rates in Agriculture. Bureau of Agricultural Economics, Washington, D.C. Reports 1–10, issued May 1945–June 1946." *Rural Sociology* 13(5):277–80.

Tenny, Lloyd S. 1947. "The Bureau of Agricultural Economics in the Early Years." *Journal of Farm Economics* 29 (4:Part II):1017–26.

Thompson, C. W., and G. P. Warber. 1913. *Social and Economic Survey of a Rural Township in Southern Minnesota*. Minneapolis: University of Minnesota. Studies in Economics 1.

Tolley, Howard R. 1943. *The Farmer Citizen at War*. New York: Macmillan.

Torbert, Edward N. 1941. "Columbia Basin: Studies in Progress." *Land Policy Review* 4(10):3–9.

Treadway, Walter L., and Emma O. Lundberg. 1919. *Mental Defect in a Rural County: A Medico-Psychological and Social Study of Mentally Defective Children in Sussex County, Delaware*. Washington, D.C.: GPO. U.S. Department of Labor, Children's Bureau Publication 48.

True, Alfred C. 1928. *A History of Agricultural Extension Work in the United States, 1885–1923*. Washington, D.C.: GPO. USDA Misc. Publication. 15.

Truesdell, Leon A. 1926. *Farm Population of the United States: An Analysis of the 1920 Farm Population Figures, Especially in Comparison with Urban Data, Together with a Study of the Main Economic Factors Affecting the Farm Population*. Washington, D.C.: Bureau of the Census. Census Monographs VI.

Turner, Ralph. 1940. "The Cultural Setting of American Agricultural Problems." In *Yearbook of Agriculture, 1940*, 1003–32. Washington, D.C.: GPO.

University of Missouri, College of Agriculture. 1937. "Proceedings of the First Midwestern Conference on Rural Population Research, April 23–24, 1937." Mimeo. Columbia: University of Missouri, College of Agriculture AES.

USDA, BAE. 1930. "The Institute of Methods of Rural Sociological Research Held at the Bureau of Agricultural Economics December 31, 1929–January 4, 1930: A Summary Report," and "A Supplement to the Report of the Institute of Methods of Research in Rural Sociology. Part 1: Report of the Committee on the Case Study Method. Part 2: The Case Study Method, by Dr. Ernest W. Burgess, University of Chicago." Mimeo. Washington, D.C.: USDA, BAE [DFPRL].

———. 1940. *Communities and Neighborhoods in Land Use Planning*. Washington, D.C.: GPO. County Planning Series 6. USDA, BAE, and USDA, Extension Service cooperating.

USDA, BAE [DFPRW]. 1940. "Significant Social Facts for County and Community Planning Committees to Know about Their County." Mimeo. Washington, D.C.: USDA, BAE [DFPRW].

———.1943. "Study of Six-County Experimental Rural Health Programs and FSA Health Associations and Groups. For administrative use." Dittoed. Washington, D.C.: USDA, BAE [DFPRW].

USDA, BAE, and Farm Security Administration. 1942. "Backgrounds of the War Farm Labor Problem." Mimeo. Washington, D.C.: USDA, BAE [DFPRW].

USDA, Inter-Bureau Committee on Postwar Agricultural Programs, Land Settlement Work Group. 1945. *Farm Opportunities in the United States: Outlook, Problems, Policies.* Washington, D.C.: USDA.

USDA, Statistical Reporting Service. 1969. *The Story of U.S. Agricultural Estimates.* Washington, D.C.: USDA. Misc. Publication 1088.

U.S. Bureau of the Census. 1933. *Fifteenth Census of the United States: 1930, Population,* Vol. 11. Washington, D.C.: GPO.

———. 1953. *Census of Population: 1950,* Vol. II, Part 1. Washington, D.C.: GPO.

U.S. Congress, House of Representatives. 1946. *Hearings on Agriculture Appropriation Bill for 1947.* 79th Congress, Second Session. Washington, D.C.: GPO.

———. 1947. *The South's Health: A Picture with Promise.* Washington, D.C.: GPO. Reprint from *Hearings on Study of Agricultural and Economic Problems of the Cotton Belt, Subcommittee on Agriculture, House of Representatives,* July 7 and 8, 1947. 80th Congress, First Session.

———. 1951. *Research and Related Services in the United States Department of Agriculture, Vol. 3.* Prepared for the Committee on Agriculture of the House of Representatives, 81st Congress, Second Session. Washington, D.C.: GPO.

U.S. Congress, Senate, Committee on Education and Labor, Subcommittee on Wartime Health and Education. 1946. *The Experimental Health Program of the United States Department of Agriculture.* Prepared by T. Wilson Longmore, Carl C. Taylor, and Douglas Ensminger. Subcommittee Monograph 1, 79th Congress, Second Session. Washington, D.C.: GPO.

U.S. Department of Agriculture. 1914, 1915. *List of Workers in Subjects Pertaining to Agriculture and Home Economics in the U.S. Department of Agriculture and in the State Agricultural Colleges and Experiment Stations.* Washington, D.C.: GPO.

———.1941. *New Settlement in the Mississippi Delta.* Washington, D.C.: USDA, BAE. Misc. Publication 442.

———. 1948. *Long-Range Agricultural Policy. A Study of Selected Trends and Factors Relating to the Long-range Prospect for American Agriculture for the Committee on Agriculture of the House of Representatives.* 80th Congress, Second Session. Washington, D.C.: GPO.

———. 1964. *Changes in Farm Production and Efficiency: A Summary Report.* Washington, D.C.: USDA. Statistical Bulletin 233.

———. 1954. *Farm Population: Migration to and from Farms, 1920–1954.* Washington, D.C.: AMS No. 10.

U.S. Department of Agriculture, Bureau of Agricultural Economics. 1923–49, annual report. "Farm Population Estimates." Mimeo. Washington, D.C.: USDA, BAE [DFPRL].

———. 1942. "War Time Work Program of the Bureau of Agricultural Economics." Mimeo. Washington, D.C.: USDA, BAE.

U.S. Department of Agriculture, Bureau of Agricultural Economics, Division of Farm Population and Rural Welfare. 1942. "Annual Report: Division of Farm Population and Rural Welfare, July 1, 1941 to June 30, 1942." Typed. Washington, D.C.: USDA, BAE.

U.S. Department of Agriculture, Bureau of Agricultural Economics, Division of Farm Population and Rural Welfare. 1945. "Field Instructions for Work in Sample Counties. For administrative use." Dittoed. Washington, D.C.: USDA, BAE [DFPRW].

U.S. Department of Agriculture, Office of the Secretary. 1919a. *Report of the Committee Appointed by the Secretary of Agriculture to Consider Plan of Organization, Scope of Work, and Projects for the Office of Farm Management, and Methods of Procedure in Making Cost of Production Studies.* Washington, D.C.: GPO. Circular 132.

———. 1919b. *Report of Committee Appointed by the Secretary of Agriculture to Consider the Subject of Farm Life Studies as One of the Divisions of Research Work of the Proposed Bureau of Farm Management and Farm Economics.* D.C.: GPO. Circular 139.

U.S. Department of the Interior, Bureau of Reclamation. 1941. *Columbia Basin Joint Investigations: Character and Scope.* Washington, D.C.:GPO.

U.S. Department of the Interior, Bureau of Reclamation. 1947. Carl C. Taylor et al., investigators. *Columbia Basin Joint Investigations, Problem 10, Pattern of Rural Settlement.* Washington, D.C.: GPO.

U.S. Department of the Interior, Bureau of Reclamation. 1949. Marion Clawson et al., investigators. *Central Valley Studies, Problem 24, The Effect of the Central Valley Project on the Agricultural and Industrial Economy and on the Social Character of California: A Report on Problem 24.* Washington, D.C.: GPO.

U.S. Department of the Interior, Bureau of Reclamation and USDA, BAE. 1946. Carl C. Taylor et al., investigators. *Columbia Basin Joint Investigations, Problem 27, Rural Community Centers.* Dittoed. Washington, D.C.: U.S. Department of the Interior, Bureau of Reclamation and USDA, BAE.

Vaughan, Theo L., and Herbert Pryor. 1946. "Prepayment Medical Care in Nevada County, Arkansas." *Rural Sociology* 11(2):137–47.

VonTungeln, George H., Ellis L. Kirkpatrick, C. R. Hoffer, and J. F. Thaden. 1923. *The Social Aspects of Rural Life and Farm Tenantry, Cedar County, Iowa.* Ames, Iowa: Iowa State College of Agriculture and Mechanic Arts AES. Bulletin 217. Contributed by Rural Sociology Section. USDA, BAE [DFPRL] cooperating.

Vasey, Tom, and Josiah C. Folsom. 1937a. *Survey of Agricultural Labor Conditions in Todd County, Kentucky.* Washington, D.C.: USDA, Farm Security Administration. BAE [DFPRL] cooperating.

———. 1937b. *Survey of Agricultural Labor Conditions in Concordia Parish, Louisiana.* Washington, D.C.: USDA, Farm Security Administration. BAE [DFPRL] cooperating.

Wakeley, Ray E. 1931. *The Communities of Schuyler County, New York, 1927.* Ithaca: Cornell University AES. Bulletin 524. USDA, BAE [DFPRL] cooperating.

———. 1957. "Sociological Research on Farmers' Organizations and Agricultural Cooperatives." *Rural Sociology* 22(3):274–80.

Wallace, Henry A. Various years. *Report of the Secretary of Agriculture*, annual reports. Washington, D.C.: GPO.

Wallrabenstein, Paul P., and Louis J. Ducoff. 1957. "Farm Employment and Farm Wage Rate Services." In *Major Statistical Series of the U.S. Department of*

Agriculture, Vol. 7: *Farm Population, Employment and Levels of Living*, 8–14. Washington, D.C.: GPO. Agriculture Handbook 118.

Ward, Florence E. 1920. "The Farm Woman's Problem." *Journal of Home Economics* 12(10):437–57.

Warren, Roland L. 1963. *The Community in America*. Chicago: Rand McNally. Revised 1972, 1978.

Wells, O. V. 1949. "Agricultural Economics Research: Some Notes on the New Journal." *Agricultural Economics Research* 1(1):9–10.

Wells, O. V., J. D. Black, Paul H. Appleby, H. C. Taylor, Howard R. Tolley, Raymond J. Penn, and T. W. Schultz. 1954. "The Fragmentation of the BAE." *Journal of Farm Economics* 36(1):1–21.

Whetten, Nathan L., and Henry W. Riecken Jr. 1943. *The Foreign-Born Population of Connecticut, 1940*. Storrs, Conn.: Storrs AES. Bulletin 246. USDA, BAE [DFPRW] cooperating.

White, Helen R. 1953. "Population in Farm-Operator Households." In *Farms and Farm People: Population, Income, and Housing Characteristics by Economic Class of Farms; a Special Cooperative Report*, 45–64. Washington, D.C.: GPO. USDA, BAE [DFPRL], Division of Statistical and Historical Research, and Division of Farm Management and Costs; and USDA Bureau of Human Nutrition and Home Economics, Family Economics Division cooperating.

Whittaker, Milo L. 1929. "Rural Community Organization: A Comparative Study of Two Rural Communities in Northern Illinois." Mimeo. Washington, D.C.: USDA, BAE [DFPRL] cooperating.

Williams, Edward B. 1990. Interview by Yvonne Beauford Oliver. August 3.

Williams, Faith M. 1935. "History of Studies of Family Living." In Faith M. Williams and Carle C. Zimmerman, *Studies of Family Living in the United States and Other Countries: An Analysis of Material and Method*, 6–13. Washington, D.C.: USDA. Misc. Publication 223.

Williams, Robin M., Jr. 1946. "Some Observations on Sociological Research in Government during World War II." *American Sociological Review* 11(5): 573–77.

Williams, Robin M., Jr., and Howard W. Beers. 1943. *Farmers on Local Planning Committees in Three Kentucky Counties, 1939–1940*. Lexington: University of Kentucky AES. Bulletin 443. USDA, BAE [DFPRW] cooperating.

Willits, Fern K., Linda M. Ghelfi, and Michele E. Lipner. 1988. "Women in the Rural Sociological Society: A History." *The Rural Sociologist* 8(2):126–41.

Wilson, M. L. 1938. "New Horizons in Agricultural Economics." *Journal of Farm Economics* 20(1):1–7.

———. 1940. "Beyond Economics." In *Yearbook of Agriculture, 1940*, 922–37. Washington, D.C.: GPO.

Wooten, H. H. 1965. *The Land Utilization Program, 1934 to 1964: Origin, Development, and Present Status*. Washington, D.C.: USDA, ERS. Agricultural Economic Report 85.

Woytinsky, W. S., and Louis J. Ducoff. 1953. "Employers." In W. S. Woytinsky and Associates, *Employment and Wages in the United States*, 34–347. New York: The Twentieth Century Fund.

Wynne, Waller, Jr. 1943. *Culture of a Contemporary Rural Community: Harmony, Georgia.* Washington, D.C.: USDA, BAE [DFPRW]. Rural Life Studies 6.

Yoder, Fred R., and A. A. Smick. 1935. *Migration of Farm Population and Flow of Farm Wealth.* Pullman: State College of Washington AES. Bulletin 315. Contributed by College Department of Sociology and Division of Farm Management and Agricultural Economics. USDA, BAE [DFPRL] cooperating.

Young, Donald. 1955. "Sociology and the Practicing Professions." *American Sociological Review* 20(6):641–48.

Young, Kimball. 1939. "The Relation of the Administrator to the Farmer and the Expert." *Standards of Value for Program Planning and Building: Proceedings of School for Washington Staff of BAE,* 93–103. Mimeo. Washington, D.C.: USDA, BAE.

Zimmerman, Carle C. 1938. *The Changing Community.* New York: Harper & Brothers.

Zimmerman, Carle C., and John D. Black. 1926. *The Marketing Attitudes of Minnesota Farmers.* St. Paul: University of Minnesota AES. Technical Bulletin 45. Contributed by University Division of Agricultural Economics. USDA, BAE [DFPRL] cooperating.

Zimmerman, Carle C., and Carl C. Taylor. 1922. *Rural Organization: A Study of Primary Groups in Wake County, NC.* Raleigh: North Carolina AES. Bulletin 245. Contributed by North Carolina State College, Department of Agricultural Economics. USDA, Office of Farm Management and Farm Economics, Division of Farm Life Studies cooperating.

Zimmerman, Julie N. 1994. "Recovering Rural Sociology's Past: The Division of Farm Population and Rural Life, U.S. Department of Agriculture, 1919–1953." Presentation, Rural Sociological Society annual meeting. Portland, Ore.

———. 1999. "Hagood, Margaret Jarman." In John A. Garraty and Mark C. Carnes, ed. *American National Biography,* Vol. 9, 791–92. New York: Oxford University Press.

Zimmerman, Julie N., and Olaf F. Larson. 1989. "The World Agricultural Society, 1919–1927: The Beginnings of International Rural Development Organizations." Presentation, Rural Sociological Society annual meeting. Norfolk, Va.

Index

A *Basis for Social Planning in Coffee County, Alabama* (Shafer), 200
A *Census Analysis of American Villages* (Fry), 67
A *Place on Earth: A Critical Appraisal of Subsistence Homesteads* (Lord and Johnstone), 211–12
A *Systematic Source Book in Rural Sociology* (Galpin, Sorokin, and Zimmerman, eds.), 26, 265
acreage limitation law, 51
Adams Act of 1906, 270
African Americans
  farm labor, 130, 173–74
  farm population studies, 172, 186 n. 2
  farm tenancy studies, 150, 152–53, 186 n. 5
  federally supported research, 22 n. 2
  fertility studies, 180
  land tenure studies, 72–73, 167, 176–77, 180–81
  levels and standards of living, 176–77, 178
  locality group studies, 95, 108, 166, 177, 179, 181, 231
  migration, 16, 57, 62, 173, 178, 180
  reconnaissance surveys, 45, 52–53, 179–80, 182–83, 186 n. 8
  rural, 174–80
Agricultural Adjustment Act of 1933, 194
Agricultural Adjustment Administration (AAA), 5, 35, 41, 162, 195, 197, 264. See also Land Policy Section
  crop reduction programs, 131
  Greene County (Ga.), 231, 232
  land utilization, 7, 223–24, 230
  operator turnover studies, 166
  rural rehabilitation noncommercial loan program, 208
agricultural economics, 13, 48–49
agricultural history and geography, 23 n. 11
Agricultural History Society, 219 n. 1
Agricultural Marketing Act of 1929, 192
Agricultural Marketing Service, 29, 281

Agricultural Planning Board, 225
Agricultural Research and Marketing Act of 1946, 276 n. 1
Agricultural Research Service, 281
Agricultural Situation (Hagood and Ducoff), 244
Ajure, Oscar, 56 n.5
Alabama, 100, 122, 128 n. 6, 174, 193, 200
Alabama College, 40, 100
Alexander, Frank D., 172, 182, 183, 184, 255 n. 12
  Coahoma County study, 52, 179–80
Alexander, Will W., 27, 230
Allen, R. H., 153–54
Allport, Gordon W., 272
Alston, John, 186 n. 6
Amarillo (Tex.), 2, 39
American Agricultural Colleges and Experiment Stations, 12
American Association for Agricultural Legislation, 17–18, 23 n. 10
American Association for the Advancement of Science, 167
American Country Life Association (ACLA), 17, 22, 26, 28, 77
  International Country Life Movement committee, 18
  local government, 116
American Farm Bureau Federation, 7, 17, 31, 53, 125, 179–80
American Farm Economics Association, 134
American Farmers' Movement, 124
American Fork (Utah), 95
American Home Economics Association, 19, 258
American Red Cross, 16–17
American Sociological Association (ASA), 2, 9, 13, 23 nn. 6, 8, 26, 28, 29, 36, 219 nn. 1–2, 275, 281
  Committee on Sociology in Latin American Countries, 275
  Rural Section, 2, 13, 26
  Rural Sociology Section, 273, 276